UNIVERSAL SALVATION?

The Current Debate

UNIVERSAL SALVATION?

The Current Debate

Edited by

Robin A. Parry and Christopher H. Partridge

William B. Eerdmans Publishing Company
Grand Rapids, Michigan / Cambridge, U.K.

For

Eva Madeleine Ludlow
(born on Monday 10th February 2003 in Cambridge, UK)

and

Evan Alexander Reitan
(born on Wednesday 15th May 2003 in Stillwater, Oklahoma)

The LORD bless you and keep you.

First published 2003 in the U.K. by Paternoster Press
an imprint of Authentic Media,
P.O. Box 300, Carlisle, Cumbria, CA3 0QS, UK
www.paternoster-publishing.com

and 2004 in the United States of America by
Wm. B. Eerdmans Publishing Co.
255 Jefferson Ave. S.E., Grand Rapids, Michigan 49503 /
P.O. Box 163, Cambridge CB3 9PU U.K.
www.eerdmans.com

Printed in the United States of America

09 08 07 06 05 04 7 6 5 4 3 2 1

ISBN 0-8028-2764-0

Contents

Foreword

GABRIEL FACKRE

In this work evangelicals are talking to one another about the controverted question of universalism. It's a conversation worth overhearing by the wider theological world. Indeed, the authors are much in dialogue with those reaches already, for careful attention is given to the history of the issue in the church universal, and to the contemporary debate in circles beyond, as well as within, evangelicalism.

The opening chapters give the most thoughtfully wrought argument for universalism to date from within the contemporary evangelical community. But then, the author of the same, Thomas Talbott, must face incisive evangelical critiques of his position, biblical, theological and philosophical, though he does get support in this volume from others in those categories who share his views, and a chance to answer the charges against his position in a tightly-argued closing chapter.

Ecumenical Christianity, as well as the evangelical community, will be enriched by listening in on this dialogue. On matters of authority, the primacy of Scripture is given its due, tradition is taken seriously and reason is honoured in the development of points of view, pro or con. All three are standard markers for classical Christian faith. Further, most of the inherited arguments for and against universalism are methodically investigated, with due recognition of majority and minority points of view within historic Christianity. And, as noted, as good a case for universalism as is current is made by Talbott, as is the counter-case by his critics, with meticulous attention by all to the biblical data.

Especially instructive for wider audiences is the seriousness with which the issue of sin is taken by the contributors. That is, the question of universalism as treated here presupposes the radical breach of God's intentions. Given the fall, how can the declared purpose of redemption be fully carried out? For the culture at large, and for vast stretches of contemporary theology, Karl Menninger's 1977 book title is as pertinent as ever, *Whatever Became of Sin?* We need to hear from those who take sin seriously.

That said, it is also worth asking how this exchange might be heard by other Christian traditions. And further, how the evangelical debate itself might be edified by questions posed by those traditions to the participants. As a thought experiment Foreword to this stimulating work here are several queries stemming from these matters.

Talbott's three propositions, focal to the exchange, are set forth so that one cannot, logically, agree to all of them (God wills salvation for everyone; God's salvific will is sovereign; some will not be saved). The proposer chooses to hold to the first two and reject the third, and that on the grounds of Scripture, tradition and reason. His critics will not let the third go, and seek to assimilate it with interpretations of the other two. An observation: Talbott's threesome bears a resemblance to the three assertions at the heart of the ancient problem of evil. The question of theodicy, whether it be raised in the formula of Epicurus, the agony of Job, the reality of the Holocaust, or the recent popular book by Rabbi Kushner, *When Bad Things Happen to Good People*, is about the justification of God in the face of undeserved suffering. Put otherwise: How can we believe in an all-good and all-powerful deity, given the magnitude of evil? In many of the efforts at an answer, one of the three propositions gets eliminated. Either the power of God is reduced to that of a finite deity ; the love of God is put into question (all suffering is traceable to human fault or mysterious divine purposes); the reality of evil disappears (defined as educative or denied as illusory).

In matters of a biblically-grounded Christian theodicy, however, the three are non-negotiables. What to do? Current eschatological theologies say that we have smuggled a culturally-shaped despotic view of power into our conceptualizing of the problem. Power, Christianly understood, is in the future tense when 'God *will* be all in all' (1 Cor. 15:28) and nothing '*will* separate us from the love of

God in Jesus Christ our Lord' (Rom. 8:39), retroactively mending every flaw, not instant-and-everywhere control. In the time between Easter and Eschaton, it's a battle, with the world, the flesh and the devil given latitude to work their ways. Yet,

> the Old Dragon in straighter limits bound,
> Not so far casts his usurped sway,
> And, wroth to see his Kingdom fail,
> Swinges the scaly horror of his folded tail.
> (John Milton, '*On the Morning of Christ's Nativity*')

Thus, evil is real but the loving God will exercise an eschatological omnipotence. This does seem to give greater logical coherence to the maintaining of the three non-negotiables. But it also leaves unanswered just how evil is countermanded retroactively, for all Pannenberg's efforts to make sense of such. Theodicy can be *explored* along the lines of the reconceptualization of power, but it cannot, finally, be *explained*. If we are not to deviate from Scripture, we must adhere to its holding together of the three non-negotiables, in a coherence known only to God. The last word is Paul's as he struggled with the theodicy of Israel, 'O depth of wealth, wisdom and knowledge in God! How unsearchable his judgments, how untraceable his ways! Who knows the mind of the Lord?... Source, Guide and Goal of all that is – to him be glory forever! Amen' (Rom. 11:33–34, 36).

Does the theodicy inquiry illuminate the universalism question? Interestingly, Moltmann, here discussed, transports his eschatological confidence about final justice vis-à-vis sufferers into the arena of universalism vis-à-vis sinners. But in doing so, has he eliminated proposition three? If Talbott's threesome parallel the theodicy trinity, then this is not a good move.

There is a parallel between these two problematics, hinted at in fugitive references to theodicy throughout. Yet, with it may go the fact that Christians can no more eliminate one of the three in the Talbott taxonomy than they can in the theodicy equation. Let the reader see how Talbott's critics handle this. By tacitly dropping one of the first two? By reinterpreting one or the other as the eschatological theodicies do? Or by pressing the human logic as far as it will go, and then admitting that we deal here with a Pauline mystery to be explored, but not explained? Paul Jewett, echoing the latter in his inquiry into the related issue of election and human responsibility, concludes that we have to do with a paradox comparable to that of the Chalcedonian formula, one not penetrable by human reason. (See his *Election and Predestination* and also Donald Baillie's 'paradox of grace' in *God Was in Christ*). God grant us humility before ultimate mysteries known only to 'the mind of the Lord.'

Another imported ecumenical query is related to the two meanings of hope in Christian historical discourse. One meaning, as in the World Council of Churches' 1954 assembly theme, 'Christ, the Hope of the World,' is the 'sure and certain' noun usage. Given Easter, there will be an Eschaton. We need to get that message of hope out to a hopeless world. A second meaning of the word has to do with aspiration rather than accomplishment, the conditional rather than the unconditional. Here hope is often a verb rather than a noun, as in Paul's comment on Timothy's possible appearance in Philippi, 'I hope there to send him as soon as I see....' (Phil. 2:23 NRSV). Karl Barth's view of the *apokatastasis* is of the second sort, as in these words from *Church Dogmatics* IV/3/1: 'We are surely commanded to hope and to pray... cautiously yet distinctly that... His compassion should not fail, and that in accordance with His mercy which is "new every morning" He "will not cast off forever".' (Lamentations 3:22f, 31) [478]. Of course, this 'universal reconciliation' is *not* a doctrine for Barth as is too often charged. He explicitly denies that: 'No such postulate can be made even though we appeal to the cross and resurrection of Jesus Christ' (477). It is not 'an article of faith' but rather an 'article of hope' in the second sense of that word.

Is this view considered in this work? The historical chapters take some note of it and parallels in Von Balthasar and others. However, it does not fit the typology, hardly describable in Talbott's words as 'a vague hope of some kind.' Of course, it is an awkward position, violating the canons of Aristotelian logic. If all the world takes part in Christ's humiliation and exaltation, as Barth argues, how can it be that everyone is not saved? The logic of Barth's theology runs up against the firmness of his commitment to the divine sovereignty. At the end of the day, our rational standards are not the last word. Who is Aristotle to tell the majestic God what to do? At work here is a Reformed stress on the divine freedom that trumps our human logic.

Another observation from the wider theological dialogue: Kudos for the attention given here and there to the theory of postmortem encounter with Christ, with its patristic roots, nineteenth century development by missionaries and their mentors, and twentieth/twenty-first century voice in the debate about religious pluralism (as in *What About Those Who Have Never Heard?* John Sanders, [ed.], Downers Grove: IVP, 1995). To be remembered is that in most of its versions, the option of a 'No' is present in this view of 'divine perseverance', along with the paradox of a free but graced 'Yes', so it is not linked, as such, with universalism, but can entertain that option as an 'article of hope.' It should be noted that this second kind of hope presupposes the real possibility of the alternative future of double destination, and therefore cannot be included as a variety of universalism, either by those who would like to write it off as a heresy or ring it in as support for universalism from the twentieth century's best known theologian.

This evangelical ecumenical finds in this work a landmark discussion among evangelicals, with ecumenical constituencies – academic and ecclesial – having much to learn from the give-and-take.

Contributors

David Hilborn is Theological Adviser to the Evangelical Alliance UK, and an Associate Research Fellow of the London Bible College. With Ian Randall, he co-authored the history of the Evangelical Alliance, *One Body in Christ*. He edited the Alliance reports *Faith, Hope and Homosexuality* and *'Toronto' in Perspective*, and co-edited *The Nature of Hell* and *God and the Generations*. He is also the author of *Picking Up the Pieces*, a study of evangelicalism and postmodernity. David is an ordained Anglican minister and lives with his wife and two children in Acton, West London.

Don Horrocks spent 25 years in the business world in corporate banking and management consultancy. He completed a PhD in 2001 on the soteriology of Thomas Erskine of Linlathen (forthcoming). He has headed up the Evangelical Alliance's Policy Commission for four years, editing books on *Transsexuality* and *Modifying Creation: GM Crops and Foods*, and has been their Public Affairs Manager since 2001. A Research Associate at London Bible College, Don is married with 3 children, and enjoys mountain walking.

Thomas F. Johnson is Professor of Biblical Theology at George Fox University in Oregon. He wrote a commentary on the Johannine epistles for the New International Biblical Commentary series and has been a dean and a president of two colleges. He and his wife, Prof. Michele Johnson, take American college students on bi-annual tours of the UK and Ireland.

Morwenna Ludlow published her first book on universal salvation in the thought of Gregory of Nyssa and Karl Rahner and she has continued to write on the historical development of universalist ideas in Christianity. She was until recently S.A. Cook Bye-Fellow at Gonville and Caius College, Cambridge, where she was working on a research project about how modern systematic theologians use the Church Fathers in their writings, with a particular focus on contemporary readings of Gregory of Nyssa. In October 2003 she will take up the post of Career Development Fellow at Pembroke College, Oxford. Her current research project is to celebrate, along with her husband and awe-struck 3–year-old daughter, the birth of the newest member of the family – Eva Madeleine.

I. Howard Marshall is presently Honorary Research Professor of New Testament at the University of Aberdeen where he taught from 1964 to 1999. He is the author of many academic articles and books including commentaries on the Greek text of Luke (NIGTC) and the Pastoral Epistles (ICC) and most recently edited the sixth edition of Moulton and Geden's Concordance to the Greek New Testament. He was married to Joyce (died 1996) and has four married children and seven grandchildren. When he is not removing weeds from his garden, he enjoys walking and climbing the local mountains.

Robin Parry was a teacher of A Level Religious Studies and Philosophy in Worcester for ten years before becoming commissioning editor for Paternoster Press. He has published articles in academic journals and books, and is co-editor of *The Futures of Evangelicalism*. His PhD is soon to be published as *Old Testament Story and Christian Ethics: The Rape of Dinah as a Case Study*. When not churching it, working, washing up, romancing/annoying his wife or playing with his daughters he can be found watching science fiction or detective dramas.

Christopher Partridge is Professor of Contemporary Religion at Chester College, Chester, England. His research and writing focuses on new religions and alternative spiritualities in the West. Chris is the editor of *Fundamentalisms*, a book on *UFO Religions* and, with Theodore Gabriel, *Mysticisms East and West*. He is the author of *H.H. Farmer's Theological Interpretation of Religion*, and has edited H.H. Farmer's second series of 1951 Gifford Lectures, *Reconciliation and Religion*. Chris is also the reviews editor for the journal *Ecotheology* and has a taste for obscure indie music.

Eric Reitan is an Assistant Professor of Philosophy at Oklahoma State University, Stillwater. He publishes regularly in the areas of social and political philosophy, environmental ethics, and the philosophy of religion. He has published several articles defending Christian universalism, and was frantically trying to complete work on a book-length treatment of the subject before his first child, due Spring 2003, deprived him of his powers of concentration. He failed.

John Sanders is Professor of Philosophy and Religion at Huntington College in Indiana, author of *No Other Name: an Investigation into the Destiny of the Unevangelized* and *The God Who Risks: A Theology of Providence*. He and his wife have five children and eight pets (the pets are far easier to keep under control). He is an enthusiast for canoeing in the Canadian wilderness.

Daniel Strange is the coordinator of the Religious and Theological Students Fellowship, part of UCCF. His PhD, *The Possibility of Salvation Among the Unevangelised* has been published and he has co-edited two books with Philip Duce: *Keeping Your Balance: Approaching Theological and Religious Studies* and *Getting Your Bearings: Engaging with Contemporary Theologians*. He loves his wife, his three kids, cricket and jazz.

Thomas Talbott teaches philosophy at Willamette University in Salem, Oregon and has published many articles in philosophical and theological journals on universalism. In addition to his theological and philosophical interests, he is an enthusiastic hiker and backpacker. He also loves classical music, gardening, and (occasionally) watching the world's most popular sport – football (not American 'football' but the *real* thing).

Jerry L. Walls is Professor of Philosophy of Religion at Asbury Theological Seminary in Wilmore, Kentucky and Senior Speaking Fellow for the Morris Institute for Human Values. He is author of two philosophical explorations of the afterlife: *Hell: the Logic of Damnation* and *Heaven: the Logic of Eternal Joy*. He has also written *Why I Am Not a Calvinist* (forthcoming) and co-authored a book on C.S. Lewis and Francis Schaeffer as Christian apologists.

Introduction

ROBIN PARRY & CHRISTOPHER PARTRIDGE

> I wish I could say that God is too loving, too kind, and too generous to condemn any soul to eternal punishment. I would like to believe that hell can only be the anteroom to heaven, a temporary and frightful discipline to bring the unregenerate to final moral perfection.

So wrote Kenneth Kantzer in 1987.[1] Like many Christians he wants to believe that God will eventually save everybody, but sadly such a universalist belief is not even an option. Or is it? That is the question under the microscope in this volume.

A Typology of Universalisms

In order to better understand the following debate it will help to have a map of the theological terrain onto which the different contributions can be plotted. The word 'universalism' can be used in a range of different ways and it is worthwhile setting out a typology of universalisms to better understand the family of views under discussion in what follows.

Multiracial Universalism

There is a sense in which *all* Christians could be considered to be 'universalists'. Since the early days of its existence the Christian church has stood by the claim that God's people are a multiracial group composed of persons from every nation. This view could be labelled 'multiracial universalism' and all our contributors would defend it. Often academic theologians will speak of the universalism of a text such as Isaiah and it is to this kind of universalism that they generally refer.[2] However, this is not the kind of universalism that is under debate in the following pages.

Arminian Universalism

A second kind of 'universalism' is one that divides Christians (our authors included). According to this kind of universalism God desires to save all people. Not simply all *types* of people (i.e. Jews *and Gentiles*), but each and every individual. It should be noted that this kind of universalism does not commit the one who holds it to a belief that God will actually achieve his desire to save all. It is enough that God desires to save all and offers salvation to all. Human freewill is often held to be the reason why God does not achieve his purposes of universal salvation. The Arminian tradition in theology affirms this kind of universalism (represented in this volume by Howard Marshall and Jerry Walls), as does the more recent Open Theism (represented here by John Sanders).

Not all Christians can agree that God desires the salvation of each individual. The Augustinian/Calvinist traditions would maintain that God always achieves his purposes. If God did intend to save every individual then he would do so. Given that only a few respond to the Christian gospel, this must mean that God did not intend to save every individual. The Calvinist holds a very high view of divine sovereignty and does not see human freedom as a problem to God when exercising his providential control. So the mainstream Calvinist would affirm 'multiracial universalism' but not 'Arminian universalism'. In this volume the standard Calvinist position is represented by Daniel Strange. However, 'Arminian universalism' is not the view under debate in this book.

Strong Universalisms

A third kind of universalism could be called 'strong universalism'. In fact, it is better thought of as a family of quite different views rather than a single intellectual position. What 'strong universalisms' have in common is that they agree with the Arminian universalists that God does indeed desire to save all individuals, but they go on to add that *God will achieve his purposes*. Thus all individuals will in fact be saved. Strong universalisms can be thought of, for our purposes, as coming in at least three forms.

First, there are non-Christian versions of strong universalism. These are views developed within the religious thought systems of non-Christian religions according to which all individuals will eventually attain the 'ultimate good'. How this 'good' is conceived and how it is achieved will vary considerably from one system to the next. However, this book will not be concerned with such non-Christian strong forms of universalism and none of our authors represent such views.

Second, there is what could be described as 'pluralist universalism'. This is the view that sees all the major religious systems as different paths to the same goal. The most famous proponent of this view is John Hick. Hick's universalism is not obviously compatible with Christian theology in that it achieves its end only by pushing Christ and his atonement to the periphery as merely one route to salvation. It is not, however, pluralist universalism that is debated in the following pages.

Third, there is what we could call 'Christian universalism'.[3] Although this is a wide family of views, they share in common (a) the commitment to working within a Christian theological framework and (b) the claim that all individuals will be saved through the work of Christ. It is this kind of universalism that is debated in the following pages. It ought to be emphasised that the different types of universalism outlined here are abstractions. As Morwenna Ludlow's essay (Chapter 10) demonstrates, Christian universalists often developed universalist ideas that were motivated by a mixture of Christian and non-Christian philosophical ideas. Many of the Christian universalists she discusses were not the 'pure' type considered here but hybrids.

One problem that Christian universalists have often encountered is that they have been confused with pluralist universalists and then dismissed on the basis of misrepresentation of their views. This book seeks to avoid such misrepresentations and *all of our contributors acknowledge the Christian theological impulse behind the kind of universalism under consideration*. Another problem is that Christian universalists have often held unorthodox views on certain issues and it has been easy to dismiss their universalism because of the heterodoxy of other beliefs they have held (see Ludlow's chapter). However, we need to be careful not to declare 'Christian universalism' guilty by association. There is no obvious reason why Christian universalists need hold unorthodox views about the Trinity, the incarnation, the Church, the atonement (although, see the essay by Strange), the Bible or any central Christian beliefs (with the obvious exception of traditional Christian views on hell). The question addressed in this volume is whether universalism is a belief compatible with orthodox Christianity. Does it find warrant from Scripture, reason and tradition?

Christian universalism is, as noted above, not a single view but a range of views and it is important to understand this. One may, for instance, dismiss Christian universalism on the basis of an element in the system of a particular universalist theologian. However, if that element is not essential to universalism one may well find another Christian universalist who takes a different view on the element in question. Hence, it would be useful to set out some of the issues that Christian universalists disagree about:

- Is universal salvation something that Christians can reasonably *hope for* or is it something they can be *certain of*? Ludlow and Walls point out that most Christian theologians who have been universalists have held to a form of 'hopeful universalism', whilst both Talbott and Reitan in this volume defend a form of 'certain' or 'dogmatic universalism'.
- Do the hell texts in the Bible explain merely a possible destiny that is deserved but will never occur (as J.A.T. Robinson famously argued), or the real but temporary fate of the damned (as Talbott and most of the early Christian universalists argue)? In other words, will anyone ever experience the horrors of hell?
- Will the devil and his demons be saved? Most Christian Universalists would either say, 'no' (in light of Rev. 20:10) or remain agnostic. Some would say 'yes' (in light of Col. 1:20).
- Is universalism a possible Christian position among others or *the* authentic Christian position?
- Is the New Testament consistently universalist (Talbott), or does it hold in tension more than one view on the ultimate destiny of the unsaved (Hillert, J.A.T. Robinson)?

- Must one have conscious faith in Christ to be saved (exclusivist universalists) or can one be saved through Christ without having heard of Christ (inclusivist universalists)? Of course, one can be an exclusivist (like Daniel Strange) or an inclusivist (like John Sanders) without being a universalist.
- Do humans have indeterministic freedom (Adams) or not (Schleiermacher)? Or is some mediating position possible (Talbott)?
- Is God's just punishment to be understood in retributive terms or restorative terms (Talbott)? Or both?
- Is God free *not* to chose to love and save all (Barth[4]) or, constrained by the very nature of his being, is God bound to love and save all (Talbott)?

The Interpretation of Particular Texts

The debate about Christian universalism is a debate about the interpretation of particular texts as well as certain key theological themes. It is worth outlining some of the issues relating to both of those foci.

It is agreed by all sides that certain biblical texts *seem* to teach the final destruction of the lost (whether that be understood in terms of eternal conscious torment or annihilation) whilst others *appear* to teach the salvation of all. There appears to be a tension within the biblical teaching, even within the teachings of a single author like Paul, and the question is how to handle that tension. The 'options' appear to be as follows:[5]

One could argue that all the texts can be harmonised in such a way that they can be seen to teach the same thing. If a harmonisation of the texts can be achieved without twisting them it is clearly desirable. However, the harmonisation could work in two directions.

Traditionally Christians have taken the hell texts as clear and have thus re-interpreted the so-called 'universalist' texts in such a way that they are not seen to teach universalism. So the universalist texts may be understood as teaching that *some* people of all *types* will be saved (i.e. Jews *and Gentiles*), or as expressing God's *desire* to save all but not a prediction of what will actually happen, or as Paul getting carried away with his rhetoric as he extols Christ. This is the traditional Christian position. In this book Howard Marshall defends this view.

Alternatively, one could take the 'universalist' texts at face value and then try to re-interpret the hell texts in such a way that they do not teach the *everlasting* fate of the damned but only a temporary one. This was the stance of the early Christian universalists and most Christian universalists through history. In this book Talbott represents this position.

Many have resisted the urge to harmonise biblical teachings and have felt that the tension between the texts must be maintained. However, this could be understood in various ways.

One could argue that the Bible hopelessly contradicts itself and so we must choose the texts which seem to us to be either more numerous, closer to the theological heart of the Bible or, slightly cynically, the ones we like best. Other texts must be pushed to the periphery.

John Robinson argued that the New Testament contained two irreconcilable visions of the fate of humanity – eternal damnation and universal salvation. The damnation texts set out very clearly the fate sinful humans *deserve* whilst the universal salvation texts set out the fate that, by God's grace and through the atoning work of Christ, sinful humans will *actually* receive. Both damnation and salvation texts are important and both are 'true'. To reject Christ is to face the reality of hell. However, in the end, as a result of the post-mortem work of God, nobody will reject Christ and in this sense hell is only hypothetically a reality.

M.E. Boring argued that Paul employed the notion of limited salvation when using the image of God as a judge and the idea of universal salvation when he used the image of God as a king. The two images must be retained, as must the teachings of universal *and* limited salvation. 'Because they are affirmed together, the ultimate logical inferences belonging to each are never drawn. Paul affirms both human responsibility and the universal victory of God's grace. As propositions, they can only contradict each other. As pictures, they can both be held up, either alternatively, or occasionally, together, as pointers to the God whose grace and judgement both resist capture in a system, or in a single picture.'[6] A sophisticated development of Boring's approach is found in Sven Hillert's book *Limited and Universal Salvation*. Hillert argues that Paul never directly addresses the issue of either limited or universal salvation. All the key texts are actually parts of arguments with quite different foci. In particular, Paul uses his doctrine of justification by faith to unite believers but never to divide believers from non-believers. The doctrine of election *seems* to forever divide believers (the elect) from non-believers (the non-elect) but Paul shows that he is quite capable, at least in the case of Israel, of arguing that non-elect Jews can become elect Jews (by believing the gospel) and that in the end 'all Israel', as opposed to part of Israel, 'will be saved' by accepting their messiah. In texts where Paul seems to speak without qualification of a final division between saved and lost there are grounds for thinking that he avoids such qualification for rhetorical and pragmatic reasons to do with the specific situations he addresses. Thus, says Hillert, we cannot be sure whether Paul saw the division between lost and saved as final or temporary. On the other hand, pragmatic considerations also underlie the universal salvation texts. In these Paul is primarily concerned with the unity of believers although he makes no attempt to guard himself against strong universalist interpretations. Like Boring, Hillert wants to maintain both universal and limited salvation perspectives as relevant in different contexts.

The Theological Debate

This debate is not simply about how to interpret specific texts. It is very much to do with key themes in Christian theology such as the love and justice of God, human freedom and divine sovereignty, the atonement, divine election and the nature of God's victory over evil.

In the opening chapters Talbott draws attention to the universalist claim that even if no particular texts spoke of universal salvation, the logic of other theological claims could push one in a universalist direction. In particular, the universalist would maintain that God's love for his creation is not consistent with the claim that God does not wish to redeem it. If God truly loves a creature his desire will be to save that creature and if God truly loves *all* his creatures then his desire will be to save *all* his creatures. If God is love then God must love all people and desire their salvation. To achieve this goal Christ died, not merely for a limited number of people, but for *all* people. These claims are shared with a great many non-universalist Christians and have *prima facie* biblical support. However, when combined with the theological claim that ultimately God will achieve his goals for creation one can see that the pull of universalism arises from claims internal to Christian theology itself and is not obviously an alien import. To complicate matters though, the claim that God will ultimately achieve *all* his purposes for creation is one that orthodox Christians disagree over. Whilst those of an Augustinian/Calvinist persuasion will have no problems with it, those of Arminian inclination will draw back. God has given humans freedom to choose to reject his purposes for them. If humans keep on rejecting God's offer of salvation, God could only save them by disregarding their freedom, and thereby treating them not as persons but as objects. Those in hell are those who refuse salvation. Marshall, Walls and Sanders stand in this tradition. Thus the debate about universalism is closely related to the debate about human freedom and divine sovereignty. It may seem that universalists would stand with Calvinists and reject any notion of 'freedom' that allowed humans to resist God's will for them, but this is not necessarily the case. Some universalists, such as Schleiermacher, have indeed defended a view of freedom that makes our choices compatible with total divine determination. Nevertheless, it would be true to say that most recent universalists have embraced non-determinist notions of freedom (i.e. that human freedom is not compatible with God's determining human choices). This poses a problem for the universalist because it is not immediately clear how God could ensure that all people will *freely* embrace salvation if he does not determine their choices. This has been a major reason for many contemporary theologians rejecting universalism (in this volume Walls and Sanders reject universalism largely for this reason). In response, Reitan and Talbott argue that if a person is *fully informed* about sin and the offer of salvation in Christ then rejecting salvation would be utterly irrational. So irrational, in fact, that it makes no sense to speak of such a person as 'free' at all but rather under the rule of some psychological malfunction. All that God has to do is ensure that *at some point* everyone will be 'fully informed' and he can guarantee that they will freely accept Christ. H.H. Farmer similarly argued that the coerciveness of truth leads to universal salvation in a way that respects human freedom and therefore does not depersonalise the divine-human relationship. That is to say, truth compels decision in a way that is not felt to be an overriding of human personality: 'we feel that it is of the very essence of personality that it can thus be brought under a thrusting and overpowering impact of truth.'[7] Hence, God in his manifold wisdom 'could bring even the most evil and recalcitrant soul to a situation, either in this world or the next, where the truth is presented with such compelling force and with such coincidental co-operation of internal conditions, that it cannot be resisted any longer – a situation where he can do no other than surrender at last'.[8] Strange and Sanders both argue that such approaches underestimate the depth and irrationality of sin. This issue has been the subject of much debate in recent philosophy of religion and this book will certainly not settle the matter.[9]

Another theological issue is the nature of God's just punishments. Are God's punishments purely retributive? That is to say, are they simply God's giving creatures what they deserve irrespective of the effect for better or for worse upon them? The traditional doctrine of hell has worked with a purely retributive notion of final judgement and Strange ably represents this position. Sinners must be sent to hell *because hell is what sinners deserve*. This view, when combined with the notion of hell as eternal conscious torment, does raise a well-known problem. How could eternal conscious torment ever be the *just* punishment for the finite sins of any individual?[10] It seems to many that such a punishment would be massively disproportionate. There are strategies for defending the justice of eternal conscious torment (see Strange's essay), but this problem is part of the reason for the steady flow of theologians away from the traditional notion of hell towards a variety of annihilationist positions.[11] Annihilation is not obviously undeserved and retains the retributive aspect of divine wrath. In theory a universalist could maintain a purely retributive view of hell in either the everlasting torment or the annihilation modes so long as they also maintained that everyone would be delivered from hell before it was too late (i.e. before eternity has expired or the fire has consumed) or, as with John Robinson, that hell is a hypothetical reality that all will be spared due to God's grace. However, it has been more common for universalists to understand God's justice as restorative justice and his punishments as corrective. Certainly this is often the case for God's judgements in history. Hellfire is educative in that it makes the sinner aware of the horrors of their sin and their need for salvation. So universalists may understand God's just punishments as wholly restorative (e.g. Talbott) or as both retributive and restorative. In defence of this interpretation of hell they argue that if God is love then *all* God's actions must be loving and this includes his sending people to hell. God's punishment of the damned must be both a just and loving action. The question remains, however, whether non-universalists cannot also see hell as a loving action. Walls and Strange argue that hell could be a manifestation of divine love in Arminian and Calvinist ways respectively.[12]

Another key question concerning hell is whether God gives those in hell a second chance to repent. Clearly most universalists have answered in the affirmative. The mainstream of the Christian tradition, however, has seen hell as the final state of the lost with no further chances for repentance. Those who see the damned as damned forever have traditionally maintained that they are getting what they deserve and that God is under no obligations to give them any more chances. However, this view is possibly problematic. If God loves those in hell, certainly a common view amongst Christians, then why would he not rescue one who called to him from hell and trusted in Christ's atonement? God's *justice* would not seem to require him to leave them in hell. If God can forgive sinners in this age without being unjust it is not clear why his justice would require him not to forgive those in hell. It is also hard to see why God's love would motivate him to not save people from hell. With these issues in mind, following C.S. Lewis some recent theologians, including Jerry Walls, have argued that the door to hell is shut *from the inside*. Those in hell could be saved if they so wished but they are so much in hatred of God that they never (rarely?) would choose to accept God's grace. They are fixed in their corruption and opposition to God. The universalist maintains that it is awkward to imagine that God would send people to a hell that has the effect of hardening its occupants against him when he could, they maintain, have a hell that would educate them and draw them towards him. This debate continues.

All Christians affirm that in the end God's kingdom will triumph over all opposition. The universalist debate, we have seen, focuses attention on the nature of that triumph. Is God's final victory one in which all creatures are reconciled to God and lovingly accept his Lordship and worship him (the universalist view), or is it one in which those who continue to resist him are *forced* to bow the knee like a defeated army (the mainstream view)? The image of military defeat is clearly biblical, but the question is whether this imagery is to be taken at face value (Marshall) or as a metaphor for salvation (Talbott). Would the destruction of God's enemies equate to a defeat for God (Talbott) or not (Walls, Sanders, Strange)?

So the universalist debate goes to the heart of Christian theology. It raises questions about the doctrine of God. Does God love everyone? Does God desire to save everyone? Is God able to achieve his purposes for his creatures? What do we mean when we say that God and his punishments are 'just'? What is the nature of the final victory of God? It raises questions about atonement and reconciliation. Did Christ die for everyone? Is Christ's atonement effective for all those Christ died for? What is the nature of reconciliation? It raises questions about human nature, human freedom and divine providence. Can humans freely resist God at all? If so can they do so *forever*? Is a *fully personal* divine-human relationship one that is *freely* entered into? The debate about universalism thus reaches far beyond specific texts about hell or universal salvation. Indeed, the broader theological debate is often more determinative for the stances of theologians than the debates about specific texts.

Scripture, Reason and Tradition

To properly evaluate universalism requires the resources of Scripture, reason and tradition. This volume aims to bring Christian universalism under the scrutiny of those resources. All the responses combine insights from Scripture, reason and tradition (threads that cannot truly be disentangled) but it may help to artificially organise the contributions as follows:

Scripture

Two biblical scholars put the exegetical case for universalism to the test and reach differing conclusions. Howard Marshall maintains that Talbott has misunderstood the biblical texts and that there is no biblical case for universalism. Tom Johnson, whilst finding fault with some of Talbott's exegesis, thinks that Scripture teaches a much wider view of mercy than is often thought and that it even leaves open the *possibility* of universal salvation. That said, in the final analysis, he tends to the view that final annihilation seems a more likely fate for the damned.

Reason

Two philosophers consider the case for universalism and come to radically differing conclusions. Jerry Walls argues that a good case can be made for a more traditional notion of hell and that Talbott's arguments fail to settle the case for universalism. Eric Reitan, on the other hand, argues that the philosophical case for universalism is very strong. We also bring two quite different theologians together. Both Daniel Strange and John Sanders argue that universalism is flawed, but do so for quite different reasons. Sanders is sympathetic to the case for universalism but ultimately rejects it because it cannot, he argues, account for human freedom. Strange rejects it as incompatible with important theological concerns central to the traditions of Calvinist Christianity.

Tradition

The mainstream Christian tradition since the time of Augustine has clearly been against universalism. The most important theologians of the Christian church have rejected universalism as have many Christian denominations and this is not something Christians can simply ignore. The wisdom of the centuries must be weighed *very* seriously before being rejected. Morwenna Ludlow traces the story of universalism through the ages and argues that although it has always been a minority tradition within orthodox Christianity it has almost always had some presence amongst otherwise orthodox believers (and some rather heterodox ones also). David Hilborn and Don Horrocks show that whilst evangelicals have more or less consistently rejected universalism, there have always been a small number of 'evangelicals' (?) who have had varying degrees of universalist sympathies.

This book does not aim or claim to provide the right answers, but rather to provoke *informed* discussion of an important and neglected area of Christian theology. Although Tom Talbott has the 'final' word this is in no way intended to suggest that he has dealt conclusively with all the objections raised against universalism or that the debate is over. The intention is, on the one hand, to show that the debate is not closed after the initial responses and, on the other hand, to encourage you, the reader, to make your own response and, hopefully, join in the debate (perhaps on the book's website: www.universalsalvation.net). If it achieves this end we shall be happy.

Notes

1 K.S. Kantzer, 'Troublesome Questions', *Christianity Today*, March 1987, p. 45. Thanks to William Bromley for drawing attention to this quotation in his unpublished book *Until He Finds It: A Journey of Exploration Into Final Human Destiny*.
2 E.g. Gelston (1992).
3 Hart (1992) makes the helpful distinction between pluralist universalism and Christian universalism.
4 There is much debate about whether the theologian Karl Barth really was a universalist. *If* he was then he would hold the position indicated above.
5 We simply describe the positions here and make no attempt to evaluate them.
6 Boring (1986), p. 292.
7 Farmer (1936), p.257.
8 Farmer (1948), p.146. On Farmer's universalism see Partridge (1998).
9 In defence of this argument see Talbott (1990c, 1999c, 2001b) and Reitan (2001). Against it see Walls (1992), Craig (1991, 1993), M. Murray (1999).
10 See Adams (1975).
11 See Fudge (1994); Powys (1998).
12 See too Stump (1986). There is also the related question of whether eternal hell, even annihilation, is a mechanical abstraction from a personal moral universe. Is victory in a moral universe achieved in the destruction of a sinful person, or in the recreation of that person into what s/he ought to be, central to which is divine-human reconciliation?

PART I

A Case for Christian Universalism

1

Towards a Better Understanding of Universalism

THOMAS TALBOTT

A Brief Autobiographical Note

As a young man growing up in a conservative evangelical church, it never occurred to me even to question the widespread assumption that, according to the Bible as a whole, a host of sinners, including some of my own loved ones, would eventually be lost forever without any further hope of redemption. Indeed, all of my early theological reflections and immature struggles took place within the context of this one unquestioned assumption – which was also the context, therefore, in which I first began to reflect seriously upon the nature and character of the Christian God.

The early catalyst for such reflection was the historical debate between the Augustinians (or the Calvinists, as some of my Augustinian friends liked to call themselves) and the so-called Arminians.[1] The Augustinian idea that salvation is wholly a matter of grace, and an irresistible grace at that, did not seem initially compelling to me, even though it seemed to accord perfectly with Pauline theology. St Paul himself, I thought, could not have made the point any clearer than this: 'For by grace you have been saved through faith, and this [the faith] is not your own doing; it is the gift of God, not the result of works, so that no one may boast' (Eph. 2:8–9).[2] But whenever I tried to combine in my own mind this doctrine of free and irresistible grace with the traditional understanding of hell, the idea of grace seemed to evaporate altogether. For where is the grace in a doctrine of limited election? Is God being gracious to an elect mother, for example, when he makes the baby she loves an object of his 'sovereign hatred'[3] and does so, as in the case of Esau, even before the child has done anything good or bad?[4] To my mind at least, such a combination of beliefs carried the obvious implication that God is anything but just, anything but loving, and (contrary to repeated declarations in the New Testament) every bit the 'respecter of persons'. So despite the clear doctrine of grace that so pervades the New Testament, I found myself rejecting Augustinian theology almost from the time I first encountered it; and during my undergraduate and seminary days, I therefore put all of my energies into working out, as well as I could, an essentially Arminian, if not outright Pelagian, theology.

But though Arminianism seemed initially plausible, especially as encountered in someone like C.S. Lewis (one of my early heroes), it too eventually led to a dead end. For even though the Arminians, with their emphasis upon free will, seemed to offer the best possible *philosophical* explanation of hell, I could never quite escape the suspicion that their biblical exegesis, especially in the case of a text such as Romans 9, is at times contrived and artificial. Because I was already persuaded, even as my Arminian friends were, that free will and determinism are incompatible, I was perhaps less concerned than I should have been that the central Arminian understanding of free will is not obviously a biblical idea at all. My point is not that the Bible in any way *excludes* the so-called 'incompatibilist' understanding of free will;[5] to the contrary, I continue to believe that indeterminism is essential to the process whereby God, first, brings rational agents into being, and second, reconciles them to himself over time as sons and daughters.[6] But the harder I tried to work out a consistent Arminian theology and to harmonize it with the New Testament writings, the harder I found it to escape the fact that, according to Paul, our final destiny is already foreordained and not a matter of free choice at all. Lest I be misunderstood, I should perhaps reiterate my conviction that in no way did Paul exclude free choice or the importance of moral effort altogether; far from it. Paul himself repeatedly exhorted his readers to exert moral effort. But at the same time, Paul consistently insisted that one's election (and therefore one's ultimate destiny) 'depends not on human will or exertion, but on God who shows mercy' (Rom. 9:16). So in the end, I had to admit that Arminian theology fails to explain how free will might plausibly figure into the divine scheme of foreordination, as we encounter it in the New Testament.

Now curiously, even as I began entertaining the possibility that Paul really was serious about predestination, I also began questioning, for quite independent philosophical reasons, the very idea of a freely embraced eternal destiny in hell. In an understandable effort to preserve God's loving character and to defend the New Testament teaching that 'God is no respecter of persons', the Arminians grant ultimate sovereignty, at least in the case of the damned, to an utterly irrational human choice. As C.S. Lewis put it, 'I willingly believe that the damned are, in one sense, successful, rebels to the end; that the doors of hell are locked on the *inside*.'[7] But Lewis also recognized that union with the divine 'nature is bliss and separation from it horror';[8] and if that is true, then a *free* choice of the kind he attributed to the damned seems deeply incoherent, even logically impossible. For no one rational enough to qualify as a free moral agent could possibly prefer an objective horror – the outer darkness, for example – to eternal bliss, nor could any such person both experience the horror of separation from God and continue to regard it as a desirable state. The Augustinian idea that the damned are subjected to punishment against their will at least makes coherent sense, but the Arminian idea that the damned freely choose horror over bliss, hell over heaven, makes no coherent sense at all.[9]

In any event, the Western theological tradition seemed to leave me with a choice between an unjust and unloving God, on the one hand, and a defeated God, on the other. But of course this hardly exhausts the logical possibilities; there remains the additional possibility that it is God's very nature to love, as 1 John 4:8 and 16 appear to declare, and that he is also wise and resourceful enough to accomplish *all* of his loving purposes in the end. Why, after all, should an assumption concerning everlasting punishment be the only unquestioned assumption in a context where some are limiting the extent of God's love and others are limiting the scope of his ultimate victory? Why not at least examine the pros and cons of universal reconciliation alongside those of limited election and those of a limited victory over sin and death? When my brother Stephen, who had come under the influence of George MacDonald,[10] finally persuaded me to do just that, something remarkable happened with a kind of breathtaking suddenness. Almost from the moment I began to examine the doctrine of universal reconciliation with an open mind, something akin to a paradigm shift in science, as Thomas Kuhn has called it, or a Copernican Revolution in philosophy, as Immanuel Kant called it, took place in my theological outlook. Suddenly, everything seemed to fall into place. Paul's theological essay in Romans 9–11 finally began to make sense to me, as did the warnings against apostasy in Hebrews 10 and Jesus' remarks about the unpardonable sin.[11] Whole areas of tension between faith and reason, between the supposed teachings of the Bible and my philosophical reflections, between theology and ordinary common sense, simply dissolved and evaporated. But above all, I finally understood why the gospel really is good news, indeed the best possible news for those in our present condition, and why it should not be confused with the twisted message of fear that we humans sometimes make it out to be.

Finally, I should perhaps also point out that I now view universal reconciliation as something more than a vague hope of some kind. To the contrary, I now view it as essential to a proper understanding of salvation, essential to a Pauline understanding of grace, and essential to the inclusive nature of election. For even as many Augustinians are utterly convinced that God's salvific will cannot be defeated forever and many Arminians are utterly convinced that God at least wills the salvation of all human sinners, so I am equally convinced that *both* claims are true. In that respect, I now feel a kinship with the New Testament scholar William Barclay who could write: 'I am a *convinced* universalist.'[12]

Three Competing Systems of Theology

When I first began interpreting the New Testament along universalistic lines, I was struck by how many regarded such an interpretation as not only mistaken, but utterly unreasonable and heretical as well. I found that a good many of my Augustinian friends, who did not regard the Arminian view as heretical (only mistaken), and a good many of my Arminian friends, who did not regard the Augustinian view as heretical (only mistaken), were united in their conviction that universalism is both mistaken and heretical. This curious response started me thinking. Why should the Augustinians regard universalism as any more heretical than the Arminian view? and why should the Arminians regard it as any more heretical than the Augustinian view?

As I began to reflect upon such questions, I observed an intriguing phenomenon. With a few notable exceptions, my own interpretation of specific texts in the Bible always seemed to find support either in the writings of a first rate Augustinian scholar or in those of a first rate Arminian scholar. The exceptions, of course, were the standard proof texts for a doctrine of everlasting separation, which the Augustinians and the Arminians both accept. But the remarkable thing is this: If you simply take the Augustinian idea of God's sovereignty in the matter of salvation – that is, the idea that the Hound of Heaven cannot be defeated forever – and put it together with the Arminian idea that God at least wills or desires the salvation of all, then you get universalism, plain and simple. And though some will no doubt reject the propriety of following such theological reasoning to its logical conclusion, it is perhaps worth comparing the kind of reasoning that leads to universalism with the kind that leads to competing theological positions.

Consider the following inconsistent set of propositions:

1. God's redemptive love extends to all human sinners equally in the sense that he sincerely wills or desires the redemption of each one of them.
2. Because no one can finally defeat God's redemptive love or resist it forever, God will triumph in the end and successfully accomplish the redemption of everyone whose redemption he sincerely wills or desires.
3. Some human sinners will never be redeemed but will instead be separated from God forever.[13]

If the above set of propositions is logically inconsistent, and it surely is, then at least one of the above propositions is false. But which one? Because Christian universalists accept both proposition (1) and proposition (2), they reason deductively that proposition (3) is false. But suppose, for a moment, that they should be mistaken in this matter; suppose that proposition (3) should in fact be true. It would then follow that at least one of the other two propositions, either (1) or (2), is false. Of course, someone who believes in eternal punishment and therefore accepts proposition (3) could always leave it at that, pleading ignorance concerning which of the other two propositions is false. Similarly, someone who believes in the universality of God's love and therefore accepts proposition (1), or someone who believes in the sovereignty of God's salvific will and therefore accepts proposition (2), could also plead ignorance concerning which of the other two propositions is false. Beyond that, a Christian might even plead ignorance concerning all three of our propositions. But I know of no reputable theologian who both accepts proposition (3) with some degree of certitude and remains content simply to leave it at that. For the obvious questions are simply too pressing: Does God truly love those who are lost forever? Does his loving will then suffer an ultimate defeat? Because the Augustinians accept both the traditional understanding of hell (proposition (3)) and the sovereignty of God's salvific will (proposition (2)), they reason deductively that God's redemptive love is restricted to a limited elect; hence, proposition (1) is false. And because the Arminians accept both the traditional understanding of hell (proposition (3)) and the universality of God's love (proposition (1)), they reason deductively that God's redemptive love can be defeated forever; hence, proposition (2) is false. So there is an initial symmetry, at any rate, between the kind of reasoning that leads the Augustinians to limit the scope of God's love, the kind that leads the Arminians to limit the scope of God's ultimate victory, and the kind that leads the universalists to reject the idea of unending punishment altogether.

Of course, any good Augustinian will insist that the Bible itself limits the scope of God's love, and any good Arminian will likewise insist that the Bible itself limits the scope of God's ultimate victory. Similarly, many Christian universalists will also insist – and believe me, I know many who do – that the Bible itself excludes the idea of unending punishment. So yes, of course. *Everyone* who looks to the Bible as an authority will insist that his or her theology represents the most reasonable interpretation of the Bible as a whole. But if you simply pick up an English Bible and read it naively – that is, if you read it without bringing to it a lot of theological expectations and without imposing upon it a well worked-out theology – you will find texts that initially appear to support each of our three propositions. So let us set aside, for the moment, sophisticated exegetical disputes and simply review the obvious.

In support of proposition (1), a naïve reader of the English Bible would likely cite such texts as 2 Peter 3:9: 'The Lord... is not willing that any should perish, but [wills instead] that all should come to repentance' (KJV); 1 Timothy 2:4: God 'desires everyone to be saved and to come to the knowledge of the truth'; Ezekiel 33:11: 'As I live, says the Lord God, I have no pleasure in the death of the wicked, but [desire instead] that the wicked turn away from their ways and live'; and perhaps the clearest of all, Lamentations 3:22 & 3:31–33: 'The steadfast love of the Lord never ceases, his mercies never come to an end... For the Lord will not reject forever. Although he causes grief, he will have compassion according to the abundance of his steadfast love; for he does not willingly afflict or grieve anyone.' All of these texts seem to suggest that God sincerely wants to achieve the reconciliation of all sinners, and other texts, such as 1 John 2:2, suggest further that Jesus Christ suffered and died precisely in an effort to achieve that end. For here we read that Jesus Christ 'is the atoning sacrifice for our sins, and not for ours only but also for the sins of the entire world'. But then, if the God who seeks to reconcile the entire world to himself (see also 2 Cor. 5:19) were to fail in the effort, this would seem to represent a tragic defeat of his own redemptive purpose for the world.

Similarly, in support of proposition (2), a naïve reader of the English Bible would likely cite such texts as Ephesians 1:11: God 'accomplishes all things according to his will and counsel'; Job 42:2: 'I know that you [the Lord God] can do all things, and that no purpose of yours can be thwarted'; Psalm 115:3: 'Our God is in the heavens; he does whatever he pleases'; and Isaiah 46:10b & 11b: 'My counsel shall stand, and I will accomplish all my purpose... I have spoken, and I will bring it to pass; I have purposed, and I will do it.' These texts seem to imply that God is able to accomplish all of his purposes including, therefore, all of his redemptive purposes. Others seem to imply that God not only has the power, but will in fact exercise his power, to bring all things into subjection to Christ (1 Cor. 15:27–28), to reconcile all things in Christ (Col. 1:20), and to bring justification and life to all persons through Christ (Rom. 5:18).

But finally, in support of proposition (3), a naïve reader of the English Bible would likely cite such texts as Matthew 25:46: 'And they will go away into eternal punishment, but the righteous into eternal life'; 2 Thessalonians 1:9: 'They shall suffer the punishment of eternal destruction and exclusion from the presence of the Lord and from the glory of his might' (RSV); and Revelation 21:8: 'But as for the cowardly, the faithless, the polluted, as for murderers, fornicators, sorcerers, idolaters, and all liars, their lot shall be the lake that burns with fire and brimstone, which is the second death.' These texts may seem to imply that at least some persons will be lost forever and thus never be reconciled to God.

Lest there should be any confusion in the matter, I should perhaps point out at this point that I make no claim, in the present context, about the correct interpretation of any of the above texts that our imaginary naïve reader might cite. Neither do I make any claim about the appropriateness of lifting isolated texts from very different contexts and setting them side by side, as if one could somehow adduce evidence thereby for the content of revealed truth. I merely make the point that various texts in the Bible may initially appear to support, and in fact have been cited on behalf of, each of our three propositions. With respect to each of them, some theologians and Bible scholars have concluded that it is not a peripheral but a fundamental teaching in the Bible. The point is important enough to bear repeating: You can line up some of the most famous names in Western theology, and also some of the most famous names in the conservative evangelical tradition, in support of each of our three propositions. But as a matter of logic, not all of them can be true; at least one of them is false.

Accordingly, if we consider the matter purely as an exercise in logic – that is, without considering any textual evidence at all – we confront this alternative: We can say, on the one hand, that the Bible teaches all three propositions and is not, therefore, infallible in all of its teachings; or we can say, on the other hand, that the Bible is indeed infallible in all of its teachings, but does not really teach all three propositions.[14] In either case, those who believe that God has revealed himself in the Bible will face essentially the same hermeneutical problem, that is, essentially the same problem of interpreting the Bible as a whole: They must provide an interpretive structure that avoids a fundamental logical inconsistency in what they take to be the revealed truth about God. And that is just what each of our three competing theological systems seeks to do; each of them rejects at least one proposition in the inconsistent set with which we began.

Is Universalism Heretical?

So herein lies the context in which I would now address the question of heresy. The Augustinians, the Arminians, and the universalists are all in the same 'theological boat', at least in one important respect: They all end up rejecting a proposition that not only has some *prima facie* biblical support, but also has the support of other scholars who would defend it as a clear teaching of Scripture. In such a context one might wonder, quite apart from the general silliness of the matter, how a charge of heresy could even be expressed coherently. If it is not heretical for the Arminians to believe that God, being unlimited in love, at least wills (or sincerely desires) the salvation of all (proposition (1)), why should it be heretical for the universalists to believe this as well? And if it is not heretical for the Augustinians to believe that God, being almighty, will in the end accomplish all of his redemptive purposes (proposition (2)), why should it be heretical for the universalists to believe this as well? And finally, if it is not heretical to accept proposition (1), as the Arminians do, and not heretical to accept proposition (2), as the Augustinians do, why should it be heretical to accept both (1) and (2)?

Now as a matter of logic, there is a possible answer to this latter question and a possible way for someone who regards the Bible as a kind of final authority to argue that universalism is indeed heretical. For if the biblical warrant for proposition (3), or a doctrine of everlasting separation, were overwhelmingly greater than that for our other two propositions, then one might be in a position to argue that you could reject (3) only at the price of falling into heresy. One might then argue, in other words, that anyone who wants to escape heresy would have to reject one of the other two propositions in our inconsistent triad.

But nothing like that seems to be true at all, and here, at any rate, is how I see the matter. The biblical warrant for proposition (1), that

God at least wills the salvation of all, is simply overwhelming – so overwhelming, I believe, that those who worry about heresy, as I do not, ought to regard St Augustine as an early Christian heretic. For surely, Augustine represented a far more radical departure from tradition than did such early Christian universalists as St Gregory of Nyssa, Theodore of Mopsuestia, or even Origen. The biblical warrant for proposition (2), that Almighty God will eventually accomplish all of his will in the matter of salvation, is also exceedingly strong, as Augustine himself rightly insisted. And proposition (3) is the weakest of the three. For only (3) seems to rest upon controversial *translations* as well as controversial *interpretations*; and whereas (1) and (2) seem to rest upon systematic teachings in Paul, the texts cited on behalf of (3) are typically lifted from contexts of parable, hyperbole, and great symbolism.

But that is merely how I see the matter. Others will no doubt see things differently. Howard Marshall, for example, concludes a vigorous critique of universalism with these words: 'if the evidence for everlasting punishment... were as palpably weak as the actual evidence for universalism is, no reputable scholar would treat it seriously.'[15] I wonder, however, whether Marshall has thought through the 'strength of evidence issue' in light of our three propositions above. Suppose we concede, as Marshall himself does, a strong biblical case for the Arminian belief that God at least *wills* or *desires* the salvation of all (proposition (1)). In Marshall's own words: 'The question is not really one of the extent of God's love; that he loves all and does not wish any to perish is *clear biblical teaching*.'[16] If we accept that claim, as I think we must, then Marshall's further claim that the biblical case for universalism is 'palpably weak' is, for all practical purposes, equivalent to the claim that the Augustinian case for irresistible grace and for the ultimate triumph of God's salvific will (proposition (2)) is also 'palpably weak'. For if there is a strong biblical case that God 'loves all' and therefore wills the salvation of all and likewise a strong biblical case that God's loving will shall triumph in the end, then there is also a strong biblical case for universalism. In fact, a universalist could, if he or she so desired, simply leave it to the Augustinians, who are in no way universalists themselves, to shore up that part of the case for universalism, namely proposition (2), that Marshall evidently rejects as 'palpably weak'.

My point is that you cannot properly evaluate any one of our three propositions in isolation from the other two; indeed, you can weaken the case for any one of them simply by strengthening the case for the other two. Because Western theology includes, moreover, two *respectably orthodox* traditions, one of which holds, as Marshall does, that proposition (1) is a clear teaching of Scripture and the other of which holds, as the Augustinians do, that proposition (2) is a clear teaching of Scripture, we are entitled to conclude, I think, that the case for universalism is not nearly as 'palpably weak' as Marshall and others would have us believe. For if it were so 'palpably weak', you would expect that the respectably orthodox among us would at least agree on which part of the case *is* 'palpably weak'. So which is it, proposition (1) or proposition (2)? Should we limit the scope of God's love, as the Augustinians do? Or should we insist that God's loving will suffers an ultimate defeat, as the Arminians do? If neither of these options seems acceptable, then one is left with the belief that God loves all equally and that his loving will cannot be thwarted forever. And that is universalism.

A Concluding Comment

As our discussion so far should already illustrate, *any* interpretation of the Bible as a whole is a complex affair, where some themes and some texts will inevitably be interpreted in light of others. It is as much an art and an act of the imagination, and as much a product of philosophical reasoning, as it is of historical and linguistic study. Accordingly, our task in what follows will be to examine two prominent New Testament themes: that of Christ's ultimate victory and triumph, on the one hand, and that of divine judgement, on the other. Although these themes may at first seem difficult to harmonize, I believe that Paul explains exactly how to fit them together consistently; it is just that his explanation is so unexpected, and so contrary to some of our natural inclinations, that we are apt to miss it altogether. Once we learn to follow his lead in the matter, however, we will no longer be tempted to explain away his theme of victory and triumph or the clear universalistic thrust of his teaching.

Notes

1 The Arminians are, of course, named after Jacobus Arminius (1560–1609), who opposed the Calvinist understanding of predestination and limited election.
2 Unless otherwise indicated, all quotations from the Bible in my essay are from the New Revised Standard Version.
3 According to G.C. Berkouwer, the Dutch theologian Hermann Hoeksema described God's attitude towards the non-elect as the 'sovereign hatred of his good pleasure'. For the quotation from *Het Evangelie*, see Berkouwer (1960), p. 224.
4 The whole thing is in fact a logical impossibility. God cannot both love me and refuse to love some of my own loved ones. Neither can he both love me and refuse to love someone else, whether I now happen to love that other person or not. For why this is so and for some of the logical absurdities in a doctrine of limited election, see Talbott, (1999c), Chapter 8. See also Talbott (1990b), pp. 30–34.
5 Incompatibilism is the philosophical view that free choice is incompatible with determinism and therefore incompatible with any deterministic understanding of divine predestination.
6 See p. 262–65. For a fuller account of my view here, see Talbott (2001a), pp. 105–108.
7 C.S. Lewis (1944a), p. 115.
8 C.S. Lewis (1955), p. 232.
9 I here present a mere sketch of my thinking at this point. For a more detailed discussion of the actual arguments, see Talbott (1992b), pp. 500–503; Talbott (1999c), Chapter 11, and Talbott (2001b).
10 Perhaps the best sources for MacDonald's theological ideas are four volumes of his sermons: *Unspoken Sermons* (originally published in a series of three volumes) and *Hope of the Gospel*. Unedited versions of these sermons are now available online at the URL: http://www.johannesen.com/OnlineGMD.htm. For an edited (and condensed) version, see Hein (ed.) (1976) and (1974). For some of MacDonald's universalistic ideas, I would highly recommend the sermons entitled 'The Consuming Fire', 'Justice', and 'Light' in MacDonald (1867) as well as 'Salvation From Sin' in MacDonald (1892).
11 For a discussion of 'the unforgiveable sin' see Talbott (1999c), pp. 103–106.
12 Barclay (1977), p. 65. My italics.
13 I here express this inconsistent set of propositions rather differently, and perhaps even more precisely, than I have expressed it elsewhere. See, for example, Talbott (1995), p. 79, and (1999c), p. 43.
14 As an illustration, consider the proposition that the earth is flat, which we now know to be quite false. If we consider the matter purely as a exercise in logic, without considering any textual evidence at all, we can say one of two things: Either the Bible teaches that the earth is flat and is not infallible in all of its teachings, or it is infallible in all of its teachings and does not really teach that the earth is flat.
15 I.H. Marshall (2000), p. 24.
16 *Ibid*., p. 19. My italics.

2

Christ Victorious

THOMAS TALBOTT

Victory or Defeat?

A frequently dismissed argument against the traditional understanding of hell is that the eternal misery of those in hell would, in the end, undermine the blessedness of the redeemed. But though many dismiss such an argument on the ground that it rests upon an extra-biblical or a purely philosophical consideration, the argument in fact has some impressive biblical credentials.

Consider first Paul's offhand remark concerning his friend and fellow worker Epaphroditus: 'He was indeed so ill that he nearly died. But God had mercy upon him, and not only on him but on me also, so that I would not have one sorrow after another' (Phil. 2:27). Here Paul acknowledged an important point about the way in which love ties people's interests together even as it renders a person more vulnerable to misery and sorrow. Given Paul's love for his friend, any good that befell his friend would also be a good that befell Paul and any evil that befell his friend would likewise be an evil that befell Paul. Or, as Jesus himself put it in his much misunderstood account of the judgment of nations: 'as you did it to one of the least of these my brethren, you did it to me' (Mt. 25:40 RSV).

Even more profound than the grief Paul might have experienced over the death of a Christian brother was his 'unceasing anguish' over the spiritual health of his beloved kin: 'I have great sorrow and unceasing anguish in my heart. For I could wish [or pray] that I myself were accursed and cut off from Christ for the sake of my people' (Rom. 9:2–3). Given Paul's universalistic conclusions in Romans 5 and 11 and the ecstatic joy they induced in him (see 11:32–36), we should not, I believe, confuse this 'unceasing anguish' with a kind of ultimate despair or hopelessness. But still, Paul's own anguish over his unbelieving kin must have been every bit as intense as the anguish that Ted Bundy's mother experienced just before her son – a serial killer of young women – was executed for his crimes. I shall never forget an interview, just prior to the execution, in which a reporter asked this dear woman – a fundamentalist Christian, by the way – whether she could still support her son who had become a monster. As the camera zoomed in on her face, she literally began to shake and her eyes filled with tears, as she barely whispered the words: 'Of course I still support him. He is my son. I love him. I have to support him!' She did not, of course, support his monstrous crimes, or even object to the severity of his punishment. But she did continue to support *him* and to yearn for his ultimate redemption. All of which raises a most profound question: How could God's grace possibly reach this suffering mother unless it should also find a way to reach (or transform) her son? – and how could it reach Paul, curing him of his 'unceasing anguish', unless it should also find a way to reach his unbelieving kin?

Christians sometimes comfort themselves at this point with the words in Revelation 21:4 and elsewhere that God will one day 'wipe away every tear from their eyes', and I have no doubt that these words record the absolute truth of the matter. Our question, however, is how God might accomplish such a feat. Will he, as some seem to believe, harden the hearts of those in heaven, making them so callous that they no longer care about the fate of their loved ones in hell? Will he remove from the heart of Ted Bundy's mother, for example, all love for her son, so that she no longer yearns for his redemption? If, as Christians have traditionally believed, love is a condition of blessedness, the very thing that renders us fit for eternity, then no such option is open to God. For as 1 John 4:8 puts it: 'Whoever does not love does not know God, for God is love.' It is the tenderness at the very heart of the universe, moreover, that commands us to love our neighbour, not to mention our enemies, even as we love ourselves. But if I *should* manage to love someone *even as I love myself*, I could no more remain unaffected by this person's ultimate fate than I could remain unaffected by my own; and if my own daughter, say, should come to a bad end – even if, like Ted

Bundy, she should make herself intolerably evil and do so *by her own will* – her wretchedness would nonetheless remain my wretchedness as well. For I could never be happy knowing that she had made herself permanently miserable. Is it any wonder, then, that Paul could wish (or even pray) that he should become accursed for the sake of his own loved ones? From the perspective of his love, his own damnation would be no worse an evil, and no greater threat to his own happiness, than the damnation of his loved ones would be. Nor is God himself any less vulnerable than we are in this regard; to the contrary, his vulnerability is infinitely greater. For if his love is infinitely greater than ours, then his own suffering over the loss of a single loved one would likewise be infinitely greater than our own.

So again I ask: How might God wipe away the tears of his redeemed if producing a more callous heart in them is no answer? According to William Craig among others, God could in effect foist upon them an elaborate deception, thereby maintaining them in a state of blissful ignorance. For God could, says Craig, simply 'obliterate' from their minds 'any knowledge of lost persons so that they experience no pangs of remorse for them'.[1] Here the suggestion seems to be that God could perform a kind of lobotomy on the redeemed, expunging from their minds any memory that might interfere with their future happiness. In the case of those whose entire family is lost, this would mean, I presume, that God would expunge from their minds every memory of parents and other family members; and I doubt that Craig has any idea how much of a person's mind this would likely destroy. But in any event, such a view reduces God's victory over sin and death to a cruel hoax; his hollow 'victory' consists not in making things right, but in concealing from the redeemed just how bad things really are. And one could hardly imagine a view more diametrically opposed to Jesus' assertion that 'you shall know the truth, and the truth [not blissful ignorance and not an elaborate deception] shall make you free (Jn. 8:32 NKJV).

So again I ask: If God cannot impart blessedness by making us more callous in our attitude towards our lost loved ones and cannot do so by transforming us into blissfully ignorant remnants of our former selves, how *will* he wipe away our tears? Fortunately, the very text in which we encounter the promise provides a clear answer to our question: 'Death will be no more; mourning and crying and pain will be no more; for the first things [will] have passed away' (Rev. 21:4). In other words, God will wipe away our tears by eliminating their source, not by foisting upon us an elaborate hoax.[2] If we interpret this from a Pauline perspective, we can think of 'the first things', or 'the old order of things', as everything associated with the first Adam: all separation, alienation, sin, and death. And we can think of the new creation that replaces the old as everything associated with the second Adam: forgiveness, reconciliation, and regeneration. When the old order passes away into oblivion, when Death and Hades are themselves finally consumed in the lake of fire (see Rev. 20:14) and there is no longer any curse (22:3), neither will there be any further reason for tears. A full explanation of why all of the images associated with the final judgement turn out to represent redemptive ideas will have to await a closer look at Pauline theology. But it all boils down to something very simple: If the ultimate truth about the universe is tragic, then there can be no real consolation in the midst of tragedy; but if it is glorious, then the truth itself will in the end set us free from all anxiety, all anguish, and all sorrow.

Paul's Doctrine of the Two Adams

According to Paul, the ultimate truth about the universe is indeed glorious, and his doctrine of the two Adams, as we encounter it in Romans 5 and 1 Corinthians 15, illustrates just how glorious that truth really is.

What we encounter in these texts is a magnificent vision of creation in two stages. The first Adam, according to Paul, 'was from the earth, a man of dust' and 'became a living being'; the second was not from the earth, but 'from heaven' and 'became a life-giving spirit' (1 Cor. 15:45, 47). The first Adam thus represents the first stage in the creation of God's children: the emergence of individual human consciousness in a context of ambiguity, illusion, sin, and death; the second Adam, or Jesus Christ, represents the second stage: the divine power that successfully overcomes all sin and death and therefore all separation from God, so that the true Sons and Daughters, or the true creations of God, can emerge.[3]

But why do I suppose that in Paul's scheme of things every human being who ever lives will finally be reconciled to God? Why do

I suppose that the work of the second Adam will be *that* successful? I doubt that Paul could have made it any clearer than he did in Romans 5. Observe first the parallel structure of 5:18:

> Therefore just as one man's trespass led to condemnation for all [humans],
> so one man's act of righteousness leads to justification and life for [them] all.

The whole point of such a parallel structure, so typical of Paul, is to identify a single group of individuals and to make two parallel statements about that single group of individuals, and the effect is therefore to eliminate any possibility of ambiguity. The *very ones* who came under condemnation, as a result of the first Adam's act of disobedience, will eventually be brought to justification and life, as a result of the second Adam's act of obedience. Or, as Paul put it in verse 19: the very ones who were *constituted sinners*, as a result of the first Adam's act of disobedience, will be *constituted righteous*, as a result of the second Adam's act of obedience. Again, I do not know how Paul could have expressed himself any more clearly than that.[4]

But there is more, as anyone who consults the context will quickly discern. For in 5:12 Paul identified the group or class he had in mind with great clarity; it is, he said, *all* human beings, or more accurately, all humans who have sinned. Then in verse 15 he distinguished within that single group or class between 'the one' and 'the many' – 'the one' being Adam himself, who first sinned, and 'the many' being those who died as a result Adam's sin. As John Murray has pointed out:

> When Paul uses the expression 'the many', he is not intending to delimit the denotation. The scope of 'the many' must be the same as the 'all men' of verses 12 and 18. He uses 'the many' here, as in verse 19, for the purpose of contrasting more effectively 'the one' and 'the many', singularity and plurality – it was the trespass of 'the one'... 'the many' died as a result.[5]

In the same context, moreover, Paul insisted that 'the one', namely Adam, is 'a type' of Jesus Christ (v. 14), presumably because Jesus Christ, the second Adam, stands in the same relationship to 'the many' as the first Adam did. But with this difference: 'if the many died by the trespass of the one man, how much more[6] did God's grace and the gift that came by the grace of the one man, Jesus Christ, overflow to the many' (v. 15 NIV). It seems to me indisputable, therefore, that Paul had in mind one group of individuals – 'the many', which includes all human beings except for the first and the second Adam – and he envisioned that each of the two Adams stands in exactly the same relationship to that one group of individuals.[7] The first Adam's act of disobedience brought doom upon them all, but the second Adam's act of obedience undid the doom and will eventually bring justification and life to them all.[8]

Paul's teaching here is so explicit, and so clear, that even the opponents of absolute universalism have sometimes conceded, as Neal Punt does, that 'Romans 5:18 and its *immediate context* place no limitation on the universalistic thrust of the second "all men".'[9] Nor can you challenge the universalistic thrust of our text merely by insisting that, according to Paul, a person's salvation occurs only when certain conditions, such as faith in Jesus Christ, are met. For if all will be saved in the end, then it already follows that all of the relevant conditions of salvation will be met as well. So with this in mind, consider Howard Marshall's argument in the following passage:

> Furthermore, we must ask what is the force of 'all' in this passage. I suggest that 'all' in Rom. 5 really has primarily in view 'both Jews and Gentiles and not just Jews': that is the point that Paul is concerned to make. He is of course referring to *all* mankind and not just saying 'some Jews and some Gentiles', but the thrust of the section is that Christ's action, like Adam's, affects both Jews and Gentiles. The one/many contrast is used of both Adam and Christ to show that both affect the whole human race and not just the Jews. So Paul's aim is not necessarily to assert that all will be saved but that the work of Christ is for all, and that he alone is the Saviour in virtue of the one saving event of his death.
>
> Eternal life is the precious gift of God in Christ, and it is received by faith. There is no question of all people automatically receiving life apart from faith in Christ.[10]

As a universalist, I can accept everything Marshall says here – everything, that is, except the inference he draws, which strikes me as a rather obvious non sequitur. In particular, I wholeheartedly agree that there is no question in Romans 5:18–19 'of all people automatically receiving life apart from faith in Christ'. But how is this even relevant to the question of whether God will eventually bring all people to a point where they have faith in Christ and are therefore saved?[11] I can also accept, insofar as I understand it, Marshall's remark about 'the force of "all" in the passage'. Because the Jews in Paul's day regarded as a Gentile anyone who was not a Jew, Paul's 'all humans' clearly implies 'both Jews and Gentiles and not just Jews'. But again, how is this even relevant to the following inference: 'So Paul's aim is not necessarily to assert that all will be saved but that the work of Christ is for all, and that he alone is the Saviour in virtue of the one saving event of his death'? Marshall seems clearly to have confused a question of *reference* with that of *predication*. The question of reference concerns what group of individuals Paul had in mind when he wrote the words '*eis pantas anthrōpous*'; the question of predication concerns what it is he actually said about this group of individuals. Did he say that they would all be saved, or merely that, for example, they would all have an opportunity to be saved? The latter question has nothing to do with 'the force of "all"' and everything to do with the meaning of 'justification of life' in 5:18 and 'will be constituted righteous' in 5:19. As John Murray has pointed out, moreover: 'The righteousness and the justification with which verse 18 deals can be nothing less than those which issue in everlasting life, and the expression "justification of life" is itself capable of no other interpretation.'[12]

Put it this way: Only two options are available to those who would reject the clear universalistic thrust of Romans 5:18–19. One can insist either (a) that Paul did not literally have in mind *all human beings* when he identified his 'all' or (b) that he literally meant 'all human beings' but his statement carries no implication of actual salvation. In general, the Augustinians take the first alternative, arguing that, although Paul's statement clearly implies that every member of his reference class will eventually be saved, he did not literally have in mind all human beings; instead, he had in mind 'all of the elect' or some humans from all nationalities and all classes. The Arminians take the second alternative, arguing that Paul really did have in mind all human beings but his statement, they insist, carries no implication of actual salvation; instead, it implies only that Christ died for all and made salvation available to all.

It seems to me, however, that neither of these alternatives has any plausibility at all. For as Marshall himself acknowledges, Paul 'is of course referring to *all* mankind and not just saying "some Jews and some Gentiles",' nor does Marshall even try to argue that 'justification of life' or 'being constituted righteous' carries no implication of actual salvation. So we are left with the conclusion that Paul was indeed referring to all human beings and did indeed claim that they would all be saved in the end.

The Reconciliation of all things in Christ

Unlike those who believe that God will never destroy sin completely, but will instead keep it alive throughout an eternity of hell, universalists and annihilationists agree that God will utterly destroy sin in the end and destroy it forever. But whereas the annihilationists believe that God will do this by annihilating some of his own loved ones, the universalists believe that God will do it in the only way possible short of annihilating the objects of his love: by saving them from their sins.

So let us now consider two texts that may help us to understand this matter a little better. In his letter to the Philippians, Paul anticipated a time when 'at the name of Jesus every knee should bend, in heaven and on earth and under the earth, and every tongue confess that Jesus Christ is Lord' (2:10–11); and in his letter to the Colossians,[13] he went so far as to declare that the very same 'all things' created in Christ – including 'all things in heaven and on earth . . . visible or invisible, whether thrones or dominions or powers' (1:16) – would in the end be reconciled to God in Christ (1:20). Once again, we could hardly ask for a clearer or more specific statement; in Colossians 1:20, Paul applied the concept of reconciliation, which is explicitly a redemptive concept, not only to all human beings, but to all of the spiritual principalities and dominions as well.[14]

It is within this context, I believe, that Paul himself understood the nature of Christ's victory, the defeat of Christ's enemies, and the destruction of sin. But consider how some have tried to limit and minimize the victory. A standard argument at this point is that in Colossians 1:20 and Philippians 2:10–11 Paul had in mind, not reconciliation in the full redemptive sense, but a pacification of evil powers, a mere subjugation of them against their will. Peter O'Brien, a respected New Testament scholar of conservative outlook, puts the argument this way:

> The reconciliation of the principalities and powers is in mind. They are one category whatever others are included. Yet these forces are shown as submitting against their will to a power they cannot resist. They are reconciled through subjugation (cf. 1 Cor. 15:28).[15]

Is O'Brien right about this? Was it really Paul's teaching that some spiritual beings will merely be subjugated and not reconciled to Christ in the full redemptive sense? If that *were* Paul's teaching, then it would have been quite incoherent. For so long as a single will remains in a state of rebellion against Christ, so long as a single person is able to cling to his or her hatred of God, at least one power in the universe – namely, the power of that person's will – is not yet in subjection to Christ. As a paradigm of subjection, therefore, consider Christ's own subjection to the Father, as Paul depicted it in 1 Corinthians 15:28. If Christ's will were in conflict with the Father's on some important issue, if he *wanted* to act contrary to the Father's will but simply lacked the power to do so, would he truly be in subjection to the Father? Of course not. The very suggestion seems incoherent. And yet, in the very passage that O'Brien cites, 1 Corinthians 15:28, Paul drew a parallel between the subjection of all things to Christ and Christ's own subjection of himself to the Father; so that very passage shows, it seems to me, that Paul did not in fact hold the incoherent idea that O'Brien attributes to him.

And similarly for Philippians 2:10–11 and Colossians 1:15–20. When Paul suggested that every tongue shall *confess* Jesus Christ as Lord, he chose a verb that throughout the Septuagint implies not only confession, but the offer of praise and thanksgiving as well; and as J. B. Lightfoot has pointed out, this verb also has such implications of praise 'in the very passage of Isaiah [45:23] which St Paul adapts...'[16] Now a ruling monarch may indeed force a subject to bow against that subject's will, may even force the subject to utter certain words, but praise and thanksgiving can come only from the heart, as the Apostle was no doubt clear headed enough to discern.[17] Quite apart from the matter of praise, moreover, either those who bow before Jesus Christ and *declare openly* that he is Lord do so sincerely and by their own choice or they do not. If they do this sincerely and by their own choice, then there can be but one reason: They too have been reconciled to God. If they do not do this sincerely and by their own choice, if they are forced to make obeisance against their will, then their actions are merely fraudulent and bring no glory to God; a Hitler may take pleasure in *forcing* his defeated enemies to make obeisance against their will, but a God who honours the *truth* could not possibly participate in such a fraud.

Now despite such considerations as these, O'Brien cites Colossians 1:21–23 as a reason for denying that, according to Paul, all will gladly be reconciled to God.

> Although all things will *finally* unite to bow in the name of Jesus and to acknowledge him as Lord (Phil. 2:10, 11), it is not to be assumed that this will be done gladly by all. For as the words following the hymn (Col. 1:21–23) indicate, the central purpose of Christ's work of making peace has to do with those who have heard the Word of reconciliation and gladly accepted it. To assert that verse 20 [of Colossians 1] points to a universal reconciliation in which every man will finally enjoy celestial bliss is an unwarranted assumption.[18]

But remarkably, O'Brien seems to have gotten it exactly backwards. For in the very text that O'Brien cites, Paul put all doubt to rest concerning the *kind* of reconciliation he had in mind. He even set forth his own readers as an example: 'And you who were once estranged and hostile in mind, doing evil deeds, he has now *reconciled* in his fleshly body through death, so as to present you holy and blameless and irreproachable before him' (1:21–22 emphasis mine). How anyone could cite such a text in support of the view that in 1:20 Paul had in mind something less than true reconciliation is a mystery that I find myself unable to penetrate. Even in 1:20 Paul specified clearly the kind of reconciliation he had in mind; he did so with the expression 'making peace through the blood of his cross'. And in Philippians 2:6–11, he likewise explained the exact nature of Christ's exaltation; he did so by pointing to Christ's humble obedience 'to the point of death, even death on a cross'. So just what is the power of the cross, as Paul understood it? Is it the power of a conquering hero to compel his enemies to obey him against their will? If that had been Paul's doctrine, it would have been strange indeed. For God had no need of a crucifixion to *compel* obedience; he was quite capable of doing that all along. According to the New Testament as a whole, therefore, God sent his Son into the world, not as a conquering hero, but as a suffering servant; and the power that Jesus unleashed as he bled on the cross was precisely the power of self-giving love, the power to overcome evil by transforming the wills and renewing the minds of the evil ones themselves.

So the blood of the cross does bring peace, but not the artificial kind that some tyrannical power might impose; it brings true peace, the kind that springs from within and requires reconciliation in the full redemptive sense. It seems to me without question, therefore, that Paul envisioned a time when all persons would be reconciled to God in the full redemptive sense.

'So that God may be all in all'

Another explicit statement of Paul's that many try to explain away is 1 Corinthians 15:22: 'For as in Adam all die, even so in Christ shall all be made alive' (KJV). According to Marshall, Paul does not here 'affirm that all die in Adam and all will certainly come to life in Christ…'.[19] But in fact that is just what Paul's sentence says. Contrary to what Marshall would have us believe, Paul in no way restricted himself to the following claim: 'Wherever death and resurrection take place, they are due respectively to Adam and Christ.'[20] Nor did he say merely that all those *in Christ* would be made alive. To the contrary, he said that in Christ shall all be made alive.[21] And the whole point of the parallel construction here, as in Romans 5:18, is to pick out a single group of individuals or a single reference class, roughly all human beings (see v. 21), and to make two parallel statements about that single group of individuals. The *very same* 'all' that died in Adam shall be made alive in Christ.

It also seems clear to me that the verses following 15:22 effectively reinforce and expand its universalistic thrust. A host of commentators disagree, however, and Marshall, for one, appeals to these very verses in an effort to show that Paul's second 'all' is more restrictive than the first. 'Death of course is universal', he writes, 'but this is not necessarily so of resurrection. Indeed, the next verses show that Paul thinks of resurrection only of "those who belong to Christ".'[22] But just how is Marshall's second sentence even relevant to the first? Certainly Paul endorsed:

(P) Only those who belong to Christ will be made alive.

But by itself (P) neither entails nor is evidence for

(Q) Not all who die in Adam will be made alive.

So unless Marshall is prepared to foist upon him a fallacious argument, Paul's acceptance of (P) is no evidence at all that he also accepted (Q). Beyond that, Paul's reference to 'those who belong to Christ' is just what one would expect if Paul believed that Christ achieved a complete victory over sin and death. For if Christ's victory provided a guarantee that all who die in Adam will be made alive in Christ, then it likewise provided a guarantee that this very same all will eventually belong to Christ as well.

Taking a cue from this, one might observe that verse 23 speaks not only of those who belong to Christ, but of those who belong to him *at the time of his coming*; and perhaps some would see here an additional reason to restrict the second 'all' of verse 22. For surely, some may reason, not all who die in Adam will be made alive *at the time of Christ's coming*. But where did Paul commit himself to the view that no one would be made alive after Christ's coming? Here it is important not to collapse Paul's three-stage progression into two stages. After informing us that 'in Christ shall all be made alive', Paul went on to say: 'But each in his own order' (v. 24). It is as if Paul had in mind a procession or a parade, and he quickly listed three segments of the procession: At the head of the procession is Christ, the first fruits; behind him are those who belong to Christ at his coming; and behind them are 'the remainder' – that is, those at the end of the procession[23] – who are there when Christ 'hands over the kingdom to God the Father, after he has destroyed every ruler and every authority and power' (v. 24).[24] But despite Paul's image of a procession in three stages, few commentators seem prepared to interpret '*eita to telos*' (literally 'then the end') to mean 'then the remainder'.[25] So I shall not insist upon such a controversial point here. For even if we understand 'then the end' to mean something like 'then comes the end of the ages or the end of redemptive history', Paul made one point absolutely clear: The end will not come until Christ's victory and triumph are complete; that is, until 'he has put all his enemies under his feet' (v. 25), until he has destroyed the last enemy, which is death (v. 26), and until 'all things are subjected to him' (v. 28).

We thus approach the very heart of the matter. Citing essentially the same objection that we dealt with in O'Brien above, Marshall writes:

> The resurrection is followed by the subjugation of his [Christ's] enemies... But it must be noted that subjugation is not the same thing as unification and reconciliation. Paul teaches the destruction of the cosmic forces opposed to Christ, including death.[26]

Now Marshall is right: Paul clearly taught that Christ will destroy death and a host of other cosmic forces inimical to the interest of humankind. So how should we understand this? Universalists believe that the same God who commands *us* to love *our* enemies loves his own enemies as well. But God does not love sin or death or anything that separates us from him, and Paul also referred to these as enemies. So here we must distinguish carefully between the sense in which such personified evils as Sin and Death and various cosmic forces are enemies and the sense in which real people under the power of such evils are enemies. Christ destroys enemies of the first kind (non-persons) by obliterating them, that is, by eliminating them from his creation entirely.[27] When he does destroy sin and death and various cosmic forces, he likewise destroys enemies of the second kind (sinful persons) in the only way possible short of annihilating them: by redeeming them while they are yet enemies. For only enemies of the second kind (persons) are possible objects of God's redemptive love.

Now according to Paul, we all came into this earthly life as enemies (see Rom. 5:10) and as children (or vessels) of wrath (Eph. 2:3). Saul of Tarsus was thus an enemy who had to be destroyed. So were the very unbelieving Jews who were also objects of God's mercy (see Rom. 11:28–32). Indeed, every Christian represents the defeat of an enemy and the destruction of something. For how could Christ possibly save us from our sin without also destroying our sinful nature? And how could he possibly accomplish his task of reconciling us to God without defeating and placing under his feet the enemy that we once were? The very last enemy that Christ shall destroy is death, which in the larger context of Pauline thought includes all separation from God. When he finally overcomes all separation from God, all persons will then be in subjection to Christ not in the sense of being subjugated against their will – Marshall is quite mistaken about that, as we saw above – but *in exactly the same sense* that Christ places himself in subjection to the Father (15:28). Then and only then will the Father truly be 'all in all', because then and only then will all persons belong to him, or at least *know* that they belong to him, through his Son.

So herein lies the Christian universalist's understanding of God's ultimate victory, which is also a key to a proper understanding of divine judgement. God is too pure (read 'too loving') to allow evil of any kind to survive forever in his creation. He will not, therefore, merely quarantine evil in hell, but will instead destroy it altogether even as he regenerates the evil ones themselves. And that will be the subject of my third and final chapter.

Notes

1 Craig (1991), p. 306. [Editors: the most detailed defence of Talbott's argument for universalism from the bliss of the redeemed is now Reitan (2002)].

2 The context of Revelation 21:4 also alludes, of course, to the second death (see 21:8). But unlike first-order death and all the separation it entails, the second death is not an enemy to be defeated or destroyed. For my own understanding of the second death and why it is the very thing required to wipe away our tears, see Chapter 3.

3 My own view is that the creation of 'rational, independent, and self aware beings such as ourselves' may pose something of a dilemma even for an omnipotent being. As I have expressed it elsewhere, 'Perhaps some of the very conditions essential to our creation in the first place and to the emergence of our unique personalities are themselves obstacles to a perfect union with God – obstacles that God must subsequently overcome in a variety of complex ways *after* we have already come into being'; Talbott (2001a), p. 104. If this is true, then Paul's doctrine of the two Adams and of creation in two stages has, I believe, real philosophical significance.

4 For a review of some of the strained efforts to avoid the clear universalistic implication of our text and for an excellent discussion of the text itself, see Bonda (1998), pp. 103–111.

5 J. Murray (1960), pp. 192–193.

6 Concerning the expression 'how much more', de Boer aptly comments: 'Unless the universalism of vv. 18–19 is taken strictly, as I think it should and must be, "how

much more" is turned into "how much less", for death is then given the last word over the vast majority of human beings and God's regrasping of the world for His sovereignty becomes a limited affair': Boer (1988), p. 175.

7 A familiar claim at this point (one that has, so far as I can tell, no coherent sense) is that Paul often used 'all' in a limited sense. Moo thus writes: 'That "all" does not always mean "every single human being" is clear from many passages, it often being clearly limited in context (cf., e.g., Rom. 8:32; 12:17, 18; 14:2; 16:19)' (Moo, 1996, pp. 343–344). But though Moo's claim is in one sense obviously correct – the 'all' in the statement, 'all rocks have weight', for example, obviously does not mean 'every single human being' – there seem to be several confusions here. First, not one of Moo's examples has any relevance at all to Romans 5:18, where Paul identified his reference class with great care and where the parallel structure of his sentence eliminates all ambiguity. Could you explain away the statement, 'All men are created equal', in America's Declaration of Independence simply by uncovering other instances, perhaps in some personal letters, where the authors also used 'all' in an ambiguous context? Of course not. Second, Moo fails to distinguish between two very different sorts of contexts: those where 'all' is combined with a relevant noun, which explicitly fixes the reference class, and those where it is not combined with a relevant noun. The latter contexts have no relevance at all to the former. Third, Moo's interpretation of Romans 12:17 and 18, where Paul did speak explicitly of all humans, is simply mistaken. Given Paul's own view that all sinners are without excuse, having the moral law written on their hearts, he also held, presumably, that on some level, at least, all (adult) humans do know what is noble (see v. 17), whether they admit to it or not. In verse 18, moreover, he merely said, '*If it is possible, so far as it depends on you*, live peaceably with all' (my italics); so here too he literally meant *all people*. And finally, even in a case of obvious hyperbole, such as Romans 16:19, Paul's 'all' clearly meant 'all people'. It is just that in a case of hyperbole the thing said is literally false, as Paul's own readers in Rome were no doubt fully aware. For more on this sort of point, see Talbott (1999c), pp. 56–62.

8 Hultgren expresses the point powerfully: 'As Adam was the head of humanity in the old eon, leading all to destruction, so Christ is the head of humanity in the new age which has dawned, leading all to justification and life. The grace of God in Christ amounts to "much more" than the trespass of Adam and its effects (5:17). All of humanity is in view here without exception' (Hultgren, 1987, pp. 54–55). Similarly, as Käsemann remarks, the central idea here, as in Romans 11:32 and 1 Corinthians 15:22, is that 'all powerful grace is unthinkable in the absence of eschatological universalism...' (1980).

9 Punt (1980), p. 14. Moo also concedes that a 'growing number of scholars argue that this [apparent universalism of 5:18] is exactly what Paul intends to say' (1996, p. 342).

10 I.H. Marshall, (2000), p. 20.

11 It is truly astonishing how many commentators draw virtually the same fallacious inference at this point. Like Marshall, Moo contends that 'the deliberately worded v. 17, along with the persistent stress on faith as the means of achieving righteousness in 1:16–4:25, makes it clear that only certain people derive the benefits from Christ's act of righteousness' (1996, p. 344). Similarly, Moule contends that 'the whole Epistle, and the whole message of St Paul about our acceptance' of Christ counts against a universalistic interpretation of Romans 5:18 (1975, p. 151). But these are clearly fallacious inferences: From the premise that only those who accept Christ and

place their faith in him will be 'justified unto life', it simply does not follow that some people will never place their faith in Christ and will therefore never be 'justified unto life'.

12 Murray (1960), p. 203.

13 Even if Paul was not the author of Colossians, as some scholars have argued, the old hymn or creedal statement reproduced in 1:15–20 is surely one that Paul would have endorsed.

14 Writes Dunn: 'What is being claimed is quite simply and profoundly that the divine purpose in the act of reconciliation and peacemaking was to restore the harmony of the original creation, to bring into renewed oneness and wholeness "all things", "whether things on the earth or things in the heavens"' (Dunn, 1996, p. 104). In a similar vein, Ephesians 1:10 speaks of God's plan 'to gather up all things' in Christ, 'things in heaven and things on earth'. Concerning that text, Andrew Lincoln writes: 'The summing up of all things in Christ means the unifying of the cosmos or its direction toward a common goal. In line with this letter's close links with Colossians, a similar thought about Christ and the cosmos had been expressed in the Colossians hymn in terms of reconciliation and *with explicit soteriological connotations* (Col. 1:20)' (Lincoln, 1990, p. 33 my italics).

15 O'Brien (1982), p. 56.

16 Lightfoot (1963), p. 115. It is also noteworthy that the context of the remark in Isaiah 45:23 is a redemptive one: 'Turn to me and be saved, all the ends of the earth.' As for the reference in verse 24 to those who come to the Lord and are ashamed, it seems that these are ashamed on account of their past anger against the Lord; such shame is quite compatible with a sincere confession that all salvation is from the Lord. On this point, see Bonda (1998), p. 203.

17 Indeed, Paul explicitly said as much in Romans 10:9: 'if you confess with your lips and believe in your heart that God raised him [Christ] from the dead, you will be saved.' In 1 Corinthians 12:3, he went so far as to insist that 'no one can say "Jesus is Lord" except by the Holy Spirit.'

18 O'Brien (1982), p. 57.

19 I.H. Marshal (2000), p. 19.

20 Ibid.

21 As de Boer observes, 'the translation "all who are in Christ" for v. 22b is not warranted by the syntax and is insupportable in view of v. 22a. One can scarcely translate the latter "all who are in Adam die", if such a translation is meant to imply that some people are not "in Adam" and therefore do not die' (1988, p. 112).

22 I.H. Marshall (2000), p. 19.

23 Just as the end of a rope is one extremity of the rope ('Almost drowning, the man desperately grasped the end of a rope'), so the end of a procession is its final stage. As Conzelmann, who rejects such an interpretation, at least acknowledges: 'In favour of this interpretation one can point to the fact that the phrase appears in the course of a series' (1975, pp. 270–271).

24 Note, however, that 'the remainder' or those who are there when Christ hands over his kingdom also belong to Christ. They are simply those who are reconciled between the time of Christ's coming and the time at which he hands over his kingdom to God. So there is no implication here that non-believers will be made alive, and the fallacious inference that 'the remainder' would have to include non-believers, or some who do not belong to Christ, is one reason, I believe, that many reject this interpretation. See, for example, Thiselton (2000), pp. 1230–1231.

25 In the lexicon translated by W.F. Arndt and F.W. Gingrich, Walter Bauer (following H. Lietzmann and J. Weiss) lists 'the rest' or 'the remainder' as a possible interpretation in the present context, and the NRSV lists it as an alternative reading as well. D.E.H. Whitely likewise admits that such an 'interpretation cannot be ruled out as impossible', though he goes on to insist that 'it is certainly less probable than the normally accepted rendering' (1964, p. 271). Most commentators, however, seem to agree with Conzelmann that 'that there is no evidence for this meaning of "*telos*"' (1975, p. 271). Are Conzelmann and others right about that? One of the basic meanings cited in Bauer is '*the last part, close, conclusion* esp. of the last things, the final act in the cosmic drama'. If we suppose that 'the remainder' is a meaning radically different from this, then we will conclude, mistakenly, that there is no evidence for such a rendering. But 'the remainder' is simply the end of the procession, the final stage in Paul's three-stage 'each in its own order'. When we read in Matthew 26:58 that Peter followed Jesus at a distance, entered the courtyard, and sat with the servants 'to see the end' ('*idein to telos*'), we understand that he was there to observe the final act of the unfolding drama. When Paul said that the end of the world-age (literally 'the ends of the ages') *has come* ('*katēntēken*' – note the perfect tense) upon us (1 Cor. 10:11), he evidently meant, among other things, that the final act of the cosmic drama was beginning to unfold. And similarly, when Paul said 'each in its own order' and listed three stages, it is perfectly natural to take 'then the end' as the third and final stage. The widespread assumption that this is an unnatural or artificial rendering is, I believe, unsubstantiated.

26 I.H. Marshall (2000), p. 19.

27 According to Hendrikus Berkhof, however, the Greek verb '*katargeō*' 'means literally "to make ineffective," "to disconnect" [rather than 'to annihilate']. The Powers are put out of commission as enemies (verse 26), which means in the light of... other texts... that at the same stroke they are reinstated in their proper function within Christ's lordship' (1977, p. 42). So in that sense, 'God reconciles the Powers – and not only men – with Himself through Christ's death' (ibid., p. 41); that is, Christ's victory over the cosmic forces restores them to their proper functioning. A strength of this view is that it accords perfectly with Paul's use of the term 'reconcile' with respect to 'all things' in Colossians 1:20. But a possible weakness is that in 1 Corinthians 15:26 Paul also applies the term '*katargeō*' to death, which is not reconciled but absolutely destroyed (see Berkhof's own comment about this on pp. 40–41). The solution to the difficulty, I believe, is simply to recognize that, in Paul's scheme of things, the destruction (or the annihilation) of sin and death, along with the destruction of the old person or the sinful nature, is just what makes possible the new creation in Christ. See Chapter 3 below.

3

A Pauline Interpretation of Divine Judgement

THOMAS TALBOTT

Justice as an Expression of Mercy

People sometimes say, as if it were a weighty consideration, that God is not only loving, but also holy; he is not only merciful, but also just. What is the point of such a remark? Suppose I should say that God is not only loving, but also wise. This second remark, like the first, is no doubt true, and might even have a real point in an appropriate context. But neither remark justifies the idea that God sometimes acts in unloving ways. For if God is love, as 1 John 4:8 and 4:16 declare, and it is therefore his very nature to love,[1] then it is logically impossible that he should fail to love someone or should act in an unloving way towards anyone. It is as impossible for God to act contrary to someone's ultimate good, in other words, as it is for him to believe a false proposition or to act unjustly.

And where is the biblical warrant, I would ask, for the popular idea that mercy and justice are separate and distinct attributes of God? Where does the Bible even hint that God's mercy permits something that his justice does not, or that his justice demands something that his mercy does not? Christians sometimes picture God, I fear, almost as if he were a schizophrenic whose justice pushes him in one direction and whose mercy pushes him in another. But when we turn to St Paul, we encounter a direct and explicit challenge to this whole way of thinking.

Perhaps the clearest example of such a challenge is the eleventh chapter of Romans, where we discover that, according to Paul, God's severity towards the disobedient, his judgement of sin, even his willingness to blind the eyes and harden the hearts of the disobedient, all express a more fundamental quality, namely mercy. In 11:7 Paul thus wrote: 'What then? Israel failed to obtain what it was seeking. The elect obtained it, but the rest were hardened' (or blinded). He then asked: 'have they [the non-remnant who were cut off and hardened] stumbled so as to fall?' (v. 11). Did God's severity towards these unbelievers, in other words, imply an ultimate rejection of them? And his reply was most emphatic: 'By no means!' By the end of the following verse, he was already speaking of their full inclusion: 'Now if their stumbling means riches for the world, and if their defeat means riches for the Gentiles, how much more will their full inclusion mean!' (11:12). And three verses later he was hinting that their acceptance would mean 'life from the dead' (9:15). He then generalized the whole thing even as he revealed a fundamental mystery about God's redemptive activity: God blinded the eyes and hardened the hearts of the unbelieving Jews, we discover, as a means by which *all* of Israel might be saved (11:25–26) – all of Israel including those who were blinded and hardened. We need not here enter into the controversy of whether Paul meant to include dead Israelites in his 'all Israel', though I think he clearly did.[2] Certainly his statement in no way *excludes* them. But whether Paul explicitly had in mind dead Israelites or not, his whole point was to illustrate how God's justice is an expression of mercy. His *specific* point was glorious enough: Though his unbelieving kin were in some sense 'enemies of God' (11:28), they nonetheless became 'disobedient in order that they too may now receive mercy' (11:31 NIV). But the general principle (of which the specific point was but an instance) is even more glorious: 'For God has imprisoned *all* in disobedience so that he may be merciful to *all*' (11:32).

According to Paul, therefore, God is always and everywhere merciful, but we sometimes *experience* his mercy (or purifying love) as severity, judgement, punishment. That also explains, by the way, the important role that choice and moral effort play in Pauline theology. For though Paul clearly rejected the idea that we choose freely between different possible eternal destinies, arguing instead that our destiny is wholly a matter of grace, he nonetheless stressed the importance of choice. 'Note then', he wrote in 11:22, 'the kindness and the severity of God: severity toward those who have fallen, but God's kindness toward you, provided you continue in his kindness; otherwise, you also will be cut off.' So how we encounter God's love in the future, whether we encounter it as kindness or as severity, is indeed, Paul declared, up to us – a matter of free choice, if you will. But our ultimate destiny is not up to us, because God's severity, no less than his kindness, is itself a means of his saving grace. In particular, God's severity towards the unbelieving Jews was, according to Paul, but one of the means whereby God would save all of Israel in the end. What our free choices determine, then, is not our eternal destiny, which is secure from the beginning, but the means required to achieve it. For the more tenaciously we cling to our illusions and selfish desires – to the flesh, as Paul called it – the more severe will be the means and the more painful the process whereby God shatters our illusions, destroys the flesh, and finally separates us from our sin.

Paul himself called this a mystery (11:25) and admitted that God's ways are, in just this respect, 'inscrutable' and 'unsearchable' (11:33), but nothing could be clearer than Paul's own glorious summation in 11:32. For here, once again, we encounter a parallel structure where the first 'all' determines the reference of the second. According to Paul, the *very ones* whom God 'shuts up' to disobedience – whom he 'blinds', or 'hardens', or 'cuts off' for a season – are those to whom he is merciful. His former act is but the first expression of the latter, and the latter is the goal and the *purpose* of the former. God hardens a heart in order to produce, in the end, a contrite spirit, blinds those who are unready for the truth in order to bring them ultimately to the truth, 'imprisons all in disobedience so that he may be merciful to all.'

Understanding Romans 9

Romans 11:32, where Paul declared the full extent of God's mercy, is the culmination of a theological argument that begins in chapter 9 and extends through chapter 11. It is here that Paul took up the problem of Jewish unbelief and systematically defended his view that, contrary to what many of his own kin believed, God has every right to extend his mercy to all human beings including Gentiles. In the early stages of his argument (Rom 9), we encounter several examples of the severity of God's mercy; and if we stop reading around 9:25, we are apt to find some of these examples hard to swallow. But once we begin to interpret Romans 9 in light of Paul's own conclusion that even God's severity expresses his mercy, Romans 9 ceases to be a problem at all.

God's Severe Mercy to Pharaoh

Consider first the severity of God's mercy to Pharaoh, the hardening of Pharaoh's heart (see 9:17–18). How, one may wonder, could this possibly qualify as an expression of mercy to Pharaoh? The answer depends, no doubt, on how Paul himself understood the hardening of a heart. Did he understand it as an instance of God's causing someone to sin? The Hebrew word most commonly used in the Exodus account to which Paul refers is '*ḥāzaq*', which literally means 'to strengthen'; it is the same word that appears throughout the Old Testament in the formula 'be strong and of good courage'. Following this usage, it seems reasonable to say that God strengthened Pharaoh's heart and gave him the courage to stand in the face of the 'signs and wonders' performed in Egypt. God consistently hardened (or strengthened) Pharaoh's heart, remember, in connection with a specific command: 'Let my people go!' Why would a merciful God do that? In the context of the story in Exodus, one possibility is this: Though Pharaoh had exalted himself over the Hebrews for years, he was essentially a coward who could never have stood the pressure, apart from the strength that God gave him, once things began to get difficult in Egypt. It is often that way; cowardice often prevents us from doing the wrong that we secretly wish to do. In the case of Pharaoh, God gave him the strength not to be cowed too easily; God gave him the *courage* to sin, if you will, but it hardly follows that God was the sufficient cause of the sin itself.[3]

Accordingly, the hardening of Pharaoh's heart was an expression of mercy in two respects: First, it revealed to Pharaoh the destructive nature of his own sin, and second, it revealed to the Egyptians something of the nature of God. For as the Lord declared to Moses, 'The Egyptians shall know that I am the Lord, when I stretch out my hand against Egypt and bring the Israelites out from among them' (Ex. 7:5). These great historical events brought real hardship to the Egyptians, even as they did to the Israelites; but they were also a revelation to the Egyptians, even as they were to the Israelites. Within the context of Paul's own argument, moreover, God's actions towards Pharaoh and the Egyptians were no different from his actions towards the Israelites or anyone else.[4] If at one time or another God 'imprisons' all the descendants of Adam in disobedience and does so for a merciful purpose, it is hardly surprising that he should do the same thing to Pharaoh.

Vessels of Wrath and Mercy

Consider next Paul's distinction between the vessels of wrath and the vessels of mercy in 9:22 and why he could not possibly have had in mind a distinction between those who are, and those who are not, objects of God's mercy. In the first place, the vessels of wrath of which he spoke were the unbelieving Jews, the very ones concerning whom he later made two claims: (a) that 'as regards election they are beloved, for the sake of their ancestors' (11:28), and (b) that 'they have now become disobedient in order that they too might receive mercy' (11:31 NIV). In Paul's scheme of things, therefore, those *individuals* who are vessels of wrath, no less than those who are vessels of mercy, are objects of God's mercy; it is just that, for a person's own good, God's purifying love sometimes takes the form of wrath. Secondly, if Paul was indeed the author of Ephesians, as I believe he was, then he clearly assumed that the same individual can be a vessel of wrath at one time and a vessel of mercy at another; he also assumed that every individual who is now a vessel of mercy was at one time a vessel of wrath. For as he said in his letter to the Ephesians, using a slightly different metaphor, all Christians were at one time 'children of wrath' (Eph. 2:3). But then, if Paul himself was a vessel of mercy who was at some earlier time a vessel of wrath (call him Saul), a paraphrase that captures part of the meaning of 9:22–23 is this:

> What if God, desiring to show his wrath and to make known his power, has endured with much patience Saul, a vessel of wrath fit for destruction, in order to make known the riches of his glory for Paul, a vessel of mercy which he has prepared beforehand for glory…?[5]

And what this paraphrase illustrates is again only what Paul himself explicitly stated in 11:32; namely, that those whom God has 'imprisoned' in disobedience – the vessels of wrath whom he has endured with much patience – are precisely those to whom he is merciful. By literally shutting sinners up to their disobedience and requiring them to endure the consequences of their own rebellion, God reveals the self-defeating nature of evil and shatters the illusions that make evil choices possible in the first place.

Esau I have Hated

Consider, finally, the quotation in 9:13 from the Prophet Malachi: 'I have loved Jacob, but I have hated Esau.' As a clue to the meaning of God's so-called 'hatred' here, consider Jesus' remark that 'Whoever comes to me and does not hate father and mother, wife and children, brothers and sisters... cannot be my disciple' (Lk. 14:26). Did Jesus mean that we are literally to hate the members of our family? Did he even mean, as some have suggested, that we are to love them less than we love Jesus? Quite the contrary: An absolute loyalty to Jesus of the kind that his hyperbole implied would require that we love our family more, not less. For it was precisely Jesus who commanded us to love others even as we love ourselves; it was also Jesus who pointed out (in the parable of the sheep and the goats) that anything less than a perfect love for those whom Jesus loves is likewise a less than perfect love for Jesus himself. Accordingly, if 'to hate' our family in the relevant metaphorical sense implies an absolute loyalty to Jesus, then it also implies a perfect love for our families as well.

And similarly for God's so-called hatred of Esau, as Paul understood it: It was nothing less than a perfect expression of God's love for Esau. For election, as Paul understood it, was inclusive, not exclusive. The election of Isaac and Jacob, for example, carried no implication of rejection for Ishmael and Esau, nor did the election of Abraham imply the rejection of all others, living at the time, whom God could have put in his historical position but did not.[6] Yes, as Paul understood it, God *does* choose or elect individuals for himself and, yes, such election *is* an expression of God's saving grace. But the election of an individual inevitably reaches beyond the elected individual to incorporate, in a variety of complex ways, the community in which the individual lives and, in the end, the entire human race. That is why the election of Abraham was ultimately a blessing to all nations (Gal. 3:8), including Esau and his progeny, and why the idea of a 'remnant, chosen by grace' (Rom. 11:5) played such an important role in Paul's argument that God is merciful to all (11:32). The remnant is always a pledge on behalf of the whole; it is the proof that God has not rejected the whole (see 11:1–6) and also the proof that 'the word of God' or his 'purpose of election' has not failed (9:6).

But if all of that is true, just what is the metaphorical sense in which God hated Esau? Here we must come to appreciate a perfectly natural way of talking. When he contemplated the election of Jacob, Paul clearly had in mind the struggle between Jacob and Esau for the birthright and for their father's blessing. Now, as the brothers themselves perceived the struggle, their interests had come into conflict; hence it was not possible that both should have their perceived interests satisfied. Any arbitration of the matter would have to favour one set of perceived interests over the other, so one of the brothers would inevitably seem to be favoured and the other disfavoured. According to Paul, moreover, God had already decided the matter even before the brothers were born: In the struggle for the birthright, Jacob would win, not because he deserved to win, but in order that God's 'purpose of election' – that is, the means by which he extends his mercy to all, including Esau – might continue. So, even before the twins were born, declared Paul, Rebecca 'was told, "The elder shall serve the younger"' (9:12). That, I want to suggest, gives the full meaning of God's so-called 'hatred' of Esau. It is a thoroughly anthropomorphic idea, a *human* way of speaking – even as, so Paul told us in Romans 3:5, his own talk about the wrath of God was a human way of speaking. God's 'hatred' of Esau implies nothing more than this: Esau lost – and was destined to lose – in a struggle that he wanted, or thought he wanted, to win.

Nor will it do to say with John Murray that God's 'hatred' of Esau implies, at the very least, 'disfavour' or a 'positive outflow of his displeasure' towards a sinner.[7] That may be true enough, but it is also beside the point. For God's 'hatred' is no different from his love in this respect. According to Murray, 'the mere absence of love or favour hardly explains the visitations of judgment mentioned' in Malachi 1:1–5,[8] to wit: 'I have hated Esau; I have made his hill country a desolation and his heritage a desert for jackals... I will tear down, until they are called the wicked country, the people with whom the Lord is angry forever.'[9] But then, neither would a 'mere absence of love' explain such judgements as these upon the house of Jacob: 'The Lord God has sworn by himself... "I abhor the pride of Jacob, and hate his strongholds; and I will deliver up the city and all that is in it"' (Amos 6:8); 'Then the mountains will melt... and the valleys will burst open, like wax near the fire, like waters poured down a steep place. All this is for the transgression of Jacob and for the sins of the house of Israel' (Mich. 1:4–5). It is not the mere *absence* of God's perfecting love that explains such judgements as these; Murray is right about that. It is rather the *presence* of such love that explains such judgements as these. For does not God's love for Jacob imply a rejection of all that is false within Jacob? – and does not his love for Israel likewise require that he destroy her wickedness forever? If so, then God's *love* for Jacob is no different, in that respect, from his so-called *hatred* of Esau. For surely, God's 'hatred' of Esau also implies a rejection of all that is false within Esau, and his 'hatred' of Edom requires that he destroy her wickedness forever. So if there is any difference at all between God's 'hatred' and his love, it lies only in this: From a certain human perspective, such as Esau's perspective in his struggle with Jacob or Edom's perspective in her struggle with Israel, God's perfecting love will consume the very thing that, in our present condition, we continue to hold dear.

But even as God's perfecting love destroys, like a consuming fire, all that is false within us, so our perspective is bound to change. According to the account in Genesis, Esau eventually did forgive his cheating brother and the two did come to love each other as brothers. In fact, the account of their reconciliation is one of the most moving stories in the entire Old Testament: 'But Esau ran to meet him [Jacob], and embraced him, and fell on his neck and kissed him, and they wept' (Gen. 33:4). So complete was their reconciliation and so sincere was Esau's forgiveness that Jacob declared: 'for truly to see your face is like seeing the face of God, since you have received me with such favor' (33:10). Yet, this man, in whom Jacob was able to see the very face of God, is one whom, as some would have it, God had already rejected and had destined for eternal perdition even before he was born.

Destruction and Redemption: Two Sides of the Same Coin

If the only part of the Bible now extant were the letters traditionally attributed to Paul, no one, I suspect, would even doubt Paul's universalism. For in this entire corpus there is but one text, 2 Thessalonians 1:9, that one could, with any plausibility at all, set over against the various universalistic texts discussed so far; and even that text is badly mistranslated in some of our English Bibles. It is badly mistranslated because the eternal destruction of which the text speaks is not destruction *away from* the presence of the Lord, but instead destruction that precisely *comes from* the presence of the Lord; the idea of someone continuing to exist but being excluded from the presence of the Lord makes little or no grammatical sense in the context.[10]

Our main question, however, is how to understand the concept of *destruction* here. According to Leon Morris:

> The nature of the punishment is 'eternal destruction'. The noun is used in 1 Cor. 5:5 of the destruction of the flesh with a view to the saving of the spirit. In that passage Paul clearly does not view destruction as annihilation, for there is no likelihood that he thought of such a one as being saved in a disembodied state. This has its relevance to the verse we are discussing, for it indicates that the word does not signify so much annihilation as the loss of all that is worthwhile, utter ruin.[11]

But this surely is confused. In the first place, Paul clearly did view destruction as annihilation – that is, the annihilation of the thing destroyed, namely the flesh. But in 1 Corinthians 5:5 the primary meaning of 'flesh' is not 'body'; hence the destruction of the flesh is not the destruction of the body and does not imply disembodied existence. It implies instead the destruction of sin or a sinful nature. As Morris himself has put it in another context: 'The flesh in this sense denotes the whole personality of man as organized in the wrong direction, as directed to earthly pursuits rather than the service of God.'[12] And the flesh in this sense must be annihilated entirely. So Morris' remark about a disembodied state has no relevance at all in the present context. Neither does 'destruction' signify, for the individual whose flesh is destroyed, 'the loss of all that is worthwhile, utter ruin.' It no doubt does imply the ruin of *something*; but within the context of 1 Corinthians 5:5, it could not possibly imply the ultimate ruin of the individual whose flesh is destroyed. For *that* individual, it implies just the opposite: the *gain* of all that is worthwhile, utter blessedness; for Paul here presented 'the destruction of the flesh' and 'the salvation of the spirit' as two sides of the same coin. So here, anyway, *destruction* is explicitly a redemptive concept, and not only that: Paul presented Satan himself as an (unwitting) agent of the redemption: 'you are to hand this man over to Satan for the destruction of the flesh, so that his spirit may be saved in the day of the Lord.'

Note also two additional points about the context of 1 Corinthians 5:5: First, the sin concerning which Paul was so exercised, a man's living with his father's wife, was one that he regarded as utterly heinous; it was 'of a kind that is not found even among pagans' (5:1). And second, the punishment he prescribed had a real retributivist flavor to it: 'Let him who has done this be removed from among you' (5:2 RSV). Paul went on to pronounce judgement on the man in the name of the Lord Jesus (5:4) and ordered the Corinthians to deliver him 'to Satan for the destruction of the flesh.' Given the harsh tone of Paul's remarks – as harsh as anything we encounter in the first chapter of 2 Thessalonians – one might never have guessed that Paul intended the punishment for the man's own good, had Paul not explicitly said so; his tone was not the kind that would suggest a mere chastening of a believer, something akin to parental chastisement. And yet, as frightening as the idea of delivering someone to Satan may be, the resulting destruction of the flesh is precisely what would make possible, Paul seemed to think, the redemption of the man himself. Paul thus demonstrated how, on his own view, even harsh punishment, the kind that may appear vengeful and unforgiving, can in fact serve a redemptive purpose.

It is an important point. From the language of retribution – which loving parents use quite frequently, by the way – you simply cannot infer the absence of a corrective purpose. Given Paul's explicit statement, we know that the *destruction* of which he spoke in 1 Corinthians 5:5 served a corrective purpose. But the absence of such a statement would have in no way implied the absence of such a purpose. For as Paul explicitly stated in Romans 11, God is merciful to all and even God's severity serves a redemptive purpose.[13] Depending upon his interests at a particular time, therefore, Paul could describe one side of the redemptive process as divine judgement upon a sinner and the destruction of the old person, or he could describe the other side as the birth of a new person. When the old person, the 'vessel of wrath', is destroyed, the new person, the real person, the 'vessel of mercy... prepared beforehand for glory' is unveiled. When Saul, an enemy of Christ, is defeated, Paul, a servant of Christ, is born. In a very real sense, therefore – the Pauline sense, if you will – both Abram and Saul were utterly destroyed and destroyed forever; what they had thought themselves to be, what they had *called* themselves, no longer existed, and so it was altogether appropriate that their names should be changed.[14]

So herein lies, I believe, the theological significance of name changes in the Bible. According to Revelation 2:17, anyone who perseveres and conquers will receive a *new name*, and that new name is also written, presumably, in the Lamb's book of life. If the old name, the one that the new name replaces, is not in the book of life, then perhaps we all have a name – the old one – that was never 'written in the book of life from the foundation of the world' (17:8). If so, then for as long as 'the inhabitants of the earth' go by their old name, or cling to the false self, they are in danger of being cast into the lake of fire (20:15). But just what is it, I ask, that the lake of fire finally consumes and destroys? It could hardly be the image of God that remains in even the worst of human sinners, nor could it be the 'vessel of mercy' that God 'has prepared beforehand for glory'. It is instead the flesh, the sinful nature, the false self that the lake of fire finally consumes and destroys. For the whole point of fire as an image is that fire consumes something, and throughout the Bible, therefore, fire is a symbol of both judgement and purification, two sides of the same coin. Once they have been purified in the lake of fire, even the kings of the earth, those most vile of all men who had stood with the beast and the false prophet (Rev. 19:19), will be free to enter the New Jerusalem through gates that never close and never shut anyone out (Rev. 21:24–26).[15]

Observe also that Death and Hades are both cast into the lake of fire. Do we not have here a perfect symbol for the final destruction of death? As Paul himself predicted, the 'last enemy to be destroyed is death' (1 Cor. 15:26); and at the end of Revelation 20 we thus see death itself being consumed or destroyed in the lake of fire. This is also called 'the second death', which is simply the death of death: the time when Death itself dies everlastingly. But in Pauline theology death is more than a physical process; it is also a spiritual condition and includes everything that separates us from God. Accordingly, the final destruction of death must also include a final destruction of everything that separates us from God. Those who endure the second death will, for reasons of a kind already given, suffer a great loss and will no doubt experience the final destruction of their sinful nature as if it were the very destruction of themselves. Still, like those failed Christian leaders whose false works must also be consumed, they themselves 'will be saved, but only as through fire' (1 Cor. 3:15).[16]

The Sheep and the Goats

Evelyn Uyemura, an English professor and poet, sometimes likes to say: 'We do not read the Bible the way it is; we read it the way we are.' In many ways, the Bible is like a mirror: the more we peer into it, the more we are apt to see a reflection of ourselves. And nowhere is this more evident, perhaps, than in the words of Jesus. For Jesus steadfastly refused to address in a systematic way abstract theological questions, especially those concerning the age to come. His whole manner of expressing himself, the incessant use of hyperbole, metaphor, and riddle, of parable and colourful stories, was intended to awaken the spiritual imagination of his disciples and to leave room for reinterpretation as they matured in the faith; it was not intended to provide final answers to their theological questions. That people should disagree over which words of Jesus to take literally, over the intended import of his colourful expressions, especially those in an apocalyptic context, and over how to put it all together is therefore hardly surprising. Neither is it surprising that those who reject Paul's universalism, like those who reject his doctrine of grace, inevitably seek support for such rejection in the colourful language of Jesus.

Now I have claimed that, according to Paul, Christ's victory over sin and death will eventually result in all sinners (or the entire world) being reconciled to God. I have also claimed that Paul teaches us exactly how to reconcile such universalism with another New Testament theme, that of judgement and the punishment of sin. For, according to Paul, divine judgement is always an expression of mercy and divine justice always an expression of love. God punishes sin, in other words, for exactly the same reason that he forgives sin and for exactly the same reason that he sent his Son into the world: to deliver us from evil. But however consistent it may be with harsh judgement, Paul's universalism, as I have interpreted it, is obviously inconsistent with any doctrine of a final and irrevocable rejection. So we now confront the claim that in Matthew 25:46, at least, Jesus himself endorsed such rejection and did so by drawing a parallel between the sheep and the goats: between those who go into eternal life (*zōēn aiōnion*) and those who go into eternal punishment (*kolasin aiōnion*). Accordingly, to sharpen the issue a bit, I now propose to consider just two propositions:

1. According to Jesus in Matthew 25:46, God will irrevocably reject some human sinners and subject them to unending punishment.
2. According to Paul in Romans 5:8, Christ will victoriously bring justification and life to all human sinners.

Observe first that, although it is quite possible (as a matter of logic) that both of these propositions should be true, they are both true *only if* Jesus and Paul held contradictory beliefs on the matter in question. If they did not hold contradictory beliefs, then at least one of the above propositions is false. But which one? We have already examined the exegetical arguments against proposition (2) and have found them wanting. So it is now time to consider proposition (1) more carefully. But given our space constraints in this volume, I shall here restrict myself to the following rather minimal thesis: The exegetical grounds for rejecting (1) are much stronger than are those for rejecting (2).

Consider first the matter of context. Whereas Romans 5:8 appears in the midst of a systematic theological discourse, Matthew 25:46 appears as the conclusion of a colourful apocalyptic story. For my own part, I take quite literally the main point of the story, which is a powerful point about the inclusive nature of love ('as you did it to one of the least of these my brethren, you did it to me' RSV). But I wonder how many are prepared to take literally the apparent implication that salvation is essentially a matter of doing good works, or that those who enter into eternal life have merely received a just compensation for their acts of kindness. For even as the text includes a parallel between eternal life and eternal punishment, so it also includes a parallel between good works and bad works. Indeed, all of those who fail to perform the required acts of kindness, which is to say all of us at one time or another, are destined for eternal punishment. So anyone who finds Jesus' apocalyptic story difficult to square with Paul's universalism should likewise find it difficult to square with his doctrine of grace. And if one holds that our failure to perform the required acts of kindness is what *would have condemned us eternally*, had it not been for Christ's atonement, then one could just as easily hold that eternal punishment is what our fate *would have been*, had it not been for Christ's atonement. On the latter interpretation, Jesus' apocalyptic warnings help to underscore our terrible plight, apart from outside help, and what would have been in store for us, had it not been for the 'one act of righteousness' that 'leads to justification and life for all'.[17]

In no way, however, is a universalist *required* to accept such an interpretation. My whole point is that, given his penchant for parable, riddle, and colourful story (sometimes explicitly designed to conceal his real meaning from his audience), Jesus' surface meaning is often misleading (to the unwary) and his deeper meaning often the subject of dispute.[18] Beyond that, the very meaning of the Greek adjective '*aiōnios*', which some of our English Bibles translate as 'eternal' or 'everlasting', has been the subject of dispute. For though the adjective literally means 'age enduring' or 'that which pertains to an age', Plato gave it a special and much deeper meaning. In accordance with his distinction between 'time' ('*chronos*') and 'eternity' ('*aiōn*'), Plato used the adjective '*aiōnios*' to designate the timeless realm, that which exists without any temporal duration or change at all.[19] And this Platonic usage seems to have had a profound impact upon the Hellenistic period, where the word '*aiōn*' acquired great religious significance by becoming 'the name of a god of eternity'.[20] It also seems to have influenced the New Testament writers to some extent, as Paul illustrated when he wrote that 'what can be seen is temporary, but what cannot be seen is eternal' (2 Cor. 4:18). But curiously, the same term is also used repeatedly in the Septuagint and occasionally in the New Testament in contexts where it could not possibly mean 'eternal' or 'everlasting'.[21]

So the question inevitably arises: How should we understand the two uses of '*aiōnios*' in Matthew 25:46? The first point I would make is that on no occasion of its use in the New Testament does '*aiōnios*' refer to a *temporal* process of unending duration. On a few occasions, as when Paul spoke of a 'mystery that was kept secret for long ages (*chronois aiōniois*) *but is now disclosed*' (Rom. 16:25–26), the adjective does imply a lengthy period of time. But on these occasions, it could not possibly mean 'eternal' or 'everlasting'. On other occasions, its use seems *roughly* Platonic in this sense: Whether God is eternal (that is, timeless, outside of time) in a Platonic sense or everlasting in the sense that he endures throughout all of the ages, nothing other than God is eternal in the primary sense (see the reference to 'the eternal God' in Rom. 16:26). The judgements, gifts, and actions of God are eternal in the secondary sense that their causal source lies in the eternal character and purpose God. One common function of an adjective, after all, is to refer back to the causal source of some action or condition.[22] When Jude thus cited the fire that consumed Sodom and Gomorrah as an example of *eternal fire*, he was *not* making a statement about temporal duration at all; in no way was he implying that the fire continues burning today, or even that it continued burning for an age. He was instead giving a theological interpretation in which the fire represented God's judgement upon the two cities. So the fire was eternal not in the sense that it would burn forever without consuming the cities, but in the sense that, precisely because it was God's judgement upon these cities and did consume them, it expressed God's eternal character and eternal purpose in a special way.

Now even as the adjective '*aiōnios*' typically referred back to God as a causal source, so it came to function as a kind of eschatological term, a handy reference to the age to come. This is because the New Testament writers identified the age to come as a time when God's presence would be fully manifested, his purposes fully realized, and his redemptive work eventually completed.[23] So just as eternal life is a special quality of life, associated with the age to come, whose causal source lies in the eternal God himself, so eternal punishment is a special form of punishment, associated with the age to come, whose causal source lies in the eternal God himself. In that respect, the two are exactly parallel. But neither *concept* carries any implication of unending temporal duration; and even if it did carry such an implication, we would still have to clarify what it is that lasts forever. If the life associated with the age to come should be a form of life that continues forever, then any correction associated with that age would likewise have effects that literally endure forever. Indeed, even as eternal redemption is in no way a temporal process that takes forever to complete, neither would an eternal correction be a temporal process that takes forever to complete.[24]

So it all boils down, perhaps, to how we understand divine punishment and its essential purpose. Is it an end in itself? Or is it a means to an end, indeed a means of grace, as I believe that Paul clearly taught? In support of my contention that Jesus in no way rejected this Pauline view, it is perhaps worth pointing out that '*kolasis*' – which, according to the Greek scholar William Barclay, 'originally meant the pruning of trees to make them grow better'[25] – was a standard Greek word for remedial punishment. I do not mean to make too much of this point, as if lexical considerations alone could be decisive one way or another here.[26] But according to Aristotle, 'there is a difference between revenge and punishment; the latter (*kolasis*) is inflicted in the interest of the sufferer, the former (*timōria*) in the interest of him who inflicts it, that he may obtain satisfaction.'[27] Plato likewise argued that a person 'becomes better in soul if he is justly punished.'[28] Indeed, Barclay went so far as to declare that 'in all Greek secular literature *kolasis* is never used of anything but remedial punishment'[29] – which may be a bit of a stretch, since the language of correction and that of retribution often get mixed up in everyday usage.[30] But that the Gospel writer chose the word '*kolasis*' at least suggests that he had in mind an eternal correction of some kind; and even if he had chosen the word '*timōria*', you cannot infer the absence of an underlying corrective purpose from harsh language alone, as we have seen. So the sum of the matter is this: Nowhere did Jesus even hint, much less explicitly state, that the punishment associated with the coming age would be utterly useless as a means of correction. Paul, however, not only hinted, but explicitly stated, that Christ's one act of righteousness leads to 'justification and life for all'. For this reason and the others mentioned above, it is far more reasonable, I believe, to reject the claim that Matthew 25:46 teaches unending punishment (proposition (1) above) than it is to reject the claim that Romans 5:18 teaches universal salvation (proposition (2)).[31]

Conclusion

Like many of my conservative evangelical friends, I tend to view the entire Bible through a Pauline lens. But unlike most conservative evangelicals, I see no way to escape the conclusion that St Paul was an obvious universalist. His teaching on this matter was so clear and so explicit that in the end we must explain the mystery of why so many seem to have missed it – though 'missed it' is perhaps the wrong expression. For the very lengths to which some have gone in an effort to explain away Paul's straightforward statements about all human beings indicate that they have not missed his universalism entirely. But none of us should underestimate, perhaps, the power of the faulty philosophical ideas that we bring to the text and thus impose upon it. If you impose upon the Bible the faulty idea that God's justice and mercy are in conflict,[32] you will inevitably conclude that punishment is a matter of justice, not mercy, and forgiveness a matter of mercy, not justice. You will then take the biblical warnings concerning future punishment as proof that God could not possibly be merciful to all, despite what Paul explicitly said. You will also conclude that Jesus came to save us not from our sin, but from the terrible justice of God.

As I see it, however, the Christian message is just the opposite of that. God sent his Son into the world not for the purpose of saving us from the justice of God, but for the purpose of *establishing* that very justice, which is also altogether merciful, in us. When every evil is finally destroyed, every wrong finally set right, and every opposing will finally transformed, then and only then will the scales of justice finally balance; then and only then will God truly be all in all.

Notes

1 For a defence of the claim that 'God is love' expresses a truth about the very nature of God, see Talbott (1999b). Much of the same material also appears as Chapter 7 of Talbott (1999c).

2 As Bonda has put it: 'The only argument adduced against this view [that Paul literally had in mind *all* Israel] is that the dead are excluded from this number. But this exclusion wreaks havoc with the interpretation of Romans 11:26a… It denies that God's redemption in Christ includes all generations since Adam, while this is precisely the

point Paul wants to make. If we grasp that, then we know that if all Israel will be saved, this will include all Israelites who have died' (1998, p. 184). See footnote 28 on p. 184 [editors: see also Bell (2003)].

3 I am less inclined than some to try to make something of the idea that Pharaoh hardened his own heart several times before God hardened it. As I see it, this means only that Pharaoh managed to keep up his own courage for a while. Had God not provided him with some additional strength, he would have caved in much earlier than he did.

4 Indeed, Isaiah 19 makes just this point: 'The Lord will strike Egypt, striking and healing; they will return to the Lord, and he will listen to their supplications and heal them' (19:21). But see the entire chapter.

5 The paraphrase is intended to startle and to make explicit something implicit in Paul's own words. The objection will be that Paul himself had in mind a contrast between such vessels of wrath as Pharaoh and the unbelieving Jews, on the one hand, and such vessels of mercy as the apostles and other Christians, on the other. He was not, in other words, consciously intending to contrast his own former life as an unbeliever with his present life as a believer. But even if that should be true, and I fail to see how one could know this for sure, it strikes me as irrelevant. For if Paul's own statement about the vessels of wrath and the vessels of mercy is true, and if Paul himself, like all other Christians, came into the world as a vessel of wrath (so that we are not dealing here with an eternally fixed category), it follows that God endured with much patience the unbelieving Saul in order to make known the riches of his mercy to the believing Paul.

6 One might claim that the election of Jacob was, at the very least, a rejection of Esau as a recipient of the birthright and his father's blessing. But given Paul's inclusive understanding of election, Jacob's election was every bit as much an expression of God's desire to save Esau as it was an expression of his desire to save Jacob.

7 John Murray (1960), p. 22.

8 Ibid.

9 Compare this use of 'forever' with its use in Jonah 2:6.

10 The reason that some translators inject into the text the idea of being *excluded* or *shut out* from the presence of the Lord is that the Greek '*apo*', like the English 'from', can sometimes mean 'away from' – as when, for example, the kings of the earth and others cry out to the mountains and rocks, 'Fall on us and hide us *from* (*apo*) the face of the one seated on the throne and *from* (*apo*) the wrath of the Lamb . . ..' (See L. Morris, 1959, p. 206, and Bruce, 1982, p. 152). When we try to hide or to conceal ourselves *from* the presence of the Lord (an impossible task) we are indeed trying to get *away from* that presence. But in 2 Thessalonians 1:9 there is no verb, such as 'to hide' or 'to conceal', and no other grammatical device that would give grammatical sense to such a rendering. In the absence of such a device, it is no less grammatically awkward to translate '*olethron aiōnion apo prosōpou tou kuriou*' as 'eternal destruction *away from* the presence of the Lord' than it would be to translate '*kairoi anapsuxeōs apo prosōpou tou kuriou*' (Acts 3:19) as 'refreshing times *away from* the presence of the Lord'. Indeed, just as the presence of the Lord brings refreshment to the obedient, so it brings destruction upon the disobedient.

11 L. Morris (1959), p. 205.

12 See Morris' entry on 'flesh' in J.D. Douglas (1962), p. 426.

13 For an important (and exhaustive) study of the New Testament understanding of punishment, both divine and human, see C. Marshall (2001). According to Marshall,

as summarized in his conclusion, 'the New Testament looks *beyond retribution* to a vision of justice that is finally satisfied only by the defeat of evil and by the healing of its victims, by the repentance of sinners and the forgiveness of their sins, by the restoration of peace and the renewal of hope – a justice that manifests God's redemptive work of making all things new' (p. 284).

14 In the case of Paul, a more accurate statement would be: It is altogether appropriate that Christians no longer call him by his Hebrew name.

15 Concerning the open gates, Eller writes: 'Open gates have no meaning at all unless there is traffic to use them. Rather certainly, there is no traffic from the new Jerusalem: Why would anyone want to leave? and where is there to go, except to the lake of fire? The gates must be "open" for the sake of *incoming* traffic. John says as much in verses 24, 26, and 27: "shall bring into it", "shall be brought into it", "shall enter". Yet there is no place for any traffic to come from *except the lake of fire*. What other interpretation possibly can be given to John's emphasis upon the open-gatedness of the city?' And concerning the incoming traffic, Eller writes: 'Both of these – "the kings of the earth" and "the wealth and splendour of the nations" – are terms John has used often enough, consistently enough, and with enough pointed overtone, that it simply is inconceivable that he could have written them this time offhandedly, carelessly, without thinking of what he was doing... In that lake of fire something has happened to these kings that makes them entirely different people, gives them an entirely different significance than they had before. If the kings of the earth are here... it can be only because their names now are to be found "in the Lamb's roll of the living"' (Eller, 1974, pp. 200–201).

16 Does the redemptive character of the lake of fire undermine the necessity of Christ's atonement? Not at all. Punishment can indeed reveal to us the error of our ways and provide additional incentives to repent. But when the misery and torment that sin inevitably brings into a life finally induces someone, even in this life, to repent and submit to Christ, this in no way undermines the necessity of Christ's atonement. So why should it be any different in the lake of fire? The point is that punishment alone could never accomplish what Christ did. It could never cancel out, for example, all the harm we have done (think of the harm that Ted Bundy did to his victims, to their families, and even to his own mother). Neither could it restore a broken and repentant sinner to health and life. Only the power of the Cross can do that. For the power of the Cross is, in the end, the power of resurrection, the power to restore life; and so, the only road out of the lake of fire leads right to the foot of the Cross and then beyond to the New Jerusalem.

17 This is in fact just what the Augustinians hold with respect to a limited elect. But, of course, the Augustinians also deny that God's redemptive love extends to all human beings.

18 After considering some of Jesus' 'fearsome pictorial language', e.g., 'the weeping and gnashing of teeth, the outer darkness, the worm not dying and the fire not being quenched', J.I. Packer writes: 'One has to ask, soberly I hope, and reverently, how the Lord could have made the fact of eternal punishment for the impenitent clearer than he did? What more could he have said to make it clear if passages like this do not make it clear?' (1998, p. 175). Curiously, Packer asks his question without even considering how a George MacDonald, or a Gregory of Nyssa, or any other universalist might explain such 'pictorial language'. But in any event, the answer to Packer's question seems to me rather obvious. Had it been Jesus' intention to address the question of universal salvation (or any other theological question) in a clear and

systematic way, I'm sure he was capable of doing so. He did not have to express himself in hyperbole, parables, and riddles, after all. He did so, in part, because he was far more interested in challenging us and in transforming our hearts than he was in imparting correct doctrine.

19 See Timaeus 37d.

20 See Hermann Sasse's entry on '*aiōn*' and '*aiōnios*' in Gerhard Kittel, *Theological Dictionary of the New Testament*, vol. I, p. 198. Sasse also writes: 'The *aiōn* speculations of Alexandria [around 200 BC], where Judaism picked up the Greek word *aiōn*, had a profound influence on syncretistic Gnosticism.'

21 For a New Testament example, see Romans 16:25–26 (discussed below).

22 A selfish act, for example, is one that springs from, or has its causal source in, selfish motives.

23 In this way, the New Testament writers managed to combine the more literal sense of 'that which pertains to an age' with the more religious and Platonic sense of 'that which manifests the presence of God in a special way'.

24 Even as an adjective can refer back to the causal source of some action or event, so it can also describe the effects of some action or event. A harmful act, for example, is one whose effects are harmful to someone or another. And perhaps more to the point, an eternal transformation or an eternal change would not be an unending temporal process at all; it would instead be an event of limited duration that terminates, decisively, in an irreversible condition. It would be, in other words, an event of limited duration whose effects literally endure forever. So as Christopher Marshall rightly points out: 'But punishment is a process rather than a state [contrary to life, which is a state], and elsewhere when "eternal" describes an act or a process, it is the consequences rather than the process that are everlasting (e.g., Heb. 6:2, "eternal judgment"; Heb. 9:12, "eternal redemption"; Mk. 3:29, "eternal sin"; 2 Thes. 1:9, "eternal destruction"; Jude 7, "eternal fire"). Eternal punishment is therefore something that is ultimate in significance and everlasting in effect, not in duration' (2001, p. 186, n.123). But whereas an annihilationist believes that the relevant effect is the annihilation of a person created in God's own image, a universalist believes that the relevant effect is the annihilation of a sinful nature or that which is utterly contrary to the image of God in us.

25 Barclay (1977), p. 66.

26 In the very nature of the case, lexical considerations alone could never settle the issue. You cannot decide between retributivist and non-retributivist theories of punishment, for example, simply by consulting a dictionary. You must instead think through a host of subtle philosophical issues. Neither can you *establish* that Jesus rejected retributivist theories of punishment simply by doing a word study on '*kolasis*'. Far more relevant, to my way of thinking, is that Jesus commanded us to love our enemies, so that we may be perfect *even as our Father in heaven is perfect* (Mt. 5:44–48), and that he explicitly rejected the principle of equal retaliation (Mt. 5:38–42).

27 *Rhetoric* 1369b, 13.

28 *Gorgias* 477a. In *Protagoras* 324, Plato also appealed to the *established* meaning of '*kolasis*' as support for his theory that virtue could be taught: 'For if you will consider punishment (*kolasis*), Socrates, and what control it has over wrong-doers, the facts will inform you that men agree in regarding virtue as procured.'

29 Barclay (1977), p. 66.

30 A person filled with hatred and seeking vengeance, pure and simple, might employ, for example, the language of correction: 'I'll teach him a lesson he'll never forget!'

And similarly, a parent who seeks to teach a child a lesson might employ retributivist sounding language: 'If you go out into the street one more time, you will wish you hadn't!' Because linguistic usage is so fluid and so individual, one would expect a word like '*kolasis*' to be used in both remedial and non-remedial contexts, even if it was a standard word for remedial punishment. In Jewish literature, moreover, the word clearly was used in retributivist-sounding contexts – as 2 Macc. 4:38 illustrates: 'Inflamed with anger, he immediately stripped off the purple robe from Andronicus, tore off his clothes, and led him around the whole city to that very place where he had committed the outrage against Onias, and there he dispatched the bloodthirsty fellow. The Lord thus repaid him with the punishment [*kolasin*] he deserved.' But in fact, as harsh as this may sound, it is in no way inconsistent with Plato's contention that one 'becomes better in soul if he is justly punished'.

31 I fully appreciate that a lot more needs to be said not only about some of Jesus' other apocalyptic remarks, but about Matthew 25:46 as well. But one cannot do everything at once, particularly when working under severe space constraints, and my primary purpose in this essay has been to argue that Paul, who claimed to have received his message from the risen Lord, was a universalist. Beyond that, I have suggested only that Paul's universalism (no less than his doctrine of grace) is compatible with Jesus' account of the judgement of nations in Matthew 25. As for a host of related matters (including some of Jesus' other remarks), I shall now wait to see how the subsequent discussion unfolds.

32 For a clear and thorough explanation of why divine justice and divine mercy are logically equivalent concepts in the Old Testament, see Brinsmead, (1983), Part 1, pp. 1–10. For an exhaustive defence of a similar view with respect to the New Testament, see C. Marshall (2001), pp. 35–95. For a powerful and moving sermon defending the idea that God's justice and mercy are one, see 'Justice', in MacDonald (1867), *Series Three*; and for a philosophical defence of the view that divine justice and divine mercy are exactly the same attribute, see Talbott (1993). Much of the same material appears as Chapter 9 of Talbott (1999c). As for *exegetical arguments* for the widespread view that divine justice and divine mercy are different attributes in tension with each other, I am unaware of any. But Packer does have this to say by way of criticizing John Robinson: 'Does the New Testament anywhere lead us to believe that justice and love are identical? I would not have thought so. But Robinson insists on it.' (1998, p. 177). Packer, however, provides no supporting argument and instead moves on to other matters.

PART II

Biblical Responses

4

The New Testament Does *Not* Teach Universal Salvation

I. HOWARD MARSHALL

Introduction

God desires the salvation of all human beings, whether or not his desire will be fulfilled. Statements such as John 3:16, 1 Timothy 2:4 and 2 Peter 3:9 have this as their obvious meaning. On one side of this statement we have the Augustinian and Calvinist view that despite this general desire God's purpose was to save only a limited group of foreordained people ('the elect'), and that he will certainly accomplish this purpose. These scholars generally deal with the texts already listed by stating either that 'all' here signifies 'all kinds of people' (such as both Jews and Gentiles) rather than 'all individual people' or that these statements refer to a general offer of salvation to the world which is compatible with a specific effectual calling of only some to salvation.[1] On the other side we have scholars, such as Talbott, who insist that the New Testament teaches, by implication if not directly, that what God desires he will certainly achieve, and therefore all people will be saved. Talbott's defence falls into three parts. Part 1 is autobiographical and introductory and identifies the two main themes of Christ's victory and divine judgement. Part 2 is essentially concerned with Paul's teaching and concentrates on the passages which appear to teach a universal appropriation of salvation, especially through the analogy between Adam and Christ. Evil will be destroyed but all humanity will be redeemed. Part 3 examines divine judgement in Paul. Judgement is seen as redemptive and restorative, a painful process that leads to final salvation. Retribution can have a redemptive purpose. 'According to Paul, divine judgement is always an expression of mercy.'[2]

Putting Things in Context

Due to space constraints Talbott confines himself to Paul's teaching and does not place it in its broader context of New Testament teaching about sin and its consequences.[3] Nevertheless, part of my response to him must be to re-emphasise that the uniform assumption and teaching of the New Testament authors is that there will be a final judgement, the outcome of which will be justification for some and condemnation for others, and that there is no indication that these outcomes are anything other than final. The intensity of the New Testament appeals to people to repent and believe lest they suffer final separation from God is such that it is difficult to believe that this separation is purely temporary and will come to an end.

This point is important because it means that the likelihood of a different perspective emerging anywhere is diminished. We have to ask whether it is more likely that Paul's outlook is one that he shares with Jesus and the rest of the New Testament writers, or that a small number of texts in Paul whose interpretation is debatable must determine the interpretation of the rest of the New Testament.[4]

By New Testament times there was a clear Jewish understanding of two things. First, the Old Testament taught that sin could lead to judgement in this world, such as national exile and disaster, natural disasters and individual illness and suffering. Certainly Jesus himself taught that suffering was not an infallible pointer to preceding wrongdoing for which the suffering was a judgement – innocent suffering is a reality – but nevertheless there is plenty of evidence that sinners were warned against impending judgement in this world. Second, it was also recognised that there was judgement after death followed by entry into the Age to Come (or 'the Kingdom of God'; or 'eternal life') or exclusion. This was the framework of thought within which Jesus and the early Christians operated and which they accepted.

The teaching of Jesus as it is portrayed in the Synoptic Gospels invites people into the Kingdom of God and warns them in the strongest terms about the consequences of rejecting the gospel. There are the dangers of losing their own souls (Mk. 8:36) and of being denied by the Son of man (Mk. 8:38; Mt. 10:33). The latter of these sayings is a reference to the judgement at which the Son of man acts as witness for the prosecution or as judge; either way, it is affirmed that eternal destiny depends on one's response to Jesus now. To some he would say, 'I do not acknowledge you' and 'many will try to enter and will not be able to' (Lk. 13:24). He also spoke about the one sin which could never be forgiven, the sin against the Holy Spirit, which is to be understood as the sin of refusing to see and acknowledge the work of God in Jesus himself (Mk. 3:28 f.). The force of this saying is not that other sins will certainly be forgiven but rather that this sin represents an attitude which is unforgivable because it is a rejection of the God who forgives.

More specifically Jesus warns that sinners and those who lead others into sin will suffer an unimaginable fate and be cast into Gehenna, a place of unquenchable, everlasting fire (Mk. 9:43–47; cf. Mt. 5:22, 29 f.; 10:15; 11:20–24; Lk. 12:5). We have no evidence for any Jewish belief in the ultimate restoration of those condemned to Gehenna.

These pieces of fairly explicit teaching[5] are confirmed by the teaching in various parabolic sayings and parables. Jesus warned that angry, unforgiving people will be like debtors who will not escape until they pay the last penny (Mt. 5:25 f.; cf. Lk. 12:58 f.). The unmerciful will be like people handed over to the jailers until they pay their debts (Mt. 18:23–25).[6] The parable of the Great Supper suggests that some will exclude themselves from the kingdom (Lk. 14:15–24). In its Matthaean version the parable closes with the comment that 'many are invited, but few are chosen' (Mt. 22:14).[7] The parables of the tares and the dragnet are explicitly interpreted to mean that some will be cast into the furnace of fire (Mt. 13:40–42, 49 f.). Unprofitable servants, foolish bridesmaids, and those who showed no charity to the needy will also be cast out into outer darkness (Mt. 25).

Over against this material must be placed the commitment of Jesus to seeking out and saving the lost (Lk. 19:10). His appeal was not accepted by everybody. But there is no hint in the Gospels that he continues to seek out sinners in the next world until he is completely successful.

It may readily be granted that some of this material may be due to the Evangelists (or the tradition) elaborating on the teaching of Jesus and giving it an emphasis or even a fresh direction that was not present in the original material. This could especially be the case in Matthew where references to 'weeping and gnashing of teeth' are multiplied. So was the teaching of Jesus significantly different from the presentation in the Gospels? I believe that a survey of critical scholarship would justify my claim that the picture presented by the Evangelists is a uniform one. In any case, the teaching summarised above is an integral part of the New Testament material; whether or not the actual wording goes back to Jesus, this was the impression that he made upon the church and how he was remembered.

It may be objected that the attitudes of Jesus presented here are in line with Jewish thinking. He is simply reflecting the ideas of his time, and we do not find the heart of his message here. We can therefore the more easily reject these ideas as time-bound and not fully assimilated into his theology. But it is fallacious to suggest that because some of Jesus' teaching about future judgement is also found in Judaism it is therefore somehow of lesser importance and is not to be taken seriously. We must beware here of the kind of error committed by some redaction critics who argue that what authors take over from tradition is not really part of their own thinking. There is no evidence that the material cited is an unassimilated part of the teaching of Jesus that doesn't really cohere with the rest of his message.

But Jesus clearly disagreed with Judaism on the basic principle that all (physical) Israel would be saved. He emphasised the need for all Jews to enter into a right relationship with God and not to trust in their hereditary position.

From the universalist side it can be urged that the teaching of Jesus has the character of warning rather than unconditional prophecy. He uses the imagery available at the time to paint the destiny of sinners in the grimmest way in order to show how serious sin is. But there is no guarantee that the slots reserved for the impenitent will necessarily be filled. The sayings stand there purely as warnings. We would need to have texts which leave it beyond any doubt that some people are condemned to everlasting perdition.

This brings us to a point of considerable importance. One way of affirming universalism might be by denying the fact of divine judgement, but this route is not a viable option since the event of a final judgement is so clearly present in the New Testament. Rather one must offer evidence that there will ultimately be nobody who will fall under its condemnation or argue that 'final judgement' is not really final.[8] It is precisely the evidence for these possibilities which is lacking. For example, Luke 13:22–30 gives no hint whatever that the door will remain permanently open: it has been closed and nothing is said about reopening it. Why is Jesus' teaching always couched in terms of final rejection with never a hint that the rejection might not be final if people will only make a post-mortem repentance?

We are left, therefore, to hypothesise that universalism was a belief held by Jesus that he did not communicate directly to his friends. In the absence of positive evidence one could speculate along the lines of, 'The possibility cannot be excluded that...' But there is nothing whatever to suggest that Jesus believed that God would bring about the ultimate salvation of all, and we have no justification for interpreting his statements about ultimate separation in some other way.[9] If we attribute to Jesus an underlying universalism, we make nonsense of the beliefs and attitudes that he openly expressed. John 5:40, 'You refuse to come to me to have life', and the outcome of the sowing of the seed in the parable of the Sower express his frustration and sadness over his mission.

Universalism in Paul?

In the last couple of decades there has been a re-thinking of the traditional doctrine of eternal punishment among some evangelical scholars. There have been two facets in this discussion.

The first is a recognition that the Bible does not teach the immortality of the human soul, but regards immortality rather as the gift of God. Therefore, people are not naturally immortal.[10]

The second is the recognition that there are types of imagery by which the Bible presents the fate of those who do not inherit eternal life, one suggesting conscious torment that never ends, while the other suggests an irreversible act of destruction. While traditional theology has interpreted the latter imagery in the light of the former, one current trend is to argue that the former way has priority in interpretation, not least because the concept of a God who consigns some human beings to endless, conscious suffering is irreconcilable with what we know of the love of God. There are some writers who seem to confuse this understanding of the nature of hell with ultimate universalism, but the two concepts must be kept distinct.[11] The proposal is relevant because acceptance of this understanding of hell as destruction rather than as eternal suffering removes one of the arguments for universalism, namely that the alternative makes out God to be a monster and also makes it hard for the saved to be happy in heaven while they know that other people are suffering in hell.[12]

Victory or Defeat?

This leads me into the first of Talbott's arguments in which he raises the question of whether the existence of the lost in hell would undermine the bliss of the redeemed.[13] A traditional standard reply to this point is that the redeemed will be sufficiently sanctified that they share the attitude of God towards the lost in that they are being justly punished for their rejection of goodness and therefore their lot is not to be regretted. Talbott responds to this kind of argument by noting how a Christian like Paul could have tremendous longing for the salvation of other people even though he recognised that they were sinners deserving of judgement (Rom. 10:1), and how strange it would be if this attitude did not persist in the heavenly state when (surely) feelings of love for the lost must also be sanctified as well as recognition of the justice of their condemnation.

Paul could speak of his own willingness to be accursed for the sake of his Jewish brothers and sisters if that might lead to their salvation (Rom. 9:2–3). This shows that Paul thought that they would be damned if they did not respond to the gospel. It is unlikely that the agony displayed by Paul was simply because the Jews were not participating in salvation there and then; his concern is surely with their future salvation and deliverance from damnation. The possibility that he was thinking of a temporary period of damnation for himself to save them from a temporary period of damnation sounds like clutching at a straw and can be ruled out, especially if there is an echo of Exodus 32:31 f. present. If Paul's anguish is purely over a state that he knows will one day be reversed, then this anguish is not a true parallel to the sense of loss that a person may feel over the final destruction of a loved one. Or are we to assume that the temporary fate of the damned is so painful that God could be accused of inflicting excruciating pain upon them so that they might eventually cry out for mercy and believe? That picture of God is not significantly different from that of a God who inflicts unending torment upon people, and nothing material has been gained.

Talbott's ultimate answer to the problem is not that God will cause the redeemed to forget their lost loved ones, but that God will destroy death. I agree that an eternity in which eternal punishment continues alongside eternal bliss in some kind of cosmic dualism is unstable and inherently unsatisfactory. Therefore, the proposal that God will destroy death and hell is helpful, but I would amend it by saying that the destruction of death includes the destruction of those who have died. At the same time we may also recollect that in human experience we constantly lose people and things that matter to us, but we live with these experiences; we tend to mourn more for our own loss than for the people who have died and have lost the opportunity of continuing life.

Romans 5

Paul generally presents his teaching within the same kind of framework as the teaching of Jesus, with a recognition of universal sinfulness and the prospect of the wrath of God being revealed now and in the future against sinners. The coming of Jesus is to deliver us from the wrath to come, and the message of Paul is summed up in the appeal to be reconciled to God. The acceptance or rejection of the gospel is a life and death issue. There are some texts which have been interpreted to suggest a different view. We need to ask whether such a view could be harmonised with the rest of Paul's teaching, and, more basically, whether the interpretation of the texts themselves is exegetically justifiable.

Foremost among these texts for Talbott is Romans 5:12–21; one might almost say that it becomes the lens through which he views the rest of the NT. The precise purpose of this paragraph is debatable, but the conclusion drawn from it is clear. Essentially there is a comparison and contrast between the actions of Adam and of Christ. The former committed sin and as a result sin and death passed upon all people inasmuch as all sinned; through one man's sin many were constituted sinners (Rom. 5:12, 19). So there is a contrast between the singularity of the actor and the plurality of those affected by his action. Similarly, there was the righteous action of the one person Jesus Christ, as a result of which a plurality of people will be constituted as righteous and therefore acceptable to God; they will experience life. Behind this action of Christ lies the grace of God which operates to give sinners what they do not deserve and for which they have not worked.

Thus there is a contrast between the singularity of the actors Adam and Christ and the great number who were affected by their actions, expressed by 'one' and 'many'. 'Many' is used in a Hebrew sense in which it is contrasted with 'one' or 'few' and means 'a larger number, a majority' that can in fact include everybody. When Paul speaks of the many who were constituted sinners and died, he means literally 'everybody'. Earlier in the letter he has established that 'all', whether Jews or Gentiles, are sinners and face judgement. Now it is possible that Paul's argument is simply to establish that sinners in danger of judgement may be found among both Jews and Gentiles, and there is no doubt that part of his purpose is to emphasise that Jews may be sinners under judgement just as much as Gentiles. But the force of his argument goes beyond this point to underline that 'Jews and Gentiles alike are *all* [as individuals] under sin' (Rom. 3:9). In the main line of his argument he is concerned with how people may be justified before God, and there is no suggestion that there is anybody who is already righteous and does not need to be justified in this way.

But now what about the scope of the effects of the righteous deed of Christ? The words 'many' and 'all' are used in the same kind of way here. Paul uses 'all' three times (Rom. 5:12a, 12b, 18a) of sinners and once of the justified (5:18b), and he uses 'many' twice of sinners (5:15a, 19a) and twice of the justified (5:15b, 19b). Part of his purpose is to make it credible that the action of the one person Christ is efficacious for all, by arguing from the universal effects of Adam's action. It is in fact 'greater' because it produces life rather than death (Rom. 5:17) and also because the condemnation followed one sin but the gift is a response to many trespasses (Rom. 5:16), and there may perhaps be the implication that whereas those affected by Adam's sin sinned themselves and so were worthy of death, those affected by Christ's righteous act did not contribute righteousness of their own; in fact Christ's righteous act is a response to their sinful deeds (Rom. 5:16).[14] This gracious act took place in the past (Rom. 5:15), but the results are future (Rom. 5:17, 19, cf. 21).

The effects of Adam's sin were inevitable and universal, in that all people were constituted sinners, and apparently were so constituted even before they themselves committed acts of sin. But are the effects of Christ's righteous act similar? The universalist claim is that there is exact parallelism at this point. The non-universalist notes that throughout Paul's writings people are put right with God by faith, and this is particularly true of the language of justification and righteousness that is dominant at this point in Romans. Faith is evidently the *sine qua non* for justification here and now. Therefore Paul's teaching here is to be construed in the sense that Christ's one action is the only basis for justification and life for all people but that it is made operative through faith. So the 'many' and the 'all' are indeed all people, but the gift becomes a reality for them only when they believe. People do not experience the gift of salvation until they become believers; apart from Christ they do not receive the gift of the Spirit, they do not have peace with God, and they do not share in the fellowship of the body.[15]

It is, then, the people who were rendered sinners by Adam's sin for whom justification is available through Christ. The question is simply whether Paul's language here requires that all of the former will in fact be justified. Are there grounds for supposing that all people will in fact become believers? Not all people become believers and enjoy the blessings of salvation in this life. Is there reason to suppose either that God grants them life after death without requiring that they believe or that somehow he brings them all to faith at that point? There is a telltale giveaway when Talbott slips a word into the text and says that God 'will *eventually* bring justification and life to them all'.[16] His view is that they undergo some kind of judgemental suffering that brings them to realise their need of salvation and thus they are brought to faith in Christ and so are saved.[17] But where is there evidence that there is this 'eventual' action of God? Is there anything in Paul that would make such possibilities credible?

For Talbott the answer is that the statements 'the result of one act of righteousness was justification that brings life for all people' and 'the many will be made righteous' mean what they appear to say, and therefore an action by God to bring all people to salvation must be assumed.

Talbott states that there are only two options for the non-universalist: either 'all' is not 'all-inclusive' (e.g. it refers to 'both Jews and Gentiles, but not necessarily all Jews and Gentiles') or 'salvation' is potential rather than actual. For the universalist 'all' is and 'salvation' is actual, but only 'in the end'.[18] Once again the idea of something happening after death is smuggled in.

Talbott then states that I reject the first option but offer no arguments for the second option. He also argues that Moo and I make a fallacious inference from the rest of the letter that 'only certain people derive the benefits from Christ's act of righteousness'. He states:

> From the premise that only those who accept Christ and place their faith in him will be 'justified unto life', it simply does not follow that some people will never place their faith in Christ and will therefore never be 'justified unto life'.[19]

The logic is correct. So what Talbott takes Romans 5 to teach is that the many who will be made righteous in Romans 5 are people who will be saved as a result of their having believed. The passage is then taken to imply that God will act in the future to bring these people to belief. Talbott, therefore, must postulate (a) that God will act in the future to bring these people to belief and (b) that he will be successful in every single case. Somehow people will be overwhelmed by the love of God, even if it causes them intense suffering, and so they will yield to his entreaty.

There are thus two ways in which Romans 5:19 can be read. It can mean 'many will be made righteous [provided that they believe]'. But, if so, the outcome remains open in that Paul is not specifying whether this condition will be fulfilled. Alternatively it could mean many [will believe] and be made righteous'.

The point at issue is a simple one. According to Talbott Paul's statement is that all individuals without exception who have sinned will come to belief and salvation, and since it is evident that not all do so in this life we must postulate that they will be given a further opportunity after death and that God will so act as to induce them to believe. The alternative is that Paul's statement means that all individuals will be saved provided that they believe, and it is left open whether they will do so; since we have no evidence for a post-mortem opportunity to believe, we cannot assume that all individuals will eventually be saved. The context favours the second view.

1 There is no positive evidence anywhere for the view that there will be a post-mortem opportunity for salvation or for the view that this will inevitably lead to the salvation of all. The burden of proof is on those who assert these two propositions.[20]
2 The passage itself is concerned with justification that leads to eternal life. But justification is something that Paul thinks of as the state of believers now in this life *prior to the judgement*, and he does not use this language for what happens at the final judgement or subsequently.
3 Romans 5:17 refers to those who receive the gift of God. This phrase clearly limits the scope of those who are saved through Christ to those who believe.
4 The whole context of Romans 1–5 is concerned with people in this life.
5 Since judgement was 'final' for Jews, Paul would need to have spelled out the fact that it was not final quite clearly for it to be apparent to his readers. But he never says anything like 'Get right with God now; otherwise you will endure the wrath of God until you do'. There is no problem with taking v. 18 to refer to the actual effects of Adam's sin and to the potential results of Christ's righteous action, making 'justification that leads to life' a possibility for all people.[21] In v. 19 the point is again the way in which the action of one person affects a vast plurality of people, and the action of Christ makes righteous the many who accept his gift of life.

The structure of Paul's theology is the same as in 2 Corinthians 5, where he teaches that God was in Christ reconciling the world to himself, and then issues the invitation; 'we implore you on Christ's behalf; be reconciled to God' (2 Cor. 5:20). Here there is equally no doubt about the universal scope of what God has done in Christ. But equally clearly the divine act of reconciliation must be accepted, and there is a danger of not doing so (2 Cor. 6:1). Acceptance of reconciliation, otherwise expressed as 'faith', is essential. The gospel message is not simply an announcement of God's offer of reconciliation: it also is a call to faith and acceptance.

In Romans 5 Paul is not preaching the gospel. Rather he is explaining how it is that Jews and Gentiles alike are saved in exactly the same way by God. He therefore goes back behind Abraham to Adam, to argue that corresponding to the universal sin arising from Adam there is the universal provision of salvation through Christ, and his point is to stress the universal provision for both Jews and Gentiles; the law is seen as a side issue. He is not concerned at this point with how salvation is received but rather with the universality of the provision, and the way in which it is through Christ that God operates. It is therefore not surprising that there is nothing explicit here on the response of faith.

To sum up: we could express the nub of the issue by saying that we have a problem with the exegesis of certain passages, principally Romans 5, which speak of the salvation of 'all'. One solution is to interpret these passages in the light of others which show that salvation comes only to those who believe and to claim that these passages refer to the universal divine provision which may or may not be accepted by people. The other solution is to interpret these passages as referring to a universal acceptance of salvation on the assumption that God will somehow bring all people to faith in the future state. The question is whether there is any evidence that would justify this assumption. Romans 5 itself is not evidence for this assumption; it is the passage that requires explanation. At most it might be held to offer a prejudice that other passages might be interpreted in such a way.[22]

Romans 11

In Romans 11 Paul is still dealing with the problem of the Jews who have not followed the way of faith but that of works; some Jews have believed and are now numbered among 'the elect'. Others, however, have been hardened, and this hardening is seen as a judgement of God upon their lack of faith. This temporarily hardened part of Israel will eventually be saved, and so 'all Israel' will be saved after the full number of the Gentiles has been saved.

Now this salvation may be associated with the parousia of Christ, since Romans 11:26 f. is traditionally understood to refer to this. I would not want to establish a case on the basis of a minority understanding of the text, but it seems more likely to me that this verse refers to the original coming of Christ, as a result of which the people of Israel will be saved: the point of the quotation is that by means of Christian preaching God, through Christ, will turn Jacob from their sins; in other words, God's covenant offering life to Israel still stands despite the existing refusal of the (majority of) Jews to accept Christ and their hardening of heart.[23]

Be that as it may, there appears to be a 'final appeal' to the Jews to repent and believe, to which they will respond. Clearly, however, this primarily affects those then living. Paul appears to be very much concerned with what happens in this world.

God's having mercy on 'all' corresponds to his binding of everyone over to disobedience. The point being made is that the scope of God's mercy is the same as that of his condemnation, and nobody is excluded from the possibility of mercy. Here in Romans 11:32 the reference in 'all' is doubtless primarily to both Jews and Gentiles and not necessarily to every individual Jew and Gentile.

But what about the phrase 'all Israel will be saved'? Primarily it means that Jews who have been hardened will now respond to the gospel and be saved, just like those Jews (including Paul himself) who had not been hardened but already believed and belonged to the 'remnant' (Rom 11:5). Does it mean that *all* such Jews will be saved? It is well-known that in the Mishnah it can be asserted that all Israel will be saved but that alongside this comes a statement that lists self-evident exceptions to the rule, the Gentiles and godless Israelites (*Mishnah Sanhedrin*. 10). Moo establishes convincingly to me that the phrase refers to Israel as a corporate entity without the implication that every single Jew is included.[24]

Here we have something different from Talbott's post-mortem experience of a corrective judgement that should not be confused with it. This is an action of God directed to the living. But what about Jews who have already died? Are they included in 'all Israel'? It is not clear to me that Paul's horizon here extends to include them, but let us assume for the sake of the argument that it does. Although nothing explicit is said about a post-mortem event, let us consider the possibilities.

The New Testament generally accepts that there will be a resurrection of non-believers to judgement (Jn. 5:29); when Paul says that we shall all appear before the judgement seat of God (or Christ; Rom. 14:10–12; 2 Cor. 5:10), this will include those who have already died. Other passages which refer to the parousia describe the salvation it brings to believers and the judgement that will be executed on the opponents of the gospel, but say nothing about it being an occasion for the conversion of anybody. There is absolutely nothing to suggest that this judgement will in fact be the occasion for the justification of those hitherto unrepentant. Consequently, there is no basis for the suggestion that in Romans 11 it is the parousia of Christ which leads to the conversion of all who have died and have not previously not believed.[25]

But if all this is correct, we are still left asking in what context the final restoration of the unrepentant and unbelievers takes place. The final judgement is never described as anything other than that – judgement. It is those who have already been justified and reconciled who will be saved from the wrath of God (Rom. 5:9–11). Where is there any evidence for a future beyond that judgement?

Finally, Bell makes the point that, although (in his view) Romans 11 teaches the salvation of 'all Israel', it does not expect all Gentiles to be saved.[26] Consequently, he sees a clash between Romans 11:25–32 where only some Gentiles are saved and Romans 5:18f. in which he finds universal salvation. His solution is that in Romans 5 Paul presents a mythical view of universal participation in Christ's death which takes precedence over the historical framework in Romans 11.[27] But clearly this will not do. It is inconceivable that Paul would have two contradictory views in the one letter, especially when he is writing under such strong emotion regarding the salvation of Jews and Gentiles in Romans 9–11, and Bell's statement that 'on the last day all will in fact have come to faith'[28] is not in fact substantiated in his essay.

Philippians 2:9–11

Here Paul states how God has exalted Jesus 'that... every knee should bow... and every tongue confess'. Two observations can be made. First, the statement is one of purpose, and it does not necessarily follow that the purpose will be fulfilled. The point is simply that God intends that Christ shall have the same honour from all people as that to which he himself is entitled. Second, the statement rests upon Isaiah 45:22–25 where God calls on all people to turn to him and be saved. Everybody will bow before him. His opponents will 'be put to shame, but in the Lord all the descendants of Israel will be found righteous and will exult.' Here, therefore, there is still a division between the opponents and the righteous. There is a question perhaps whether those who are 'put to shame' will then be saved,[29] but the passage does not say so; certainly elsewhere in Philippians the opponents of the gospel will be destroyed (Phil. 1:28; cf. 3:19). Universalists argue that the confession in Philippians 2:11 is not 'forced' but voluntary and salvific, but who could possibly come to this conclusion in the light of 1:28 and 3:19? Further, the language used here is paralleled in Romans 14:10–12 where the context is one of judgement on the disobedient.

Talbott rejects the idea of 'subjugation' on the grounds that God's victory is incomplete so long as anybody can cling to their hatred of God. But the New Testament plainly uses the language of judgement and destruction to describe what God will do. This is clear from 1 Corinthians 15:24–28 where the vocabulary of destruction and subjugation is used. There are 'dominions, authorities and powers' to be subjugated and destroyed, so that the people of God and the new creation may live in peace. Talbott's suggestion that the subjugation here is like that of Christ to the Father[30] ignores the mention of destruction. The willing subordination of Christ is different from the destruction of hostile powers. He also claims that the language of confession implies praise and thanksgiving. And forced confessions are no confessions. Talbott's response is that the power of the cross is the appeal of self-giving love which can overcome all evil and transform it.[31]

1 Corinthians 15

The key verse here is 1 Corinthians 15:22. Against my interpretation that it means 'Wherever death and resurrection take place, they are due respectively to Adam and to Christ', Talbott asserts that it means 'The very *same* all that died in Adam shall be made alive in Christ.'[32]

But in the context Paul is establishing that it is through Christ that resurrection takes place, and he is using the argument by analogy, that if death came about through a human being, it makes sense that resurrection also comes about through a human being (1 Cor. 15:21). That is the point at issue, rather than the extent of the resurrection. He goes on to say; 'For as in Adam all die [i.e. just as all who are in Adam die], so also all who are in Christ will be made alive'. There is the possibility of confusion because 'all who are in Adam' are in fact all human beings without exception, whereas 'all who are in Christ' are not necessarily all human beings. This is confirmed by v. 23 which describes the resurrection of Christ followed by 'those who belong to him' at his coming;[33] To bring in the rest of humanity Talbott then translates *to telos* as 'the remainder', rather than as 'the end'. But this translation is rejected by virtually all commentators[34] and Talbott's appeal to an earlier generation of scholars is inadequate to justify it; he is right not to insist upon it. There is, therefore, no contextual evidence to justify the view that all people will be in Christ and will be made alive.[35]

What Talbott depends upon is his claim that 'Only those who belong to Christ will be made alive' does not imply 'Not all who die in Adam will be made alive'; but this claim is irrelevant. What is needed is evidence that 'all will belong to Christ'. But Paul does not provide this. The implication of v. 23 is that it is those who already are Christ's people who will be resurrected when he comes (cf. 1 Thes. 4:14, 16). There is nothing said to imply that some (other) people will become Christ's people after he has come.

Talbott distinguishes between the cosmic powers opposed to God who will be destroyed and the sinful persons, but he says that the latter are 'destroyed' by redeeming them while they are yet enemies.[36] But he then modulates this to 'destroying our sinful nature'. This is inadmissible, since whenever Paul uses 'destroy' (*apollumi*) of human beings he refers to a judgement upon them that destroys them with no suggestion that their sinful nature is destroyed but they themselves are spared.[37]

Colossians 1:20

Colossians 1:20 is not different in principle from 2 Corinthians 5. Here again God acts to reconcile to himself 'all things, whether things on earth or things in heaven'. The recipients of the letter have experienced this reconciliation, but the ultimate aim of reconciliation is achieved only 'if you continue in your faith, established and firm.' Thus the condition of faith is essential. Accordingly, the only question is whether there is any evidence that suggests that God will bring all people to faith, whether in this world or after death. But again we have found none. The language of this letter is of defeat of the powers opposed to Christ (Col. 2:15) and of the coming of the wrath of God on human sinners (Col. 3:6).

Divine Judgement

Space prevents a full consideration of Talbott's discussion of divine judgement. The thesis here is that all that God does is merciful, that his severe, painful judgement is an act of mercy to lead people to contrition and ultimate salvation. We can choose whether we experience his mercy as kindness or severity, but either way God will use it to bring us to salvation, creating in us that willingness to accept his love.

That God does act correctively in judgement may readily be granted (cf. the succinct example in Judges 3:7–11). But this does not prove that God will do this to all people without exception and that there are no limits to his patience (cf. Rom. 2:4 f.). If that punishment is eternal or everlasting, the implication is clearly that the punished are beyond redemption (2 Thes. 1:8 ff.). Moreover, the fact that God's judgement is merciful does not carry the corollary that people will necessarily respond to that mercy. Talbott's assertion that people have freedom of choice as to the means whereby they achieve their eternal destiny but not as to the destiny itself is arbitrary and unsupported from the New Testament.[38]

Matthew 25:31–46

Talbott recognises that this could be the Achilles' heel of his interpretation since it appears to prophesy not just 'harsh judgement' but 'final and irrevocable rejection'.[39] He offers four arguments in favour of an interpretation congenial to his thesis: 1. The text is not to be taken literally. If it is, it would teach salvation by works. 2. The meaning of *aiōnios* is disputed, but it never refers to an unending temporal period. 3. The word for punishment (*kolasis*) refers to remedial punishment. 4. Jesus was not attempting to teach theology but to challenge and transform by use of vivid language. We may note by way of reply:

1. Like Jesus, Paul also teaches that final judgement is on the basis of works (which may be understood as the evidence of faith and not as works worthy of reward). So this principle can be accepted without any greater problems than we have in the case of similar statements in Paul. There is no problem about taking the teaching of the passage seriously.
2. There is scholarly agreement that in the New Testament *aiōnios* does mean 'never-ending' (like *aidios*), although the force of this term may be conditioned by the context; there is no good reason to take it otherwise here.[40] If the punishment is not everlasting, neither is the life given to the righteous (Matt. 26:45b).
3. Talbott's point shows at most that the statement could be open to an understanding as corrective punishment. But he has not shown that such an understanding is demanded or is even likely.
4. We may grant that what Jesus is doing is to warn how awful is the fate of those who fail to do good to their fellow-beings. To do so he uses the existing imagery of judgement. But he does this consistently to express the terrible outcome of a sinful life.

Clearly the parable does not teach universalism, and it cannot even be said to be compatible with it.

Conclusion

Talbott's form of universalism attempts to do justice to the reality of judgement and is no easy option. It also recognises that there is no salvation outside of Christ and faith in him. To that extent it is more congenial than cruder forms. It leaves the urgency of evangelism unimpaired. It emphasises again the universality of God's offer of salvation in Christ to all people. It thus implicitly argues against any view which suggests that there is a 'hidden agenda' with God whereby he actually purposes to save only a specified, limited group of persons whom he has previously chosen, although the gospel is addressed in general terms to all humanity.

However, he replaces this hidden agenda by a different one in which all that God says about the consequences of rejecting the gospel is ultimately seen to be unreal because the (unspoken) message is really: 'You would do better to repent and believe the gospel now because otherwise you will be subjected to intense pain inflicted by the wrath of God until you respond to his love and freely accept salvation.' Stated thus, it is patently obvious that this is not what the New Testament preaches or teaches. There is nowhere any suggestion that the final judgement still leaves the door open for repentance. Indeed, Revelation is very pessimistic that the preliminary judgements that it describes would lead any or many to repentance (Rev. 9:20 f.; 16:9, 11).

Talbott's claim is that this hidden agenda is necessary in order to make sense of those passages which might seem to suggest that all will (believe and) be saved. I have argued that there is no indication that there will be a future scenario in which people will be brought to faith. Had this been what the New Testament authors intended, they must surely have made it far more clear. The character of future judgement as restorative is simply not there. The church is left with the urgency of preaching the gospel to all the world both so that people may enjoy the blessings of salvation both here and hereafter and also so that people may not suffer the wrath of God and eternal separation from him. To make universalism credible, there must be some clear evidence that the process of 'final' judgement will lead to *all* who undergo it repenting and believing (even if *some* repented that would not prove the point), but none has been provided. Otherwise, it makes better sense to interpret Romans 5 and similar passages in line with the very clear teaching of the rest of the New Testament.

The major weakness in the universalist view is thus that in attempting to explain the few texts which it interprets to refer to the salvation of all people it has to offer an unconvincing reinterpretation of texts about God's judgement and wrath and to postulate an unattested salvific action of God in the future. It is one thing to prophesy a large-scale entry of Gentiles into salvation within history followed by a large-scale conversion of Jews that may possibly be associated with the parousia. It is quite another to postulate some other event or process after death for those who have already died. Two possibilities are suggested. One is that at the parousia/final judgement Christ makes a loving appeal that wins over those previously unrepentant. The other is that the unrepentant will undergo some kind of suffering which will make them realise how lost they are and cause them to turn to God in faith and repentance. They endure the wrath of God, but the point of the wrath is to lead them to repentance. The difficulty with both views is that there is no evidence whatever for them; they are pure speculation. The New Testament does not teach nor imply universal salvation. It teaches the reality of a final judgement on the impenitent and sadly it states that some will be lost. That is why there is such an urgency to proclaim the gospel to all the world.

Notes

1 I have difficulties with the Augustinian/Calvinist position, since I do not believe that it does justice to the 'universal' statements in the New Testament; see I.H. Marshall (1989).

2 p. 44. Since my space for reply is limited, I must apologise for any apparently dogmatic assertions made without producing adequate supporting evidence and argument.

3 p. 52, n. 31

4 There is, of course, the possibility that Paul could be in disagreement with the other writers, but evangelical scholars would want to argue for an underlying unity and harmony.

5 Talbott, p. 54, n. 18, may perhaps be implying that Jesus did not speak directly on these issues but only in figures of speech. The evidence cited suggests otherwise.

6 Universalists may toy with the idea that these sayings imply the possibility of ultimate deliverance once the debt is paid, but they stand quite isolated, and it is probable that they are simply metaphors expressing the impossibility of release. In the fantastic world of Mt. 18:24 the debt of 10,000 talents is unimaginably large and unrepayable. In general, allegorisation of the details of parables is a dubious procedure.

7 The force of 'chosen' cannot be discussed here. It certainly includes the nuance of responding positively to the invitation. In any case the present text expresses particularism and not universalism, and there is no indication that the exclusion is temporary until those who do not respond come to a better frame of mind.

8 Admittedly the term 'final' is not used of the judgement in the New Testament, but this is a helpful way of distinguishing the judgement associated with the parousia from previous acts of judgement.

9 The logical difficulties into which one gets by insisting on their subjective reality but objective emptiness are seen in J.A.T. Robinson's discussions.

10 Harris (1983).

11 Cf. the discussion in Hilborn & Johnston (2000), pp. 24–34.

12 I consider that the case for understanding hell as the state of total destruction is well-founded.

13 pp. 15–18.

14 Boer (1988), pp. 174., defends universalism here, on the grounds that if death has the last word over the vast majority of humanity the 'much more' is really 'much less' (cited by Talbott, p. 28, n.6). But Paul evidently thinks that the conquest and overcoming of death by Christ is much more than what Adam did, and it is sufficient that the offer of life is there to humanity. De Boer further argues that Paul's division of humanity elsewhere into those perishing and those being saved is provisional, and that the imagery of 'firstfruits' indicates that those who are now believers foreshadow a harvest of cosmic salvation. But the 'firstfruits' imagery does not imply that the whole of humanity will be redeemed, and no other reason is offered for the 'provisional' character of the division within humanity.

15 The question of what happens to those who have never heard of Christ is not directly answered by Paul. He is more concerned to ensure that as many people as possible do hear the gospel.

16 p. 20.

17 Talbott rightly does not take up the possibility that by suffering they somehow expiate their sins and so are accounted righteous. Their salvation rests on the fact that Christ died for them and it is appropriated by faith. This understanding of the basis and means of salvation (by grace through faith) is thoroughly evangelical.

18 p. 21–22.

19 p. 29, n. 31

20 In Rom. 10 people believe only if they have had the good news preached to them by God's messengers. An eschatological proclamation of the gospel (by God himself?) is never mentioned.

21 It will be clear that I do not think that the New Testament limits the scope of the atonement.

22 We can pass over Romans 8, since the references to 'the whole creation' (vv. 19–22) clearly are to the non-human sectors of the universe and cannot by any stretch include 'human beings who do not yet believe'

23 For this interpretation see, for example, N.T. Wright, (1991), pp. 250 f..

24 Moo (1996), pp. 720–23.

25 As I have maintained elsewhere, the only possible allusions to a preaching of the gospel to the dead (1 Pet. 3:19: 4:6) should be interpreted otherwise; see Achtemeier (1996).

26 Bell (2002a), p. 417, n. 1.

27 Ibid., pp. 430–2.

28 Ibid., p. 429.

29 p. 30, n. 16.

30 p. 28.

31 p. 25.

32 p. 25.

33 So rightly, Bell, (2002a), p. 428.

34 Details in Thiselton, (2000), pp. 1230 f.. Similarly Boer (1988), p. 222, although he is a defender of universal resurrection elsewhere in the passage.

35 'The unqualified 'all' of verse 22 is given further specification in the sentence immediately following: it is 'those who belong to Christ' who will be raised at the time of

his coming... [Paul] says nothing one way or the other in this passage about the resurrection and judgement of unbelievers' (Hays, 1997, p. 264). Hays further comments that 'Many of Paul's other statements make it difficult to suppose that he held such a view: within 1 Corinthians alone, see 1:18; 2:6; 3:17; 4:5 and 6:9–10' (ibid.).

De Boer (1988), p. 112, asserts the universal reference of 'all' in v. 22b. He has two arguments. The first is syntactical. The translation 'all who are in Christ' is impossible in view of the parallelism with v. 22a. That is correct, but the point at issue is rather that just as all who die do so 'in Adam', so also all who will be made alive will do so 'in Christ'. Clearly Paul wants to assert that, just as there is death, so also there is life, but his main point is to establish the reasonableness of belief that life can come through a man (Christ) by analogy with the fact that death came through a man (Adam). De Boer's second point is that the believers in v. 23 are a representative rather than an exclusive group, but he does not substantiate this assertion. Finally, he holds that 'those who have fallen asleep' in v. 20 is not restricted to believers; but this phrase takes up the phrase 'those who have fallen asleep in Christ' in v. 18 and should be understood in the same way.

36 p. 27.

37 Rom. 2:12; 14:15; 1 Cor. 1:18; 8:11; 15:18; 2 Cor. 2:15; 4:3, 9; 2 Thes. 2:10. Cf. Phil. 1:28; 3:19; 1 Tim. 6:9.

38 Since this article is a reply to Talbott, it has not been possible to devote space to Hillert (1999). The author argues for two different perspectives in Paul, but I have not been persuaded by his arguments.

39 p. 44.

40 So, for example, BAG, s.v.; H. Balz in *Exegetical Dictionary of the New Testament* I, pp. 46–8; J.P. Louw and E.A. Nida, *Greek-English Lexicon of the New Testament* (New York: United Bible Societies, 1988), I, p. 642.

5

A Wideness in God's Mercy: Universalism in the Bible

THOMAS JOHNSON

Introduction

Definitions and Understandings

The Bible teaches the universal saving and sovereign grace of God, who, out of love for all people and all creation, has provided ultimate reconciliation and restoration for all. While the Bible affirms the awful possibility that some may reject God's love and be lost, it also allows us to hope that no one will ever be eternally separated from the love of God in Jesus Christ our Lord.

According to the Bible, God is a universalist. From Genesis to Revelation, God's saving purposes always have in view all human beings, as well as their natural environment. This broad universalism sets the overall tone for the Bible's teaching on salvation.[1] God wants all people to be saved (1 Tim. 2:4) and has indeed reconciled them all to himself through Christ (2 Cor. 5:19).

How different is the traditional view that only those who have made a conscious decision[2] in this life to accept Christ as their personal Saviour will be saved and that everyone else, i.e., the vast majority of human beings who have ever lived (with exceptions usually made for the mentally handicapped and small children), will endure a hell of eternal conscious torment![3] This chapter also takes the view that Scripture teaches that unrepentant unbelievers will be destroyed after the last judgment. They will cease to exist, all the rest will be saved, and no one will be in hell forever. It may also be true that human beings are not naturally immortal and that eternal life is a gift to believers.[4]

Authority and Interpretation

Writers on the biblical message of salvation often treat the relevant passages without due consideration of their historical, cultural, and human context. What the Bible says and what it teaches are not the same thing. Only the overall teaching of the Bible (on a particular issue) can be considered authoritative for Christian faith, not the apparent teaching of any specific passage. Individual passages must be placed in the context of the broader teaching of the Scripture as a whole. It may also be the case that the Bible teaches more than one thing or has more than one emphasis, and that these teachings might be in tension with each other.[5]

Further, no one does presuppositionless exegesis of Scripture,[6] or interpretation without some pre-understandings or theological commitments. There are always larger theological issues to be taken into account before one can pronounce that 'this is the teaching of the Bible' on a given subject. We as interpreters are changed by our readings of the Bible. Our theology is continually being revised, modified, and deepened as we submit ourselves to God's word. It is not helpful, therefore, to come to the study of 'universalism' with our minds already made up, as is often the case.

The weight of Christian tradition is also difficult to evaluate. Some think that because a preponderance of church theologians in past centuries has held a particular view that this throws the burden of proof on those who would disagree. Yet it is unlikely that the Reformation would have occurred if the Reformers had not appealed to Scripture behind the tradition of the church. It is still the case that truth is determined by neither the ancientness of the view nor how many people have held it. Let tradition make us cautious but not foreclosed.

Given the above, it is best that we be both generous and wary in our reading of each other's interpretations of Scripture, especially on controversial issues. We should not too readily say that a particular view is unbiblical or without Scriptural warrant, especially if it is a view that is contrary to or challenges what we already believe. We should also not too readily believe that a particular exposition is the 'truth of Scripture', especially if it coheres with what we already believe.

The Problem of Corporate Wholes

Part of the problem in using the biblical texts to argue for or against universalism is that most of the biblical passages involved are talking about groups of people: Israel, the Jews, the Gentiles, all the nations, all peoples, and even Adam and Christ as corporate wholes. In the West, especially since the Enlightenment, we have been preoccupied with individuals, their beliefs, destiny, and salvation. How can I as an individual be saved?[7] The Bible, for the most part, does not reflect this preoccupation. So, we have trouble making the Bible, answer our modern questions.

It is easy to show in the Old Testament that God has always been concerned about all people as a corporate whole. Though God chooses to have a special focus on Israel, God does so for the sake of all people. Whether we are speaking of Israel or all the nations, Jews or Gentiles, we are dealing with people or nations as a whole, not with the salvation or destiny of individuals. We want to know whether every single person, every individual Sumerian, Egyptian, Mayan, Bantu, or Chinese, who ever lived got an opportunity to make a personal decision for God! It is not that our modern questions are not important; it is simply and frustratingly that the Bible was not written to answer them. The Scriptures come from very different times and places, each with their own cultural assumptions, and they can be used only indirectly and along with other sources of authority, such as the teaching of thoughtful Christians before us, clear thinking, and Christian experience to work out or educe principles, theological and moral, by which to think and live Christianly today.

Universalism in the Old Testament

The kind of universalism we find in the Old Testament is the broader definition we discussed above. In the Old Testament God shows passionate interest in the whole of creation, all people, as well as their environment.[8] For example, in the Psalms the theme of

God's universal love and concern for all is prominent. God rules the nations and is sovereign over all the earth (22:27–28; 46:10). God loves all people,[9] and the nations as a whole are called to praise and honour God.[10]

God called Abraham and formed his people Israel so that all might come to know and worship God. The Old Testament demonstrates God's faithful determination that all people might know him and serve him as Lord. This is especially evident in Isaiah. Several passages witness to God's desire that all the nations, all peoples, come and worship him. God's deeds are to be made known among the nations (12:4). God's servant, usually Israel in Isaiah's Servant Songs (though see 49:5–6), will bring forth justice to the nations (42:1, 3–4). This might mean judgment, but 42:6–7 makes it clear that salvation is in view, opening the eyes of the blind and releasing prisoners from darkness. Israel as light to the nations is re-emphasized in 49:6, 'that my salvation may reach to the end of the earth.' All nations and tongues will come and see God's glory (66:18), since Israel's returning exiles will 'declare my glory among the nations' (66:19). 'All flesh shall come to worship before me, says the Lord' (66:23).

It is widely acknowledged that for most of the Old Testament that 'the traditional view in ancient Israel [was] that there is no real life after death, except in the minimal sense of a shadowy existence in Sheol, the land of the dead.'[11] Only two passages clearly affirm a resurrection from the dead: Isaiah 26:19[12] and Daniel 12:2,[13] though it is intimated in Ezekiel 37, Psalm 49:15 and Psalm 73:24–25. The Old Testament affirms the justice of God in blessing the righteous and punishing the wicked, but it has almost no eschatological framework in which to carry this out. Our search for passages that discuss eschatological salvation and judgment will prove more fruitful in the New Testament.

Universal Salvation in the New Testament

The Gospel of Matthew

The broad universalist theme of God's love and concern for all people is prominent in Matthew's Gospel even though it is directed to a Jewish-Christian audience. Matthew is remarkably inclusive and sensitive to God's mission of salvation to non-Jews. Jesus is the light that has dawned on the Gentiles in fulfilment of prophecy (4:15–16; 12:18, 21).[14] Rather than the narrower and more ethnic term, 'Messiah', Jesus prefers 'Son of Man', a broader term that, in addition to its apocalyptic nuance (Dan. 7:13 ff.), more closely identifies him with all humanity (Ps. 8:4).[15] Jesus' disciples are to be lights to the world and carry the gospel to all the nations.[16] He invites to his rest all who are weary and heavy laden (11:28), counts as his close relative everyone who does the will of his Father in heaven (12:50; cf. Mk. 3:35; Lk. 8:21), and pours out his blood for many for the forgiveness of sins (26:28; cf. Mk. 14:24). Some, like the Roman centurion at the cross will confess that Jesus was God's Son (27:54; cf. Mk.15:39). We continue to see that God, though working within his covenant relationship with Israel, always has in mind his universal saving purpose.

Does that saving purpose extend to all individuals with the result that all will be redeemed? This meaning appears to be called into question by numerous passages in the teaching of Jesus in Matthew that speak of hell.[17] Anyone who says, 'You fool!' will be liable to hell (5:22). Those whose bodies cause them to 'stumble' are in danger of hell (5:29–30; 18:8–9). We are commanded to fear God who can destroy both body and soul in hell (10:28). Jesus warned the scribes and Pharisees that, as children of hell, they were in danger of being condemned to hell (23:15, 33). There are also other descriptions of punishment after death, such as:

- 'destruction' (7:13, in contrast to life),
- not entering the kingdom of heaven (7:21),
- 'outer darkness' with 'weeping and gnashing of teeth' (8:12; 22:13; 25:30; cf. 13:42, 50; 24:51),
- being burned up with fire,[18] a 'furnace of fire' (13:30, 40–42, 49–50), or 'eternal fire' (18:8–9; 25:41; also called 'eternal punishment' in 25:46, in contrast to 'the kingdom' and 'eternal life' – vv. 34 and 46),
- perishing (10:28; 18:14; 21:41),
- and being tortured or cut in pieces and put with the hypocrites (18:34–35; 24:51).

Several considerations come into play when we reflect on these statements. They are all taken from apocalyptic and parabolic contexts, where Jesus is using hyperbole and exaggeration to warn of the consequences of sin, i.e., a life of evil conduct reflective of a character not in conformity with the will and nature of God. It is better to take these images seriously but not literally. Some people are warned of condemnation or destruction due to mistreatment of others (5:22, 29–30; 18:34–35; 21:41; 23:15, 33; 24:51; 25:31–46). Others are condemned because of displayed or implied evil character (5:29–30; 7:13–14; 13:24–30, 36–42, 47–50; 18:8–9; 24:51). The way to destruction is broad (7:13–14). Many are called but few are chosen (22:14). It is very difficult to enter the kingdom of heaven (19:23; cf. Mk. 10:23–24).[19] Only those who become like little children enter the kingdom (18:3; 19:14) and those who do the will of the Father in heaven (7:21). Sometimes the cause of a person being condemned is not specified (8:12; 10:28). One man is sent to outer darkness for not having the proper clothing at a wedding banquet (22:11–13), another for not earning interest on his master's money (25:24–30), and a third God will torture until he or she learns to forgive (18:34–35)![20]

Despite the hyperbolic and parabolic language, if there is a literal hell, then these texts imply an eschatological separation of the righteous from the wicked (by whatever standard is applied) at death or after judgment. Are the wicked lost forever? Do they suffer forever? What is the nature of hell? Some kind of punishment after death is certainly implied. But unless the reader already begins with an understanding of hell as eternal, conscious punishment, it is not clearly taught in Matthew's Gospel.

Hell is suffering, but is the fire or darkness (note the conflicting images) restorative,[21] or does it end in the final destruction of those who finally persist in their self-chosen path of rejection of God's loving will for them,[22] or is it, in accordance with to the traditional view, the everlasting conscious suffering of the damned?[23] We do not know whether the weeping and gnashing of teeth are remorse and repentance leading to life, or the prelude to their destruction (7:13; 10:28), being burned up in the eschatological fire (13:30, 40, 42, 49–50). The clearest passage, Matthew 25:31–46, the parable of the sheep and the goats, speaks of an eschatological separation to 'eternal life' (the kingdom) and 'eternal punishment' ('eternal fire').

But here we face the problem of whether *aiōnios*, 'eternal,' refers to a qualitative state (the life or punishment appropriate to the age to come) or quantitative (everlasting in duration).[24] Either or both meanings are possible. There is no reason to assume or read into the passage that some are lost forever. Their punishment in eternity, punishment that all deserve (for all have sinned), may burn away all that keeps them from the full realization of the image of God in which they were created.

In the Sermon on the Mount Jesus teaches his disciples that they are to be perfect as their Father in heaven is perfect (5:48), for he makes his sun and rain to fall on both the righteous and the wicked, and calls us to love and forgive our enemies, as God also does (5:43–47). The way to life is open for all through the mercy and forgiveness of God.[25] Will anyone finally persist in refusing God's love?

Gospel and Letters of John

The Gospel and Letters of John have at their centre a theological presentation of the person and work of Christ. Our consideration of universalism here will also be Christ-centred. After briefly reviewing some of John's christological themes, we will look at the concept of eternal life in relation to faith, the judgment/condemnation/wrath motif, and then a concluding word about the nature of God in these documents.[26]

Christological themes.
Jesus is the Logos, God's agent in creation (1:3, 10). He is also 'the light of all people' (1:4), the light that enlightens everyone (1:9), and 'the light of the world' (8:12; 9:5; cf. 12:46). Jesus is the Saviour of the world, the one who takes away the sins of the world (1:29), the one whom God sent to save the world (3:17; 12:47; 1 Jn. 4:14). Closely related to his role as Saviour, is Jesus' death as 'the atoning sacrifice' (*hilasmos*), 'not only for our sins, but for the sins of the whole world' (1 Jn. 2:2; 1 Jn. 4:10). Jesus is also the life/resurrection. As Logos he is life itself (Jn. 1:4; 14:6; cf. Gen. 2:7), and he is 'the resurrection and the life' (11:25). He is the bread of God (true bread of heaven, bread of life – Jn. 6:48), sent to give life to the world (6:33; 1 Jn. 4:9). Eternal life is in the Son, so that to have the

Son is to have life, and without him we do not have it (1 Jn. 5:11–12).

Faith and eternal life.

Another set of passages teaches that one enters into this life through faith or believing in Christ (or in the one who sent him, 5:24). Indeed, to encourage this faith is the very purpose of this Gospel (20:31). Out of love for the world God gave the Son, 'so that everyone who believes in him may not perish, but may have eternal life' (3:16; 3:36; cf. 10:26–28). It is God's will that all who 'see the Son and believe in him may have eternal life' (6:40). Those who believe in Christ will enjoy resurrection life (11:25–26), and they know that this life is theirs (1 Jn. 5:13).

Judgment/condemnation/perishing.

The alternative to having eternal life is perishing (*apollumi*, 3:16; 10:28), condemnation (5:29), enduring the wrath (*orgē*) of God (3:36), or simply, death (5:24). God did not send the Son to condemn the world but that the world through him might be saved (3:17). Those who believe in Jesus are not condemned, unlike those who reject him (3:18). Light and darkness also function as contrasting elements of divine judgment. Those who do evil hate the light and love darkness, while those who do what is true and good come to the light (3:19–21). Jesus has the authority to judge humankind, separating those who have done evil from those who have done the good (5:27–29; cf. 9:39). Those who reject him on the last day will find that his word is their judge (12:47–50).

The character of God.

Finally, as with the other Gospels, the nature or character of God is an important consideration in assessing the outcome of salvation. God's essential nature is love (1 Jn. 4:8, 16) and light (1 Jn. 1:5). Whatever God does must be in accord with his character. It was out of love that God sent the Son to save the world (3:16–17), and his light enlightens (1:9), delivers from darkness (12:46), and cleanses us from sin as we walk in it (1 Jn. 1:7).

In *summary*, the Fourth Gospel and 1 John strongly emphasize the universal love of God. God created all things through the Word and sent him into the world to be its Saviour. In Jesus, God takes away the sins of the whole world and gives life to all who believe in him. Those who reject the Light of the world are in darkness and in danger of perishing, but it is God's purpose to save the whole world through Christ. All who do what is genuinely right, good, and loving show evidence of the Father's work in their lives. In the end what matters most is that God is love, holy love, love that seeks to save the world.

The Letters of Paul

Paul's letters contain many passages that are relevant to universal salvation. We will focus our discussion on the ones most often raised in this connection.

Romans

Some of the strongest arguments for the ultimate victory of God's universal love come from the Apostle Paul's letter to the Romans. We will examine the relevant passages under five headings:

Everyone Needs the Gospel

Paul begins his teaching strategy in Romans by stating his theme (1:16–17: the gospel is God's power for saving everyone who has faith), and then by demonstrating conclusively that all people need this gospel. All are qualified because all are sinners: Gentiles (1:18–32), moralistic judges (2:1–16), and the Jews (2:17–3:8). All have sinned and fallen short of the glorious nature of God that, according to Jewish teaching, humanity once enjoyed before the fall (3:9–23).[27] This situation came about, according to Romans 5:12–21, because of all humanity's participation in the sin of Adam. Because of his trespass, sin came into the world and spread to all people, causing death and condemnation for all.

The Gospel (Salvation or Justification) is For All

In answer to the universal human predicament, Paul makes explicit that the gospel is the power of God for saving everyone who believes; it is good news for all people, Jews and Gentiles (1:5, 14–16; 14:8–9). God has provided, as a gift of his grace, righteousness (justification) and redemption for all who believe (3:22–24), regardless of their ethnic origin; God is the one God of all people, Jews and Gentiles (3:28–30).[28]

This is stated in even stronger terms in Romans 5. All sinners in Adam have received the free gift of God's saving grace (i.e., life, justification) through Jesus Christ (5:15–17). This applies to all who are in Adam, affected as they are by the one man's trespass (5:12, 17). Just as 'one man's trespass led to condemnation for all, so one man's act of righteousness leads to justification and life for all (5:18; cf. 6:23). The theological basis for this claim is the universal application of the death and resurrection of Jesus. He died and rose for all. All people have been put right with God through Jesus Christ (5:19). God's grace and its consequences are greater than the consequences of Adam's sin.[29] In God's economy, grace now has the dominion, not sin. It is hard to see how the gospel can be good news if the vast majority of people who have ever lived are condemned to an eternal hell.

A somewhat parallel argument occurs in Romans 11. There, Paul maintains that God will, in the end, be merciful to all. A blindness or hardening has come upon Israel at present (11:7–10, 25) with the result that the gospel of God's mercy has come to the Gentiles (11:25, 30). It has meant the 'reconciliation of the world' (11:15). Eventually Israel's 'full inclusion' (11:12), or 'their acceptance' will be life from the dead (11:15), and by God's universal mercy 'all Israel will be saved' (11:26, 31). 'For God has imprisoned all in disobedience so that he may be merciful to all' (11:32). There is a wideness in God's mercy that is far beyond human understanding. His wisdom, knowledge, judgments, and understanding are unfathomable (11:33).[30]

How God will apply this universal saving benefit to all is not stated in Romans 5, but throughout this epistle Paul clearly teaches that people receive this salvation (life, justification, and redemption) by faith (believing) in Jesus Christ the Lord (10:9–10).[31]

Salvation for Only Some?

There are other passages in Romans that have been interpreted to suggest that God's salvation is limited only to a few. Romans 8:28–39 speaks of 'those who love God, who are called according to his purpose' (v. 28), 'those whom he foreknew' (v. 29), and 'God's elect' (v. 33). Are these passages intended to teach us about the scope of the God's saving work? No, they are focused on the wonderful benefits believers in his saving work receive.[32] God is planning a 'large family' (v. 29). We who believe have the privilege of entering that family in this life and of experiencing the vice-grip of God's love on our lives now.

Certain verses in Romans 9 have been taken to mean that God condemns some for all eternity and only saves a few elect ones. God chose Jacob, not Esau (9:11–12). God has mercy and compassion on whomever he will (9:15, 18) and hardens the heart of whomever he chooses (9:18). Some are vessels of wrath, while others are vessels of mercy (9:22–23). But these texts must be interpreted in their context in Romans. We have already seen in Romans 1:18–3:31, 5:12–21, and in Romans 11 that God's 'strategy' is to show that all stand condemned, that all have sinned and need the gospel, that all deserve God's wrath, that all are in Adam and under the sentence of death, that some are hardened that others might be included so that eventually all may be saved, and that God has 'imprisoned all in disobedience so that he may be merciful to all' (11:32).

God's judgment

No one will escape the judgment of God (14:10); 'each of us will be accountable to God' (14:12). God will judge the world (3:6), judging everyone, with absolute impartiality (2:11), according to their deeds (2:6–10) and through Jesus Christ (2:16). All people will fall under his sentence of condemnation (2:3; 5:16; cf. 11:32). But some with hard and impenitent hearts, who have been self-seeking and done evil, will experience God's wrath on the day of judgment (2:5, 8–9), while others who have done good and sought immortality and what is honourable will be rewarded with God's shalom (2:7, 10). For those already in Christ, there is no condemnation (8:1); they have already begun to enjoy God's *šālōm* (5:1). In the end, 'says the Lord, every knee shall bow to me, and every tongue shall give praise to God' (14:11).

God's Love

God's saving plans for all people arise out of his love. Believers experience that love when the Spirit of God is poured into their hearts (5:5). But, as in the Synoptic Gospels, God also loves his enemies. God loved us when we were enemies, still sinners and outside of Christ. He loved us so much that he died for us. If God loved us this much when we were his enemies, now that we have been reconciled to God by Christ's death, we have nothing to fear from God's wrath (5:8–10).

In fact, we have nothing to fear at all. Though all kinds of fearful things may happen to us (8:35b–36), nothing will ever be able to separate us from the love of Christ (8:35a, 37). There is no power or circumstance in all creation, neither in life nor in death, that will ever be able to separate us from God's love for us in Christ (8:38–39). The love of God is unconquerable and inescapable.[33]

1–2 Corinthians

Paul's universalism derives from his faith in one God, the creator of all, and in 'one Lord, Jesus Christ, through whom are all things' (1 Cor. 8:6). God's sovereignty includes all beings in heaven and on earth.

On the matter of the salvation of all, Paul invokes his Adam/Christ typology in 1 Corinthians 15 in the context of an extended argument about the necessity of resurrection. 'As all die in Adam, so all will be made alive in Christ. But each in his own order: Christ the first fruits, then at his coming those who belong to Christ' (1 Cor. 15:22–23; cf. 15:49). There has been some disagreement about how to interpret the opening of the next verse (v. 24). The phrase *eita to telos* might be a reference to persons, i.e., a third group in Paul's order of resurrection procession, and so be translated: 'then come the rest.'[34] But it is far more natural and common to interpret *telos* as a reference to time: 'Then comes the end,' as in nearly all modern translations and commentaries,[35] especially in the light of the temporal conjunction *hotan* that begins the next clause.

Even if v. 24a is not a reference to the resurrection to life of all the rest of humankind, Paul states clearly in v. 22 that all persons will be made alive in Christ.[36] When he makes this assertion more specific in v. 23, he mentions first Christ himself, then 'those who belong to Christ.' How are we to understand this? There are two apparent alternatives, and both are problematic. Christ may be understood as the forerunner, the first fruits, of a general resurrection of all persons, who come alive only because he rose from the dead. They all 'belong to Christ' because he has redeemed them all and reconciled them all to God (2 Cor. 5:14–15, 19). The problem is, however, that 'those who belong to Christ' usually refers in Paul's letters to Christian believers.[37] On that alternative, it is difficult to make sense of Paul's assertion that '*all* will be made alive in Christ.' The answer that the second 'all' does not mean 'all,' while the first 'all' ('as all die in Adam') does, is patently unsatisfactory.

Three solutions are possible. It may well be that Paul has a genuine universalist hope here, contending that the sovereign grace and love of God will ultimately prove victorious over all sin and unbelief. It may also be that Paul is speaking in broad, general terms, while not ruling out that some (few?) might reject God's provision of new life in Christ. Thirdly, perhaps Paul envisions Christ as the beginning of a whole new creation. Adam heads the old creation, and in it all who have come from him, who belong to him, die. Christ, by contrast, heads a new creation (2 Cor. 5:17). One enters it by being reconciled to God in Christ (2 Cor. 5:18–19) and by being made alive with him in the resurrection at his coming (1 Cor. 15:22–23). There is no one else in the new creation. Just as all the people in the old creation were Adam's and died, so all persons in the new creation belong to Christ and live. He saves them by his atoning death (2 Cor. 5:19, 21) and makes them 'imperishable' and 'immortal'[38] by their restoration to his image (1 Cor. 15:47–49) in the coming resurrection (1 Cor. 15:42–57). In this sense, the two 'alls' in 1 Cor. 15:22 are compatible if not exactly coordinate.

As a result of Christ's reign, every ruler, authority, and power hostile to God, all God's enemies, will eventually be destroyed, including 'the last enemy,' death (15:24–26). Then Christ will hand over the peaceable kingdom to God, and God will be 'all in all' (15:28).

Philippians

Four verses in Philippians pertain to our subject. Phil. 2:10–11, coming at the end of the early Christian hymn in 2:6–11 that Paul uses to reinforce his teaching on humility (2:1–5), says,

> so that at the name of Jesus every knee should bend,
> in heaven and on earth and under the earth,
> and every tongue should confess that
> Jesus Christ is Lord, to the glory of God the Father.[39]

This is the ultimate, universal submission of all beings to Christ. Is it voluntary or involuntary, glad or forced? The strongest argument in favour of the former is the word 'confess' (*exomologeō*). *Every use of this word in the New Testament connotes a voluntary confession.*[40] This includes all uses of the cognate verb, *homologeō; and the related noun, homologia.* Inherent in the nature of confession is willing and, sometimes, joyful acknowledgement. It will not do to suppose that the humble confession of Phil. 2:11 is a reluctant and forced confession from Jesus' conquered enemies.[41]

Two passages in Philippians speak of the 'destruction' (*apōleia*): of the Philippian Christians' persecutors (1:28) and of those who are 'enemies of the cross of Christ' (3:19). 'Their end is destruction' (3:19). Paul entertains the possibility that some of those who oppose Christ's work will not attain the salvation awaiting believers (1:28) or gain a resurrection body (3:21).

One way to bring together the diverging eschatological emphases of these two sets of texts from Philippians is to understand that all powers and persons who persist (if any do) in their opposition to Christ and reject God's salvation in Christ will be destroyed, leaving all remaining powers and believers to bow in glad submission to Christ the Lord. One might alternatively hope that God will destroy that in them which was God's enemy (though he always loves them) and that, in the end, through the fire of hell, they may yet be saved.

Ephesians

One of the distinctive features of Ephesians is its emphasis on the universal sovereignty of Christ. As in Philippians 2, God raised Christ from the dead and seated him at his right hand 'far above all rule and authority and power and dominion' and gave him a name 'above every name that is named,' now and forever (Eph. 1:20–21). This is the same sovereignty God has, who is 'Father of all,' and 'above all and through all and in all' (4:6).

Once, all people were under God's wrath (2:3), and, if they continue in their disobedient rebellion and sin, they will experience God's eschatological wrath and miss the kingdom (5:5–6). But God's mercy, love, and grace abounded richly to save us (Gentiles, aliens and strangers from the commonwealth of God's people – 2:11–16). We who were dead in sin God made alive with Christ (2:3–5). It is entirely God's doing; our part is to say the 'thank you' of faith (2:8–9). This is all part of God's Christ-centred 'plan for the fullness of time, to gather up all things in him' (1:9–10).

The NRSV's 'gather up all things in him' does not capture the flavour of the Greek text's *anakephalaiōsasthai ta panta en tō Christō*. Better is the NASV's, 'the summing up of all things in Christ,' or the RSV's 'to unite all things in him,' or the NIV's 'to bring all things in heaven and on earth together under one head, even Christ.' It is God's will and definite purpose (1:9) to sum up all things in the universe in Christ. The word was used in Greek rhetoric to sum up or recapitulate an argument. In Romans 13:9 Paul uses it to say that love sums up the whole law.[42] Lincoln points out that the prefix *ana-*, indicates 'a restoration of harmony with Christ as the point of reintegration.'[43] God plans to redeem, restore, and reunite his entire broken and fragmented cosmos in Christ (cf. Rom. 8:18–23), including all beings not just humanity. The historic inclusion of the Gentiles through the Pauline mission is just one part of God's plan of universal reconciliation accomplished through the cross of Christ. (2:11–16).

Colossians

As in Ephesians, Colossians emphasizes the creational sovereignty of Christ. As God's image and agent in creation (1:15–16), 'he himself is before all things... so that he might come to have first place in everything' (1:17–18). He is the head of every ruler and authority (2:10), having disarmed the powers and triumphed over them through his death on the cross (2:14–15). Christ's sovereignty is for a purpose, *the universal reconciliation of all things to God*, which God accomplished in him (1:20).[44]

As to humanity, God raised us to new life with Christ and forgave us all our sins (2:13–14). But some reject what God has done for them and continue in disobedience; they are warned that 'the wrath of God is coming' (3:6). There is much in the universe and in humanity that needs correcting, purging, and destroying. How God's wrath will be applied we do not know; *that* it will be applied is assured.[45]

1–2 Thessalonians

Eschatology is a principal topic in 1–2 Thessalonians. Paul's (possibly) earliest writing is alive with expectation of Christ's near return.[46] The Thessalonians are waiting for God's Son to come from heaven. He will deliver them from 'the wrath that is coming' (1 Thes. 1:10). That wrath of God has already come upon Judean Jews (1 Thes. 2:14) who had been persecuting Paul (1 Thes. 2:16).[47] But the Thessalonian Christians can be confident that 'God has destined us not for wrath but for obtaining salvation through our Lord Jesus Christ' (1 Thes. 5:9). In Paul's theology, God's wrath is the working out in human history of his righteousness (Rom. 1:16–18; 2 Thes. 1:5). Sin has consequences, and God's wrath, represents God's holy and loving judgment on all that is not in conformity to his good purposes for people and the world. God's righteousness is determined to set things right and to display his just and holy character in view of sin and evil in the world (Rom. 3:25–26).[48] It might be construed as part of God's redemptive plan or as the final, eternal working out of destruction against disobedient, hardened and finally impenitent sinners (2 Thes. 1:8–9; 2 Thes. 2:10, 12). The writer of 2 Thessalonians[49] contemplates the possibility that some, who are perishing (2 Thes. 2:10), will be destroyed (*avelei*), annihilated (*katargēsei*) forever from the presence of God (2 Thes. 2:8), especially 'the lawless one,' whom the Lord Jesus will destroy when he is revealed (2 Thes. 2:3, 8).

The Pastoral Epistles

One of the characteristic phrases of the Pastoral Epistles is 'God our Saviour.' It occurs five times in 1 Timothy and Titus (1 Tim. 1:1; 2:3; Tit. 1:3; 2:10; 3:4) and almost nowhere else in the NT.[50] God is called Saviour because he 'desires everyone to be saved and to come to the knowledge of the truth' (1 Tim. 2:4), has saved us 'according to his own purpose and grace' (2 Tim. 1:9; Tit. 3:4–7), and has provided the one mediator between God and humanity, Christ Jesus, 'who gave himself a ransom for all' (1 Tim. 2:6; cf. 2 Tim. 1:9–10). God's universal saving intent is seen also in Titus 2:11: The 'grace of God has appeared, bringing salvation to all.' In a remarkable statement, Paul[51] says that Christians have set their hope on God, 'who is the Saviour of all people, especially of those who believe' (1 Tim. 4:10), implying that God is also the Saviour of those who do not yet believe. God's intention and action to save all people could not be stated more clearly.

God alone 'has immortality' (1 Tim. 6:16). It did not exist as a possibility for humankind before Christ abolished death and brought life and immortality to light through the gospel' (2 Tim. 1:10; cf. 1 Cor. 15:53–54).

Hebrews, 2 Peter, and Jude[52]

Hebrews

A prominent feature of the Letter to the Hebrews is its set of warning passages (2:1–4; 3:7–4:11; 5:11–6:12; 10:19–39; 12:14–29). These state that only those who persevere in faith and obedience will be saved (5:8), while those who fall away in disobedience and unbelief will be lost or destroyed (10:39), or miss the rest God has prepared for his people (3:18; 4:11). In fact, the author apparently believes that repentance is impossible for those who have fallen away from the faith and back into sin (6:4–6; 10:26; 12:17). Hebrews also warns of certain and fearful judgment in the Age to Come (9:27). It will include 'fire that will consume the adversaries' (10:27) and destroy the devil (2:14), 'for indeed our God is a consuming fire' (12:28). There is nothing here of hell as eternal conscious punishment. A universalist might see these passages as warnings and note that the author of Hebrews does not think that they really apply to his readers (6:9). Or, he may hold that in the end all will come to repentance and faith, though for some it may be through the consuming fire of God's love. An annihilationist might understand that the judgments in Hebrews are not hypothetical and that indeed the unrepentant may fall away and be destroyed in eternity.

Finally, it is helpful to note that Hebrews contains several instances of the adjective 'eternal'. In nearly every case, they refer, not to unending time, but to the quality of eternity, the kind of life that characterizes the age to come. 'Eternal judgment' is not a judgment that lasts forever but one that takes place in eternity (6:2).[53] 'Eternal redemption' might refer to the duration of salvation but could just as easily mean the Christian's heavenly redemption (9:12), especially in view of the contrast between the earthly sacrifices of Israel's priests and Christ's priestly role in the heavenly sanctuary. The 'eternal Spirit' is not the long-lasting Spirit but the divine Spirit (9:14). Christians also have an 'eternal inheritance,' the reward and blessing of the age to come (9:15). This important point needs to be remembered when we are assessing the meaning of verses that speak of eternal punishment and eternal life.

2 Peter – Jude

There is a close literary relationship between 2 Peter and Jude.[54] They treat some of the same themes in some of the same terms. Both have a strong flavour of the apocalyptic language of destruction and judgment. Despite this, the writer of 2 Peter reminds his readers of the patience of the Lord, who does not want (or is not willing, *boulomenos*) anyone to perish (*apōlesthai*) 'but all to come to repentance' (2 Pet. 3:9). God wants everyone to be saved and enter Christ's 'eternal Kingdom' (2 Pet. 1:11) or eternal life (Jude 21).[55] This is a surprisingly common New Testament theme.

2 Peter and Jude are both replete with words of judgment against the false teachers (2 Pet. 2:1–2) and ungodly intruders (Jude 4) who are disrupting Christian communities. They are bringing condemnation (*krima*) and destruction (*apōleia*) on themselves (2 Pet. 2:1, 3). Like the cities of Sodom and Gomorrah, the ungodly will be reduced to ashes (*tephrōsas*, 2 Pet. 2:6, NRSV: 'condemned... to extinction') 'by undergoing a judgment of eternal fire' (Jude 7). Indeed, a coming eschatological fire will destroy everything in heaven and earth (2 Pet. 3:7, 10, 12). Like irrational animals, 'born to be caught and killed,' the ungodly will be destroyed by fire (2 Pet. 2:12; 3:7). Even now, the fallen angels and the unrighteous are being kept in a punishment of 'deepest darkness' until the final judgment (2 Pet. 2:4, 9, 17; 3:7; Jude 6, 13).

The Book of Revelation

The joyful theme of the Book of Revelation is the victory of the Lamb (11:15–17; 12:15; 17:14; 19:15–16). Several passages that include all creation show that God continues to have in view, even in the eschaton, his plan for all humanity. The redeemed come from every 'tribe and language and people and nation' (5:9; 7:9–10; 14:6). The 144,000 of Revelation 14 are the firstfruits of all humanity (14:4), the opening wedge of a great tide that will come to worship God and the Lamb. There will be a new heaven and a new earth centred in a new Jerusalem, where God will dwell with humanity (21:1–3). All the nations will walk in his light (21:24) and be healed by the tree of life in its midst (22:2). Revelation closes with an open invitation to all: 'Come, and let everyone who is thirsty come. Let anyone who wishes take the water of life as a gift' (22:17).

Prior to this final victory, there will be a time of judgment. Judgment is a prominent theme in the second half of the Revelation (11:18; 14:7; 15:4; 20:4, 11–15). It is one of the roles of the Messiah (19:11), and his/God's judgments are righteous and true (16:7; 19:2). It takes concrete shape, first, in the judgment against the evil city, Babylon (17:1; 18:8, 10, 20) and, finally, in the last judgment and destruction of the devil, the unrepentant dead, and Death and Hades themselves (20:10, 11–15; 21:8; cf. 14:11). All are repaid according to their works (2:23; 20:12; 22:12; cf. 14:13). One of the primary reasons for judgment is a lack of repentance on the part of human evildoers (2:16, 21–22; 9:20–21; 16:9, 11; 21:8).

Judgment will take the form of God's wrath against sin (11:18; 14:19; 15:1; 16:1) and will result in the affliction (14:10; 19:20; 20:10, 15) and destruction (11:18; 17:8, 11) of 'the beast' (17:8), those who worship false gods and destroy the earth (11:18; 14:9), impenitent sinners (21:8), and those not written in the book of life (20:15). Some are in the book of life, and apparently some are not (3:5; 13:5; 17:8; 20:15; 21:27).

We also read that the 'nations' are to be judged. Revelation is ambivalent about the nations. On the one hand, they will be punished with wrath (19:15). On the other hand, the nations have been victims of the powers of evil, deceived and forced to do wrong (14:8; 18:23; 20:3, 8). But the ultimate hope is that 'all nations will come and worship before you' (15:4). In the final vision of the new universe, the nations walk by the light of the Lamb, 'the kings of the earth will bring their glory' into the holy city (21:24, 26) through the open gates of the New Jerusalem (21:25), and the tree of life produces leaves 'for the healing of the nations' (22:2). The nations are not cast into the lake of fire, but the powers which had deceived them are (19:20; 20:10; cf. 20:14).

Some have held that those thrown into the lake will be purified in it and eventually make their way into the open gates of the heavenly city.[56] This is not impossible, though Revelation does not make it explicit. The purposes and duration of hell are left in the hands of the Lord and the Lamb.

And this consideration leads to an important issue that must be addressed: the nature of this punishment in hell, whether John's images of it are to be taken literally, how it coheres with other New Testament teaching on the same topic, and finally how we are to understand it.

In 14:10–11 those who made the mistake (either willingly or under coercion) of worshiping the beast will be 'tormented with fire and sulphur', and Jesus and the angels will watch them suffer. The 'smoke of their torment goes up forever and ever', and there is no rest for them day or night. In 19:20 the beast and the false prophet, both symbolic figures of opposition to God and God's people, are 'thrown alive into the lake of fire that burns with sulphur.' In 20:10 the devil is added to the lake of fire and sulphur, 'and they will be tormented day and night forever and ever.' In 20:14–15 Death and Hades are also thrown into the lake of fire, along with 'anyone whose name was not found written in the book of life.' Finally, in 21:8 various kinds of sinners, including 'the cowardly' or fearful, unbelievers or faithless people, all liars, and people guilty of sexual immorality, also take their place 'in the lake that burns with fire and sulphur, which is the second death.'[57]

Revelation is apocalyptic literature; at least the sections under consideration are. It is characteristic of apocalyptic to use images, pictures, metaphors, and symbols to convey the teaching or principles behind the figurative language. John uses a wide variety of images from a wide variety of sources, and sorting out their meaning is the hardest part of the exegetical task.[58] It is not always possible to tell what John meant to convey through his images and where to draw the line between symbol and the thing symbolized.

Most would agree that it is mistake to read apocalyptic literally, as if it were 'future history.' It has been a common hermeneutical principle to let didactic passages establish teachings and then find them illustrated or fleshed out in symbolic passages.[59] Therefore, since so much is at stake in these texts one must use the greatest caution in interpreting them and err, if necessary, on the side of the less specific and more general. Revelation assures us that God is in control of history, that Christ will ultimately reign in victory over all the evil powers, including sin and death, that his victory is our victory so that the people of God will be triumphant, even if through suffering, in the age to come, and that finally God will judge and destroy evil and those who have caused it once and for all.[60]

We have also seen throughout our study of the Bible's teaching on universalism that, while there is a strong theme of God's loving plan to save all people, the main teaching about the ultimate destiny of those who persist in unrepentant rebellion against God and the good is they will be utterly destroyed. Only the book of Revelation introduces the element of everlasting[61] conscious punishment in a highly pictorial and symbolic passage. To allow this one set of passages from an apocalypse to dictate the teaching of the rest of Scripture is unwise and improper when seeking to form a sound and faithful biblical eschatology.

Finally, mature Christian readers need to ask themselves whether they are prepared to take literally passages that portray Jesus watching the unending torment of sinners, such as fearful unbelievers, liars, and people guilty of sexual sins, in the light of Jesus' attitude toward sinners during his ministry. The extreme imagery of the Apocalypse forces us to choose between pictures of Jesus and leads us to seek interpretative solutions more consistent with the nature of God as revealed in Christ.

Conclusion

The case for universalism is stronger than is usually realized. God's saving love for the world is a prominent biblical theme from Genesis through Revelation. God is the Lord and Saviour of all and does not want any to perish but all to be saved. God provided salvation, forgiveness, justification, and reconciliation for all, indeed for all creation. Eventually, everyone will confess Jesus Christ as Lord. Yet, we do not know how God's judgment works out with respect to individuals. Paul speaks most often about the eschatological salvation of groups or corporate wholes.

The traditional view that the vast majority of people who have ever lived will suffer in a hell of eternal conscious torment is inconsistent with the biblical data. It has to be read into the texts from later teachings in church history. Only Revelation's apocalyptic, symbolic treatment of hell comes close to this position. Most of the relevant New Testament texts teach the destruction of finally impenitent unbelievers and the gift of life and immortality to repentant believers. There is no biblical doctrine of the natural immortality of the soul.

Thomas Talbott makes good use of the 'positive' texts of the New Testament to defend his position on universalism. Passages such as Romans 5:12–21; 11:11–35; 1 Corinthians 15:20–28; 2 Corinthians 5:17–20; Ephesians 1:10; Philippians 2:10–11; Colossians 1:20; and 1 Timothy 2:3–6 can be understood to teach that God has provided salvation for all people and that universal reconciliation of all things is God's eschatological goal. The objection that salvation is only for those who believe does not reach Talbott, since he would agree. All will, on his view, come to believe and be saved, as an outcome of their encounter with God, in all his beautiful and purifying holiness and love.

Talbott's position is weaker with respect to the 'negative' New Testament texts. Several passages appear to teach the final destruction of rebellious and impenitent evildoers. Faith and character are inseparable, so that the New Testament consistently speaks of the salvation of those who believe and do the good and the destruction of those who reject God and work evil. Talbott believes that hell is real but that it is purgative and restorative. This view rests more on good theological, philosophical, and moral grounds than on the biblical texts themselves, which leave the matter open.

The New Testament's primary teaching on the extent of salvation is that all will be saved *except* those who knowingly and wilfully reject God and God's forgiving love. People begin to do this in this life by their response to God through the way they live and the character they develop. Those who persist in rebellion will perish. Talbott cannot conceive that any would knowingly and sanely refuse God's love and choose instead to suffer in hell or perish. Yet, humans have misused their God-given freedom from the beginning, and people who have been deforming their souls all their lives by choosing against the good and for evil may not any longer see the presence of God and heaven as a desirable environment. Recently, a friend said to me, 'Maybe there are not two places, heaven and hell, but just one place, heaven, and to some it seems like hell.' In that case, God's love would be the consuming fire destroying all who refuse the light to their eternal loss. Yet, the mercy of God is wide, and the grace of God is great. Will anyone finally persist in refusing the inescapable love of God?[62]

Notes

1 Gen. 1–11; Rev. 21:1; Isa. 65:17; 66:22; 2 Pet. 3:13.
2 The reconciling love and mercy of God for all people has been accomplished in the atoning death and life-giving resurrection of Christ. Only those who reject this gift of life will fail to enjoy eternal fellowship with God.
3 This, or something quite like it, has been the view of the majority of Christian theologians from the early centuries. See Shogren (1997); Kelly (1960), pp. 483–85; Walvoord (1996); Crockett (1996); and R.A. Peterson (2000).
4 Rom. 1:23; 2:7; 1 Cor. 15:53–54; 1 Tim. 1:16; 2 Tim. 1:10; cf. 4 Ezra 7:96; 4 Macc. 17:9–12; 18:23. These two views are sometimes known as annihilationism and conditional immortality.
5 E.g., the contrasting emphases in the Wisdom literature of the Old Testament: Job and Ecclesiastes vs. Proverbs and Job's friends.
6 Bultmann (1960).
7 See the insightful essay, 'Paul and the Introspective Conscience of the West' by Stendahl (1976), pp. 78–96.
8 There are surprising passages that tell of God's concern for animals, e.g., Gen. 1:21; Jonah 4:11; Ps. 84:3.
9 Cf. Psalm 33:5; 36:7; 62:12; 85:5; 86:15; 100:5; 103:8; 107:43; 117:1–2; 136:26; 145:8–9.
10 Cf. Psalms 67 and 96.
11 B.W. Anderson (1999), p. 321. See also Erickson (1983), p. 774: '"Sheol" was frequently used simply of the state of death, to which it was presumed all persons go.'
12 But this is a resurrection only for the faithful, not for the wicked. According to Isa. 26:14, their shades do not rise; they are destroyed and all memory of them is wiped out.
13 The apocalyptist of Daniel 12:2 foresees only a resurrection of 'many,' not all. 'Here the writer is not speaking about a general resurrection,' B.W. Anderson, (1999), p. 318; so also Hoekema (1979), p. 245. Some remain dead and are not raised, some receive eternal life, and others receive 'everlasting contempt.' Daniel 12:2 comports with none of the four debated views of the afterlife, including the traditional position. Apparently the biblical data were not designed to make the theologian's task an easy one!
14 Cf. also the worship of the Magi in 2:1–12.
15 Jesus may have chosen and used the term 'Son of Man' for just this reason: to identify himself with all people.
16 5:14; 24:14; 26:13; 28:18–20; cf. Mk. 13:10; Lk. 2:30–32; 24:46–48. Acts also repeatedly emphasizes the availability of salvation to all, especially through Peter's witness (Acts 10–11; 15:7–11) and Paul's mission (Acts 9:15; 13:47–48; 14:27; 26:17–18, 22–23; 28:28).
17 Only the Greek word *ge'enna* is properly translated 'hell.' Hades is not hell but is the realm of the dead. In Matthew it occurs in 11:23 and 16:18.
18 In Mark 9:48 (Matt. 18:8–9), in hell, 'their worm never dies, and the fire is never quenched' (9:48). This description was drawn from Isaiah 66:24, where it is applied to the dead bodies of those who have rebelled against the Lord. Is it a purifying fire, a destroying fire, or a fire of eternal conscious suffering? This passage does not give us the answer, though in context purification is suggested, since the next verse, Mark 9:49, says that 'everyone will be salted with fire,' a reference to salt's purifying

function. 'We should not read into these sayings later speculations about the eternal punishment of the wicked in hell… What occurs on the lips of Jesus here is not a developed doctrine of everlasting punishment, but an affirmation in quite conventional terminology that none could be more "lost" than they who choose to renounce the life of the kingdom and cling to the life of this world and its fleeting powers' (H. Anderson [1976], p. 238).

19 Jesus' disciples ask in astonishment, 'Then who can be saved?' (Mt. 19:25). Jesus replies that salvation 'is impossible' for human beings, 'but not for God; for God all things are possible' (19:26). Salvation rests solely upon God's grace.

20 Note that the traditional causes for a person being sent to hell, such as rejecting or not accepting Christ or the gospel, are not mentioned. If the Matthean texts are taken literally, they teach that anyone whose character and conduct are out of conformity with the will of God deserves to be punished in hell, i.e., 'the wages of sin is death' (Rom. 6:23a). But according to the good news, *all* are sinners for whom Christ died in order that they might enjoy the gift of God, which is 'eternal life through Jesus Christ our Lord' (Rom. 6:23b). Christ gave his life for the sins of the world, in order to rescue us from the punishments threatened in the Gospel of Matthew.

21 See C.D. Marshall (2001), especially pp. 175–99. There are two passages that appear to teach something close to purgatory. In Luke 12:47, Jesus tells an eschatological parable in which servants of a late-returning master receive severe and light beatings, depending on whether they knew or did not know their master's will. There is no mention of hell. Also, in another parable (Lk. 16:19–31), a rich man is seen suffering in Hades (not Gehenna), paying a penalty (temporal?) for the evil things he did in life. That purgatory is in view is too speculative, and introduces a category from the Church's later teaching, but clearly there is nothing here of eternal conscious suffering. The rich man cannot pass from Hades to Abraham's bosom until his suffering is completed, but no time is specified. Only if one already believes in the traditional hell would one see the concept here. For an alternative interpretation of this parable, see Powys (1997), pp. 218–228.

22 See Fudge (1994), especially pp. 93–143.

23 R.A. Peterson (2000).

24 C.D. Marshall (2001), p. 186 n. 123, argues that 'eternal life,' being an ongoing *state*, includes the idea of everlasting duration, but 'eternal punishment' refers to a *process*, a process whose consequences are eternal in the sense of 'ultimate in significance and everlasting in effect, not in duration.'

25 The hope of sharing in the life of the age to come depends solely on the mercy and grace of God. When Jesus commands us to love our enemies, it is because this is what God does: 'Be merciful as your Father is merciful' (Lk. 6:36). This is also what Jesus does from the cross, saying about those who are crucifying him, 'Father, forgive them; for they do not know what they are doing' (Lk. 23:34).

26 The Johannine writings also contain several broad, inclusive, non-christological statements about who receives salvation. Those who do good come to the light, so that all may see that 'their deeds have been done in God' (3:21). Those who have done good will arise at the resurrection of life (5:29). 'Everyone who has heard and learned from the Father' will come to Jesus (6:45), and the Father draws all who come to him (6:37). Anyone who resolves to do the will of God will know whether Jesus' teaching is from God (7:17). Everyone who does what is right has been born of God (1 Jn. 2:29), and everyone who genuinely loves is born of God and knows God (1 Jn. 4:7).

27 Cranfield (1975), pp. 204–05.

28 God's ultimate redemption of all includes the creation as well. Creation waits with longing for its own liberation at the time when God's children receive their redemption (8:20–23).

29 See 'much more surely' (5:15); 'abundance of grace' (5:17); 'where sin increased, grace abounded all the more' (5:20).

30 See Pinnock (1992).

31 1:16; 3:22; 3:25–26; 4:16, 23–24; 5:1; 10:17.

32 Such benefits as: God's work in all things for them, v. 28; restoration of the *imago dei* in Christ, justification, eschatological glory, vv. 29–30; and God being 'for us' and allowing nothing ever to separate us from his love (vv. 31, 35–39).

33 See Talbott (1999c), especially pp. 200–20.

34 Ibid., p. 65. See NRSV footnote.

35 See the discussion in Barrett (1968), pp. 355–56.

36 See the parallel argument in Romans 5:12–21, especially Rom. 5:18.

37 Cf. 1 Cor. 1:12: 'What I mean is that each of you says, "I belong to Paul," or "I belong to Apollos," or "I belong to Cephas," or "I *belong to Christ*";' (1 Cor. 3:23): 'and you *belong to Christ*, and Christ belongs to God;' 2 Cor. 10:7: 'If you are confident that you *belong to Christ*, remind yourself of this, that just as you *belong to Christ*, so also do we;' Gal. 3:29: 'And if you *belong to Christ*, then you are Abraham's offspring, heirs according to the promise;' and Gal. 5:24: 'And those who *belong to Christ Jesus* have crucified the flesh with its passions and desires.'

38 Cf. 1 Cor. 15:42–57. We are not naturally 'imperishable' and 'immortal.' We are given it as a gift in Christ (cf. Rom. 2:7; 1 Cor. 15:53–54; 2 Cor. 5:4; 1 Tim. 6:6; 2 Tim. 1:10). Others who lack it perish and are destroyed (2 Cor. 2:15; 3:3). There is no sound biblical reason to adopt the Platonic doctrine of the inherent immortality of souls. See the arguments in Fudge (1994) and the debate in Fudge & Peterson (2000).

39 Quoted from Isaiah 45:23, a verse that calls upon all the nations to turn to the Lord and be saved.

40 People willingly confess their sins: Mk. 1:5 (par.); Acts 19:18; Jas. 5:16 1 Jn. 1:9. They give thanks or praise: Matt. 11:25; Rom. 14:11; 15:9. They confess their faith: Matt. 10:32 (par.); Jn. 9:22; Acts 23:8; Rom. 10:9–10; 2 Cor. 9:13; Phil. 2:11; 1 Tim. 6:12; Titus 1:16; Heb. 3:1; 4:14; 10:23; 13:15; 1 Jn. 2:23; 4:2–3, 15; 2 Jn. 7. They willingly acknowledge or tell the truth: Matt. 7:23; Acts 24:14; 1 Tim. 3:16; 6:13; Heb. 11:13; Rev. 3:5.

41 Cf. 1 Cor. 15:25–26; Heb. 10:23.

42 Lincoln (1990), p. 33.

43 Ibid.

44 'The unusual feature of this passage is that it refers to the reconciliation of "all things"… and that as a past event,' O'Brien (1982), p. 53. Cf. 2 Cor. 5:19.

45 See the fine treatment of this passage in ibid., pp. 184–85.

46 E.g., 1 Thes. 4:15: 'we who are alive, who are left until the coming of the Lord.'

47 It is unknown in what form Paul thought the wrath of God had come upon the Jews of Judea. It cannot be the Jewish-Roman war and the fall of Jerusalem, unless this passage is a later interpolation, as some think possible (e.g., Bruce, 1982, pp. 43; 48–51).

48 See Borchert (1993).

49 Some think that 2 Thessalonians may be by a writer other than Paul, an inconsequential factor for those who consider the canonical New Testament authoritative for faith and life, regardless of how questions of authorship or authenticity may be resolved.

50 The only other occurrence of the exact phrase is in Jude 25. However, Mary's spirit rejoices in 'God my Saviour' (Lk. 1:47); God is the Saviour of all (1 Tim. 4:10); and Jesus is called 'our God and Saviour' in Titus 2:13 and 2 Peter 1:1.

51 The Apostle Paul is the stated author of the Pastorals. Whether he is the actual author is irrelevant to our investigation.

52 We have selected only the most relevant texts in the interest of brevity. On James, see 5:3, 9, 12, 20 and their warning of judgment, especially upon the rich. On 1 Peter, see 1:17; 4:5, 17–18 (judgment). The most difficult passage to interpret in 1 Peter is the notoriously obscure 4:6, which says that 'the gospel was proclaimed even to the dead, so that, though they had been judged in the flesh as everyone is judged, they might live in the spirit as God does.' No one really knows what this text means. 'The dead' may be Old Testament believers who, having suffered death as everyone does, get to enjoy the resurrection through the proclamation of the gospel. It would be tenuous exegesis to turn this passage into a text that supports the universal salvation of all who have died. That possibility cannot be established through this doubtful text. See the fine discussion in J.R. Michaels (1988), pp. 235–42.

53 Cf. 'eternal glory' in 1 Peter 5:10.

54 See Neyrey (1993), pp. 120–21; and Bauckham (1983), pp. 141–43.

55 These two uses of 'eternal' can be read equally well as references to the everlasting duration of Christ's kingdom and of life there or as qualitative descriptions of the nature of the that kingdom and life, i.e., as belonging to eternity or the age to come.

56 Caird (1966), pp. 279–80: 'Nowhere in the New Testament do we find a more eloquent statement than this of the all-embracing scope of Christ's redemptive work,' (ibid., p. 280). See also Boring (1989), pp. 221–22. For the traditional view, see Beale (1999), pp. 1097–1101.

57 In Harrington's view, 'The "second death," identified with the "lake of fire" here [20:14] and in 21:8 is also named in 2:11 and 20:6. In each case it is most reasonably taken to signify annihilation.' In Harrington (1993), p. 205.

58 Fee and Stuart (1993), pp. 236–38.

59 Carnell (1959), pp. 63–64. Osborne says, 'I personally believe that one reason for the use of cryptic symbols was to keep the reader from giving the future fulfilment too great a place in the message of the book,' (1991), p. 231.

60 See a similar summary in Fee and Stuart (1993), p. 239.

61 The one use of the word 'eternal' in Revelation does not connote everlasting duration but something like true, heavenly, or divine (14:6). Other terms are used in the texts of torment to connote lasting duration.

62 We may *hope* that all will be saved, but we cannot know this. So, Balthasar (1988), and Neuhaus (Aug/Sep 2001). 'Eternal damnation is certainly proclaimed in the Gospel. To what degree is it realized in life beyond the grave? This is, ultimately, a great mystery. However, we can never forget that God 'wills everyone to be saved and to come to knowledge of the truth' (1 Tim. 2:4),' Pope John Paul II (1994), p. 73.

PART III

Philosophical Responses

6

A Philosophical Critique of Talbott's Universalism

JERRY L. WALLS

A Hair's Breadth of Difference

John Wesley once famously remarked that with respect to the doctrine of justification, he hardly differed 'a hair's breadth' from John Calvin.[1] This remark is noteworthy because some of Wesley's sharpest and most persistent polemics were directed at Calvinism. Despite profound differences from Calvin at key points, at other crucial junctures the differences were negligible.

As I read Thomas Talbott's most recent defence of universalism, I found myself in agreement with so much of what he says that I often thought of Wesley's remark.

Talbott's view of the love of God is one I can heartily endorse. Indeed, there is not a hair's breadth of difference between us on this issue. Given that God's very nature is love and that his mercy endures forever, it naturally follows that he always treats his children in a loving way and promotes their well being. Even wrath and punishment, in the case of God, is the flip-side of the coin whose face is love. The doctrine of eternal hell that I accept is not premised upon a weak view of the love of God, nor upon the notion that God does not love all the persons he has created. If I believed the doctrine of eternal hell entailed that the love of God is anything less than superlative, then I would reject it in favor of universalism.

Moreover, I agree with Talbott that there are exegetical difficulties for all sides in this debate and that all sides must make exegetical decisions based on what seems most clear to them. No one involved in this dispute can fairly pronounce their view *the* biblical view if by that they mean to imply that other positions have nothing going for them in the way of textual support that, at least *prima facie*, seems to favor them. Talbott's exegesis is sustained and serious and he cannot be accused of failing to take Scripture seriously. The details of his exegesis are not my specialty here as a philosopher, and I will leave that to my colleagues to assess, but it is clear that Talbott holds his position, in significant part, because he believes Scripture teaches it.

Talbott is a careful thinker and a fine philosopher and I generally agree with how he spells out the logic of the issue and the points on which disagreement fundamentally turns. The strength of his case depends crucially on several contested philosophical judgments. I will focus my criticism on those.

Is Universalism Heretical?

Let us begin with Talbott's observation that both his Augustinian and Arminian friends view universalism as heretical. This impressed him as odd since these two traditions view each other only as mistaken, but not heretical. Moreover, he observes that most of his interpretations of biblical texts are supported either by a first rate Augustinian scholar or a first rate Armianian scholar. But what is perhaps most striking to him is this: 'If you simply take the Augustinian idea of God's sovereignty in the matter of salvation – that is, the Hound of Heaven cannot be defeated forever – and put it together with the Arminian idea that God at least wills or desires the salvation of all, then you get universalism, plain and simple.'[2]

Talbott spells out the logic of the matter more precisely in a set of three propositions that are logically inconsistent.

1 God's redemptive love extends to all human sinners equally in the sense that he sincerely wills or desires the redemption of each one of them.
2 Because no one can finally defeat God's redemptive love or resist it forever, God will triumph in the end and successfully accomplish the redemption of everyone whose redemption he sincerely wills or desires.

3 Some sinners will never be redeemed but will instead by separated from God forever.

Now Talbott is surely correct that at least one of these three must be false. Furthermore, if (3) is accepted, then one must either reject (1) or (2). Talbott is also surely correct that there are biblical texts that, at least *prima facie*, can be cited in support of each of these propositions. For anyone who takes seriously the authority of Scripture, this poses an obvious problem, as he rightly notes. 'We can say, on the one hand, that the Bible teaches all three propositions and is not, therefore, infallible in all of its teachings; or we can say, on the other hand, that the Bible is indeed infallible in all its teachings, but does not really teach all three propositions.'[3]

Now Talbott's argument here, as elsewhere, has considerable force and deserves a careful rebuttal if his universalistic conclusions are to be rejected. By way of criticism, I want to start with his bafflement that both Augustinians and Arminians are inclined to view each other as merely mistaken, whereas they both consider univeralism to be heretical. How can this be the case if joining together a central conviction from each position leads straightforwardly to universalism?

For insight on this question, let us compare Talbott's logically inconsistent trio of statements with three statements from another field of inquiry, namely, moral philosophy.

4 Capital punishment is an appropriate punishment to administer for some crimes.
5 Capital punishment is cruel and degrading.
6 No crimes are such that it is appropriate to administer cruel and degrading punishment.

As with Talbott's three statements, one cannot consistently hold all three of them. One of them must be given up. And as in Talbott's case, there are reputable moral philosophers who affirm (4) and there are reputable moral philosophers who affirm (5). Both positions are respected and defensible views within the field of moral philosophy. Moreover, both those who affirm (4) and those who affirm (5) would also insist that (6) is true.

However, one cannot legitimately join (4) and (5) and affirm both simultaneously. To do so entails this proposition that both sides would reject out of hand.

7 Some crime are such that it is appropriate to administer cruel and degrading punishment.

Both sides would reject this claim as something like the equivalent of moral heresy. Indeed, both sides would likely consider (6) the most non-negotiable proposition in the set and would probably be prepared to give up (4) or (5), respectively, if shown that their view entailed (7). Clearly then, those who affirm (4) will properly deny (5) just as those who affirm (5) will reject (4).

What this suggests is that there is really nothing at all odd about the fact that Augustinians and Arminians each may regard the other merely as mistaken, even if profoundly so, while both regard Universalists as not merely mistaken but heretical. The reason is that (3) is more of a matter of consensus among orthodox Christians than either (1) or (2) and is therefore arguably more certain for both sides. Speaking for myself, I am more certain of (1) than of (3) and I would be prepared to give up (3) if I could be shown that it were inconsistent with (1) along with my other theological convictions. But as I shall argue, there is no such inconsistency.

The next point I want to make, briefly, is that the burden of proof is on Talbott in this dispute. While there is at least *prima facie* scriptural support for universalism, just as there is for the doctrine of eternal hell, things are not equal here. The fact that Arminians and Augustinians agree that some persons will forever be lost places the burden of proof squarely on the universalists. In other words, the exegetical debate cannot be carried out in a theological or historical vacuum. If the Bible is to be read as Scripture, given as revelation by God to the Church, then it cannot be read in isolation or abstraction from the Church's interpretation of it.

This is not to say that the history of interpretation settles this matter entirely, especially since there is a minority position defending universalism going back to the Fathers. Moreover, universalism has not been rejected officially in the same way that certain Christological heresies have been, for instance. It is, however, worth noting that the Roman Catholic Church has condemned *necessary* universalism as a heresy. That is, they have rejected the view that we can say with certainty that all will in fact be saved, the very view Talbott endorses. Given the reality of human freedom, it is possible that some persons will be forever lost. The view that universalism is possibly true, however, has not been rejected. For it is possible that all persons will eventually accept grace and be saved. It has been judged an acceptable position to hope for universal salvation and to pray for it.

It is important here to distinguish two different senses of necessity, namely, metaphysical and epistemic. To say that universalism is metaphysically necessary is to say that in all possible worlds that include humans, or similar creatures, all are saved. This assumes God is a necessary being and that he necessarily has the attributes he does. Given these attributes, and the nature of human beings, it is impossible that any persons could reject God and be forever lost. Now it could be that universalism is necessarily true in this sense but that we do not know this with certainty. That is, it could be metaphysically necessary even if it is not epistemically necessary.

At any rate, the point I want to emphasize is that universalism of any stripe is a minority position, and that *necessary* universalism, even if it is not regarded as heresy, surely must bear the burden of proof. Talbott's attempt to make the case for necessary universalism hinges on two central claims that I now want to focus on for the remainder of this essay. First, he has argued in detail that the choice of eternal hell is incoherent and therefore impossible. Second, he has argued that if the punishment of hell is such that hell can forever be preferred to heaven, then we can in fact sin with impunity and even defeat God. The first of these claims is most crucial to Talbott's case so I shall deal with it at some length. Let us turn now to consider these claims.

It is Possible to Freely Choose Eternal Hell

Talbott's claim that universalism is necessarily true follows straightforwardly from his view of the love of God, along with his claim that the choice of eternal hell is incoherent. It is the combination of these convictions that renders universalism necessarily true for Talbott. It is Talbott's view, then, that universalism is necessarily true in both the metaphysical and the epistemic sense. Not only is it the case that the choice of eternal hell is impossible in the metaphysical sense, but we can know this with certainty.

Talbott's understanding of the love of God is crucial for his view. A weaker view of God's love than Talbott defends would make it relatively easy to explain how some might choose eternal hell. But given the view that God necessarily loves all persons deeply and consistently, Talbott can plausibly advance the argument that the choice of eternal hell is simply incoherent. In this book, Talbott does not spell out this argument in detail although it is crucial to his case for necessary universalism. Elsewhere, however, as he indicates, he does so and I shall examine one of his more recent arguments for this conclusion.

Talbott's case that the choice of eternal hell is incoherent is plausible because he has a very particular account of what is involved in freely choosing an eternal destiny. In short, such a choice must be fully informed, and once the person making the choice gets what he wants, then it must be the case that he never regrets his choice. This means that the person must be free from ignorance and illusion both in his initial choice as well as later. He must fully understand what he has chosen while freely persisting in the choice. Given these conditions, Talbott thinks there is an obvious and important asymmetry between choosing fellowship with God as an eternal destiny, on the one hand, and choosing hell as an eternal destiny, on the other. Whereas the first of these obviously is possible, the latter is not.[4]

Talbott's argument also hinges on his view that hell is forcibly imposed punishment, the view that he believes is clearly taught not only in the New Testament but also in much traditional theology. If hell is indeed forcibly imposed misery, then it seems unintelligible that anyone could freely choose it forever. Talbott puts the point as follows.

> But if separation from God can bring only greater and greater misery into a life, as Christians have traditionally believed, then the very idea of S [a person] freely embracing a destiny apart from God seems to break down altogether. For how could a decision to live apart from God survive without regret a full disclosure of truth about the chosen destiny?[5]

As Talbott sees it then, the forcibly imposed misery of hell will eventually move even the most recalcitrant sinners to repent and choose God for their eternal destiny. Moreover, he believes sinners will do this with their freedom intact. That is, sinners will freely respond to the punishment of hell and happily embrace God.

It is important to emphasize that Talbott insists these choices are free in the libertarian sense. This understanding of freedom involves two crucial claims: '(1) a person S performs an action A freely at some time *t* only if it should also be within S's power at *t* to refrain from A at *t*; and (2) it is within S's power at *t* to refrain from A at *t* only if refraining from A at *t* is psychologically possible for S at *t*.'[6] While Talbott expresses reservations about this analysis of libertarian freedom and plans to offer an alternative account, he thinks the doctrine of eternal hell breaks down even on what he calls the standard account. So his argument proceeds in terms of the standard analysis.

It is worth noting, however, that Talbott has elsewhere distinguished between having the power to do something, on the one hand, and being psychologically capable of doing it, on the other. As an instance of the difference, he cites Augustine's view that the redeemed in heaven will no longer even be tempted to disobey God. Indeed, they will see with such clarity that God is the source of happiness and sin is the source of misery that sin and disobedience will no longer be psychologically possible for them. But surely they will not be less free on this account, Talbott points out, nor will it be the case that they lack the power to sin. But sin will nevertheless remain a psychological impossibility for them.[7] This distinction is important because it calls into question the second condition of libertarian freedom stated above.

I accept Talbott's distinction between power and psychological ability as a helpful one. However, even with this distinction granted, there are serious problems with his claim that persons who repent under forcibly imposed punishment are free in the libertarian sense. First, the notion of ever increasing misery, misery without a distinct limit, destroys the very notion of a free choice. The reason for this is that finite beings like ourselves are simply not constituted in such a way that we can absorb ever increasing misery. At some point, we would either be coerced to submit, or we would go insane, or we would perish. We have neither the *power* nor the *psychological ability* to withstand constantly increasing misery, regardless of whether that misery is physical or emotional in nature. Our freedom, in other words, can only take so much pressure.

Where exactly the limit lies is perhaps not easy to say, but clearly there is such a limit.

For punishment to elicit a free choice that is morally significant, the person receiving the punishment must come to see the truth about himself and his actions and genuinely want to change. He must achieve moral insight in the process and willingly desire to act on that insight. He must want to change because of the truth he has seen, not merely to escape or avoid the punishment that is being forced upon him.

Consider now another passage in which Talbott alleges the impossibility of freely choosing eternal misery.

> So imagine now a person S in a state of prolonged misery or suffering or sadness, such as one might experience in hell as traditionally conceived; imagine also that S knows *all* the relevant facts about the source of human happiness and suffers no more illusions about the source of S's own misery. Given that all of S's ignorance has now been removed and all of S's illusions have finally been shattered, what possible motive might remain for embracing such eternal misery freely?[8]

Now I am inclined to agree with Talbott that a person as he describes would have no motive for remaining in his misery. On the assumption that one is at least minimally rational and desires his own happiness, then it is difficult to conceive any sort of motive to resist God in these circumstances.

As I have argued against Talbott before, the really crucial question is whether we are truly free to acquire the relevant insight or not.[9] There is more required here than merely knowing all the facts. The knowledge that finally counts is personal knowledge, it is moral understanding, a right sense of values and the like. This is the biblical sense of what it means to know God, as suggested by numerous passages. For just one instance consider Jeremiah 22:16.

> 'He defended the cause of the poor and needy
> and so all went well.
> Is that not what it means to know me?' declares the LORD.

These are the sort of factors involved in knowing in a morally significant way the source of human happiness. For the source of human happiness is a right relationship with God and other persons. And one does not gain a meaningful understanding of this without entering and growing in those relationships. As one comes to know and love God, one's understanding that God is the source of happiness grows and deepens accordingly.

The point to be emphasized here is that such insight and understanding cannot be coerced or instilled by forcibly imposed punishment. Rather, the truth must be not only discerned, but also willingly owned and appropriated if one is to achieve an understanding of God as the source of happiness that is spiritually and morally profound. Interestingly, Talbott apparently recognizes this point. He draws a distinction between two kinds of compulsion and defends what he calls the 'right' kind of compulsion, namely, that which comes from dramatic conversions such as that of C.S. Lewis. As he notes, when Lewis was finally converted, he had a sense of God closing in on him in such a way that it seemed impossible to do otherwise than to submit to God.

Over against this, Talbott repudiates the sort of compulsion defended by Augustine who was willing to employ the sword to persuade the Donatists to come back to the Church. He writes: 'A stunning revelation such as Paul reportedly received, one that provides clear vision and *compelling evidence*, thereby altering one's beliefs in a perfectly rational way, does not compel behavior in the same way that threatening someone with a sword might.'[10] Now Talbott is surely right that there is an important difference between these two kinds of compulsion, and that the latter is not only morally objectionable, but also incompatible with any meaningful sense of freedom.

However, it is somewhat puzzling that Talbott appeals to this distinction, given his view of hell as forcibly imposed punishment. As we shall shortly see, he criticizes the view of hell I defend as not severe enough. By contrast, he aligns himself with the view, common in much traditional theology, that hell is a matter of 'unbearable suffering.'[11] It is also the case that many traditional theologians hold the somewhat paradoxical view that this unbearable suffering must nevertheless be borne forever. Indeed, some even suggest that God provides the damned supernatural strength and thereby forces them to endure what could not otherwise be borne.

As Talbott notes, this picture of hell is nothing short of the ultimate torture chamber and it is most difficult, if not impossible, to see how this can be compatible with the biblical picture of God as a being who is both supremely loving and supremely powerful. Thus, theologians have been inclined to modify the traditional doctrine in one of two ways. On the one hand, they can say the punishment of hell is indeed unbearable, but not eternal, or on the other hand, they can say it is terrible, albeit bearable, and can therefore be chosen freely as an eternal destiny. Talbott obviously takes the former option.

Again, the point I want to emphasize is that is hard to see how this squares with Talbott's distinction between two kinds of compulsion, and his repudiation of compulsion by physical threats such as the sword. For those traditional accounts of hell that Talbott endorses surely include physical pain of a rather intense variety. If Talbott is to avoid outright inconsistency here, then he owes us some explanation of how forcibly imposed punishment that produces unbearable misery is not the wrong kind of compulsion.

But there is another problem with Talbott's account of the right kind of compulsion. Notice his italicized words above, namely, his appeal to 'compelling evidence' that alters one's beliefs in a perfectly rational way. Now I have no problem with the idea that evidence that is taken to be compelling can alter one's beliefs in a completely rational way. Indeed, it is arguably the very nature of rationality to be willing to alter one's beliefs in light of appropriate evidence, especially if that evidence is staring one directly in the face.

I am more dubious, however, about the notion that evidence can ever be truly compelling.[12] For the fact of the matter is that some persons simply may not wish to be rational and are prepared to dispute even such apparently undeniable truths as basic laws of logic. Moreover, there are various Cartesian styled methods of doubting even the most obvious truths and thereby giving one's skepticism an air of intellectual respectability.

But when we come to religious truth claims, it is notoriously the case that there is even more room to doubt for those who are inclined to do so. Indeed, God's very existence is a matter of debate, and it is widely agreed among philosophers that none of the arguments for his existence are entirely compelling. All of them are such that either they employ one or more controversial premises or the conclusion that God exists follows doubtfully from those premises. And things are even more difficult when we come to distinctively Christian claims such as the incarnation and resurrection of Jesus. These doctrines depend on controversial historical judgments and disputed interpretations of the biblical documents.

This is not to deny that there is good evidence in favor of belief. But there is a vast difference between adequate evidence and compelling evidence. Indeed, it is arguable that the evidence needs to be at least adequate for belief to be rational, but short of compelling, for us to be properly free in our response to it. Consider in this light Pascal's comment on the evidence for Christianity.

> The prophecies, even the miracles and proofs of or our religion are not of such a kind that they can be said to be absolutely convincing... But the evidence is such as to exceed, or at least equal, the evidence to the contrary, so that it cannot be reason that decides us against following it, and can therefore only be concupiscence and wickedness of heart.[13]

It is important for Pascal that the evidence for Christianity be at least as good as the evidence against it, for if it were not then it would arguably be irrational to believe. Such belief would have to be an act of the will to fly in the face of the evidence. But as Pascal sees it, belief is not irrational in this manner. However, faith is not merely an intellectual matter either. Rather, it is also very much a matter of the heart. That is, it is a matter of having one's heart rightly disposed, of loving the right things for the right reasons, and so on. This is part of the reason that God is hidden according to Pascal. He is not on display in order to satisfy our intellectual curiosity. Since he is hidden, we must seriously seek him in response to his prompting, and as we do so, he reveals himself to us more and more. But his self-disclosure varies according to our willingness to open our hearts to the truth and follow it.[14]

The fact that the evidence is disclosed in this fashion is also important for a correct diagnosis of the true nature of unbelief. As Pascal puts it, it is a matter of 'concupiscence and wickedness of heart.' Unbelief at the end of the day is not matter of lacking sufficient evidence. This is also why evidence alone can never be compelling if we mean by that to say that certain evidence is such that unbelief would simply be impossible in the face of it. For true faith is much more than assent to evidence or recognition of certain facts. God can and does reveal himself to us quite clearly enough to make clear the disposition of our hearts. In this sense the evidence is compelling. But neither 'compelling evidence' nor 'unbearable suffering' can guarantee the sort of free response that God desires from his creatures. Evidence can never be compelling in the relevant sense, and unbearable suffering cannot elicit a response that is truly morally free. A response that is extracted by unbearable suffering is compelled in a sense that destroys any meaningful sense of freedom.

And this brings us to the heart of the matter. In response to my earlier criticism of his views, Talbott writes as follows.

> What might Walls possibly have in mind, moreover, when he speaks of God 'interfering with our freedom'? That is, what *specific* freedom might he have in mind here? It could hardly be the freedom to make a *fully informed* decision to reject God, since absolute clarity of vision would be a necessary condition of any such freedom as that. And if, as I have argued and Walls seems to concede, a free and fully informed decision to reject God forever is logically impossible in any case, then there can be no question of God *interfering* with a freedom that was never possible in the first place. So does Walls perhaps have in mind a *less* than fully informed decision to reject the true God?[15]

Well, these are good questions so I shall attempt to answer them. My reply, in brief, is that the specific freedom I believe God cannot interfere with without destroying it is our freedom to trust and love him or not.

Let me begin to spell out what I mean by addressing Talbott's claim that a fully informed decision to reject God would require 'absolute clarity of vision.' And freely rejecting God with such clarity is precisely what Talbott says is impossible. And I agree. However, here is where I part ways with Talbott. Such absolute clarity of vision is only achieved as we progressively respond with trust and love to God's self-revelation. Absolute clarity comes when we have responded to God's gracious initiatives and have allowed him to form in us a character that is holy, like his own character. This kind of clarity is the result of coming to love God with all our heart, soul, mind and strength, and our neighbor as our self. When our character is formed in this fashion then we see with perfect clarity that God is the source of happiness and sin is the source of misery. And in this condition, we freely and gladly obey God and are no longer psychologically capable of sinning or rejecting God. This is the happy state of the blessed in heaven.

Are such persons still free? Yes, they are perfectly free within the happy limits of a character formed by the wonderful truth about God. In an important sense they still retain libertarian freedom, for their actions are not all determined. Precisely how they will honor God and express their character of holy love may be up to them. But sin and disobedience will no longer be an option for them, given the character they have formed.

But here again is where I part ways with Talbott. We must freely respond to God's gracious initiatives with trust and love in order to form this kind of character, and such trust and love cannot be compelled. When God first approaches us in his gracious initiative, our characters are far from formed in holy love, and consequently, we do not have the absolute clarity of vision that precludes sin, disobedience and rejection of God's will for us. To be sure, God informs us as fully as we can be informed in that condition.

We can then, distinguish between two senses of being fully informed. In the *ultimate sense* of this term, it means to know with profound certainty in the depths of our being and at all levels of our character that God is perfectly good and wise and that he is the indispensable source of our happiness and fulfillment. As distinct from this, we can stipulate the *initial sense* of the term, and say that one is fully informed if he is given as much truth and insight as he is capable of receiving at the current level of his character and spiritual capacities.

Now here is the point I want to emphasize. If a person is truly free then he can resist God's overtures at this point, he can refuse to trust him and consequently never form the sort of character that makes disobedience an impossibility. This is where our true moral freedom lies, the freedom that God has granted us and will not override. If we exercise this freedom as God intends, our freedom is perfected and we become the kind of persons who gladly obey him and find our happiness and fulfillment in doing so. But on the other hand, if we choose to resist God and refuse to believe that he not only knows what is best for us but also wants it, then our characters can become fully formed by evil and we may never come to trust and love God. This is damnation. Recall that the initial sin in the garden of Eden began with a failure to trust God. It was the fear that what God had forbidden was actually something good for them that led to the choice to disobey God.

Indeed, it is important to stress that the very nature of trust is that it is exercised in a context of less than full disclosure. Trust is required when information or understanding is incomplete. By contrast, when we know and understand fully, trust is no longer required. In calling us to a life of trust and obedience, God calls us to believe that his intentions for us are good and that his will is directed toward our ultimate fulfilment and happiness.

God has many means to draw his children back to him once they have chosen the way of mistrust and obedience, including punishment. Certainly punishment is often effective in correcting rebellion, but there is no guarantee that it will have this effect. While biblical exegesis is not my task here, I do want to cite a couple of texts that suggest this. First, consider Revelation 16:9, which describes the fourth bowl of God's wrath, namely, scorching heat from the sun. 'They were seared by the intense heat and they cursed the name of God, who had control over the plagues, but they refused to repent and glorify him.'[16] Now what is striking here is the defiant response to even the intense pain of physical punishment. The point is that if punishment is properly seen for what it is, namely, the attempt by a loving God to correct his wayward children, then it can induce repentance, a sincere change of mind. But if not, it will only be experienced as a hateful thing that elicits cursing and further defiance.

Consider now the story of the rich man and Lazarus, which Talbott cites as evidence for the view that hell is forcibly imposed punishment.[17] This story is apparently a parable, and as such we cannot press all the details of the story and assume each of them is intended to make a specific point. A few observations are in order, however. First, there is nothing in the story to indicate the misery of the rich man was an unbearable punishment that led to his repentance and eventual salvation. That is precisely the scenario we would expect if Talbott's theory of hell is correct.

Second, despite the rich man's misery he seems more concerned to justify himself than to repent and beg God's mercy. Although his first request is for relief from his pain, his next request is for Lazarus to be sent to his brothers to warn them so they can escape his fate. While this appears on the surface to be a loving gesture on behalf of his brothers, it may actually be an indirect attempt at self-justification. This is indicated by Abraham's response when he points out that his brothers have Moses and the prophets. When the rich man retorts that more is needed, that they would repent if someone from the dead went to them, Abraham replies: 'If they do not listen to Moses and the Prophets, they will not be convinced even if someone rises from the dead.' (Lk. 16:31).

The unspoken claim in the rich man's request is that if he had been better warned, *he* would not be there either. Indeed, his request is an appeal for compelling evidence, the sort of evidence that Talbott also thinks would be convincing and produce repentance. But the point of the parable is that the rich man is not in hell because he lacks compelling evidence. Just like his brothers, he had available to him Moses and the Prophets. And Moses and the Prophets warned against indifference to the poor, yet the rich man ignored Lazarus as he lay at his gate covered with sores. In other words, he was indeed fully informed but declined to act on the truth that was openly before him. He was fully informed in the initial sense of the term as distinguished above, but he was not compelled. In resisting the truth, he failed to form the sort of character that he would have developed had he responded to the truth that he was given.

As I see it then, hell is indeed a place of misery but not unbearable misery. This is why it can be freely chosen forever as one's eternal destiny. Talbott certainly raises an obvious question in asking what possible motive could explain such a choice. In response to this, I would begin by insisting that the choice of evil is ultimately irrational, although it has its own twisted sort of logic. The heart of this perverse logic is famously stated by Milton in words attributed to Satan: 'Better to reign in hell than serve in heaven.' In short, the damned find a certain distorted sort of satisfaction in evil and they perversely prefer that satisfaction to the true happiness of heaven.

Although this notion is somewhat paradoxical, I believe it is coherent. It has, moreover, been depicted with striking psychological plausibility in literary sources, one of the more recent and well known of which is C.S. Lewis's *The Great Divorce*. In this fantasy, Lewis describes a number of characters from hell who are given a bus ride to heaven and given the option to stay there. In a number of scenarios that seem hauntingly familiar, either with respect to attitudes in our own hearts or in persons we have encountered, Lewis describes how most of the characters decline the invitation to remain in heaven and opt to return to hell. In each case, there is some sin they cherish, some resentment or jealousy, sense of injustice or the like that they cling to as if their lives depended upon it. In each case Lewis describes the miserable satisfaction they derive from holding on to their sins and how they prefer it to the joy of heaven. Moreover, it is clear that repentance and transformation involve a certain amount of pain. While truth is not compelling, it does sometimes hurt and given the choice, rather than submit to the pain of transformation, they elect to hold on to their sins and the distorted pleasures they afford. The desire to avoid the pain of transformation is another part of the complex motivations that make sense of the choice to embrace eternal hell.

I have written to defend the intelligibility of this notion at some length elsewhere, and I will not repeat myself here. However, it is important to note that the view that hell can be preferred to heaven obviously requires a profound illusion. Those who remain in hell because they take it in some way to be better than heaven are deeply self-deceived. The ability to decline the truth about ourselves and God, and thereby deceive ourselves is an essential component of the moral freedom I have defended.[18] It is the ability to deceive ourselves that finally makes intelligible the choice of eternal hell. Let us turn now, more briefly, to Talbott's argument that this allows us to sin with impunity.

Clarifying the Nature of the Sufferings of the Damned

In arguing that the damned are self-deluded in this fashion, Talbott charges that I, along with Lewis, have in effect taken 'the hell out of hell, at least as far as the damned are concerned.'[19] After all, if the damned in some sense get what they want, is hell such a bad place after all? Indeed, Talbott argues that there is no coherent sense to the idea that the damned could forever conceal from themselves the objective horror of hell. Eventually, he maintains, those in hell must come up against the hard rock of reality and thereby shatter all their illusions to pieces. Talbott illustrates his claim with an example of someone who stuck his arm in the fire believing it would cause him pleasurable sensations. Either his experience would shatter his illusions about fire or someone or something would have shielded him from the fire and its ability to harm him and cause pain.

Likewise, if I act on the sinful illusion that I can promote my happiness and well being apart from God then either experience will shatter this illusion or someone or something must protect me from the reality of my choices. Furthermore, 'if I am able to separate myself from God without experiencing the full horror of such separation, then my belief that I can sin with impunity, perhaps even achieve a measure of what I believe to be happiness in the process, is no illusion at all. It is the simple truth of the matter.'[20]

Once again, Talbott is asking for those in hell to experience what they do not have the capacity to experience. Only one who is fully informed in the ultimate sense I distinguished above, and fully formed by the truth about God could truly understand the horror of being separated from him. Only one who fully understood the goodness of God, and had a deep sense of his beauty, as well as the joy of living in his presence, could truly grasp the horror of being separated from him forever. Only someone who had responded in trust and love to God's grace and had been deeply formed by it could see with full clarity what would be lost for those who rejected it. So, ironically, it is impossible for anyone fully to experience the horror of being separated from God. Those who are fully formed by the requisite truth and understanding are those who have freely accepted his grace and will forever enjoy his presence. Those who have not accepted his grace lack the capacity to experience in the fullest sense of the word what separation from God entails.

But even given their limited spiritual capacities, they can experience something of the horror of being separated from God and that will surely be enough to make them miserable. So it is hardly true that we can sin with impunity on the account of hell I defend. Those in hell will know why they are there. Even though they will not fully understand what they have rejected since they have not experienced it, they will know they are not happy.

So I must confess that I overstated the case in my earlier book when I said those in hell get what they want.[21] What the damned want is to be happy on their own terms. However, that is impossible. The only possible way we can truly be happy is on God's terms. So the damned choose what they *can* have on their own terms, namely, a distorted sense of satisfaction that is a perverted mirror image of the real thing. At some level they know this. Self-deception is not a matter of being unaware of truth, but of choosing not to attend to it, of turning our eyes away from it and acting as if it is not true.

A person who is doing this cannot experience a deep sense of unity and integrity. There will inevitably be a deep sense of unease and unhappiness. The rock of truth does indeed hurt when we fall against it. While it does not necessarily shatter all of our illusions, it surely remains an insurmountable obstacle for any project of self-created human happiness.

These considerations also point up why Talbott is mistaken to claim that the damned succeed in 'utterly defeating God's omnipotent love and therefore utterly defeating His justice as well.' Or as he puts it in this book, the doctrine of eternal hell implies either an unloving God or a defeated God.[22]

For Talbott to employ the rhetoric of divine defeat when talking about the love of God is cleverly misleading at best. Language of defeat is appropriate when we are talking about a contest of strength, of wit, or of will. Well, the damned do not win a contest of strength, of wit nor of will by rejecting the love of God.

God's love can be declined but it cannot be defeated. The only meaningful sense in which God's love could be defeated would be if he ceased to love those who rejected him and his love turned into hate. But in my view he never stops loving those who reject him. Rather, his love shines all the brighter by remaining steadfast in the face of such rejection. In my view, God's will was to create free creatures to whom he could offer his love, knowing that it was at least possible that some of them would reject him. His choice to create such a world means that ultimately his will is done even if things happen in that world that God does not prefer.

Even Talbott must agree that things happen in this world that God does not prefer unless he wants to say that all the atrocities down the ages have been willed and determined by God. Of course, Talbott does not want to say any such thing. So the question can be fairly pressed: do such atrocities mean God is defeated? Surely not, as Talbott will agree. There are, however, those who hold that unless literally everything that happens is willed by God, then God is less than fully sovereign. On this view to allow that anything happens that God does not will would imply a weak or defeated God. In employing the rhetoric of divine defeat Talbott reveals a curious affinity for this brand of theology. To be sure, he draws the line for divine defeat in a different place, but the fundamental idea is the same.

Conclusion

To conclude, let us recall Tabott's set of three inconsistent propositions that we considered at the beginning of this paper. I want to propose three similar propositions that are perfectly consistent.

1 Since God's eternal nature is perfect love, he sincerely extends his grace to all his human creatures and does everything he can to elicit from them a free response of trust and love.
2 Although free creatures can decline God's love, his ultimate purpose of glorifying himself cannot be defeated since his love is demonstrated whether it is accepted or rejected.
3 Some sinners will never accept God's love and will be forever separated from him.

The combination of these beliefs renders belief in eternal hell a coherent one. While I recognize that my arguments are not decisive, I would reiterate my earlier claim that Talbott and his fellow universalists bear the burden of proof. And in the spirit of Pascal, I would urge that my arguments that the doctrine of eternal hell is coherent are at least as strong as Talbott's arguments that it is not. In view of this, the burden of proof has not been satisfied and we should continue to reject universalism.[23]

Notes

1 Wesley (1931) Vol. 4, 298.A.
2 p. 7.
3 p. 10.
4 Talbott (2001b), pp. 418–21.
5 Ibid., p. 420.
6 Ibid., p. 426.
7 Talbott (1988a), p. 13.

8 Talbott (2001b), p. 423.
9 Walls (1992), pp. 129–33.
10 Talbott (2001b), p. 427.
11 Ibid., p. 417.
12 What then of testimonies like that of C.S. Lewis? It is important to note that Lewis wrote that 'before God closed in on me, I was offered what now appears a moment of wholly free choice.' Lewis (1955), p. 224. More importantly, it is crucial that Lewis was committed to following the truth, and previous to his moment of conversion he had already begun to accept, however reluctantly, truths that profoundly altered his thinking. Had Lewis not made the decision to be honest with the truth on previous occasions, he would not have felt compelled as he did when the whole matter of God's existence came to a head in his experience and thinking. For more on this matter, see Burson and Walls (1998), pp. 98–103.
13 Pascal (1966), no. 835.
14 For more on this, see T.V. Morris (1992).
15 Talbott (2001b), pp. 428–29.
16 Cf. Revelation 2:21; 11:13: 16:11, 21.
17 Talbott (2001b), p. 417.
18 For further details, see Walls (1992), pp. 129–33.
19 Talbott (2001b), pp. 429–30.
20 Ibid., p. 431.
21 Walls (1992), p. 126.
22 Pp. 4, 7, 14.
23 Thanks to Ray VanArragon and the editors of this volume for helpful comments on an earlier version of this essay.

7

Human Freedom and the Impossibility of Eternal Damnation

ERIC REITAN

Introduction

It is no secret that Christians have historically favoured the Doctrine of Hell (DH) over the more optimistic Doctrine of Universalism (DU). This preference is puzzling, insofar as it seems to commit Christians to the view that, at least in some human souls, the power of sin reigns forever victorious over God's love.[1] The preference becomes less puzzling when we learn that Christians have historically thought that DH is clearly affirmed in Scripture. But as Thomas Talbott has so aptly argued, the scriptural case for DH is far from decisive. While no one can doubt that some scriptural passages, under their most natural reading, support DH, other passages can be more naturally read as endorsing DU. Thus, even if we regard Scripture as infallible, it is not self-evident that Scripture offers more support for DH than DU. A simple review of the relevant scriptural texts cannot settle the matter. As such, it may be helpful (even necessary) to look elsewhere.

One place to look is to philosophical arguments. In recent years, Christian philosophers have had quite a bit to say about DH and DU. While a number of philosophers have challenged the coherence of DH, others have come to its defense.[2] Most contemporary defenders of DH tend to support what I will call a progressive rather than a classical understanding of DH. In brief, the classical understanding is that the sufferings of the damned are imposed upon them by God, against their will, as a just punishment for sin. They languish in hell, not because the have chosen to suffer in this way, but because they deserve it.[3] The progressive understanding – which typically takes its cue from an Arminian approach to theology – holds two things: first, that the sufferings of the damned are nothing but those that necessarily attend the state of alienation from God; second, that this state results entirely because of the free choices of the damned. On this view, God sincerely wills the salvation of all, even the most undeserving of sinners, but his will is blocked by the free choices of the creature. While he surely could override their freedom, he does not do so, out of respect for their freedom.[4]

There are numerous variants of both of these understandings of DH, but for our purposes the rough distinction above will be sufficient. Because the progressive understanding (or something close to it) is the one most commonly defended by contemporary philosophers, it will be the main focus of my comments here. Nevertheless, it is important to say a few words about the classical understanding, if for no other reason than to see why it has fallen out of favor among philosophers.

Problems with the Classical Understanding of DH

According to the classical doctrine, God imposes eternal torment on the damned as retributive punishment for their sins. Thus, while their own free choices may be what render them worthy of damnation, these choices are not the immediate cause of their damnation. Instead, God is the cause. Out of justice, he casts them to the flames. This understanding, while prevalent among medieval theologians and many conservative Christian communities today, confronts several daunting problems.[5] First, this understanding is hard to reconcile with the predominant Christian view that God loves all, even the most unrepentant sinners. How can it be loving to *impose* endless torment on them? The classical answer is that God is both loving *and* just. The punishments of the damned are imposed, not as an expression of God's love, but as an expression of his justice. The damned *deserve* their fate.

But this answer leads to a further question. According to classical theology, *all* of us deserve eternal damnation, because *all* of us have sinned against an infinite God. If God is obligated to punish according to our deserts, then why not embrace a doctrine of universal damnation? The obvious answer is that God doesn't *have* to punish according to our deserts. He is free to show mercy. But if that is true, why doesn't he show mercy on everyone? Why limit his mercy to a few? Perhaps his nature requires that he express both his mercy and his justice. Perhaps he does this by saving some who deserve damnation, while damning others. Who is saved and who is damned is determined entirely by God's supreme will, to manifest both his mercy and his justice.[6] But here we come up against numerous problems. I will highlight only one: Christians believe that God has met the demands of justice on the cross. Christ has paid the penalty for human sin. If the penalty for human sin has already been paid by Christ, how can justice be an impediment to his mercy and His love? [7] Did Christ's atonement only atone for the sins of *some* human beings, or *some* but not all sins? This would seem to derogate from the power and significance of Christ's death on the cross.

The most obvious, and I think best, solution to these problems is to say that, on account of Christ, justice is no longer an impediment to the salvation of anyone. The demands of justice have been met on the cross, so that God may express his boundless love by extending his mercy to all as a free gift. But if that is true, why isn't everyone saved? Here is where the progressive understanding of DH, with its essentially Arminian theology, emerges. This understanding is succinctly articulated by C.S. Lewis in the passage quoted by Talbott in Chapter 1: the doors of hell are locked from the *inside*.[8] The sufferings of the damned are not a punishment imposed upon them by an unforgiving God, but are instead the result of their free decision to remain alienated from God – a decision that God, out of respect for their autonomy, does not override. On this picture, Christ's atonement has fully satisfied God's wrath against sin, and God freely extends the offer of salvation to all without distinction. But some, indeed many, refuse this offer of their own free will, preferring the misery of eternal alienation from God. On this picture, God's perfect love and mercy are preserved intact, as is the all-sufficiency of Christ's atonement. Thus, at least in terms of its compatibility with other central Christian teachings, this progressive understanding of DH is preferable to the classical one.

Talbott's Case Against the Progressive Understanding of DH

But, as Talbott points out in Chapter 1, this progressive understanding, with its Arminian assumption that a free choice decides our eternal fate, is highly problematic in its own right. As Talbott puts it, no one rational enough to qualify as a free moral agent could possibly prefer an objective horror – the outer darkness, for example – to eternal bliss, nor could any such person both experience the horror of separation from God and continue to regard it as a desirable state.[9] Talbott elaborates on this idea in other writings.[10] He maintains that in order for a choice to qualify as truly free, the person making the choice needs two things: First, a full and adequate understanding of the nature of the choice (as Talbott puts it, freedom from all ignorance and deception); second, freedom from any bondage to desire (more precisely, bondage to sinful desires that the person is powerless to resist). But anyone who understands the options and is free from bondage to desire would have no motive to reject God's offer, and every motive to accept it. Furthermore, we never freely choose what we have no motive to choose and every motive not to choose. Hence, it is incoherent to speak of someone freely choosing damnation. Anyone who does choose damnation must therefore lack genuine freedom. God could save them by removing their ignorance, deception, or bondage to desire – thereby *restoring* (not interfering with) their freedom. [11]

Walls' Defense of the Progressive Understanding

Defenders of the progressive understanding of DH must offer a satisfactory response to this argument. Jerry Walls, in his book *Hell: The Logic of Damnation*, proposes an ingenious two-pronged response.[12] His basic strategy is to accept Talbott's claim that those who choose damnation are not making a free choice – but to reject the claim that God could therefore save the damned without violating their freedom. In brief, he looks in turn at both the ignorance and the bondage to desire that would make the choice of damnation possible – and he argues that both of these states could be freely chosen by the damned. Hence, if the damned are those who freely choose one or both of these states, then God could save them only by violating their freedom.

In the first part of his response to Talbott, Walls admits that someone who fully understands the nature of the choice would never freely choose damnation over salvation.[13] Thus, this choice is possible only if the person is in a relevant state of ignorance. But Walls thinks that the ignorance of the damned might be *willful* ignorance, resulting from a freely chosen act of self-deception.[14] Thus, even though the choice of damnation may not be free in itself (since it is done out of ignorance or deception), human freedom is still ultimately responsible for the choice (since human freedom is responsible for the ignorance or deception). We might say that the free choice is located in a different place: in the decision to remain ignorant,[15] rather than in the decision to forever reject God. To save the damned, then, God would have to override their free choice to remain ignorant, and thus could not save them without violating their freedom.[16]

In the second part of his response, Walls considers whether God really could liberate sinners from bondage to desire without overriding their freedom. Those in bondage to desire are those who have developed such deeply entrenched bad habits that they can no longer resist their sinful and self-destructive impulses. They have fallen so far into sin that it is no longer in their power make anything but a sinful choice. While it is easy to understand how a person in such a state could choose damnation, it is hard to see how anyone could call this choice free. Talbott thinks that if God were to liberate a person from such a state, he would not be interfering with the person's freedom precisely because liberation from this state is a necessary condition for making a free choice. He likens such a divine act of liberation to the act of a doctor who, without the consent of a patient, cures the patient of a heroine addiction. This act does not violate the patient's freedom precisely because being addicted to heroine interferes with the patient's ability to make a free choice. Liberating the patient from this addiction is therefore a precondition for the patient being able to freely consent to anything.[17]

But Walls asks us to consider a case in which the patient freely chooses to become an addict, and makes friends and family aware of this choice before the heroine robs him of his freedom.[18] In this case, it is not so clear that the doctor hasn't violated the patient's freedom. Likewise, we can imagine that someone may have freely chosen to become a slave to his sinful desires because he did not want to exercise the discipline necessary to impose order on his desires.[19] If God were to liberate such a person from bondage to sinful desires, it would violate the person's freedom. As Walls puts it,

> The sinner might resent being faced over and over with the choice either to impose order on his desires, as Swinburne put it, or allow his desires to impose their order on him. He might prefer in a settled way the latter alternative and find it ever more annoying that God will not, once and for all, let him have what he wants.[20]

Like the first part of his proposed solution to Talbott's problem, Walls essentially agrees that the choice to be damned is not in itself a free choice, but then argues that it is based on a prior choice that *is* free: in this case, the choice to become the kind of person who is a slave to sinful desires.

The Failure of Walls' Defense

Ultimately, however, Walls' response to Talbott does not work. There are problems with each part of his response, as well as a general problem with his overall strategy. I look at each of these concerns in turn.

The first problem is this: In order for self-deception to result in *eternal* damnation, it must endure forever. But is it really possible to cling *forever* to a false belief? Talbott says no. He thinks that as the damned persist in their false beliefs, and in the choices that follow upon these beliefs, their misery will only grow. Eventually, the painful reality of sinfulness will shatter their illusions.[21] Just as the alcoholics who hit bottom can no longer tell themselves that alcohol makes their lives better, neither can sinners who come face to face with the utter anguish of alienation from God continue to insist that such alienation is preferable to God's loving embrace.

Walls tries to resolve this problem, but his solution is ultimately unsuccessful. He agrees with Talbott that sinners who are confronted with more and greater suffering would eventually break down and cast aside their illusions, but he does not think that their doing so would be free. In effect, he thinks they would be *coerced* into letting go of their self-deception. Walls claims that if God were to cause those who reject him to become increasingly miserable until their illusions are finally shattered, He would be like the legal authorities in England centuries ago who, in order to convince accused criminals to enter a plea of Guilty or Not Guilty, would press them under increasingly heavy iron weights.[22]

But this analogy misses an important point. If Christianity is true, then everything that is good and valuable comes from God, and without God we are left with only misery. Thus, we need not claim that God *imposes* more and greater suffering on the damned (as the classical understanding of DH assumes). All God needs to do is permit the damned to face the *natural* consequences of their choices. What forces them to change their belief that alienation from God is preferable to union with him is not torture under God's hand, but the truth about what alienation from God involves. They discover that their belief is false because, in trying to get by without God, they experience nothing but mounting anguish.

Now, Walls might well insist that the truth they confront is eventually so overwhelming that they are no longer free to deceive themselves. But to claim that this is a wrongful violation of their freedom would be like claiming that my freedom is violated by the fact that I have clear eyesight. Because my eyesight is clear, I am not free to impose upon myself the false belief that the rangy mutt sitting on my front lawn is my long-lost greyhound Sophie. Would that God would blur my eyesight in order to increase my freedom to deceive myself!

The point is this: even if we admit that our freedom to deceive ourselves is limited in the face of reality, it does not follow that God is *violating* our freedom when he simply *allows* us to face the reality that reveals our self-deception for the lie it is. In order for the damned to persist forever in their self-deception, God would have to *shield* them from reality. He would have to blur their vision, in effect, thereby *aiding* in their self-deception. But it seems that a God who helps to hide the truth from his creatures is actually interfering with their freedom, by helping to conceal the knowledge necessary to make a fully informed choice. But even if we don't go this far, we may ask whether it is really loving to help others perpetuate a profoundly damaging self-deception, simply in order to protect their freedom to deceive themselves. It does not seem so. In fact, on this picture it would seem that God is actively taking part in the damnation of the damned, helping them along the path to hell. But surely a perfect God would refuse to play any part in such sinful and self-destructive behavior. And all that is necessary for the damned to have their illusions shattered is for God to keep his hands off.

But even if all of this is true, Walls still has his argument that bondage to desire may be freely chosen. Unfortunately for Walls, there are problems with this argument as well.

Christian orthodoxy teaches that *all* of us are in bondage to sin and cannot free ourselves. Hence, divine intervention is essential for any of us to be saved.[23] What Walls claims, however, is that some of us *freely choose* our bondage to desire – and for those of us who do, God cannot intervene to break that bondage without violating our freedom.

This answer is problematic, first of all, because it seems unlikely that anyone actually *chooses*, freely or otherwise, to be in bondage to desire. What seems more likely is that such a state sneaks up on us. We routinely act on whatever desires we have. We fail to take advantage of opportunities to develop the discipline to resist sinful desires. Eventually, we find ourselves simply unable to resist them. While our choices play a role in becoming slaves to sinful desires, we never actually choose such a state. Rather, we make a series of bad choices that have the cumulative effect of depriving us of free choice.[24] Thus, in eliminating bondage to desire, God would be removing one of the *effects* of our choices, not a state that we have chosen in itself. And insofar as this unchosen state interferes with our capacity for free choice, how can its elimination be a *violation* of our freedom?[25]

This first problem, however, is not decisive. Walls could argue that even if people do not choose *initially* to make themselves slaves to sin, they can choose it after the fact: they can *endorse* who they have become. The damned may be those who have not merely stumbled into such bondage, but who have chosen to embrace this aspect of themselves in defiance of God, thereby rebuffing the grace necessary to eliminate such bondage. This seems to be the kind of person Walls has in mind when he refers to those who have made a decisive choice for evil. They are like the addict who wants to stay addicted, affirming and embracing their bondage.[26] Thus, even if people do not set out to be slaves to sin, they may nevertheless choose to be slaves to sin in this latter sense: they choose to embrace who they have become.

But whether the choice to be a slave to sinful desires is made in advance of developing that character, or after the fact, we may still ask ourselves why anyone would make such a choice. And here lies the deeper problem with Walls' argument: He does not sufficiently consider the conditions under which choosing bondage to desire is possible.

And this leads us directly into the general problem with Walls' reply to Talbott – a problem that applies to both parts of his response. With respect *both* to the choice of ignorance *and* to the choice of embracing bondage to desire, the perplexity Talbott expresses about freely choosing damnation seems equally appropriate. Why would anyone with the power to make a free choice, and a full understanding of what such a choice involves, freely choose a state of ignorance or a state of bondage to sinful desires? According to Walls' own hypothesis, these choices (if sustained) bring about eternal damnation. Possessing full and accurate information about God is not only in our interests, but of ultimate importance to our eternal destiny. Likewise for freedom from bondage to sin. Thus, those who choose ignorance or bondage to desire are choosing something that is, in all respects, immensely harmful to them. Is it really possible to make and sustain such a choice *freely*? That is, can we imagine someone who is fully capable of choosing otherwise (that is, not in bondage to sinful desires) making one of these choices while *knowing* that doing so will doom them to eternal alienation from everything of value? If not, then anyone who chooses ignorance or bondage to desire must do so based on some pre-existent ignorance or bondage to desire. For example, they choose to remain ignorant because they do not fully understand what such ignorance entails. Hence, the choice is not free, and God would not be violating human freedom by eliminating such ignorance or bondage to desire.

If Walls tried to move the free choice one further step back (arguing that the choice to be ignorant or in bondage to desire is based on some previous ignorance or bondage to desire that was freely chosen), he would trap himself in an infinite regress. Either the choice to be in one of these states is always based on a previous choice to be in one of these states, ad infinitum, such that we never arrive at a choice that is truly free; or there is some initial ignorance or bondage to desire that is not chosen based on any prior similar state, and hence could not be the result of a free choice. In either case, God can eliminate the ignorance or bondage to desire that blocks his salvific intentions without violating our freedom.

Marilyn McCord Adams, in her fine essay 'The Problem of Hell', reminds us in vivid terms of the conditions under which human beings develop their capacity to make choices. We start out ignorant and helpless, and only gradually develop a picture of the world, influenced by others who are just as imperfect as we. From early on we are confronted with problems that we cannot adequately grasp or fully cope with, and in response to which we mount (without fully conscious calculation) inefficient adaptational strategies.[27] These strategies eventually become entrenched in our adult personalities. Having thus begun *immature*, we arrive at adulthood in a state of *impaired freedom*, as our childhood adaptational strategies continue to distort our perceptions and behaviours.[28]

We can surely imagine that someone who develops under these conditions might end up wilfully embracing self-deception or bondage to sinful desires – but it hardly seems right to claim that these choices were freely made, or that God should refuse to interfere with such choices out of respect for freedom. As Adams points out, given our broken state, we are no more competent to be entrusted with our eternal destinies than a toddler is to be entrusted with life-and-death decisions.[29]

In short, it seems that the choice to deceive oneself and the choice to put oneself in bondage to desire are choices that themselves could not be made unless one were either ignorant or in bondage to desire, and hence not free. Thus, Walls' response to Talbott collapses in on itself.

A Libertarian Defense of the Progressive Understanding

Despite these considerations, Talbott's perspective is still susceptible to an important worry. Even if we agree with Talbott that full knowledge of the facts and freedom from bondage to desire are necessary conditions for a genuinely free choice (as I think we should), it does not follow that they are sufficient conditions. A third condition may be necessary as well: namely, *the ability to have done otherwise.*

If this condition is accepted, then defenders of the progressive version of DH may have available to them a different response to Talbott than the sort proposed by Walls. According to Talbott, someone who is liberated from all ignorance and deception and bondage to desire would *infallibly* choose God's offer of salvation. That is, it is not possible for the person, given her circumstances (including what she knows, her desire structure, and her overall psychology), to choose otherwise. But if this is true, can we really say that the person's choice is free? The choice meets two of the conditions for freedom, but not the third.

A philosophical distinction may help to develop this response. In discussions about free will, philosophers distinguish between what they call compatibilist freedom and libertarian freedom.[30] A choice made freely in the compatibilist sense is one made on the basis of the agent's own psychological preferences and/or judgments about what is best, in the absence of external coercion. Free choice of this sort is called compatibilist because it is compatible with the choice being *determined* by prior conditions (upbringing, past experience, temperament, etc.) such that this person, given these conditions, *could not have done otherwise.* Libertarian free choice, however, is not compatible with this sort of determinism. A person makes a choice freely in the libertarian sense only if it is possible for the person to have done otherwise.[31]

It seems, then, that according to Talbott, those who are liberated from all ignorance, deception, and bondage to desire have compatibilist freedom, but not libertarian freedom. Their choice is free only in the sense that it is based on their own psychological preferences and/or judgments about what is best. But since, given their condition, they could not have done otherwise than accept God's offer of salvation, their choice is decidedly *not* free in a libertarian sense.

But some believe that libertarian freedom is the most valuable sort. If we are determined by prior conditions to make the choices that we do, some believe our choices lose their significance.[32] This applies especially with respect to the most important choice of all: our eternal destiny. Hence, God would see to it that all creatures retained their libertarian freedom with respect to this most critical choice. But Talbott is surely right to insist that a choice made in ignorance or out of bondage to desire is not free in *any* sense. Hence, God would have to see to it that creatures had the power to reject Him even once liberated from these states.

But if this is so, then how can we guarantee that all are saved? At first glance, it would seem that we cannot. Of course, the eternal damnation of some is not guaranteed either, but it is *possible*.[33]

The Failure of the Libertarian Defense

Or is it? On the progressive view of DH, the doors of hell are locked from the inside – that is, God never withdraws the offer of salvation. Hence, if any are damned eternally it is because they eternally reject God's offer. It's not enough to turn God down once. It must be done *forever*.

We are assuming that, to have libertarian freedom on the matter of our eternal destiny, we must be able to reject God's offer of salvation *even when* we know what we are doing and are not in bondage to sin. But this means that it must be possible for us to make a choice that we have no motive to make, and every motive not to make. To say that this is possible is not to say that it is likely. In fact, it seems clear that, however possible it may be for us to act against all our interests, it is very unlikely at any moment that we would actually do so. But in order for someone to be eternally damned, the person must not only make this unlikely choice once. The person must unwaveringly choose to reject God at every moment for the rest of eternity, *even though the person sees absolutely no good reason for doing so, has every reason not to do so, and has absolutely no compelling desire to do so*. Is *that* really possible?

It certainly seems hard to imagine anyone making such a choice. We can, of course, imagine people who are ignorant or in bondage to desire choosing forever to reject God, but this is because we can conceive of such people as having a motive for doing so – for example, the false belief that defiant self-assertion is a good thing, or the irresistible impulse to be willful. But choices made according to these motives would not be free. What we need to ask ourselves is whether it is really possible to eternally reject God despite the fact that at every moment one is free from any compelling desire to do so *and* one knows that doing otherwise would be infinitely preferable.[34]

Of course, someone may well claim that the fact that such choices are implausible and hard to imagine does not mean that they are impossible. And if we assume that people have libertarian freedom, we must assume that such a choice pattern is at the very least possible.

I have two responses to this defense of DH. First, libertarian freedom as described does not seem worth having. In fact, as described, I sincerely hope that I lack it. The capacity to eternally act against all of my motives would introduce into my life a potential for profound irrationality that I would rather do without. And if I exercise my libertarian freedom as described above, dooming myself to the outer darkness without reason, I sincerely hope that God would act to stop me – just as I hope a friend would stop me if I decided to leap from a rooftop for no reason. I would not regard the actions of that friend as a violation of any valuable freedom, but would see it as a welcome antidote to arbitrary stupidity.[35]

My second answer is more involved. Suppose for the sake of argument that humans have this sort of extreme libertarian freedom, which makes it possible to reject God even at the moment when we have every reason to accept him. By parity, we would also have the freedom to accept God even when our most muddled sensibilities (muddled, presumably, because we have freely chosen to muddle them) make that choice seem the worst possible option. In such a world, is it really the case that there can be no guarantee of universal salvation?

It seems that, given two further assumptions, we can guarantee it even then. The first assumption, made by those who accept the progressive version of DH, is that those who reject God never lose the option of changing their mind. The second assumption, in line with most of Christian theology, is that those who finally accept God's offer of salvation and come to experience the beatific vision are *confirmed* in bliss. There simply is no possible world in which the blessed, joined with God in love, fall away and become unsaved. Someone might object that this assumption implies that once we experience the beatific vision we *no longer* possess libertarian freedom. But this implication is unproblematic. Once we are united with God in love, libertarian freedom has *served its purpose*. We have attained our final end, the end for which we and all our powers – including the power to make libertarian free choices – were created. On the other hand, to *deny* this assumption is to threaten the very notion of salvation itself. It is to suggest that we are never truly saved, that the abyss of damnation forever lurks beneath us even when we have attained the blessed realm, because our libertarian freedom is so pesky and unpredictable that it could turn against our better judgment even then.

Together, these assumptions provide a guarantee of universal salvation. To see why, consider the following analogous case. Imagine a box of pennies, spread out heads-side up. Suppose that the heads-side of each penny is covered with a thin film of superglue, such that if the penny were to flip over in the box it would stick to the bottom and remain heads-side down from thereon out. Imagine that this box is rattled every few seconds. For the sake of argument, let us suppose that there is no chance of the pennies getting stuck to the walls of the box or anything like that. Let us suppose, furthermore, that for any penny that is heads-side up at the time that the box is rattled, there is exactly a fifty percent chance that after the box is rattled the penny will land heads-side up, and a fifty percent chance that it will land heads-side down. Once a penny lands heads-side down, however, it sticks to the bottom of the box and remains that way, regardless of how much the box is subsequently rattled. Let us imagine, furthermore, that the box is rattled every five seconds indefinitely, stopping only once all the pennies have landed heads-side down and become stuck that way.

In this situation, we would expect that eventually the rattling *would* stop, because eventually every single penny in the box *would* become stuck heads-side down. We expect this outcome even though every penny started out heads-side up, and even though at any given time a heads-side-up penny has a fifty percent chance of *staying* heads-side up. If the rattling continued *forever*, we would be inclined to say that this outcome is *inevitable*.

Our intuition here can be formally explained in terms of the philosophical notion of possible worlds. Let us call a penny that remains heads-side up a bad penny, and a penny that has become permanently heads-side down a good penny. For the sake of simplicity, let us suppose that the box contains only three pennies.[36] We will call these pennies A, B, and C. Before the first rattle of the box, all three pennies are bad. But after the first rattle of the box, several possibilities emerge. Each of these possibilities can be represented by a possible world – that is, a way things might possibly turn out. After the first rattle, there are eight possible worlds sharing the same initial conditions, representing eight possible combinations of heads and tails for pennies A, B, and C. To simplify things, let me focus attention on penny A. After the first rattling, there are four possible worlds in which penny A remains a bad penny, and four in which it becomes a good penny.

With one rattle of the box, there are 8 possible outcomes – in other words, there are 8 possible worlds sharing the same initial conditions (the conditions that held before the first rattling). With two successive rattles of the box, there are 27 possible worlds sharing these initial conditions. What is interesting to note is that while, after one rattle of the box, A remains bad in 4 out of 8 possible worlds (half of the possible worlds), given two rattles of the box A remains bad in only 9 out of 27 possible worlds (a third of the possible worlds). This trend continues for each successive rattle of the box: the number of possible worlds in which A remains bad represents a successively smaller percentage of the whole field of possible worlds that share the same initial conditions. As the rattles continue indefinitely, the number of possible world sharing the same initial conditions expands while the percentage of possible worlds in which A remains a bad penny steadily diminishes, approaching 0 as the number of rattles moves towards infinity. The same is true for pennies B and C. Hence, even though at any given time it remains possible that one of the pennies remains a bad penny, this possibility becomes increasingly remote as time goes on. For all practical purposes, it *is* inevitable that every penny will finally become a good penny.

Notice that this outcome does not depend on the probabilities involved. Even if we suppose that the chance of a bad penny turning good were only 20% for any given rattling, as the rattles continued indefinitely the percentage of possible worlds in which any given penny remains bad would still approach 0. It would just take longer to get there. The final outcome – assuming the box is rattled indefinitely – would still be guaranteed.

Given my initial assumptions, the case of salvation is entirely analogous to this hypothetical case. I assumed that the option of accepting God's offer of salvation is never removed, meaning that a person who has not yet accepted God's offer of salvation remains free to do so. But in order to be free to do so, it must be *possible* for the person to do so. That is, there must be some possible world in which the person does accept the offer. Thus, the person who has yet to accept the offer of salvation is like the bad penny: While the person has not yet chosen to be saved, at every moment there is some probability that the person will so choose.

I also assumed that once one has accepted the offer of salvation and entered into the presence of God, one is confirmed in that choice – one is, in fact, saved. This is like landing heads-side down in the box. One is fixed in salvation from thereon out. One becomes a good penny.

In other words, as decision opportunities continue indefinitely into the future, the probability that any one person will continue to reject God's offer of salvation approaches 0. Just like the box of pennies, in which we regard it as inevitable that given an indefinite number of rattles every penny will eventually land heads-down, so we should regard universal salvation as inevitable, given our assumptions.

Of course, to say that a probability approaches zero over time is not to say that it ever *is* zero. Thus, someone might claim that, strictly speaking, it is possible for someone to freely reject God *forever*. But the possible world in which this occurs is so remote that there seems to be no good reason to think that it is actual. More precisely, given the assumption that we remain forever free to accept the offer of salvation, we should believe in universal salvation unless we have some kind of knock-down proof that, despite the tremendous odds against it, some freakish twist of bad luck has landed us in a world where God's will is eternally thwarted in some human souls. It is hard to imagine what such a knock-down proof would look like – but scattered and conflicting scriptural passages surely don't constitute such a proof.

What all of this means is that the only plausible way to reject universalism is to say that we are not forever free to accept the offer of salvation. At some point, either the offer is withdrawn, or we lose the freedom to accept it. But each of these alternatives is problematic. If the offer is withdrawn, we would wonder why a loving God would turn His back on some of the creatures that He loves. If the damned somehow lose the freedom to accept God's offer, we can wonder why a loving God does not restore that freedom to them. In either case, the Arminian understanding of DH, according to which damnation results entirely from the free choice of the damned, must be rejected. This means that, finally, the only way to defend DH is to return to a more classical understanding. But such an understanding is, as we have seen, highly problematic for Christians.

Notes

1 For a detailed development of this idea, see Talbott (2001b). See also Adams (1993), pp. 323–324.
2 Most non-Christian philosophers regard DH as unappealing, offensive, or absurd. Bertrand Russell goes so far as to identify it as one of his chief reasons for rejecting Christianity in his frequently reprinted essay, *Why I Am Not a Christian*. Unfortunately, non-Christian thinkers do not devote much sustained philosophical attention to doctrine. Not unsurprisingly, most Christian philosophers who write on the topic defend the traditional view. They include, among others, William Lane Craig, Jonathan Kvanvig, Michael Murray, Charles Seymour, Eleonore Stump, Richard Swinburne, and Jerry Walls. Nevertheless, there are several Christian philosophers who reject DH. They include, among others, Thomas Talbott, Marilyn McCord Adams, John D. Kronen, and myself.
3 For a careful articulation of this classical understanding, see Kronen (1999). The doctrine has roots that extend at least back to Augustine, who extensively defends the notion that the damned suffer eternally in a literal fire that never consumes them. See Augustine (1931), Bk. XXI, Chs. 2–10.
4 Jerry Walls offers a book-length defence of this understanding of DH. See Walls (1992), especially Chapter 5.
5 For a more careful treatment of some of the key problems with this version of DH, see Kronen (1999); K.J. Clark, (2001); Thomas Talbott's discussions of Conservative Theism and Hard-Hearted Theism in Talbott (1990b) and Talbott (1993).
6 This is what Talbott calls the Augustinian/Calvinist theology.
7 [editors: see Crisp (2003) for a development of this concern].
8 C.S. Lewis (1944a), p. 115
9 Chapter 1, p. 5.
10 Talbott (1992b), pp. 500–503; (1999c), Chapter 11; and (1990b), pp. 34–39.
11 Talbott (1990b), pp. 36–38
12 See Walls (1992), Chapter 5, especially pp. 129–138.
13 Ibid., p. 129
14 Ibid., pp. 129–131
15 For the sake of simplicity, I will hereafter use ignorance in such a way that the state of being ignorant includes both the state of being without relevant knowledge and the state of being deceived.

16 Walls (1992), p. 133.
17 Talbott (1990b), pp. 36–37.
18 Walls (1992), p. 134.
19 Ibid.
20 Ibid.
21 Talbott (1990b), p. 39.
22 Walls (1992), p. 132.
23 Talbott asks, 'Is it not precisely the function of the Holy Spirit, according to Christian theology, to release sinners from their bondage to sin?' See (1990b), p. 36.
24 If, furthermore, these bad choices were made without a clear understanding of their ultimate implications, we might question whether these choices were genuinely free.
25 For a fuller treatment of these issues, see Reitan (2001), pp. 232–238.
26 Walls makes this point using the philosophical terminology of first- and second-order desires. The damned are those who do not merely want to sin, but want to want to sin. Thus, Walls says, good (and presumably therefore God's grace) cannot even find a foothold in their souls. See Walls (1992), pp. 120–121. It is interesting to note how at odds Walls is at this point with the traditional notion that God has the power to save anyone he chooses through an exercise of his almighty power, a notion captured by the theological term efficacious grace.
27 Adams (1993), p. 313.
28 Ibid.
29 Ibid., pp. 313–314.
30 For an accessible overview of these notions of freedom, see Robert Kane's introduction to his recently edited anthology, *Free Will* (2002), especially pp. 9–21.
31 There are some important challenges to this idea that genuine freedom in any sense involves the power to do otherwise. Harry Frankfurt, through a series of examples, raises some especially important challenges to this idea. See Frankfurt (1969). I will not address this controversy here, since the challenge to Talbott that I am considering arises only if freedom is taken to involve the ability to have done otherwise.
32 A helpful summary of the reasons for this stance is offered by Laura Waddell Ekstrom (2000), pp. 6–14.
33 This appears to be the intuition underlying Eleonore Stump's claim that it is not within God's power to ensure that all human beings will be in heaven, because it is not within the power even of an omnipotent entity to *make* a person freely will anything. See Stump (1986), pp. 194–195.
34 Someone might think that a variant on Walls' arguments can be reintroduced at this point, in order to add some credibility to the eternal rejection of God. We might hold that what is freely chosen is not the rejection of God itself, but self-deception about the nature of God and sin, or bondage to sinful desires. But neither of these choices is any easier to imagine sustained for eternity. In order for either choice to be free, it must be made in full knowledge of the facts and not on the basis of compelling desires – that is, the person must be fully capable of choosing otherwise and know full well that making this choice is utterly devastating to everything the person values. It is hard to conceive of someone making such a choice for a moment, let alone an eternity.
35 Talbott makes a similar point. See (1990b), p. 38.
36 But it is worth keeping in mind that the same reasoning would apply for any number of pennies in the box.

PART IV

Theological Responses

8

A Calvinist Response to Talbott's Universalism

DANIEL STRANGE

Introduction

Tom Talbott has presented a clear, robust exegetical and systematic defence of a 'hard'[1] 'Christian' universalism and I myself now have a much better understanding of this version of universalism. As with all theological construction, there is an 'organic' (or interconnected) quality to doctrine and part of the challenge in responding to Talbott is that he presents the reader not only with an argument for universalism *per se* but with an overarching theological paradigm which is founded on and supported by a wide range of fundamental (and disputed) presuppositions concerning, for example, the relationship between divine sovereignty and human responsibility and the nature of God in terms of divine justice and mercy.[2]

I have been given the responsibility of responding to Talbott from the position of those evangelicals who call themselves 'Calvinists', a theological paradigm built on different foundations from Talbott's (and Arminians' and Open theists' for that matter) and coming to different conclusions from his concerning the final destiny of unbelievers and the nature and duration of hell, namely, a 'convinced' separatism between believers (who go to heaven) and unbelievers (who go to hell which is both retributive and eternal), and a soteric particularity concerning God's love and the extent of the atonement.

In this response, whilst I methodologically understand and affirm the hermeneutical spiral and two-way dialogue between exegesis and systematics, I do not want to rehearse detailed exegetical questions and criticisms of Talbott's position, firstly, because this is reserved for elsewhere in this volume, and secondly, because I believe exegesis like that of Talbott's has been convincingly countered elsewhere.[3] I also do not want to simply counter Talbott's biblical evidence for universalism by citing another set of biblical texts that to me unambiguously teach a pre-mortem finality of choice, an eschatological separatism, and the existence of an eternal hell. Again the evidence can be found elsewhere.[4] Suffice it to say, I do think that Talbott's exegesis of some passages, while ingenious, requires some serious hermeneutical gymnastics which I believe compromises the traditional evangelical hermeneutic of 'historico-grammatical' analysis. As a Calvinist, the question I ask myself and attempt to answer in my chapter is this: How and why do I exegete and interpret all the texts Talbott mentions so paradigmatically differently? What is going on here theologically for us to come to completely different conclusions on this matter?

Robert Reymond states that 'every Christian will have either a God-centred or a man-centred theology.'[5] What I do want to concentrate on in this chapter is the explicit and implicit substructure of Talbott's position focussing on a number theological presuppositions that I believe under gird his universalism and which necessitate his particular exegesis and hermeneutics. I hope to show that Talbott's universalistic paradigm is in essence anthropocentric rather than theocentric and, as a result, completely incongruous with God's revelation of Himself, His creation and His gospel. I will do this in a number of stages. First, I want to briefly define what I understand by the label 'Calvinism' and dispel certain caricatures often presented. Second, I want to revisit a number of doctrinal loci that Talbott mentions in his argument: (a) sin, justice and punishment – here I will argue *for* the concept of eternal punishment; (b) the nature of divine love and mercy – here I will argue *against* the concept of universalism. Finally, I will briefly deal with Talbott's concern about Christian's in heaven being able to rejoice when there are those in hell.

Before I begin I note three caveats. First, because I have a somewhat daunting task in representing a particular theological community which is not represented elsewhere in this volume, my emphasis will be marshalling material and drawing from key thinkers from within Calvinism rather than attempting much 'original thinking' of my own. Second, space only permits me to outline the contours of a Calvinist response and so there will inevitably be a lack of sophistication and nuance in my argument. For those interested, I indicate in the footnotes more thorough treatments of the themes in question. Third, I am well aware of the grave nature and emotional sensitivity of the subject of divine punishment and hell as well as the temptation to speculate when there should be silence. However, I do believe that we must submit ourselves to the biblical revelation and to the Living God who speaks truly through his Word.

Understanding the Calvinist tradition

By the Calvinist (or Reformed) tradition, I am referring to those theologians who place themselves within the tradition represented by the Magisterial Reformers, especially John Calvin and his followers. Defining this strand is made somewhat easier by certain creedal affirmations that the majority of Calvinist theologians adhere to depending on their denominational preference. The most important of these confessions are: the Thirty-Nine Articles (1571, Anglican); the Westminster Confession of Faith (1643–1646, Presbyterian); the so-called 'Three Forms of Unity' which consist of the continental creeds (The Heidelberg Catechism [1563], The Belgic Confession [1561], and The Canons of Dordrecht [1618–1619]); the Augsburg Confession (1530, Lutheran); the New Hampshire Baptist Confession (1833, Baptist); and the Baptist Faith and Message (1925/1963).

In terms of soteriology, the Reformed/Calvinist position is often summarised by the so-called 'five points of Calvinism' that are a summary of the Synod of Dort (1618):[6] What should be noted though, is that the Calvinist tradition cannot be defined solely on these points of soteriology. The 'five points' must be seen as being a microcosm of a broader vision. As Packer notes:

> Calvinism is a whole world-view, stemming from a clear vision of God as the world's Maker and King. Calvinism is the consistent endeavour to acknowledge the Creator as the Lord, working all things after the

> counsel of His will... Calvinism is a unified philosophy of history which sees the whole diversity of processes and events that take place in God's world as no more, and no less, than the outworking of His great preordained plan for His creatures and His church. The five points assert no more than that God is sovereign in saving the individual, but Calvinism, as such, is concerned with the much broader assertion that He is sovereign everywhere.[7]

At this point I have to say something briefly concerning the relationship between divine sovereignty and human responsibility in the Calvinist worldview. The Calvinist wishes to maintain that the Bible teaches that God is completely sovereign over all events and yet we are still responsible for our actions. The Westminster Confession famously summarises this as follows:

> God from all eternity did, by the most wise and holy counsel of his own will, freely and unchangeably ordain whatsoever comes to pass: yet so, as thereby neither God is the author of sin, nor is violence offered to the will of the creatures, nor is the liberty or contingency of second causes taken away, but rather established. (III/I)

This particular view of the relationship between sovereignty and responsibility is commonly called compatibilism[8] and I will note three characteristics of this position. First, in terms of the notion of human freedom compatibilists classically maintain that freedom is simply doing as one pleases (or acting on one's preference), and the idea that freedom entails the absence of restraint and constraint. Second, compatibilism would maintain that in Scripture, human freedom has nothing to do with being outside of God's control and that God can causally determine an act and the agent be morally responsible for this act if the act is according to the agents desires. Third, compatibilists maintain that a libertarian or indeterministic view of freedom as held by Arminians, Open Theists and Talbott is both unbiblical and incoherent.[9] Finally, on this issue of divine sovereignty and human responsibility, while realising that we are pushed to the limits of our finite understanding, it is sufficient to say that a compatibilist theodicy will not want to find its solution in any form of 'freewill defence' but rather in the sovereignty of God.[10]

Understanding Sin, Justice and Punishment

What I want to do is work backwards from Talbott's thesis looking first at the nature of divine judgement. As I understand it, Talbott's thesis runs like this: The love of God (which means for Talbott that it is impossible for God to act contrary to someone's ultimate good) is the axis on which everything turns and everything must be understood in light of this basic truth. Universal salvation is therefore a necessity since the highest good for man is salvation. Because of this, Talbott's understanding of divine judgement and punishment is that they are proximate means to an ultimate end – both serve the goal of salvation and in this sense their function is restorative and remedial. Therefore, hell cannot be eternal because its function is to purify and does not exist for its own sake but for the sake of heaven. This approach resembles a post-mortem variation of an Irenaean theodicy where evil is necessary for 'soul-making.' How is one to assess such thinking? I will focus on three linked points.

The Sinfulness of Sin

Perhaps the most appropriate slogan for the Calvinist is *Soli Deo Gloria* – to God alone be the glory. The glory of God is the teleological principle from which everything takes its reference – everything exists for the glory of God. Therefore, a doctrine like sin must be defined essentially in its Godward aspect as an affront to God's glory. The root of sin is failing to glorify God as God and indeed a mocking His glory[11] with the result that a just punishment is necessary, this being an eternal punishment. Part of the problem of Talbott's argument is that he fails to understand this essence of sin and the severity of it. As Bavinck notes:

> In order to appreciate that fact of eternal punishment it is above all necessary, therefore, to recognise along with Scripture the integrity of the justice of God and the deeply sinful character of sin. Sin is not a weakness, a lack, a temporary and gradually vanishing imperfection, but in origin and essence it is lawlessness (*anomia*), a violation of the law, rebellion and hostility against God, the negation of his justice, his authority, even his existence. Granted, sin is finite in the sense that it is committed by a finite creature in a finite period of time but, as Augustine has

> already noted, not the duration of time over which the sin was committed but its own intrinsic nature is the standard for its punishment.[12]

Does Talbott truly understand the sinfulness of sin? The Puritans understood well enough. One of the most crucial texts for the Puritans in this regard is Psalm 51:4, 'Against you, you only, have I sinned.' Here we are confronted both with the exceeding sinfulness of sin and its unspeakable seriousness – it is against God! Ralph Venning wrote, 'sin goes about to ungod God, and is by some of the ancients called *Deicidium*, God-murder or God-killing… Sin is the dare of God's justice, the rape of his mercy, the jeer of his patience, the slight of his power, the contempt of his love… the upbraiding of his providence (Ps. 50), the scoff of his promise (2 Pet. 3:3–4), the reproach of his wisdom (Isa. 29:16)…'[13]

God's wrath, his divine revulsion to evil and his vigorous opposition to it is personal, passionate and permanent. God is angry with sin, it represents a negation of his being and must be exposed and attacked, God cannot be or seen to be morally indifferent to sin, he is necessarily righteous.[14] Why do I mention this?

First, I want to suggest that the primary purpose of divine punishment and therefore the purpose of hell is not remedial or restorative as Talbott thinks but rather retributive:

> Retribution, the essential theological principle underlying the reality of hell, is fundamental to the biblical concept of God. Retribution refers to God, the supreme Judge, punishing those who have rebelled against his rule. (Isa. 3:11; Matt. 25:31–46). This is not a capricious but a retrospective act that is directed toward sinful deeds (Matt. 25:31–46; 2 Cor. 5:10; Rev. 20:12). God inflicts this punishment, not to rehabilitate the sinner, but to rectify and re-establish his good and righteous rule (Rom. 2:5–11); Retribution means that sinners pay the penalty solely because they owe it. In addition, God's judgement cannot be confined to the inevitable process of cause and effect in a moral universe; these penalties and ills are not simply intrinsic to the sinful deed. Rather, retribution is God's personal wrath that inflicts an extrinsic punishment upon sinners.[15]

John Stott lists the way Scripture speaks of God's self-consistency and his obligation to judge sinners: the language of provocation; the language of burning; the language of satisfaction itself and the language of the Name.[16] Retributive righteousness cannot be seen to be discretionary as if God has the choice not to punish sin: 'The reason that God visits sin with retribution is that He hates it and it is impossible to conceive of Him not hating it... One cannot go beyond this and ask, Why? It is His nature.'[17]

On a retributive model of punishment, hell is the place where God's undiluted anger is poured out against sinners who have rebelled against him. What must be noted here is that while God is just in the degrees of punishment inflicted in hell, all sin must be punished infinitely:

> The retributive model of punishment is characterized by an idea of proportionality, expressed in the notion that *the punishment must fit the crime*... sin committed against an infinite God requires an infinite punishment, because all sin against an infinite God has infinite disvalue. The rationale behind this view is that God is infinitely great, such that every sin against God is infinitely serious (quite apart from its consequences). Nevertheless, there are infinite consequences because all sin against this God incurs an infinite demerit, since it an affront to the infinite glory and honour of God, thereby accruing an infinite disvalue.[18]

As terrible and counter-cultural as eternal punishment sounds we must maintain it if we are to be true to God and his revelation. Punishment in hell is not about making people better but is about retribution 'imposed because wrong is wrong and God is against it. Our society shudders at that idea. It pierces hardened consciences and touches a deeply buried nerve of guilt.'[19]

The Habitualness of Sin

If the above point on sin could be seen from the perspective of the doctrine of God, my second point looks at sin from the perspective of biblical anthropology. Talbott maintains that God's punishment of purification will eventually turn all sinners to saints. However, I wonder whether Talbott is too positive concerning the state of humanity. The Calvinist doctrine of sin argues that we are born with a sinful nature inherited from Adam (Rom. 5:12–19), that we are by nature 'objects of wrath' (Eph. 2:3), that we are dead in our sin.

What must be emphasised here is that sinners sin because they want to, they cannot do anything other but sin. They are slaves and captives to sin. There is a bondage of the will, *and hell does not change this*: 'a sinner cannot become innocent by being confirmed in sin.'[20]

We must remember, too, that those who are in hell continue to sin, incurring more guilt to all eternity. The divine sentence is, 'He who is unjust, let him be unjust still; he who is filthy, let him be filthy still' (Rev. 22:11). In other words, those in hell become ever more guilty and accumulate ever more sin, which deserves increasing punishment. After countless ages, they have more to answer for than when they were first condemned.[21]

Furthermore, the thing to be considered here is not so much the 'duration of the sinning' as 'the will of the sinner which is such that it would always wish to sin if it could.' He who commits sin is a slave to sin: he will and cannot do otherwise than sin. It is truly not his own doing when he is denied the opportunity to continue his sinful life. In terms of his interior desire he would not want anything other than to live forever so that he could sin forever. Who then, looking at the sinful nature of sin, would have the nerve to say that God is unjust if he visits the sin not only with temporal but also with eternal punishments.[22]

Talbott's idea that the Augustinian believes the damned are subjected to punishment *against their will* is simply untrue. An eternity in hell is a just punishment and neither the passing of time nor the amount of punishment suffered by the guilty can ever convert guilt into innocence. In Calvinist soteriology the 'deadness' of humanity means that the sinner needs the Spirit's work of regeneration, to make alive that which is dead and that both faith and repentance are a gifts from God. There is a particularity and finality in this work: particularity in that the Spirit only regenerates those God has drawn to him; finality in that the boundary of this work is pre-mortem and not post-mortem.[23]

Retribution and the Cross

Finally, I believe there are implications in Talbott's understanding of divine punishment for his doctrine of atonement. Talbott wishes to see Christ as victorious and that his victory includes all of creation. Commenting on Colossians 1, Talbott notes that 'it is within this context, I believe, that Paul himself understood the nature of

Christ's victory, the defeat of Christ's enemies, and the destruction of sin.'[24] I think this is a revealing comment not for what it says but for what it omits. I glean from Talbott's argument that his doctrine of the cross appears to include some understanding of reconciliation, redemption, expiation and destruction of the kingdom of evil but there is no explicit mention of propitiation, the notion that the cross appeases or pacifies the holy wrath of God. Why is this not mentioned by Talbott? I suggest that it is not mentioned because in Talbott's schema propitiation, which has to do solely with God's retributive justice and Christ's role as penalty bearer, is a concept of justice that Talbott rejects. However, I would want to argue that not only is propitiation an important concept in terms of the doctrine of the atonement, but is *the* most important concept because of its *Godward* reference.

> Indeed, if one reflects even for a moment on the sinful condition of the race vis-à-vis the holy character of God, it will become clear that *its Godward reference was the cross's primary reference.* The Bible plainly teaches the doctrine of the *wrath of God*. It teaches that God is angry with the sinner, and that his holy outrage against the sinner must be assuaged if the sinner is to escape due punishment. It is for this reason a death occurred at Calvary. When we look at Calvary and behold a dying Saviour for us, we should see in his death not first our salvation but our damnation being borne and carried away by him![25]

In Talbott's universalism, is there any room for the notion of penal substitution? My fear is that in rejecting the concept of retributive punishment, the cross loses much of its meaning and power, a fear shared by other Calvinist thinkers:

> Critics of eternal punishment not only fail to do justice to the doom-worthiness of sin, the rigorousness of divine justice; they also infringe on the greatness of God's love and the salvation that is in Christ. If the object had not been salvation from eternal destruction, the price of the blood of God's own Son would have been much too high. The heaven that he won for us by his atoning death presupposes an eternal death by which he saves us. The grace and good pleasure of God in which he makes us participants forever presuppose a wrath into which we would have otherwise plunged forever.[26]

> W.G.T. Shedd shows profound insight when he comments: 'The doctrine of Christ's vicarious atonement logically stands and falls with that of eternal punishment.' Let us be quite clear. If we lost hell, we will eventually lose the cross, for if there is no hell, there is no real point in the cross. Jesus did not need to come and be made a curse for sin. He did not need to enter the horror of forsakenness. The cross and hell stand together. Hell is extreme, but that is because sin is extreme and because extreme measures were taken for our salvation. We cannot survey the wondrous cross, meditate on what the Saviour suffered and assert that hell is an inappropriate punishment for sin.[27]

We will return to the implications of this in terms of the efficacy of Christ's death and its extent further on in the chapter.

Understanding the Love of God

However much Talbott and I disagree on the nature of God's justice, and theories of punishment, we have yet to speak about the love of God and how this fits in with everything I have said about God's justice and punishment. I would maintain that the hub of Talbott's universalism is his particular construal of the love of God.[28] For Talbott the love of God (which necessarily means eventual universal salvation) is the fundamental attribute of God, by which I mean that love as the eschatological destination becomes the hermeneutical lens through which he reads the biblical text and interprets all passages that speak of judgement and punishment. As he notes: 'For if God is love, as 1 John. 4:8 and 4:16 declare, and it is therefore his very nature to love, then it is logically impossible that he should fail to love someone or should act in an unloving way to anyone. It is impossible to act contrary to someone's ultimate good, in other words, as it is for him to believe a false propositions or to act unjustly.'[29] If God is love how can there exist an eternal hell? This is the essence of Talbott's 'hard' universalism which is a position derived from the nature of God and so is a 'necessary' universalism.

This simple thesis seems attractive on the surface but I want to argue that on deeper inspection the thesis is fundamentally flawed and that Talbott has an oversimplified, universalised and absolutized understanding of divine love that misunderstands key aspects of the both the nature and scope of divine love. I wish to argue that both divine love and an eternal hell are compatible. I shall demonstrate this by again outlining three connected areas pertaining to divine love and the doctrine of God.

Divine Necessity and Love

Talbott is right to object to a 'schizophrenic' picture of God whose justice pushes him in one direction and whose mercy pushes him in another.[30] Maintaining the doctrine of divine simplicity or God's necessary existence should guard against this error. Each of God's attributes is necessary for his Being:

> God cannot be God without his goodness, his wisdom, and his eternity... None of his attributes can be removed from him, and no new attribute can be added to him. Therefore, none of his attributes exists without the others. So each attribute has divine attributes; each is qualified by the others. God's wisdom is an eternal wisdom, and his goodness is a wise and (importantly) just goodness.[31]

Divine simplicity has implications for how we speak about the divine attributes. It is incorrect to speak of a fundamental attribute of God that is more central than any other attribute. Rather, all the attributes are perspectival.[32] Unlike other versions of universalism I interpret Talbott as not stating that love is more fundamental than the other attributes, rather his concern is to understand how to reconcile all the attributes of God with his particular understanding of divine love.

Let us take then the attribute of God's love. What do we mean when we say that God is love? From the perspective of God's essential and necessary being, this must be referring to the intratrinitarian love the divine Persons share with one another. This love is totally self-sufficient and complete in itself. Each Person loves the other, gives to the other and is glorified by the other. The Persons love the other Persons necessarily. God is not just loving but is love! Such a trinitarian truth helps explain a facet of *soli Deo Gloria* and stops people over anthropomorphising and misinterpreting phrases monadically like 'God's self-love' or 'God's self-centredness' to think that God is "introverted, narcissistic and self-regarding."[33] As Reymond notes: 'God loves himself with a holy love and with all his heart, soul, mind, and strength, that he himself is at the centre of his affections, and that the impulse that drives him and the thing he pursues in everything he does is his own glory.'[34] What is important to note is that the self-sufficiency of God's love means that he is not dependent on anything outside of God – God is love because God is Trinity, God is Trinity because God is love.[35] Had God not created anything, it would still be true that God is love.

Divine Freedom and Love

Having defined God's intratrinitarian love that is necessary, we must now distinguish this from the divine love that has its object not in God Himself but outside of God. Here Calvinists maintain that God's decrees of creation and redemption are not necessary because if they were God would be constrained by them. That is to say that God does not need to create or redeem to be God. Therefore his actions here are free, 'in the sense that we know nothing in God's nature that constrains these acts or prevents their opposites.'[36] God's freedom to create or not create can also apply to redemption:

> Indeed here that case for divine freedom is even stronger. For there are attributes of God that might be thought to make redemption very unlikely. God's righteousness would seem to prevent redemption altogether, for it demands punishment for sin. Does God's grace require him to redeem? Certainly not. The very idea of grace it that God is not required to give it. If God is required, even by his own nature, to give grace to us, then we have a certain claim on him. But grace excludes such claims. Here redemption is parallel to creation, as it is often is Scripture (e.g., 2 Cor. 4:6). In neither case do we have any claim upon God. Furthermore, even if God were required to redeem men, it would be hard to argue that his grace requires him to save exactly the elect. That he saves even one is amazing. Those who are lost, Scripture teaches have no right to complain against God. So although redemption reveals God's grace vividly, that attribute does not constrain him to save anyone or any particular group of people.[37]

The problem with Talbott's understanding is that divine love appears always to be equated with love for the created being giving the impression that God can only be love if there is universal salvation and almost that God is *obliged* or *constrained* to save everyone for him to be God.[38] Here I think it is important that we safeguard God's self-sufficiency and independence from creation: God does not have to love all of humanity (and eventually save them) for him to be love. Furthermore, and as hinted above, by Talbott universalising divine love he misunderstands the fundamental quality of mercy as 'underserved love.' Helm and Jenson note the logical and philosophical problems with Talbott's position:

> What is essential to such love is that it could, consistently with all else that God is, be withheld by him. If God cannot but exercise mercy as he cannot but exercise justice then its character *as mercy vanishes*. If God has to exercise mercy as he has to exercise justice then such 'mercy' would not be mercy. For the character of mercy is such that each person who receives it is bound to say 'I have no right to what I have received. It would have been perfectly consistent with God's justice had I not received it.' And so in this respect the logical character of mercy is vastly different from that of justice. A justice that could be unilaterally waived would not *be* justice, and a mercy which could not be unilaterally waived would not be mercy.[39]
>
> The New Testament presents human salvation as the product of divine grace. Salvation implies deliverance from an unpleasant consequence; grace implies ill-desert. Is it the case that I do not deserve salvation? Unless it is then I am not saved by grace. The universalists must assert either (i) that all humans deserve salvation, or (ii) that all humans will avail themselves of the means of grace (soft universalism), or (iii) that God's love necessitates that all be saved despite their ill-desert (hard universalism). The difficulty with hard universalism is that genuine human ill-desert requires salvation to be the product if divine *supererogatory* goodness. But the very notion of supererogatory goodness, i.e., good acts which God can justly leave undone, makes the claim that God is requires to perform them incoherent. Thus, if humans are ill-deserving of divine salvation, God can justly not save them. Talbott does not deny this, but his argument implies that divine love vitiates divine freedom: God's love necessitates that God perform supereogatorily good acts. I find this unintelligible.[40]

Of course, God is perfectly free to have a saving mercy on all if he so desires. However, as I have already stated, I believe there to be overwhelming Scriptural evidence to suggest that God does not have a saving mercy on all. My criticism of Talbott here is that his 'hard' universalism makes God's mercy *necessary* and this is an untenable position both for the doctrine of God and a true understanding of mercy.[41]

Interestingly, in his theological critique of universalism, Timothy Phillips uses the same kind of arguments from an explicitly Christological perspective.[42] Phillips notes that universalism undermines Jesus' prophetic work as the revelation of God and is unable to accept it because of the differences pertaining to God's love. First, and contrary to the universalist claim that God must have a saving love for the world, Jesus reveals not 'an insight into an immanent law of history'[43] but a unique and particular intervention into human history (Jn. 14:6) which shows the freeness of God's salvation and the reality of grace. Second, Jesus' contrasts between this age and the next, and the urgency of the present (Matt. 25:13; Mk. 13:32–37) limits the offer of God's saving love to this life contrary to the universalist claim where God's love is eternal: 'to take as axiomatic God's eternal pursuit of the sinner, once again subverts the finality of Christ's revelation.'[44] Finally, to say, as universalists do, that God's love for us is necessary and eternal and to maintain that God must endlessly pursue reconciliation for him to be good is an attempt to subvert God into humankind's servant – something which Jesus assails: 'God alone is King, insists Jesus. "No one is good – except God alone." For that reason Jesus demands that humanity be God's obedient servant (Matt. 6:24; Mk. 10:18; Lk. 17:7–10).'[45] Phillips concludes:

> Because God's goodness is self-grounded, anything contrary to his will is evil. Wrath and retribution, then, become reasonable expressions of his goodness. They bring about forced submission to God's will, an obedience that ought to have been there in the first place. Retribution establishes that rebellion will never dethrone God's goodness.[46]

Universality, Particularity and Love

If we are to see God's love and mercy as free and not necessary, then we are 'free' not to have to necessarily link God's love with God's salvation as Talbott does. The mistake Talbott makes (a mistake he has to make because of his doctrine of God) is to absolutize and universalise one aspect of the love of God that leads to an over-simplification. However, and as Carson points out, the love of God is a 'difficult doctrine'[47] in the sense that the Bible speaks about the love of God in different ways some which pertain to salvation, some which do not, some which focus on the temporal, some on the eternal, some which are universal in their extent, some which are particular. In Calvinist theology this is recognised and the area of systematics is complex and highly nuanced. However, for our purposes we can distinguish a threefold typology that is standard in Calvinist thought. The first is God's intratrinitarian love between the Persons about which we have already spoken. Second, there is God's universal providential but non-salvific love toward all humanity in His common grace by which he restrains sin, restrains his wrath and gives temporal blessing to all.[48] Given our sinful rebellion against God, the fact that he restrains his wrath and does not send us to hell immediately is grace indeed. What must be remembered though about common grace is that our sinful nature rejects the giver of the gift and finally it serves to condemn us:

> It is without question true that good gifts abused will mean greater condemnation for the finally impenitent... it is just because they are good gifts and manifestations of the kindness and mercy of God that the abuse of them brings greater condemnation and demonstrates the greater inexcusability of impenitence. Ultimate condemnation, so far from making void the reality of grace bestowed in time, rather in this case rests upon the reality of the grace bestowed and enjoyed.[49]

Third, we see God's particular effective and salvific love to the elect in His special grace. We have already seen some of the logical and philosophical arguments for maintaining a particularity of mercy but there is overwhelming biblical support to make the claim that God has set his affection on particular individuals, or the church in a way in which he has not done with others. The basis of this love is not located in the elect or their own loveliness but in the 'free' love of God who elects according to his good purpose. These of course are the building blocks of the Calvinist doctrines of predestination and election.

In light of these different ways to speak about the love of God Talbott's argument is inadequate because it does not see these nuances between God's universal and particular love and this leads to (a) a fusing together common and special grace with the result that (b) there is universalisation of the particular which inevitably leads (c) to his universalist conclusion which then (d) has implications for other doctrinal loci.

The Extent of the Atonement

There remains one issue we need mention and that concerns the particularity of the atonement. Let me approach this controversial area by summarising some implicit themes throughout my response. Firstly, there is the Calvinist stress on the sovereignty of God whereby God foreordains all things that come to pass but is not the author of evil. Second, is the intrinsic efficacy of Christ's death on the cross, where Christ took completely the punishment of God we deserved in an act of substitution, and so propitiated God's wrath, reconciled God to us, redeemed us from the curse of the law and power of sin and destroyed the works of the devil. Third, is God's love for creation and redemption that is free and not necessary, so enabling God to be particularistic in his mercy while not impugning God's essential loving character. Finally, there is the particularity of God's saving love whereby before the foundation of the world he chose a people for himself and determined to save them. Now, not wanting to drive a wedge between the will of the Father and the Son and wanting to hold to a unity of purpose between all three Persons of the Trinity, it is not a huge step to speak of the design or intent of the atonement and come to a particularist conclusion – what Calvinists call the doctrine of particular redemption.[50] From what I have said about the complete efficacy of Christ's cross work, Talbott is indeed correct that *if* Christ died for everyone *then* everyone will be saved. On this we are both deeply critical of Arminian soteriology that limits the efficacy of the atonement for sake of universal extension (Arminians not wanting to fall into universalism). More than this, Talbott is right that *if* God decretively willed everyone to be saved *then* all would be saved.[51] However, I believe that when pertaining to salvation (including how salvation is planned, accomplished and applied) the biblical revelation is particularistic in its vocabulary and that exegetically, systematically, and logically the divine design behind the Christ's cross-work is intended for the elect only. I am convinced of the doctrine of particular redemption!

Some Final Thoughts on the Relationship Between the Love of God and the Wrath of God

Having spent some time outlining the nature of sin, of divine justice and punishment and now divine love I want to bring all these perspectives together and try to reconcile them in the Calvinist framework. This is an extremely difficult task and requires far more space than I can give.[52] However, I think apologetically a brief sketch is required. At one level we may be content in saying that because we know something of God's nature as revealed in Scripture we know that eternal punishment will be consistent with God's justice and therefore his goodness. [53]

Can we say more than this though? It is in God's nature to judge and punish sin for eternity but that concerning God's free love and mercy *in his common grace* God loves all in some way and *in his saving grace* (including the provision of the cross) God loves some in all ways. How do God's wrath and mercy relate to each other? Is it possible to say that God's wrath is a form of his love and God's love is a form of his wrath? It is indeed possible for God to be wrathful and loving to the same individual at the same time for although God's wrath toward us is generated by our sinfulness, his love toward us is not generated by our loveliness. The cross where 'God took his own loving initiative to appease his own righteous anger by bearing it his own self in his own Son when he took our place and died for us'[54] is the most perfect, brilliant and beautiful revelation of the place where both wrath and mercy meet: 'The cross involves the harmonization in historical outworking of attributes that are united in the eternal nature of God.'[55] As Frame notes :

> God's love always observes the boundaries of his righteousness. Even in redemption, God takes enormous pains, so that in showing love, he may be just (Rom. 3:26). The sacrifice of Christ insures that God's re-

> demption is both loving and righteous, so that Scripture can even appeal to God's righteousness as a ground for the forgiveness of sins, and thus God's righteousness becomes a form of his love.[56]

But how does this all work out eschatologically? For the elect the situation is resolved in that God's wrath has been dealt with, there will be no more sin (and therefore no more wrath) and God will love his people for eternity. However, what of the reprobate who in this life received God's love shown in his common grace but who were storing up wrath for themselves on the day of judgement? Is there a temporal boundary to God's common grace? Is God's love absent when in his righteous wrath he punishes in hell for eternity? Is there an absolute bifurcation at this point (when in this life there has been a 'mingling') – God simply loves the elect and hates the reprobate? In some ways we must say 'yes' as what we see in hell is God's unrestrained wrath, a wrath that had been lovingly restrained in this life. Many Calvinists would want to say that there is no sense in which we can talk about God's grace, special or common in hell: 'There is no meaningful way to say that God loves the wicked after death.'[57] However, there may be some sense in which it is true. John Frame speculates that while it is hard to think of eternal punishment as divine benevolence there may be truth in it:

> Is God good to the lost in hell?... There is no logical problem with the possibility that God is good only to those people who are not condemned to hell, and that the condemnation of the wicked is itself a benevolence of God directed to other people: God established his justice and, for the sake of his people, exiles those who would turn the cosmos into chaos. There may be some ways, however, in which God is good even to the lost. Perhaps he is as good to them as he can possibly be given their hatred of him and the demands of his justice. And if there are degrees of punishment in hell..., then even in hell, God may exercise his benevolence by mitigating punishments. It may also be worth considering that in their very punishment of hell, God is giving a privilege to the lost – the privilege of displaying his justice and his victory in the spiritual war (cf. Rom. 9:17). Those who find no benevolence in this privilege might be advised to consider whether their standards of goodness are sufficiently theocentric... God is good to his creatures in different ways and at different times, depending on their natures and their roles in God's plan for history. His goodness does not obligate

> him to give the same blessings to all, or to give the same blessings to any creature throughout his existence. If the lost in hell are now receiving no blessings at all, they cannot complain that God was never good to them. During this life they were surrounded by God's goodness just like all other creatures.[58]

We come once again to one of the fundamental differences that separates my position from that of Talbott: the issue of particularity over and against universality. If we maintain a separatist particularity then wrath can be an expression of love not for those in hell for but those in heaven:

> The claim that God's wrath is an expression of his love is wider than the claim that it expresses love for its victim. It is also an expression of God's love for other human beings. There may be situations, such as with God's wrath against the impenitent in the final judgement, where wrath expresses love without expressing love for its object.[59]
>
> But God's wrath is nevertheless an outworking of his love. Once we understand God's love, we know it as a tough love, one that respects his standards of righteousness and burns in jealousy against those who betray it. God's wrath serves the purposes of his love, and his love is the richer for it: it bestows on his beloved the ultimate blessing of a sin-free world.[60]

In terms of teleology, it may be possible to say with Talbott that from one perspective everything God does he does to advance His purposes of love. But the crucial question remains for whom does He advance His purposes? Talbott believes it is everyone, I believe it is only the elect.

How can Those in Heaven Rejoice When There are Those in Hell?

The above section leads me nicely onto my final point where I wish to briefly respond to Talbott's argument against the traditional understanding of hell that the eternal misery of those in hell would in the end, undermine the blessedness of the redeemed. One possible response to this is that we must just trust in both the scriptural truths that state that the wicked will suffer in hell and that the righteous will be absolutely happy in heaven and leave alone questions about whether believers in heaven will be able to see sinners in hell.[61] Perhaps it is wise to stop here. However, far from believing the existence of hell was a cause of distress for the redeemed, Calvinists of the stature of Jonathan Edwards and Murray McCheyne wrote that believers will rejoice in the existence of hell.[62] The basis for their argument is not a feeling of superiority or a perverse sadism but can be summed by McCheyne himself: 'The redeemed will have no mind but God's. They will have no joy but what the Lord has.'[63] From the perspective of heaven we will rejoice in all of God's perfections including his just judgement of those who have rebelled against him. Depending on slight variations pertaining to one's understanding of the doctrine of God and where one places the 'ceiling of mystery' some are more cautious than others when reflecting on this subject. For theologians like MacLeod's conclusion is reserved:

> What must guide us in this whole area is, surely the attitude of God Himself, and that is described for us unmistakably in Ezekiel 33:11: 'As I live, saith the Lord, I have no pleasure in the death of the wicked.' This makes it perfectly plain that God himself is not excited by the destruction of the impenitent... however resolutely He condemns the defiant, His condemnation is rooted not in malice but in equity (on the basis of Hosea 11:8) that He acts with reluctance, not as one doing something he relishes, but as one doing something he must.[64]

However, others are bolder in their statements. Donnelly links his response to the slogan that has followed us through this response – *soli Deo Gloria*:

> We must remember also that hell exists for God's glory. Properly understood, it should not be an embarrassment to us. We need not speak about it in whispers or wish it did not exist. In hell, and we can say this only in trembling reverence, God's glory will be revealed in new and amazing ways, His kingly authority will be seen more clearly than has ever been possible before. Fresh aspects of his holiness and justice will be revealed to his wondering people. We can dare to believe this because Scripture teaches it. The last book of the Bible shows us the sinless inhabitants of heaven praising and thanking God for hell. The twenty-four elders fall on their faces before him saying, 'We give you

thanks, O Lord God Almighty... because You have taken your great power and reigned. The nations were angry, and Your wrath has come, and the time of the dead that should be judged' (Rev. 11:17–18). The angels of the waters praise the Lord for his judgments: 'You are righteous O Lord... because You have judged these things... and You have given them blood to drink. For it is their just due' (Rev. 16:5–6). Like all else in creation, hell exists for God's glory.[65]

Notes

1 P.T. Jensen defines 'hard universalism' as 'the view that no person *can be* finally lost... the [claim that the] salvation of all humans follows from the necessary attributes of God would qualify as hard universalism.' This is to be distinguished from 'soft universalism:' 'the view that no person *will be* finally lost... the [claim that the] damnation of some humans is logically and morally possible, but will never be actual, would qualify as soft universalism.' (10/2 April 1993), p. 236.

2 This is the *nature* of the universalist debate. See Bauckham (1979).

3 See, for example, Schreiner (2001), pp. 182–188; Reymond (1998), pp. 683–698. Reymond believes that universalism is 'so patently unbiblical' that he even ignores it as a possible option! C.f., N.T. Wright, (1979); Fernando (1991), pp. 55–127; Blanchard (1993), pp. 189–208; Blocher (1991).

4 See note 3. See also Townsend (8/3 September 1999); Beougher (2000); Crockett (1991a); Blocher (1992).

5 Reymond (1998), p. 343.

6 J.I Packer summarises them as follows: '(1) Fallen man in his natural state lacks all power to believe the gospel, just as he lacks all power to believe the law, despite all external inducements that may be extended to him. (2) God's election is a free, sovereign, unconditional choice of sinners, as sinners, to be redeemed by Christ, given faith and brought to glory. (3) The redeeming work of Christ had as its end and goal the salvation of the elect. (4) The Work of the Holy Spirit in bringing men to faith never fails to achieve its object. (5) Believers are kept in faith and grace by the unconquerable power of God till they come to glory. These five points are conveniently denoted by the mnemonic TULIP: Total depravity, Unconditional election, Limited atonement, Irresistible grace, Preservation of the saints' 'Introductory Essay' to Owen (1959), p. 4. For a recent treatment which contrasts Calvinist soteriology with Openness Theism see R.K.M. Wright (1996).

7 In Owen (1959), p. 5.

8 Other terms used are divine determinism or a 'no-risk view' of providence.

9 Some good recent defences of compatibilism and critiques of libertarianism can be found in: Frame (2002), pp. 119–160; idem., (2001), pp. 105–143; Reymond (1998), pp. 343–383; Grudem (1994), pp. 315–355; Helm (1993); Ciocchi (1994); Feinberg (1995); Nicole (2002), pp. 33–47; Carson (1990), pp. 199–229. In fact a statement from Talbott like 'God will eventually lead all people to a point where they have faith in Christ and are therefore saved' coupled with his indeterministic view of freedom will not only be incoherent to Calvinists but will be incoherent to Arminians and Open Theists as well as they will argue that such a view of sovereignty

and freedom is incompatible. I trust that the Arminians and Open Theists responding in this volume will point this out!

10 E.g., Reymond's theodicy is as follows: 'The ultimate end which God decreed he regarded as great enough and glorious enough that it justified to himself both the divine plan itself and the ordained incidental evil arising along the foreordained path to his plan's great and glorious end.' (1998, p. 377). See also Frame (2002), pp. 160–185; Helm (1994), pp. 193–216; and Feinberg (1995).

11 E.g., Rom. 1:21–25; 3:23. See Fernando (1991), pp. 99–104.

12 Bavinck (1996), p. 151.

13 Hamilton (2000), p. 12.

14 For more on the wrath of God see Strange (2001b); Lane (2001).

15 Phillips (1991), p. 54.

16 Stott (1986), pp. 124–128.

17 Macleod (1995), p. 95.

18 Crisp, 'Divine Retribution: A Defence' (forthcoming). On this idea see also Donnelly (2001), pp. 26 ff; Bavinck (1996), p. 151.

19 Donnelly (2001), p. 19. For more on the theory of punishment and its relation to the Bible and society see Townsend, (6/1 March 1997).

20 John L. Dagg, *A Manual of Theology*, 1857, reprint, Harrisonberg: Sprinkle Publications, 1990, p. 373 quoted in Donnelly (2001), p. 26.

21 Donnelly (2001), p. 26.

22 Bavinck (1996), p. 151.

23 See Blanchard (1993), p. 174.

24 p. 22.

25 Reymond (1998), p. 639. For an excellent recent defence of penal substitution see G. Williams (2001). All the papers in this collection (D. Peterson, 2001) are worth prolonged reading and reflection. See also Packer (2002).

26 Bavinck (1996), p. 153.

27 Donnelly (2001), p. 27.

28 While noting the theological imprecision of the term I want to include under the word 'love' the varied vocabulary used in Scripture – 'goodness (glorious generosity), love itself (generous goodness in active expression), mercy (generous goodness relieving the needy), grace (mercy contrary to merit and despite demerit), and loving kindness (KJV) or steadfastlove (RSV) (generous goodness in covenantal faithfulness)' (Packer, 1995, p. 418).

29 p. 32.

30 Macleod points out that 'the antithesis between mercy and righteousness is a false one. The true opposite of righteousness is not mercy but unrighteousness or injustice. In fact righteousness is itself a function of love... A God who contemplated inhumanity with indifference or indulgence would not be loving. He would be amoral. And a universe presided by One who would enact no sanctions against Belsen would not be lovely. It would be hell.' (1995), p. 97.

31 Frame (2002), p. 226.

32 This is Frame's terminology.

33 Macleod (1995), p. 185.

34 Reymond (1998), p. 343.

35 This truth has important application in terms of our understanding of personhood, see Ovey (June 1995).

36 Frame (2002), p. 236.

37 Ibid., p. 234 ff.
38 As Catherine the Great famously remarked, 'God will forgive me. It's His job'.
39 Helm (1985), p. 50. See also Helm (2001).
40 Jensen (1993), p. 239.
41 Divine simplicity does not help Talbott here. As Crisp notes: 'Whilst I agree that one of the most widely held beliefs among Christian theists is that God is essentially benevolent, I do not see that this entails that justice *requires* forgiveness... Nor do I see that that punishment is "second best" to the perfect exercise of justice in total, global forgiveness... [Talbott's] view that... justice requires forgiveness, seems to devolve upon the notion that the divine moral nature is simple, understood here to mean that, "all of his moral attributes are identical with his love." But his construal of this is such that, "his justice will be altogether merciful even as his mercy is altogether just; he will punish sinners, in other words, only when it is merciful to do so, *and he will always forgive them because that is the most loving and therefore the just thing to do*" simply does not reflect the doctrine of divine simplicity, at least as it has been traditionally articulated. For perfect being theologians like Augustine, Anselm and Aquinas, the simplicity of the divine nature means that God, as *actus purus*, is just and benevolent at one and the same time. But since they do not construe justice as perfect in forgiveness, deeming instead that it is perfect in retribution, they do not maintain that justice requires forgiveness in every instance.' 'Divine Retribution: A Defence' (forthcoming).
42 Phillips (1991).
43 Ibid., p. 49.
44 Ibid.
45 Ibid.
46 Ibid., p. 49 f.
47 See Carson (2000).
48 Still one of the best expositions of common grace is by John Murray, 'Common Grace' in Murray (1977), pp. 93–119. See also Frame (2002), pp. 429–437; MacLeod (1995), pp. 145–166; and Grudem (1994), pp. 657–668.
49 J. Murray (1977), p. 15.
50 Owen (1959) remains the most thorough defence of particular redemption. More recent and accessible treatments can be found in John Murray (1955), pp. 59–76; Reymond (1998), pp. 671–702; Packer (1995).
51 I say 'decretively' because Calvinists wish to distinguish clearly between God's decretive will and his preceptive will. There is not a Calvinist consensus on the precise relationship between these aspects of God's will. For a representative sample see Reymond (1998), pp. 356–381; Frame (2002), pp. 531–542; Piper (1995).
52 Lane outlines the issues very clearly in his essay (2001).
53 Bavinck notes that if we see an eternal inconsistency we will see a temporal one as well: 'For if eternal punishment is inconsistent with God's goodness, then temporal punishment is inconsistent with it as well. But the latter is a fact no-one can deny... Who can square this world's suffering with God's goodness and love? Still it must be possible, for it exists. Now if the question of immense suffering in this world may not lead us to question God's goodness, then neither may eternal punishment prompt us to deny it. If this world is consistent with God's love, as it is and has to be then hell is too. For aside from Scripture there is no stronger proof for the existence of hell that then the existence of this world, the world from whose misery the features of the biblical picture of hell are derived' (1996), p. 152. Donnelly makes the same point:

'Or we could approach the problem by facing up to the obvious fact of suffering in this life. People ask how a God of love can inflict endless misery on his creatures. But we could equally ask how he can permit his creature to suffer any misery at all. Yet he does. The world is full of pain and unhappiness. It is quite clear that God judges sin, and that he has done so since the Fall. We believe however, that he is love, in spite of the judgements which foreshadow the future (2001), p. 29.

54 Stott (1986), p. 175.

55 Lane (2001), p. 163.

56 Frame (2002), p. 467.

57 Crockett (1991b), p. 197, quoted in Blanchard (1993), p. 173.

58 Frame (2002), p. 413.

59 Lane (2001), p.167.

60 Frame (2002), pp. 467 ff. The idea that the elect 'benefit' from the reprobates exclusion is I think linked to the notion that for the sake of God's glory, God's common grace always serves God's special grace. See Murray (1977), pp. 22 ff.

61 See Blanchard (1993), pp. 179 ff.

62 Edwards, 'The End of the Wicked Contemplated by the Righteous' quoted in MacLeod (1995), p. 133; McCheyne (1979), p. 162.

63 Ibid., p. 334.

64 Macleod (1995), p. 134.

65 Donnelly (2001), p. 24.

9

A Freewill Theist's Response to Talbott's Universalism

JOHN SANDERS

Introduction

On a recent fishing trip I informed a long-time friend of mine that I was working on this essay. He thought it totally unnecessary to inquire into the validity of universalism and asked whether Talbott read the Bible. I replied that Talbott and other universalists do indeed read their Bibles and, moreover, have some arguments that are not easily overcome. My friend's response is rather typical of evangelicals for whom universalism is easily dismissed on the grounds that universalists reject biblical authority.[1] Most universalists, however, argue that a correct reading of scripture is to interpret the damnation passages in a way compatible with, what they consider to be, the overriding thrust of the New Testament: the universal victory of God.[2]

To his credit Tom Talbott has, over the past decade, advanced the discussion in important ways. In particular, he has sought to provide a cogent account as to how God will bring it about that all humans will be saved. That is, he has not simply remained content with claiming that all will be saved but has produced a methodological explanation regarding the way in which God will accomplish this goal. Moreover, he has tried to respond to the criticisms raised against his arguments. Some of these criticisms are ones that I have held so I welcome this opportunity to interact with professor Talbott's work.

Before I begin criticizing his arguments let me say that I am in agreement with a number of his points. For instance, with other Arminians I affirm that God intends to save everyone and reject the view that God eternally decreed specific individuals to damnation (the so-called double decree). Universalism is on the opposite end of the spectrum from 'restrictivism', the view that salvation is restricted to those who hear about Jesus and put their faith in him before they die. Restrictivism implies that the majority of the human race will experience damnation and calls into question the divine love towards those people. If forced to choose between the God of restrictivism who makes salvation so incredibly difficult to find and the God of universalism, it is not difficult to understand why many find universalism attractive.

However, as Talbott acknowledges, these are not the only options on the theological market. Freewill theism (which includes Arminianism) affirms that God intends to redeem all people. It also affirms that because God wants us to reciprocate his love God has instilled in us a freewill whereby we may do so. However, with freewill comes the possibility that humans may fail to return God's love and instead rebel in sin and harm one another. Freewill theists believe that because love cannot be forced it is possible that humans will reject God's love and they may reject it ultimately, finally and eternally. It is this last option that Talbott wishes to remove. Most of my comments will attempt to challenge Talbott's arguments on this point. However, I first want to say some things about his overall approach and one of his theological arguments in particular before returning to the issue of freewill.

Talbott argues biblically and theologically that God will save everyone in the end, then he posits a method as to how God will accomplish this: postmortem persuasion. Postmortem evangelization – the view that God evangelizes beyond the grave – is not a new position on the historical scene. In fact, this theory has some big names behind it.[3] A key advantage of this position is that it allows for the evangelization of absolutely every single human being – every single person will come face to face with our risen Lord Jesus and will have to make a decision. Hence, this view affirms a totally universal evangelization. However, the biblical evidence for it is highly questionable and it has a number of theological problems.[4]

Talbott combines postmortem evangelization with a view known in Roman Catholic circles as the 'final option theory'.[5] According to this position, all people, at the moment of death (not after death), have their consciousness enlarged so that they make a 'final' decision whether or not to put their faith in God. The soul becomes fully awake and makes a free decision in full knowledge of the truth. Although the soul becomes intently serious it remains affected by habits developed and choices made during our earthly existence. The character traits we formed in life influence but do not determine our choice for we are given the grace to choose against even our habits. This theory as well affirms a universal evangelization not dependent upon humans. Talbot agrees with elements of both of these theories but he rejects the idea that the character traits and habits we have developed will affect our ultimate decision. Furthermore, contrary to the proponents of these two theories, he rejects the idea that it will be possible to eternally reject God's invitation. Proponents of post-mortem salvation and the final option theory reject any confident assertions that universalism will occur even though some remain 'hopeful' that all will be redeemed.[6] Talbott, on the other hand, is what may be called a 'dogmatic universalist' in that he argues that this will definitely happen.

Critique

The Case of the Unhappy Redeemed

Now I will move into some specific questions and criticisms of Talbott's arguments. First, a brief word about one of his lesser theological arguments. He claims that he could never be happy in heaven knowing that his daughter had made herself permanently miserable in hell. This is quite the reversal of the claim made by some Christians long ago that our happiness in heaven would be enhanced by our awareness of the suffering of the damned! Though Talbott's claim has some appeal to me existentially, I believe there are enough significant questions to undermine any confident assertion based upon it.

To begin, my present happiness and even identity (who I am and the meaning I give to my life) are bound up with the various relationships with which I am enjoined. For instance, whether I am happy or sad is deeply affected by my wife and children. In fact, the very way I think of myself – who I am – is bound up with these relationships. Presently, I find it very difficult to imagine how I might overcome the misery that would be brought upon me should my wife die. Since my identity is closely connected to her, her death would bring about significant changes in who I am. Talbott castigates the notion that God might perform 'a kind of lobotomy on the redeemed' in order to enable them to experience happiness in the afterlife. Joking aside, I do wonder what God may have to do in heaven to my memory of my life with my wife. Jesus' statement, made in all three synoptic gospels (e.g., Mk. 12:18–25), that we will not experience marriage relationships in heaven has always troubled me for I cannot imagine who I would be under such circumstances. It seems to me that my happiness would be deeply affected by a kind of divorce for the redeemed. What God will do to my memory, I know not, but I am sure he must do something to bring about a change in my identity such that I would not be unhappy in no longer being husband to my wife. Now, if God can accomplish this for me regarding my marriage then why could God not accomplish it in the case of a loved one who permanently turned away from God's love?[7] I recognize that this might be more difficult but let us not minimize the fact that my identity and happiness are tied to both situations.

Another difficulty with this claim of eternally unbearable misery if any loved ones are not redeemed is that our misery tends to be self-centered. The grief I would experience over the death of a loved one is pretty much for what *I* would miss. It is the fact that my life is forever altered that is largely the source of my grief. Since I have very little understanding of what it will be like to 'see the face of God' (Rev. 22:4) or to experience the divine glory I find it difficult to imagine why, in the new earth, I will not grieve over the changes in my present relationships. If God can bring about such changes in me that I do not grieve over very important changes in my relationships, then it is also possible that God can bring it about that I would not be eternally miserable if someone I love rejected God's love.

Also, it seems to me that many people do, in fact, go on with their lives even now after experiencing tremendous loss. They manage to find meaning, even enjoyment, in life in spite of the fact that someone they loved committed a horrible crime. That this is far from easy to obtain I do not doubt. Nevertheless, it is possible even now to live with loss. Perhaps we will be given the ability in the new creation to live with loss just as God does. Consequently, I find unpersuasive the argument that my eternal blessedness will be ruined if everyone is not redeemed.

Freewill and Sin

At this juncture I want to turn to the major difficulty I have with Talbotts' case – the issue of freewill and sin. Let me say at the outset that I am not entirely sure that I understand his view properly so if I misstate his position I am sure he will correct me. In his 'Freedom, Damnation and the Power to Sin With Impunity'[8] Talbott says that he affirms libertarian freedom (the ability to do otherwise than you did). However, he questions whether this entails the notion that in order to be free in the libertarian sense it must be possible that when we act rightly we could also have acted wrongly. He says if that were true then we could not say that God acts freely for God is not free to do wrong. The issue regarding the type of 'freedom' God has is a thorny problem.[9] A minority position has held that God does have libertarian freedom and could act wrongly but chooses never to do so.[10] More commonly it has been claimed that God cannot even choose to commit a moral evil. Along these lines Alvin Plantinga has suggested that though God has libertarian freedom in many areas (e. g. what colour to make leaves), God lacks 'morally significant freedom' (the freedom to do evil).[11] Along these lines one could argue that in heaven we will use our libertarian freedom to ask God to confirm our characters such that we no longer have morally significant freedom to act wrongly.

It seems to me that Talbott is thinking along these lines when he asserts that we have libertarian freedom for pretty much everything but salvation. When it comes to our ultimate redemption, he says, we lack morally significant freedom for we cannot reject God permanently. In the eschaton we will be brought to a deciding point when it is no longer possible for us to choose to reject God (do evil). This is different from the more traditional view that people with both libertarian and morally significant freedom choose in the eschaton to have their characters confirmed. In this scenario the possibility existed at conversion that the person would decline, for the Holy Spirit provided the individual with 'enabling grace' not irresistible grace. That is, the person was enabled to accept God but it was still possible that the person would reject God. It is this last possibility that Talbott wishes to remove.

Talbott would agree with Nells Ferré that 'God has no permanent problem children'[12] but, unlike Ferré, Talbott does not appeal to a 'transcendent logic' by which God mysteriously gets everyone to freely put their faith in him. Rather, Talbott attempts to explain, without sacrificing rationality, precisely how it is that God brings this about. For Talbott, God takes no risks when it comes to human redemption. In this area, at least, he would agree with Augustine that 'the will of the omnipotent is always undefeated.' Chapter 2 of this book is called 'Christ Victorious' for God suffers not a single defeat regarding the salvation of humans. Nobody likes to say that God is defeated or 'fails' to achieve what he wants. It just does not sound right to say God fails. But that is exactly what is entailed in the freewill theist's position that God sometimes does not get precisely what he wants in specific situations because humans refuse to obey God.

The sense in which God may be said to 'fail' needs to be qualified. God does not fail in his overarching purposes. For instance, God does not fail in creating the world with the structures, patterns and conditions with which he desires. It was solely God's decision whether, for instance, to grant humans libertarian freedom. God did not fail in establishing the conditions within which humans could experience the divine love and freely reciprocate it. This entails the possibility that we may not reciprocate the divine love – this is the risk God was willing to take. However, if God does not control everything then it is possible that God will not get everything he wants. For instance, God wants everyone to participate in the divine love but if some use their God given freedom to refuse, then God may be said to fail to achieve everything he wanted. That is precisely the risk that freewill theists believe God took in creating us the way he did.

Scripture presents us with a God who makes himself vulnerable to being hurt by creating beings who have the freedom to reject him. This God takes risks and leaves himself open to being despised, rejected and crucified. The creator and sovereign lord is one who suffers with, because of, and for his creatures. God is the 'defenseless superior power' who in grace makes himself vulnerable to us by making it possible that his every desire may not be fulfilled. It pains God when we sin and harm others and those who ultimately reject God will pain him as well. That is the price God was willing to accept in deciding to create this sort of world. Talbott seems to agree that God has taken risks in creating us with freedom in that the harm we do to one another is not what God desires. In other words, God is vulnerable and his will is defeated by human sin every day. The evils (murders, rapes and the like) that happen now are not purposed by God and so God is not victorious in everything. However, Talbott rejects the idea that God takes the risk of some finally rejecting him. That is, Talbott believes God operates in a significantly different way regarding salvation than God operates in most other areas. Whereas God is normally a risk-taker, vulnerable to rejection, Talbott believes that in this single case – our ultimate destiny – God takes no risk for there is no vulnerability to rejection.

Why does Talbott think God operates differently in this area than in all others? One of the reasons is his understanding of Romans 9. Talbott believes the text stresses God's sovereign right to choose individuals for salvation. Though I agree with many of his explanations of specific passages in Chapter 3, I disagree that Paul is speaking about God selecting individuals for redemption. In my opinion, the Reformation debate over predestination is read into this text for it was not Paul's issue at all. That is, the Arminian-Calvinist debate is not what Paul is speaking about. In this, I am influenced by the so-called 'new perspective' school on Paul and the law. New Testament scholars such as N.T. Wright and James Dunn have argued that the issue Paul is addressing is one of divine sovereignty, but not individual election. Paul is discussing a highly controversial issue – one that preoccupies much of the New Testament – whether Gentiles first have to become Jewish in order to be redeemed by the Jewish messiah.[13] Specifically, do Gentiles who want to be followers of Jesus have to practice circumcision, keep the dietary regulations and keep the Sabbath? These three practices were the 'public' identity markers distinguishing the Jews from Gentiles. Moreover, these were established by God, so if one wanted to follow God then they must be kept. It was simply inconceivable for many Jewish Christians to believe that God would set these markers aside for demarcating the 'people of God.'

In order to participate in the redemption of the Jewish messiah, many argued that Gentiles had to practice the public badges of membership in the people of God. Paul absolutely repudiated this view. For him, God is bringing Jews and Gentiles together as the people of God solely through faith in Jesus, apart from the badges of membership. In Romans, Paul argues that both Gentiles and Jews are sinners before God (1–3) so God is free to redeem both Jews and Gentiles through the work of Christ (4–8) without observing circumcision or the Sabbath. In Romans 9–11 Paul claims that it is God's sovereign right to bring about redemption this way and he brings up various illustrations of divine election in history. Each of these is for the purpose of persuading the reader to agree that God has the right to manifest redemption in this way. Again, the text is about divine sovereignty but not about God choosing individuals for heaven.[14]

With this framework in mind I want to apply it to the issue at hand – whether God takes risks in salvation. One may get at this by asking a number of questions. Did Paul win the day with this argument? Did his fellow Jews accept Jesus as the climax of the covenant? Was he successful in achieving equal standing for Gentiles within the church apart from the badges of covenant membership? Did the salvation of the Gentiles stimulate Israel to trust God that Jesus was the messiah? It seems that God achieved some of what he desired but not all. On the one hand, Paul certainly won the day regarding Gentile salvation without them having to become identified with ethnic Israel. The enormous growth of the church among the Gentiles and its transnational character testify to God's outstanding success here.

On the other hand, the predominately Jewish composition of the early church faded from the scene since fewer and fewer Jews placed their trust in Jesus. Originally, God wanted to redeem the nations through Israel, but ends up attempting to reach Israel through converted Gentiles. In this we see the divine resourcefulness switching to alternative routes in order to achieve his purposes. Yet, God did not get everything he wanted for, in my view, God banked his strategy on the Gentile church and it has not, overall, been the agent God desired it to be in relation to Israel. This does not mean that God has given up on his goal of uniting Jews and Gentiles into one people of faith through Jesus Christ. But it was God's desire that the way Christian Jews and Gentiles lived in community in the church was to be the visible manifestation of the divine wisdom to the 'rulers and authorities' (Eph. 3:10–11).

God has achieved some of what he desired, but not everything. God took the risk of working through the disciples and others in the early church. Some of the apostolic Christians understood the direction divine providence was going while others did not and worked hard against it (witness Paul's Christian detractors). In his providential work God encounters conflict and opposition to his project and in seeking its fulfilment he experiences both victory and defeat.

That God is not always successful in his redemptive efforts is made clear by the Pharaoh of the exodus.[15] The first words of Pharaoh in the narrative set the stage for what follows. In response to the request to allow the Israelites to celebrate a feast in the wilderness he haughtily remarks that he does not have to listen to the voice of a god named Yahweh because he does not know Yahweh (Ex. 5:2). The Egyptian deities were known to him and were powerful so he paid no heed to this patron deity of the Hebrews that had let them become enslaved. A repeated refrain in the rest of the narrative is the divine purpose: 'So that you may know that I am Yahweh' (8:10; 9:14, 29; 11:6). Throughout the plagues Yahweh demonstrates the impotence of the Egyptian deities, in part, in order to evangelize Pharaoh and the Egyptians (Ex. 12:12; 18:11; Num. 33:4). To 'know' in Hebrew involves much more than mere cognitive information. God wants this hard-hearted king to enter into a redemptive relationship with himself – to orient his life towards Yahweh. Many find this difficult to believe since God 'hardened' Pharaoh's heart. On this score Talbott has it right and I would like to add some points that the hardening should not be understood deterministically.

When we hear the word 'harden' in reference to God we normally think in terms of complete control. But the three Hebrew terms used in the narrative (*kābēd, ḥāzaq* and *qāšāh*) have the general meaning of 'to make something strong' or 'heavy' or 'to encourage (reinforce) someone'. The other occurrences of these words in the Old Testament do not carry deterministic overtones.[16] If it is deterministic then one wonders why God must harden his heart more than once. Moreover, the act of hardening does not make one incapable of resisting the influence. After all, God hardened the hearts of Pharaoh's advisors (10:1) yet they plead with Pharaoh to let the Hebrews go and serve Yahweh (10:7). The same divine activity (hardening) does not produce only one sort of reaction for Pharaoh and his advisors are all hardened yet they disagree with one another. Divine hardening does not remove their decision-making capacities or their ability to take a different course of action.

That the divine strengthening still leaves Pharaoh with alternatives is indicated by the conditional language employed in 8:2; 9:2 and 10:4. God proclaims that particular judgments are coming *if* Pharaoh does not release the people. If, however, Pharaoh is so under divine control that he cannot let them go then the use of 'if' by God is disingenuous. By uttering a conditional God is saying to Pharaoh that he does not have to persist in his intransigence, he may repent. It hardly glorifies God if Pharaoh is not a genuine opponent, but merely a puppet for God to manipulate. God and Pharaoh are involved in a real conflict, one that is not settled by overwhelming divine power.

Talbott is correct that God is intensifying what Pharaoh has already decided upon – strengthening his resolve. But why, it may be asked, would God do such a thing, especially when Pharaoh is on the verge of letting the people go? I think that God is trying to push Pharaoh out of his comfort zone in the attempt to get Pharaoh to come to his senses and repent. Pharaoh is pushed by God to decide: either stick with his old deities and remain steadfast in his oppression in which case he will suffer further judgment, or repent and call upon Yahweh – the god whom he said he did not know (5:2). What God desires is the redemption of Pharaoh and to this end the plagues are deployed. However, God was unsuccessful in this. God was successful in getting many of the Israelites to put their faith in him but God did not achieve all that he desired in this story.

The biblical record of redemptive history manifests both victories and defeats for God. In taking risks God has made himself vulnerable to not achieve everything he would like. I believe this is the way God works and, unlike Talbott, I do not believe God will work differently when it comes to our ultimate destinies – God continues to take risks. Talbott, however, argues that our decisions in this life have not been fully free, being conditioned as they are by sin and fallen people. In several of his published articles, including the work here, Talbott claims that anyone choosing to reject God permanently would not be making a 'fully free and rational' decision. Rather, they would still be in bondage to sin and deception. He writes that a free choice of the kind 'attributed to the damned seems deeply incoherent, even logically impossible. For no one rational enough to qualify as a free moral agent could possibly prefer an objective horror.'[17] He criticizes Arminians for allowing an ultimately 'irrational' choice to seal our eternal destinies. Instead, he argues that such an important decision as our eternal destiny must be completely free and rational and no sane person would have any 'reason' or motive to reject God. Hence, everyone will ultimately become sane and freely choose eternity with God.

Let us examine Talbott's criteria for a fully free and rational choice. First, he claims such a decision could not involve any ignorance of the effects and consequences of the choice. We must understand the full implications of damnation and salvation. In effect, we must be given a quasi-omniscience in order to fully grasp the situation before us. Second, we cannot be deceived in any way for deception covers up the truth. If we are deceived into damnation, then, he says, we have not really understood it. If there is no deception then we must be granted the ability to be wholly wise, a sort of infinite wisdom. According to the first two criteria we must know the truth, the whole truth, and nothing but the truth. Third, God must remove any trace of bondage to sinful motives. We must be granted a moral purity that enables us to only desire the good. Hence, we not only know only truth, we want to do only the truth. We are made like God.

Again, here Talbott disagrees with proponents of the final option theory who hold that although grace will be given us to overcome our habits and character traits they will nonetheless be present with us when we make our final decision. Though Talbott criticizes Craig for suggesting that in the new creation God performs a kind of lobotomy on the redeemed such that they forget anything that causes them misery, it seems to me that Talbott is suggesting something similar. After all, exactly who is it that is standing before God in a state of full knowledge, total wisdom and moral purity? It sure is not most of us. It seems that this would involve God so altering my identity that it would be difficult to know who I am at that moment for I am made like God.

In fact, such a transformation implies that for us to make a fully free and rational choice God has to make us godlike so that we can choose God. It is a common Christian notion that at some point in the eschaton we will become confirmed in our characters or, as Eastern Orthodoxy puts it, divinized such that we become unable to sin. But that will be the culmination of our present libertarian choices.[18] Talbott appears to reverse the order: we are divinized in order to choose God. The notion that God has to remove our ability to sin in order for us to freely choose God sounds rather predestinarian since, for Talbott, this entails that we could not possibly choose to reject God. In other words, we become truly free when we have no alternative but to accept God. Such a transformation is what is required, he says, no matter how 'irresistible a means of correction such experience might be.'[19]

Of course Talbott is well aware that this idea of irresistible grace is not going to sit well with freewill theists. The only alternative, he says, left to the freewill theist is to say that God will allow some people to be deceived and make an irrational decision for damnation. Though it may not be the only option for a freewill theist it still seems a correct option to me. This is because I see sin as fundamentally irrational. That is, it makes no 'good' sense to go against God. Sin is intrinsically inexplicable – even God does not understand why we sin (Jer. 3:7). If sin was something explainable, such as a dead car battery, it could be readily fixed. But sin is not rational in this sense and cannot be 'fixed' as though it operated by mechanical laws. God is not left defenceless against our sin, however, for God can love us and attempt to overcome our irrationality with the love of Jesus. I say 'attempt' because it is not a guarantee. If sin operated along the lines of a car battery then a good mechanic would have the know-how to fix it and guarantee it.

Talbott asserts that drawing near to God is what we all really desire deep down in our hearts. If we would just think straight we would see that rejecting God and choosing damnation simply is not rational. Desiring the good is what we are naturally attracted to. It seems to me that he has a rather Platonic understanding of human nature. Plato said that if you knew the truth you would do the truth for nobody ever knowingly does what is wrong.[20] I think this view of humanity is false since we can know the truth and fail to do it. If Plato was right the solution to human wrongdoing is education. Now, being an educator myself I believe it is very important for our lives. However, I do not believe that sin can be overcome simply by education since sin is essentially irrational. Talbott appears to affirm this Platonic outlook when he says that God will so educate us that we will see the truth and consequently we will not be able to choose falsely. To see the truth is to want the truth. Hence, for Talbott, the heavenly revelation in the eschaton will produce but one result – all will accept God. But if, as I argue, the 'mystery of iniquity' just is not understandable then no matter how much education we receive it is possible that we can act irrationally. Thus, even God cannot guarantee that all people will accept his love.

Talbott's position here also renders problematic a standard Christian explanation of why God is not responsible for our sin. Indeed, he makes some disparaging remarks about the 'freewill defence'. In brief, the freewill defence is the idea that libertarian freedom and determinism are incompatible. One cannot be free in this sense and be controlled by another. Beings with libertarian freedom do not have to sin but it is possible that they will sin. Hence, God cannot create beings with libertarian freedom and *guarantee* that they never sin. According to the freewill defence, God is responsible for creating the possibility of evil arising but not for evil itself.

Utilizing the Genesis narrative it may be asked whether Adam made a free choice according to Talbott's criteria. For Talbott a fully free and rational choice is made if: (1) no ignorance is involved, only truth; (2) one is wholly wise and not deceived; and (3) one has moral purity – no sinful desires. According to these criteria Adam did not make a free choice to reject God for (1) Adam was ignorant of some things, (2) was deceived and (3) had a desire to sin. If, according to Talbott, God cannot allow us ultimately to deceive ourselves then what does this imply about Adam's deception? It would seem that God wanted him to sin! In fact, for Talbott, God could have easily provided knowledge, wisdom and moral purity to Adam and thus enabled him to make a free choice to continue in love and fellowship with God. After all, Talbott does not believe that God's providing such knowledge, wisdom and purity overrides our freedom at all. He writes: 'just what *specific* freedom does God interfere with when He shatters our illusions and corrects our faulty judgements?'[21] He does not believe God interferes with our freedom at all in such cases, rather, we are truly free when God provides us with such revelations. Therefore, according to Talbott's criteria, God did not provide Adam with the necessary revelation and purity of heart in order for Adam to make a free choice to sin. So, it seems that God actually desired Adam to sin.

A number of Christian theologians have thought the fall into sin a good thing, saying, '*O felix culpa*' (O happy fall).[22] If, however, God finds our sin 'happy' because it allows God to achieve a greater good which would not have otherwise been achievable, then how can the biblical writers portray God as implacably opposed to sin and never being 'happy' about it? God laments the wickedness of creatures (Gen. 6:6; Mt. 23:37), and the divine love does not rejoice in unrighteousness (1 Cor. 13:6). In my view, God does not want sin and it was not part of God's intentions for humanity. God desired that we experience the triune love and reciprocate that love to God and others. It was not God's intention in creating us that we should experience suffering and horrors from one another. Earlier I said that, 'Talbott seems to agree that God has taken risks in creating us with freedom in that the harm we do to one another is not what God desires.' However, it seems this is not the case and that Talbott actually believes that God intended our suffering and the harm we do to one another. God did not take a risk in giving us freewill since we were not really free at all. Instead, the evils in the world are here because God specifically wants them to exist.

Though this may sound ghastly to many readers, there is a well-known tradition that affirms this point of view. It is called the 'soul making theodicy.'[23] According to this theory, God wanted suffering and evil in order to "build" our characters, make us more mature. That is, in order for God to reach the desired end of redeemed souls it was necessary that humans do harm to one another so that we could acquire virtuous traits such as forgiveness. Talbott writes:

> As I see it, then, the purpose of the earthly realm (and even the physical cosmos as a whole) is just what John Hick and other proponents of a 'soul making theodicy' have proposed. The created universe provides an environment in which God can, first, bring us into being as

> independent, rational agents, and second, begin teaching the lessons of love as he reconciles us over time both to himself and to each other.[24]

Aside from the fact that the biblical writers affirm that God is fundamentally opposed to, rather than in favour of, sin, there are a number of other problems with the soul making theory. To begin, it seems that Talbott agrees with many proponents of this view that all evils will result in higher goods in the future, either in this life or the next. However, it is a serious question whether each and every evil or experience of suffering will produce some greater good and it is not clear that future goods justify the present evil.

Moreover, theodicists have not shown that each and every evil either serves a greater good or that each and every evil is logically necessary. When a two-month-old child contracts a painful bone cancer for which there is no cure, but only endless suffering until death, why is this necessary? Was the Holocaust necessary? Are all the murders, rapes and abused children required for God to build our characters? Some may wish to claim that God intends such suffering in order to teach the parents something, or the Jews something, or the young girl something. Indeed, numerous well-meaning believers attempt to comfort those suffering with such explanations regarding God's intentions for the sufferer. Did God want the Holocaust in order to teach us a lesson? Is such pedagogy justifiable and does it even work? One of my brothers was killed in an accident. Some years latter some Christians informed me after my conversion that his death was ordained for the purpose of bringing me to faith in Christ. My immediate question was: God killed my non-Christian brother so that I would become a Christian? But without middle knowledge God could not have known this would happen. This would mean that God goes around killing people and causing disasters in the hopes that some may then repent and confess Christ.

Some may wish to make the more modest claim that God uses, rather than causes, these evils in order to stimulate people to repentance and love. But does God always succeed in this? Even in the church I see a fair number of people who become embittered towards God – though they seldom say so publicly! They typically lead lives of quiet resignation or secretly hate God. In fact, many people do not experience growth in the face of adversity. Rather, they become embittered or overwhelmed which casts doubt on God's ability to teach. Also, in order for me to grow must my children suffer from debilitating illnesses or be abused? Furthermore, the inequitable distribution of suffering is disproportionate to the needs of the learners. It is doubtful that it can be shown that no one suffers more than is necessary for his spiritual benefit.

In my view, God does seek to bring good even out of tragedy, but there are no guarantees. God is working in the lives of those who love God to redeem even evil situations and bring forth something good (Rom. 8:28). The God who grants libertarian freedom cannot ensure that people who are suffering will respond positively to his redemptive love. Given the fellowship model of providence where God does not force his will on us it is possible that we thwart God's attempts to redeem suffering in our lives. Though God works to bring good out of evil, God cannot *guarantee* that a greater good will arise out of each and every occurrence of evil

It seems that, for Talbott, God could have begun with fully free and rational beings who would only love and care for one another. That is, God could have created humans with the freedom to never sin. Apparently, however, God wanted the horrors of this life in the hopes our characters would improve. But if we are fully free and rational only when we choose the good and refuse evil, then God could have created us that way and so there would not be any need to improve our characters for they would be perfect to begin with. Even granting that the horrors of this life do help some people to mature, many people do not mature in response to suffering and many (those who die) never get the opportunity to mature. Talbott responds that in the afterlife every single person will respond positively to the suffering they experienced. How so? God will use irresistible grace, grant us full knowledge, wisdom and moral purity so that we all make free and rational decisions to improve our characters. As I said before, however, it seems the transformation of our characters, Talbott envisions, implies that God must recreate us in order for us to make the choice to accept God and so our "choice" in the eschaton is of no real consequence.

Moreover, if God can use irresistible grace at the end to ensure we are free and rational then why did God not do so at the beginning and spare us the evils that we execute on one another? Would this not have been a better world? Talbott thinks not. '[S]uch an instantaneous transformation would be far less worthwhile than a learning process whereby rational agents choose freely, experience the consequences of their free choices, and finally learn from experience why love and reconciliation are better than selfishness and separation.'[25] In response to this I want to say a number of things. First, there would have been no 'transformation' since we would have been created this way in the first place. Furthermore, if God imbued us from the beginning with full knowledge, wisdom and moral purity, then we would not need to learn that love is better than selfishness for we would already know it. Of what specific benefit is it to learn from experience? If God is omniscient, never deceived, and holy and thus is incapable of selfishness, then God did not learn that love was better and he had no need to learn from experience. Why should we have had to? Also, his remark that 'rational agents choose freely' implies that we can be rational and freely choose to do evil so that we can learn that this is not the best way. But Talbott has already said those who sin are not rational and are not free. What he should say is that it was good for God to make us unfree (in bondage to sin) and irrational so that we might come to appreciate freedom and rationality. Again, it would seem that God can appreciate freedom and rationality and God has no need to go through bondage and irrationality in order to arrive at this appreciation. So why do we have to go through this horrendous process? Overall, it appears that Talbott has moved much further in the Calvinist direction than simply on the issue of election. It seems he would have God say in preparing to create us, 'Let us bring forth evil that good may result.'

Conclusion

In conclusion, though professor Talbott has advanced the discussion and put forth a number of worthy arguments, I remain unpersuaded that universalism is true. At best, I think his arguments support a 'hopeful' rather than a 'dogmatic' universalism. However, I have brought forth a number of criticisms that, I believe, render even this conclusion problematic. My main criticisms are: (1) it seems Talbott, contrary to his own estimation, is committed to some form of an eschatological lobotomy on the redeemed; (2) his understanding of divine risk taking is too limited; (3) his criteria for 'free and rational' choices means that neither Adam nor ourselves have ever been free or rational; (4) that these criteria imply that God has to make us godlike in order for us to choose God; (5) that he seems to understand sin in a mechanical sort of way that is readily overcome by proper education; (6) that God seems morally culpable for bringing forth evil in the world; and (7) that his use of a soul making theodicy puts him further away from Arminianism than perhaps he believes he has gone. Professor Talbott no doubt has replies to many or all of my criticisms and I look forward to them. At the very least, I hope that my essay provides some grist for his mill.

Notes

1 See Cameron (1987). N.T. Wright argues that universalists are attempting '*Sachkritik*, the criticism of one part of Scripture on the basis of another' (1979, p. 55). The universalist Nels Ferré argues that while the New Testament does teach both universalism and eternal damnation, universalism is more consistent with the emphasis of the New Testament as a whole (1951, p. 244). Howard Marshall has insightfully pointed out how even evangelicals practice a form of *Sachkritik* (Marshall, 1988). It is certainly a form of theological criticism when evangelical Calvinists argue that biblical passages that assert God's desire to save all human beings cannot mean what they seem to mean since that would lead to universalism.

2 For a survey of the various arguments used for universalism and a critique see Chapter Three of Sanders (1992) now reprinted by Wipf and Stock Publishers.

3 For a survey and historical bibliography of this view see Sanders (1992), pp. 178–214. In the early church it was put forward by stalwarts such as Athanasius and Cyril of Alexandra (see MacCulloch, 1930). The view was reborn in the nineteenth-century via such luminaries as Isaac Dorner (1890), pp. 130–135. Recently, Yale theologian George Lindbeck has argued for it. See Lindbeck (1974 and 1984), pp. 46–72. Evangelical Gabriel Fackre (1995) affirms it.

4 See Sanders (1992), pp. 205–210.

5 Ibid., pp. 164–167 for discussion.

6 Gabriel Fackre, for example.

7 One reviewer of this paper questioned whether this could really occur without positing conditional immortality.

8 Talbott (2001b).

9 For an overview of the various positions see Sanders (1998), pp. 316–318 n. 59.

10 Davis (1983), pp. 86–96.

11 Plantinga (1980).

12 Ferré (1951), p. 229.

13 For the 'New Perspective' applied to Romans 9–11 see N.T. Wright (1992); Dunn (1988); and Sanders (1998), pp. 120–124.

14 Talbott holds that one's election is not dependent upon human will but on God (Rom. 9:16). In one sense this is correct. It is solely God's decision to show mercy to humanity through Jesus and God has shown mercy to 'all' (Rom. 11:32). But the issue in Romans 9 is not about choosing individuals for heaven but about God's mercy in bringing Gentiles into the people of God solely by faith in Jesus. In 9:16 Paul is referring back to Exodus 33:12–20 where Moses made several requests to God but God agreed to only some of his requests. In 33:19–20 he tells Moses that Moses has requested something he cannot handle. God does, however, provide something to Moses – he will display his goodness to him – but when, where and how God has mercy is not for Moses to know. Hence, Paul says, in effect, even the great Moses did not get everything he wanted – it depends upon what God wants to do and what God wants to do in Paul's day is not what the Jewish leaders of the Christian community think God should do. It does not depend upon their will, however, but on God's. Also, I believe that the New Testament writers speak of election to salvation in corporate rather than individual terms. On this see Klein (1990).

15 For further discussion see Sanders (1998), pp. 58–61.

16 For example, Deut. 1:38; Josh. 11:20; Judg. 3:12; Ezra 1:6; and Ezek. 3:7–9.

17 p. 5.

18 See Habermas and Moreland (1992), pp. 150–1 and Sennett (1999): pp. 69–82.

19 Talbott (2001b), p. 432.

20 Plato, *Protagoras*, 358; *Meno*, 77–8; *Laws*, 731.

21 Talbott (2001b), p. 429.

22 As does Paul Helm (in good Calvinist fashion). Helm (1994), pp. 214–215.

23 One of the most articulate recent defences of this position is John Hick's (1978), pp. 201–364.

24 Talbott (2001a), p. 105.

25 Ibid., p. 107. On the next page Talbott claims that without sin there would have been no need of Jesus' redemption. True, but if no redemption was necessary, one could affirm the 'Scottist' view that it was still possible that the incarnation would have occurred in order to produce greater fellowship with God. We simply do not need sin and evil in order to have meaningful relationships with God or for the incarnation to have significance. See Sanders (1992), p. 103.

PART V

Historical Responses

10

Universalism in the History of Christianity

MORWENNA LUDLOW

The Early Church

Origen (c.185–254) was the first person systematically to argue that all people will be saved and to offer an explanation as to how that might be possible. He was closely followed by Gregory of Nyssa (c.335–395).[1] These men were steeped in both the Christian and the pagan Hellenistic culture of their day. They were scholars both of philosophy and of the Bible and it is sometimes difficult to separate out these different strands in their writing. However, when it comes to their eschatology there seem to be four main influences on their thought.

The first is the gnostic idea of life as a period of discipleship in which one grows in the true knowledge (*gnōsis*) of God. The eschaton is thus viewed as the achievement of the most perfect knowledge of God possible. God is sometimes seen as a father-figure or teacher who uses seemingly harsh punishments to drive home his lessons (which helped Christian writers explain some puzzling episodes of apparent divine cruelty in the Old Testament).

The idea of punishment as educative had been present in Greek philosophy at least since the time of Socrates; it was Plato, however, who seems to have added to this the idea of punishment being medicinal. This idea is the second influence on patristic universalism. It is transformed in the Christian context – particularly by Origen –

into the image of God as a divine physician who, 'in his desire to wash away the sins of the our souls... makes use of penal remedies of a similar [healing] sort, even to the infliction of a punishment of fire on those who have lost their soul's health.'[2]

These two related ideas of reformative punishment – for educating and for healing – allowed Christian theologians to articulate their belief that in all things God acted for the good. In opposition to those who suggest that justice and goodness are two different qualities Origen argues that '[God] is not good without being severe, nor severe without being good; for if he were only good without being severe, we would only have had more contempt for his goodness, and if he were severe without being good, perhaps we would have despaired of our sins.'[3] This argument has been of enormous importance in the history of universalism.[4] More specifically, the ideas of punishment as education and healing allowed Origen and Gregory to explain the punishment of hell as a reformative and thus temporary state.[5]

The third influence on the eschatology of Origen and Gregory is the Stoic idea of the restoration of the cosmos to its original state.[6] The Stoics believed that when the planets reached the place in the heavens which they occupied when they were first created there would be a world conflagration (*ekpurōsis*), followed by the recreation or restoration of the world – the *apokatastasis* (literally, a setting back to the beginning). From this specific astronomical meaning, the term came to refer simply to the end of the world: this is the meaning which it appears to have in Acts 3:21, where Peter mentions 'the time of the restoration of all things' (*apokatastaseōs pantōn*). In other words, the expression originally had no soteriological implications at all. However, it gained its connection to universal salvation through its use in the interpretation of 1 Corinthians 15:28. Origen and Gregory reasoned that, since the Father created the world through the Son, the submission of the world to the Father in the Son is akin to the return of all things to their original state, in a manner loosely analogous to the Stoic astronomical return. But, of course, the return in Christian eyes was not literally a return to the start of a cycle, but a fulfilment and perfection of creation. Although it has been argued that Origen had a cyclical view of time in which creation, fall and salvation would be endlessly repeated, this view has recently been rejected.[7] This consummation was seen as universal because God is described in 1 Corinthians 15:28 as being 'all in all (*panta en pasin*)'. This phrase then became associated with the phrase 'the restoration of all things' (*apokatastaseōs pantōn*) from Acts. Hence, although the word *apokatastasis* is used in several different ways by Origen and Gregory, it subsequently came to be used as a sort of short-hand to mean 'the salvation of all things/people', particularly after a universalistic idea of the *apokatastasis* was anathematised in 543 and 553.

The fourth and most important influence on Origen and Gregory is the Bible. Ultimately, it is Scripture, and especially 1 Corinthians 15:28 which grounds their belief. Perhaps because he was aware that opposition to Origen's theology was already growing, Gregory of Nyssa is particularly keen to ground his belief in universal salvation in Scripture: besides 1 Corinthians 15:28, he uses Philippians 2:10: 'so that at the name of Jesus every knee should bend, in heaven and on earth and under the earth, and every tongue should confess that Jesus Christ is Lord to the glory of God the Father'.[8] He even tentatively suggests that the words 'under the earth' refer to demons who will also be saved.[9] Elsewhere, Gregory uses the techniques of allegorical interpretation to derive universalistic ideas from Scripture: thus Psalm 59 asserts that sinners will not be destroyed but will be restored; the feast of the tabernacles indicates the eschatological universal feast around God, the story of the Egyptians and the plague of darkness suggests that sinners (the Egyptians) will not stay in the darkness of Gehenna for ever.[10] Thus, although modern scholars might question their interpretation of Scripture, the writers themselves were convinced that their views were Scriptural.

It should be noted that despite the apparent certainty with which his views on universalism are expressed, Origen does not include it in his list of clear and certain doctrines in the prologue to *On First Principles*, and we are to assume that he regards it as speculation, albeit speculation grounded so far as possible in Scripture. There is even some evidence that he later denied that he ever taught that the devil would be saved.[11] Gregory shows a similar circumspection when he mentions universal salvation, sometimes attributing the idea to a character other than himself in a dialogue, or prefacing his remarks with the comment that 'some people claim'. Nevertheless, his whole theological system is directed towards the conclusion that all people will be saved.

Origen's theology was very influential in the Eastern Church, but more in its general method than in its specific conclusions about universal salvation. Those who did accept his universalism, however, developed it in a more extreme form. For example, Didymus the Blind (c.313–398) saw the resurrection as purely spiritual, the restoration as part of a cyclical movement of the universe and salvation as being the unity of all souls in God, beyond all multiplicity.[12] Similarly, Evagrius Ponticus (346–399) taught the destruction of human bodies at the Last Judgment and the transformation of the soul alone in the future life. No clear pronouncement on universalism is extant, but he does speak of all rational beings bowing to God and of there being a time when there will be no more evil.[13] Theodore of Mopsuestia (c. 350–428) was accused of being a universalist, but there is no evidence from his writings to support this.[14]

The first concerted opposition to Origenism was led in the late fourth century by Epiphanius of Salamis (315–403), Theophilus of Alexandria (d.412) and Jerome (c.345–420).[15] Their anxieties were never purely about Origen's universalism (they were also concerned about the subordinationist elements in his doctrine of the Trinity) and when they did discuss eschatology they seem less worried about the simple claim that all people would be saved, than Origen's supposed claims that the devil would be saved, that souls pre-existed and 'fell' into bodies as a punishment, that all would eventually receive an equal reward in heaven and that the resurrection would be spiritual.[16] Of far more consequence was an attack in the 420s by Augustine of Hippo on 'those compassionate Christians who refuse to believe that the punishment of hell will be everlasting'. He says that Origen was 'the most compassionate of all' because he suggested that the devil would be saved, and that the church has rightly rejected his teaching for 'this opinion and a number of others, in particular his theory of the incessant alterations of misery and bliss, the endless shuttling to and fro between those states of predetermined epochs.'[17] Augustine's authoritative influence over subsequent Western theology was such not only that nearly everyone assumed that Origen had unequivocally asserted these things (even though, as we have seen, that is very questionable) but also that they disapproved of any eschatology similar to his.

The controversy was renewed in the sixth century. Philoxenus of Mabbug (c.440–523) taught a universal but spiritual resurrection and Stephen bar Sudaili (c.480–c.543) a far more extreme doctrine of the final substantial union of all creatures with God.[18] An extreme form of Origenism was also taken up by some Palestinian monks. Subsequently, the doctrine of the 'apokatastasis' was anathematised by Justinian in 543 and at the Fifth Ecumenical Council of Constantinople in 553. Again, universal salvation was condemned specifically in connection with (and, arguably, specifically *because* it is connected with) the ideas of the pre-existence of souls, their 'fall' into human bodies, and a spiritual resurrection. Although the anathemas mention no-one by name and were provoked by the sixth century controversy over Origenism in Palestine, most subsequent Greek writers took the condemnations to refer to Origen and to his fourth century followers Didymus the Blind and Evagrius of Pontus – but not, interestingly, to Gregory of Nyssa.[19]

For obvious reasons, very few theologians felt inclined to assert the apokatastasis in the centuries after it was explicitly anathematised. Even the two writers who are often cited as being universalists – Maximus the Confessor and John Scotus Eriugena – seem ambivalent on the issue. Although Maximus (580–662) speaks of Christ uniting all creation, he qualifies this by saying that 'the mystery of salvation belongs to those who desire it, not to those who are forced to submit to it.'[20] He believes that all human nature shares in a movement towards God, but sees this to a large extent as a potentiality which must be activated by individual free will.[21] Interestingly, Maximus comments on the three types of use of the word '*apokatastasis*' by Gregory of Nyssa: all focus on the concept of restoration and none is universalistic.[22] It is possible, then, that Maximus is trying to defend Gregory against charges of Origenism.

The Irish philosopher John Scotus Eriugena (c.810–c.877) is more sure that there will be a universal restoration: he has a complex cosmology which centres on the idea that the universe has moved from unity to division and will return to its original state. However, he distinguishes three modes within the general return. First, the material world will simply return to its 'causes' (which seem to be akin to Platonic Forms, residing in the mind of God).[23] Second, there will be 'the general return of all human nature saved in Christ to the pristine state of its creation and... to the dignity of the divine image...'[24] Thirdly, the elect 'will cross superessentially above all the boundaries of nature into God himself, and will be one in him and with him'.[25] Eriugena himself relates the distinction between the second and third modes to the myth of the garden of Eden, by saying that although all humans will return to Paradise only some will eat of the tree of life.[26] Thus, although there is a universal *restoration*, it is unclear to what extent one can see this as a universal *salvation*, given that there is still a distinction between those who are elect and those who are not (although there is no concept of damnation or eternal punishment).

The Middle Ages

It was several centuries before any other western theologian matched Eriugena's expertise in Greek patristic sources. However, a few of his pantheistic ideas influenced philosophers such as Amalric of Bena (d. c. 1207), a lecturer in logic and theology at the university of Paris.[27] Exactly what Amalric believed is uncertain, but his beliefs clearly disturbed the Catholic hierarchy sufficiently for them to demand a public recantation from Amalric in 1206. Eriugena's work the *Periphyseon*, which had not been suspected of being heretical until the thirteenth century, was condemned in 1225 because of its influence on Amalric.[28]

Besides a general pantheist idea that God pervades the whole universe, Amalric seems also to have the view that those believers who remained faithful to him could no longer sin. This was widely assumed to have influenced a group of educated Parisians – who were consequently known as Amaurians – who were condemned in 1210. Of the fourteen, three recanted and were imprisoned for life; the rest were burnt at the stake. They had turned Amalric's philosophical pantheism into a popular movement: teaching that 'all things are One, because whatever is, is God', they concluded from this that all believers could count themselves God. This clearly could – and did – lead to a rejection of traditional ecclesiastical, legal and social norms. They believed that the ages of God the Father and God the Son had now been surpassed by the age of the Spirit, who was incarnate in all true believers. Possibly, they were universalists, for they taught that 'they would lead all mankind into… perfection. Through them the Holy Spirit would speak to the world; but as a result of its utterances the Incarnation would become ever more general, until soon it would be universal.'[29] However, this belief was somewhat contradicted by other assertions that after a world catastrophe only a remnant would survive and enjoy bliss with God.

The belief in the possibility of communion with the Holy Spirit in this life, in the sinlessness of believers and in a consequent amorality, particularly with regard to sexual relations, survived in the movement known as the Brothers and Sisters of the Free Spirit.[30] Existing from the thirteenth to the fifteenth centuries, spread over a wide geographical area and with many disparate adherents, it was, as one commentator has remarked, more 'a personal turning away from the church than an organisational alternative to it'; it 'was a state of mind as much as a settled body of doctrine'.[31] It appealed to popular enthusiasm (at all levels of society) for asceticism, a more mystical approach to religion and a rejection of the institutional church's claim to have power over the soul through doctrines such as that of purgatory. Their pantheist beliefs included two fundamentals, which in combination produced a doctrine of universal salvation – although salvation in a sense unrecognisable to most orthodox Christians. First, their pantheism meant that evil, sin and the punishments for sin did not truly exist, for God was in and was all things. Secondly, unlike many Neoplatonists who suggested that God was all in all at the beginning and would be so at the end, they believed that God was in all things here and now. This lead in effect to a radically realised universalist eschatology: not a belief that all people *will* be saved, but that they *already* are.[32] In fact, the implication of the doctrine of the Free Spirit is that people are not really saved from anything at all, except perhaps from their ignorance in thinking that there was such a thing as sin. Adherents sometimes derided the doctrines of hell and purgatory as inventions of the church, which fitted with their usual anti-clerical attitude.[33] Because they believed in the complete communion between the soul and God, they rejected any form of mediation, whether by the Church or by Christ. One exception is William Hilderniss who appears to have believed that all things have already been saved through Christ's merits on the cross, that their personal virtue counted nothing to their salvation, that they were already resurrected in Christ's resurrection and that hell did not exist.[34] There are intimations here of a later 'hyper-Calvinist' version of universalism, which we will examine later.

A few traces of universalism can be seen in the beliefs of some Cathars.[35] In general, Catharism was a strongly dualist movement, opposing the traditional Christian God (responsible for the creation of all spirit) with a powerful devil (responsible for the existence of all matter). The purpose of Cathar practice was to release adherents so far as is possible from the obstruction of evil matter, so that on their death they could be released from the body to enjoy communion with God. Those who did not achieve purity in this life would be reincarnated until they did. In the absolute dualism of some Cathar systems, the evil principle was co-eternal with God and would always remain. However, in the 'mitigated dualism' of some other systems, the evil principle originally derived from God and fell from his angelic status; in these systems there is sometimes the suggestion that (as in Origen) the end will be like the beginning and all evil will disappear. There were also reports that the Albanenses (a Cathar group) believed that the judgment had already past and that hell and eternal fire or punishment were in this world, not in the afterlife. Nevertheless, Cathar ritual was almost entirely preoccupied with the purity of individuals in the here and now and they appear to have been more interested in cosmic myths of the beginning of the world, than of the end.

It should be clear from this discussion that the theology espoused by the Cathars and the believers in the Free Spirit was of a very different nature from that of Origen, Gregory of Nyssa, Maximus and Eriugena (for all the claims of the Eriugena's influence). These Fathers always considered themselves part of the catholic Church and they were steeped in its tradition. The sects, on the other hand, were consciously opposing the Church with a new way of thinking and were minimally influenced by Christian tradition. Both sects had an extremely loose interpretation of Scripture and both denied the doctrine of Christ: the Free Spirit doctrine denied him any significant role and the Cathars denied his incarnation. Finally, it is easy to see why they did not stress the eventual universalism of their system: like most sects both groups were geared to gaining new adherents through proclaiming the special advantages of being perfected in this life; these promises would inevitably be undermined if people were told that in the end everybody would be saved anyway. In this era of intense ecclesiastical scrutiny of Christian belief – particularly through instruments such as Inquisition – it is perhaps not surprising that an unorthodox idea like universalism appeared only in extremist and sectarian groups who rejected the authority of such ecclesiastical powers.

The Reformation

The teachers of the doctrine of the Free Spirit rejected the concept of purgatory partly because it was associated with the powers of the Church, which they denied. But, as we have seen, it also reflected an underlying universalist tendency in their theology. In the Reformation, however, individuals and groups who denied purgatory because it seemed to imply that the Church had power over divine grace were sometimes also accused of universalism when this was not justified. The debate over grace went further than the issue of purgatory, however, and divided not only reformer from Catholic, but reformer and reformer. It is with these disputes over the nature of divine grace that the history of universalism is deeply intertwined.

Hans Denck (c.1495–1527) is the person most frequently cited as being a universalist in this period.[36] His key works were written in the last two years of his life as he travelled around various Germanic cities studying, preaching and (usually) being expelled by the local authorities. He died of the plague while still a young man. Denck was a trained scholar: he studied and taught Greek, Latin and Hebrew and was attracted by some aspects of humanism, probably specifically by Erasmus. Although he was disenchanted with the mainstream Reformation, he was never leader of a clearly-definable religious sect. He accepted re-baptism at the hands of Balthasar Hubmaier, and thus is often referred to as an Anabaptist, but re-baptism was never central to his own preaching. He had strongly egalitarian views, but these did not lead to the revolutionary political beliefs of some extreme Anabaptists.

Denck was accused on at least three occasions of teaching universal salvation in the style of Origen. For example:

> [Denck] so misused his mind that he defended with all efforts the opinion of Origen concerning the liberation and salvation of those who are condemned. The bountiful love of our God was praised so much…

> that he seemed to give hope even to the most wicked and most hopeless people that they would obtain salvation, which would be granted to them someday however distant it might be.[37]

However there is no evidence in Denck's writings for precisely this view. What Denck *does* argue is that God wills all to be saved and that he has provided a means for this salvation: Christ. Christ, the Word, is present to all people, whether they realise it or not, but the incarnation of the Word in Jesus revealed God more directly to humankind. Thus Scripture is a valuable, although not absolutely necessary means of revelation. Denck rejects the idea of Christ's death as a substitutionary punishment and instead argues that salvation is through the imitation of Christ's perfect life of divine love. Through the grace of the Word's presence and the example of his life, we are able to be transformed – Denck is quite close to the Greek Fathers' notion of divinisation. However, although Denck clearly believes that all people *can* be so transformed he never predicts that they will: he is insistent that human freedom is necessary for salvation. According to Denck, sin is its own punishment and results in hell: a feeling of complete abandonment by God, which results in a deep desire for and turning towards God. In some places Denck suggests that some people will never emerge from this state of hopelessness, hinting that the fate of each person is sealed in this life. Denck is very uninterested in eschatology.

Why was Denck accused of preaching universal salvation? First, his ideas are similar to those of Origen: particularly the stress on freedom, on divinisation and the idea that sin is a punishment which can lead to repentance. A second reason is that some of his opponents may have assumed that his basic propositions entailed universal salvation. For those who stressed above all God's irresistible grace in election, it may have been difficult to understand that Denck asserted that God willed all to be saved, that Christ lived and died for all, and that in the end some people might be able to resist salvation. What evidence we have for universalism among other teachers of the 'radical reformation' suggests a very similar conclusion: that although several suggested the possibility that all might be saved, or claimed that Christ died for all, few if any seem to have confidently predicted that in the end God would be 'all in all'.[38]

The Seventeenth Century

In Denck we can see elements of both mysticism (God present in spirit to all people) and liberal humanist rationalism (a belief in the importance of human freedom; seeing universal salvation as part of a theodicy). These continued to develop in the subsequent centuries. In particular, as the works of Origen became more widely available, one can find universalist theologies which are directly influenced by Origen's theology, whether this is acknowledged or not. Prominent among universalist writers at this time are some associates of the Cambridge Platonists, who were greatly interested in Origen and Neoplatonism.[39]

The *Letter of Resolution Concerning Origen and the Chief of his Opinions* was published anonymously in 1661 and is now generally considered to be the work of George Rust (d.1670), Anglican Bishop of Dromore in Ireland. In this work, the author defends the idea of universal salvation on the grounds that God made all things out of love and 'for the good and happiness of the things themselves'; this was incompatible with creating creatures who would suffer for ever in hell. Like Origen, the author insists that God's wisdom, justice and mercy are identical, so that punishment must be for the purpose of correction, not retribution. The defence of Origen is clearly taking place in the context of contemporary debates over the doctrine of the atonement: the author rejects a penal substitution theory of the atonement, which sees punishment as owed to God by sinners and paid by Christ, rather than as a providential tool for bringing them back to God. Some punishment takes place in this life; sinners will also be punished in hell after their death. Although that punishment is not eternal, Rust stresses that it will be 'very long, great and intolerable' and he emphasises the necessity of pain for conversion. He is impatient with those who claim that hell is eternal, whilst 'having easie wayes of assuring themselves that it shall not be their portion'.

George Rust became a friend of Lord Conway and his wife, Anne Conway (d.1679). The latter was an extraordinarily learned woman, able to read Latin, Greek and Hebrew and very well read in philosophical and mystical works. Throughout her life she suffered from a permanent and severe headache for which she was constantly seeking a cure. This appears to have influenced her belief in universal salvation, for she became convinced that the only explanation for her condition which could fit with the idea of a good God, was that she had sinned terribly in a previous life and that she had been reincarnated into a life of suffering in order to purify herself from that sin. To an even greater degree than Rust she was convinced of the necessity of pain for salvation:

> every pain and torment excites or stirs up an operating Spirit and life in everything which suffers... through Pain, and the enduring thereof... and so the Spirit... is made more Spiritual, and consequently more Active and Operative through suffering.[40]

She outlined these beliefs in a work published posthumously in Latin. In this she stated he belief in universal salvation: with time, all souls would turn to God, since evil is finite and there will come a point when the soul must come to the nadir of sin and turn to rise to God. By contrast, God, the Good, is infinite and the soul's journey into divinity will never cease. This argument is very similar to one used by Gregory of Nyssa. Because of this and her belief in a Christianised form of reincarnation, which has strong Origenistic elements, one can surmise that she had read some universalistic Church Fathers as well as more recent sources. Conway eventually became a member of the Society of Friends.

Anne Conway was encouraged in her scholarship by one of her doctors, Francis van Helmont (fl. 1670–9). He too wrote a work defending universal salvation in a similar way to Rust, placing particular emphasis on the fact that divine justice requires all punishment to be reformative. Like Rust, he emphasises that divine punishment will be long and very painful – lest anyone should think that his doctrine was an encouragement to immorality.

Two further universalist writers of this period were Independent ministers and chaplains to Oliver Cromwell. Peter Sterry (1613–1707) was the teacher and mentor of Jeremiah White (1613–72), whose work more clearly asserts universal salvation. White believes that God's love demands that all punishment will be reformative, but warns that this should not encourage anyone to sin: the last chapter of his book *The Restoration of All Things* (published posthumously in London in 1712) is sternly entitled 'Being a Warning to Sinners'. He stands out, however, for having a more sophisticated analysis of the divine nature: because unity of love and justice are perfectly united, he argues divine punishment is *both* good in itself (because everything that God does is good) *and* good for those being punished (because God loves his creation). Perhaps most interesting is the fact that he attempts to square a doctrine of universal salvation with a doctrine of double predestination, by asserting that the division of elect and reprobate is a temporary measure for the purposes of illustrating the divine grace. He consequently puts less emphasis than the other writers on human free will. White's book is peppered throughout with scriptural quotations and there are several passages of extended exegesis; his book is prefaced with a list a quotations from earlier advocates of universal salvation, including Origen, Clement of Alexandria and Gregory of Nazianzus.

Jane Lead (1623–1704), was the author of *The Enochian Walks with God* (1694), which purports to be an account of a mystical experience in which the nature of post-mortem punishment was revealed to her. It is a simpler and more unsophisticated work than those dealt with above, containing more poetical description in a biblical style of prose and less philosophy. Nevertheless, it contains the same elements: an emphasis on divine love, on punishment as reform (with a stress on its purificatory or purgatorial function), on the length and painfulness of that punishment and on the eventual reconciliation of all sinners to God. The most remarkable thing about Lead was that unlike the others she preached her ideas openly and a small congregation known as the Philadelphians gathered round her in London. They had various millenarian beliefs, but they were not sectarian and always claimed to remain within the Church of England. Although the Philadelphians died out as a congregation in 1730, Lead gained a sizable, but very disparate and never organised following on the Continent, especially in Holland and Germany. Her influence spread partly due to the energy of her disciple Francis Lee (1661–1719).[41] Her interest in the mystical writings of Jacob Boehme, appealed to many such as the radical German pietists Johann and Johanna Petersen, who began openly preaching and writing about universal salvation at the turn of the seventeenth and the eighteenth centuries – although they had clearly been convinced of the truth of the doctrine for some years before. Johann Petersen in particular echoed the apocalyptic speculation and the focus on purificatory punishment found in Lead's work, with an emphasis on a Lutheran doctrine of justification, which stressed that believers had only a passive role in their own salvation.[42] The Petersens themselves had a significant impact both on their aristocratic patrons and on later pietist groups, a few of which later emigrated to America.

These writers seem to mark a significant renewal of interest in universalism amongst those who held otherwise more or less mainstream Christian beliefs and who had no sectarian ambitions. Nevertheless, Lead's congregation was the beginning of a new phenomenon: universalism as a faith confessed by a congregation as that which identified them – as opposed to a secret belief published only in private.

Eighteenth and Nineteenth Centuries

Although universalism was still a highly controversial belief to hold, it gradually became more acceptable to preach and write about it in public. Consequently, this period saw both the expansion of universalist congregations and the public espousal of universalist positions by eminent theologians of several denominations.

Universalist congregations

The development of universalist congregations is extremely complex, partly because of the controversial nature of universalism itself and partly because universalists became sectarian groups who had a tendency to proliferate, split and re-unite with great rapidity. However, it is possible to identify four main sources and two main forms of universalist thought in this period.[43] The sources are: first, a liberal humanism (often influenced by the Greek fathers and Arminianism) which emphasised the goodness of God, reformative punishment and the value of human free will; second, mysticism, sometimes neoplatonic, sometimes apocalyptic in character; third, a reaction against the harshness of Calvinistic double predestination, often by converts to Calvinism; and, fourthly, a strong interest in egalitarian political aims, such as the opposition to slavery.

The first form of belief in universal salvation is what Rowell dubs 'purgatorial universalism': a form which stressed the necessity of post-mortem punishment to reconcile all people to God. The second might be called hyper-Calvinism, for it accepted Calvinism's doctrines of predestination and atonement but simply claimed that they applied to all people, not just a remnant.

Liberal humanism and mysticism tended to lead to the first form of universalism. Some Calvinists reacted against Calvinism by turning to purgatorial universalism, others reformed it into hyper-Calvinism. Many members of each group were influenced by and encouraged in their egalitarian political views, for universalism coincided with their instinct that all people were loved equally by God – and should, therefore, by loved equally by their fellows.

A few examples of the more famous universalists will suffice to show the complexity of groupings in this period. Among the purgatorial universalists one finds Elhanan Winchester (1758–1816), author of *Dialogues on The Universal Restoration* (1788).[44] Winchester was American, but made a missionary journey to Britain, founding a congregation in London and converting, amongst others, William Vidler (1758–1816) who took over leadership of the congregation on Winchester's return to America. Vidler and his congregation later converted to Unitarianism, whilst retaining their universalist beliefs.

In the group of hyper-Calvinist universalists one can place James Relly (1722–88), who took Paul's words 'just as one man's trespass led to condemnation for all, so one man's act of righteousness leads to justification and life for all' (Rom. 5:18) to mean that an ontological unity of all people had already been established in Christ, such that conversion to faith was the recognition of this union, not the task of perfecting oneself under fear of post-mortem punishment. Since the debt for sin has already been paid by Christ to God, there would be no punishment after death. Relly's disciple, John Murray (1741–1815) held very similar views: he alleged that Winchester's doctrine of 'purgatorial satisfaction' denied the satisfaction made by Christ. The hyper-Calvinists were frequently accused of antinomianism, that is of believing that that since that were already justified they had no reason to try to act virtuously. Both criticisms were, on the whole, equally ill-founded.

Murray travelled to America and founded the First Universalist Church in Massachusetts and the conflicts between different universalists were repeated on American soil. Murray's writings were criticised by a universalist with an Arminian background, Charles Chauncy (b.1704), who saw Murray's views as 'an encouragement to libertinism'[45] and who defended the idea of reformative punishment after death.

In the early days of universalism in America these sorts of disagreements were minimised because of the smallness of the groups and their main object of defending themselves against their considerable opposition. The next generation, however, was more seriously disturbed by the 'Restoration controversy' (1817 to c.1831) between Hosea Ballou and his Restorationist opponents. The latter were followers of Winchester who defended the need for purgatorial punishment to restore sinners to God, such as Edward Turner (1776–1853). Ballou accused them of paying too much attention to 'Grecian philosophy' and too little to Scripture, and of believing in effect that people could save themselves through virtuous behaviour.[46] Ballou recognised the roots of an opposing type of universalism in Calvinism, but he was far from being a hyper-Calvinist himself. He criticised the whole idea of a vicarious atonement made by Christ, whether it applied to a part or the whole of humanity, and rejected the doctrine of the Trinity. Instead, Ballou argued that God rewarded and punished people in this life, and that after death each individual would be transformed in such a way that all could participate in the kingdom. Ballou's view became known as 'Death and glory' or 'Ultra Universalism' by his opponents. What is theologically very interesting about his view is that it combined a strongly rationalist and Unitarian viewpoint (particularly with regard to the interpretation of Scripture), which had usually been found among universalists of the 'purgatorial' type, with a denial of post-mortem punishment. His case usefully reminds one of the variety and complexity of universalism in this period.

Ballou had such influence that during the controversy some Restorationists left the universalist churches in America, often becoming absorbed into Unitarian congregations. But after Ballou's death the tide turned and by the end of the nineteenth century nearly all American universalists believed in the necessity of some form of punishment after death.

Individual Universalists

The debate on universalism did not just concern members of these congregations, however. It began gradually to be publicly debated in the Enlightenment academy. Because both Christians and proponents of rational religion tended to agree broadly on the issue of immortality, debate focused on the eternity of hell.[47] Philosophers asked whether the threat of an eternal hell was an effective deterrent and, if it was, whether the sort of good behaviour induced by the threat of hell was truly virtuous. They thought that for some Christians a faithful conviction of their own salvation by grace had turned into a self-righteous attitude which assumed that hell existed, but only for other people.[48] On the other hand, there was still, as there had been for centuries, a deep-rooted ambivalence about public discussion of the issue:

> the denial of hell was regarded as subversive, because of its importance as the chief moral sanction. Men were wary of publishing their doubts about hell because of the personal risk involved in admitting to disbelieving in hell, and because of genuine moral scruples concerning the collapse of the fabric of society if such views became widespread.[49]

Friedrich Schleiermacher (1768–1834) was the first really influential theologian since the Patristic period to consider universalism. He had doubts about the traditional notion of hell from a young age, and when he was a mature scholar asked in a journal whether the doctrine of the eternal punishment of sinners could fit with the 'eternal fatherly love of God'.[50] In an appendix on the subject in *The Christian Faith* he argues that the biblical evidence for eternal damnation is inconclusive and challenges the coherence of the idea of an eternal punishment: if the punishment were physical it simply could not go on for ever, he asserts, and if it consisted of the pains of conscience 'we cannot imagine how the awakened conscience, as a living movement of the spirit, could fail to issue in some good'.[51] His assumption is that good punishment is reformatory, bringing with it 'a sharpened feeling for the difference between good and evil'. Eternal punishment would render the state of the blessed imperfect, whether they were aware of hell or not (for Schleiermacher, ignorance would not be bliss[52]). Therefore, Schleiermacher suggests that one should admit the force of the 'milder' view 'that through the power of redemption there will one day be a universal redemption of all souls'. This is, however, by no means a forceful and absolute defence of universalism and elsewhere in *The Christian Faith* Schleiermacher is cautious about making statements about the concept of judgment and the afterlife.[53] It is important, nevertheless, that he steers away from a notion of universalism which involves the idea of the 'sudden recovery of all souls for the Kingdom of Grace' after death, and sees the process of reformative punishment after death in parallel with 'the complete purification of the soul due to the appearance of Christ' and a growing 'receptivity for the knowledge of Christ'.[54] There is much here that reminds one of Origen (whom Schleiermacher occasionally cites) and Gregory of Nyssa. Schleiermacher's views on eternal punishment influenced the ideas of some of his pupils and universalism continued to attract attention throughout the heyday of German liberal Protestantism.[55]

Søren Kierkegaard (1813–55) also had doubts about the traditional Christian concept of hell, and seems to have hoped for universal salvation, despite the pessimistic tone of his theology. He once replied to a question about hell: 'If others go to hell, then I will go too. But I do not believe that; on the contrary I believe that all will be saved, myself with them – something which arouses my deepest amazement.'[56] His hope was based neither on a philosophical system, nor on philosophical objections to the notion of eternal punishment, but on a profound faith in the saving power of Christ.

Hope for the salvation of all was not just confined to great thinkers such as these. Although there were not universalist congregations in continental Europe of the sort found in Britain and America, a hope for the salvation of all people became popular among some groups from Württemberg in Germany which were strongly influenced by pietism. Particularly notable were Johann Albrecht Bengal (1687–1752) and his pupil F.C. Oettinger (1702–1782) and the evangelists Johann Christoph Blumhardt (1805–80) and his son Christoph Friedrich Blumhardt (1842–1919).[57]

In Roman Catholic countries, on the other hand, there was a profound hostility to the discussion of the idea of universal salvation and those who did discuss it tended to be poets or philosophers, not priests or theologians of the Church.[58]

In Britain deep passions were aroused by some debates of the latter half of the nineteenth century. In 1853 F.D. Maurice (1805–72), lost his position as Professor of theology at King's College London, for supposedly affirming universal salvation in the last of his *Theological Essays*. In fact, his beliefs were more complex and tended towards the hope that all might share eternal life, rather than towards strict universalism.[59] A particularly controversial aspect of his thought was his discussion of the meaning of eternity. He wrote: 'eternity is not a mere negation of time... it denotes something real, substantial...'; for him it meant more than simply 'without beginning and without end'.[60] Consequently the expressions 'eternal life' and 'eternal punishment' express something about the *quality* and *nature* of divine life or punishment; they do not necessarily refer to a future or an endless state:

> The eternal life is the righteousness, and truth, and love of God which are manifested in Jesus Christ... to men that they may be partakers of them...[61]
>
> Eternal punishment is the punishment of being without the knowledge of God, who is love and of Jesus Christ who has manifested it.[62]
>
> The state of eternal life and eternal death is not one we can refer only to the future... Every man knows what it is to have been in a state of sin, knows what it is to have been in a state of death. He cannot connect that death with time; he must say that Christ has brought him out of the bonds of *eternal* death. Throw that idea into the future and you deprive it of all its reality, of all its power.... And if you take from me the belief that God is always righteous, always maintaining a fight with evil, always seeking to bring his creatures out of it, you take away everything from me, all hope now, all hope in the world to come.[63]

Further controversy was caused by H.B. Wilson's contribution to *Essays and Reviews* (published 1860), in which he expressed a hope that after death there might be found 'nurseries... and seed-grounds, where the undeveloped may grow up under new conditions – the stunted may become strong, and the perverted restored', so that eventually 'all, both small and great, shall find a refuge in the bosom of the Universal Parent, to repose, or be quickened into higher life, in the ages to come, according to His Will'.[64] Another storm was provoked in 1877 when F.W. Farrar

(1831–1903) preached five sermons on hell in Westminster Abbey: in these he stated that he could find 'nothing in Scripture or anywhere to prove [that] the fate of any man is, at death, irrevocably determined'.[65]

Other writers who took a universalist line included the Anglican Bishop John Colenso of Natal (1814–1883) (who felt that the doctrine of eternal hell was actually a hindrance not an encouragement to mission), the Anglican Andrew Jukes and the Baptist Samuel Cox (1826–1893) – but these men were less influential than Farrar, Wilson and Maurice and provoked less controversy.[66] All three assumed that there would be some sort of purificatory process after death.

The Twentieth Century

Geoffrey Rowell notes a change of tone in discussions of the afterlife after the First World War: in particular there is much more pessimism about the human capacity for evil, which tempers some of the more liberal humanistic discussions of the previous years. In addition, there are several other social, political and intellectual developments which influenced discussions of universalism in the twentieth century. So, for example, while universalists have perhaps always defended their beliefs with an appeal to the incompatibility of an eternal hell with a loving God, this argument was given extra force by those wanting to stress that divine justice is entirely different from human attempts at justice which were shown to have failed so much in that century. Added to this was a familiar theodicy: how else can one explain how God could allow the terrors of the twentieth century unless there is some vastly overriding good outcome at the end of time? Similarly, although some universalism had been stimulated by missionary encounters with other religions (e.g. Colenso), with the breakdown of colonialism and the advent of large-scale emigration from former colonies, Western Europeans have grown more used to the idea of living next to people of other races and religions as neighbours, rather than as subjects. Improved communications through media and travel meant that westerners knew more about other cultures. This raised the obvious question: are good adherents of other religions condemned to hell? In particular, the Holocaust called Christians to reflect on their relations to Jews. The increase of atheism or agnosticism raised a similar sort of question, both in the increasingly secular societies of Western Europe and the Americas and in the politically atheist regimes of the eastern bloc, especially the Soviet Union.

Added to these factors were various changes in scientific understanding. In psychology, an awareness of the complexities of human intentionality and of the influence of the social and cultural environment caused theologians to rethink the notion of choosing God: those who justified hell on the grounds that it was freely chosen were challenged to consider whether there is ever such a thing as a totally free choice. Scientific discoveries about the apparently small niche that human beings occupy both in the vastness of the cosmos and the long evolutionary history of life on our planet have caused many to question the supposed Christian doctrine of the supremacy (or uniqueness) of humanity: instead of talking about the salvation of some humans, should we be talking of the renewal and perfection of the whole universe? This theme has been picked up in particular by feminist and ecological theologies.

Finally, although the idea that all people might be saved was still highly contentious, it was not dangerous to discuss: members of more conservative churches might have faced censure for espousing the doctrine, but they were highly unlikely to lose university posts or to face public outrage. Even the Roman Catholic Church has tolerated the open expression of hope for the salvation of all, provided that the anathematised Origenist doctrine of the *apokatastasis* is denied.

In fact, perhaps the most distinctive feature of twentieth century universalism has been its attitude of hope. Few theologians are so bold as to predict that all people will be saved, although it is notable that analytic philosophers of religion who are universalists usually express their conclusions with more certainty than systematic theologians. This is evident, for example, in the writings of Thomas Talbott and John Hick, whose work is characterised by a clarity and desire for coherence, which tends to result in their affirmations of universal salvation sounding very confident.

Hick discusses universalism in the context of theodicy: how can an omnipotent and loving God allow so much evil?[67] His answer is not just his famous 'Irenaean' view of human development (that it is better for people to grow to moral and spiritual maturity rather than to be created so that they cannot sin), but also that eventually there will be no more evil in the world. Hick argues that this is compatible with the sort of human freedom he advocates in the Irenaean model, because ultimately the sort of freedom that it is important to have is not the freedom to choose who we are (for that is impossible), but the sort of freedom to be able to respond as creatures of God to the God who created us. Ultimately, however much we struggle against him, we will turn to God because he has created us with a bias toward him, which, can be clouded but never obscured by sin. Hick suggests that some people will take a long time to turn to him, requiring long periods of reform after death. His views thus lie broadly in the tradition of purgatorial universalism discussed above.

Probably the most confident of theologians on the question of universal salvation is Jürgen Moltmann.[68] Yet he expresses this hope not through the clarity and logic of the analytic philosophers, but by grounding it precisely in the ambiguity caused by setting the victory of Christ next to the horrors of human sinfulness and hell:

> If we follow the method of providing christological answers to eschatological questions, then in trying to measure the breadth of the Christian hope we must not wander off into far-off realms, but must submerge ourselves in the depths of Christ's death at Golgotha. It is only there that we find the certainty of reconciliation without limits, and the true ground for the 'restoration of all things', for universal salvation and for the world newly created to become the eternal kingdom.[69]

Moltmann's hope is founded on his theology of the cross: because of the crucifixion Christ the all-powerful judge of all cannot be envisaged without also envisaging the desolate Christ who was accused, condemned and died in solidarity with all people. Thus God's justice is revealed not as retaliatory, but rather as creative. The Christian eschatological hope, based on this revelation from the cross, must be that Christ's judgment will put things right, once and for all: hence the last judgment is not about division but it is 'nothing other than the universal revelation of Jesus Christ and the consummation of his redemptive work'.[70]

Another strongly Christological emphasis is found in the eschatology of Hans Urs von Balthasar (1905–88).[71] Just as Moltmann saw

Christ entering a state of God-forsakenness on the cross on Good Friday, Balthasar sees this state of God-forsakenness in terms of Christ's descent into hell on Easter Saturday. By revealing how even Christ entered into the depths of human experience, the cross and Easter Saturday thus ground the firm theological conviction that there are no limits to God's love. For Balthasar, by entering into the worst of hell, Christ brings God's love even into the darkest place so that he can redeem even those who have abandoned God most completely. Balthasar is perhaps a little more cautious than Moltmann: he does not claim that it is absolutely certain that Christ's descent to hell will achieve the salvation of absolutely all humans, for the outcome is dependent on how humans use their freedom. Nevertheless, Christ's descent into hell (plus other scriptural indications of God's overwhelming love) does give Christians the right to *hope* for the salvation of all.

An exploration of this right to hope, and an investigation of the tensions involved in a proper Christian concept of hope feature in the works of two more influential theologians. The thought of the German Roman Catholic theologian Karl Rahner (1904–1984) is pervaded with a profound sense of the mystery of God.[72] The eschatological implication of this is that nobody can predict what God will do – Rahner very consciously distances himself from the determinism he sees at the heart of Origen's theology.[73] The two other foundations of Rahner's eschatology are a belief that something has already been achieved by Christ on the cross – that salvation does not simply lie in the future – and that God communicates himself to absolutely all people. The result of this communication as a universal openness to God which is present (albeit not consciously) in every moment of human life means that our present experience of salvation is one in which we are *constantly* presented with a decision: to choose or not to choose for God. Because this choice is free, we *cannot* predict that everybody will respond with a 'yes' to God: we can neither presume on our own salvation, nor assume that we know what others have decided. This conclusion about the possibility of hell, however, is held in tension with Rahner's belief that Christ has already been victorious over sin.[74] His view is thus more than a vague optimism that perhaps all will be saved although perhaps some will not; rather, it could be summed up as a hope which lies between prediction and paradox: Rahner believes that Christ's life, death and resurrection has revealed God's victory over sin, but he holds this conviction in a world in which the outworkings of that sin are still ever-present.[75]

Whereas Karl Rahner's soteriology is based around decision, the Protestant Karl Barth (1886–1968) focuses on the notion of election.[76] Nevertheless, at the centre of both theologies lies the idea of God as simultaneously self-revealing and yet mysterious – which means that both men refuse to predict God's deeds. Their differences lie in the fact that while Rahner's eschatology tries to elucidate the human response to God's self-revelation, Barth's is more concerned to show how that self-revelation presents itself to us as something which has chosen us: as election. Because of the tradition of Reformed Protestantism out of which Barth was writing, the question of whether he believed in, or hoped for universal salvation has become a very controversial one and has been hotly debated. The problem is exacerbated by the fact that the *Church Dogmatics* was not complete when Barth died and that the remaining volume(s) was to be on the doctrine of redemption. One must acknowledge that Barth consistently denies a systematic doctrine of universalism, or of the apokatastasis – that is, any doctrine which attempts to predict the outcome of God's actions. However, Barth's emphasis on the sheer freedom of God's actions cuts both ways: one cannot limit God by predicting that God *cannot fail* to save all people; but on the other hand one cannot limit him by saying that he *cannot* save all people. Consequently, Barth emphasises that we cannot impose limits on God's love. Furthermore, Barth's rethinking of Calvin's doctrine of election points in the direction of universalism: put very simply, he sees *Christ*, not humanity as the object of election, so that while previous doctrines of election have taken the ideas of election to salvation and election to damnation and applied them to two different groups of people, Barth applies them both to the one, single person of Christ: Christ died for *all*, and that *all* have died in him, whether they know it or not. The expected corollary to this would be that Christ rose for all, and that all will rise in him, but Barth never clearly draws that conclusion. Instead, a little like Rahner, he draws a contrast between the absolute victory of Christ on the cross and the still sinful character of the age in which we are now living.[77]

Postscript

The intention of this chapter has been neither to provide an exhaustive account of all those people who have advocated universal salvation, nor to defend any particular belief by recourse to a close examination of the traditional doctrines of the Church. Rather, my aim has been to show not only that there has been a more or less continuous tradition of universalism within (and on the penumbra of) Christianity, but also that there has been a wide variety of universalist beliefs. So often, a belief in universal salvation is taken to be a uniform thing, motivated by one or two narrow theological aims: on the contrary, this chapter reveals the diversity of contexts and motivations which have contributed to different universalist views. The debate over universalism is thus broader than a simple opposition of 'Origenist' and 'Augustinian' theologies. It is also broader than merely the question of whether all will be saved, for it inevitably raises the questions 'how?' and 'why?' Nevertheless, what is also striking is that most of the writers I have examined, despite their many speculations have ultimately based their convictions on the biblical promises that God wills all to be saved and that in the end, God will be all in all.

Notes

1 For surveys of Origen's eschatology see Daniélou (1995), Chapter 5 and several essays in Crouzel (1990). For a study specifically of universalism see Müller (1958). Gregory of Nyssa's views on eschatology and universalism, together with the secondary literature, are studied in Ludlow (2000), Chapters 1–3.

2 Origen (1936), II:10:6 (a parallel between the fire of hell and cauterising a wound); c.f. Origen (1976–77) XII:5 (surgery) and Origen (1936), II:10:6 (bitter medicine).

3 Origen (1976–77), 4; see also Origen (1936), II:5:3.

4 [Its influence can be seen in Talbott's version of universalism – The Editors].

5 Origen held that after death the just would be educated further towards perfection in 'schools for souls' (1936, II:11:6); those who had not turned to God in their lifetimes would undergo painful but finite punishment (Ibid., I:6:3–4, Ibid., III:6:5). Gregory of Nyssa emphasises the latter idea (1917), p. 48, pp. 82–3 (1988) p. 451; see also Ludlow (2000), p. 34; pp. 82–5.

6 For a more detailed discussion of the development of the term '*apokatastasis*' see Ludlow (2000), pp. 38–44.

7 Daley (1991), p. 58.

8 Gregory of Nyssa (1988), p. 461; see also Ludlow (2000), pp. 77–82.

9 Gregory of Nyssa (1988), p. 444.
10 Gregory of Nyssa (1995), pp. 211–12; *Idem* (1988), p. 461; *Idem.* (1978) Part II, section 82.
11 Daley (1991), p. 58.
12 Ibid., p. 90
13 Ibid., p. 91
14 Ibid., p. 114
15 See E.A. Clark (1992), Chapter 3.
16 Our only evidence of the Synod in Alexandria in 400 which condemned Origen mentions his doctrine of pre-existent souls, not universalism (Ibid., p. 109).
17 Augustine (1931), XXI:17.
18 Pseudo-Dionysius writes of spiritual creatures uniting with God, but not universally: Daley (1991), pp. 183–4.
19 Ibid., p. 190.
20 *Ambigua ad Joannem* 14 (*Patrologia Lingua Graecae* 91:1309c4–11); *Expositio orationis dominicae* (*Corpus Christianorum Graecorum* 23, lines 154 ff).
21 *Ambigua ad Joannem* (PG91:1392c9–d10)
22 *Quaestiones et Dubia* 13
23 *Periphyseon* V:21 & 39
24 Ibid., V:39
25 Ibid. V:39
26 Ibid. V:36
27 On Amalric (otherwise referred to as Amaury of Bène) and the Amaurians see Cohn (1970), pp. 152–6.
28 Ibid., pp. 152–3; Amalric was also condemned by the Lateran council of 1215: Cross and Livingstone (1983), p. 48.
29 Cohn (1991), p. 155.
30 On this movement see Leff (1967), Chapter IV; Cohn (1991), pp. 152–86
31 Leff (1967), p. 310, p. 400.
32 Some versions seemed to suggest that the universal communion with God would happen in the future: see Cohn (1991), pp. 172–73: '…whatever existed was bound to yearn for its Divine Origin; and at the end of time everything would in fact be reabsorbed into God… This doctrine amounted of course to an assurance of a universal, though impersonal salvation; and the more consistent of the Brethren of the Free Spirit did in fact hold that heaven and hell were merely states of the soul in this world and that there was no afterlife of reward and punishment.'
33 Leff (1967), p. 374.
34 Ibid., p. 396
35 Most works on the Cathars are not interested in their eschatology; for tangential references to universalistic tendencies see, e.g. R.I. Moore (1994) pp. 218 ff.; Peters (1980) pp. 125, 130 (on the Albanenses); Costen (1997), p. 65.
36 For a fuller account of Denck's theology and more detailed references to his works, see Ludlow (forthcoming).
37 Cited by Kiwiet (1957), p. 242.
38 Denck, Ziegler, Bader and Pocquet allegedly argued for the possibility of the salvation of demons and several characteristics of radical reformation thought tend in the direction of universalism: G.H. Williams (1962), pp. 832–45. However, further research is needed to determine whether any radical reformers were in fact universalists.

39 Of the following, George Rust was a former pupil of the Cambridge Platonist Henry More; Conway and Van Helmont were friends of More; Sterry and White were associated with the Cambridge Platonists. On this group, and for the sources of quotations, see Ludlow (2000b); D.P. Walker (1964), pp. 104–55.
40 Conway, *The Principles of the most Ancient and Modern Philosophy* (ET 1692), p. 193, quoted by Almond (1994), p. 23.
41 Rowell (1974), p. 40.
42 D.P. Walker (1964), p. 240.
43 This scheme is adapted from Rowell (1971). For further detail on developments in America see Conrad Wright (1955), Chapter 8 and *The Dictionary of Unitarian and Universalist Biography* published online at www.uua.org/uuhs/duub.
44 Winchester also edited a later edition of White (1798).
45 C. Wright (1955), p. 191.
46 Ballou (1849).
47 Rowell (1974), pp. 28–29.
48 See D.P. Walker (1964), pp. 40–43 and Rowell (1974), p. 29.
49 Rowell (1974), p. 29; c.f. D.P. Walker (1964), pp. 4–7. Obviously, many Christians were reluctant to raise doubts about hell because they assumed that Scripture clearly affirmed the eternity of hell; furthermore, a denial of an eternal hell was often linked to a denial of Christ's full divinity (many Unitarians, for example, tended towards universalism). See Rowell *op cit*, p. 30.
50 'Ewige Höllenstrafen', *Theologische Zeitschrift* 1 (Berlin 1819), p. 109, cited in Müller (1964), p. 3.
51 Schleiermacher (1989), pp. 720–2.
52 [editors: this is a precursor to Talbott's argument in Ch. 2]
53 Ibid., §162–3
54 In Ibid., §162:1, p. 714–15
55 For example, the Zurich systematician Alexander Schweitzer and the Dane Henrik Nikolai Clausen: Müller (1964), p. 17.
56 Cited by Müller (1964), p. 17 (my translation).
57 Moltmann (1996), p. 23; Müller (1964), p. 5.
58 See Müller (1964) on France (pp. 12 14) and Italy (pp. 15–16).
59 Maurice (1853), pp. 442–478.
60 Ibid., p. 465.
61 Ibid., p. 449.
62 Ibid., p. 450.
63 Ibid., pp. 475–6.
64 Quoted in Rowell (1974), pp. 116–17
65 Farrar (1878), p. 82 ff..
66 Rowell (1974), pp. 117–18; pp. 129–132; Travis (1980), p. 16; Müller (1964), pp. 9–10. Colenso's views were published in his *Village Sermons* (1853) and his *Commentary on Romans* (1861); Jukes' in *The Second Death and the Restitution of All Things* (1867); Cox's in *Salvator Mundi* (1877).
67 See Hick (1976), pp. 242–261; (1985), pp. 341–345.
68 Moltmann (1996), pp. 235–255.
69 Moltmann (1996), p. 250; *Idem.* (1999)
70 Ibid..
71 Balthasar (1988) and (1990) Ch. 4.

72 For a way into Rahner's eschatology see Rahner (1978a), Rahner (1978b) Chapter IX. For a full study of Rahner's eschatology and his universalism in particular, with detailed bibliography, see Ludlow (2000a) Chs. 4–7.

73 See Ludlow (2000a), p. 142.

74 Ibid., p.143

75 Ibid., pp. 243–248.

76 Barth (1956); *idem.* (1956–1976), II.2, Ch. VII pp. 3–506; *idem.* (1949) sections 17–20, 24 (especially section 20 'The Coming of Jesus Christ the Judge').

77 On this tension, see, for example, Barth (1956–76) IV/2 p. 511, cited by Colin Gunton 'Salvation' in Webster (ed.) (2000), p. 146.

11

Universalistic Trends in the Evangelical Tradition: An Historical Perspective[1]

DAVID HILBORN & DON HORROCKS

Talbott and 'Evangelical Universalism'

Thomas Talbott is a philosopher, not a historian. Even so, it is striking that despite his avowed evangelical heritage, and his professed debt to the 'enduring value' of that heritage,[2] he largely ignores precedents within the evangelical tradition for the universalism he promotes. Of course, many evangelicals would say that this is simply because there are few, if any, precedents to cite – and certainly, the traditional view of universalism and evangelicalism is that they are mutually exclusive.[3] In a historical survey of universalism, Richard Bauckham associated the doctrine with 'less conservative' theologians, and barely mentioned anyone who could be classed as an evangelical.[4] Likewise, while charting the recent growth of more radical soteriologies among evangelicals, Daniel Strange has nevertheless concluded that 'even those evangelicals who are very optimistic about the numbers of people who will eventually be saved still do not believe in universalism; for it is not a matter of degree to move from the belief that the majority of humanity will be saved to a belief that all will be saved, but a matter of kind.' In fact, Strange's assessment of the current scene leads him to declare that he knows 'of no published evangelical who holds to the doctrine of universalism.'[5]

Plainly, however, such assessments beg the question whether there are *any* conditions under which an evangelical who did embrace universalism could continue to be classed as 'evangelical' – and if so, what those conditions might be. We shall return to this question at the end of this paper, but it should be acknowledged from the outset that Talbott himself does not offer a straightforward 'test case' for it, since he seems fairly unconcerned about whether his own belief in universal salvation disqualifies him *ipso facto* from being categorised as an evangelical.[6] Still, in what follows we shall show that from time to time, some who might *on certain grounds* be defined as 'evangelical' have, in practice, held either universalist or universalistically-inclined views. Granted, it will also become clear that the grounds in question, and the precise mode or shade of universalism adopted in each case, may be debatable: as Jerry Root notes, there are 'about as many varieties of universalism as there are people writing about it'.[7] Granted, too, we shall see that opinions differ as to which of these varieties, if any, might be compatible with an authentic evangelical theology. Yet in a book presented as an in-depth study of Talbott's universalist convictions, it would be remiss not to examine ideas from his evangelical lineage which prefigure the ideas that he is now propounding.

Evangelicals and Universalism in the Post-Reformation Period

While there is some debate about whether the *cultural* phenomenon of 'evangelicalism' as we know it today derives directly from the Reformation, from post-Reformation Puritanism, or from the later period of Pietism and revivalism,[8] the basic *doctrinal* pillars of the movement – from justification by faith, through crucicentrism and the priesthood of all believers, to the primacy of Scripture – owe their shape in large part to the theology of the Reformers.[9]

Just as Augustine laid the ground for the anathematising of universalism at the Second Council of Constantinople (553),[10] the magisterial Reformers revealed their own considerable debt to Augustine when they repudiated universalism in no uncertain terms. For Luther in particular, universalism represented an offence against the key principle of justification by faith alone. Without such justification by faith, he was adamant that it would be impossible for anyone to escape 'sin, death [and] hell.'[11] Inasmuch as it had located salvation in cosmic restitution rather than the victory of Christ on the cross, the universalism systematised in the third century by Origen in his doctrine of *apokatastasis* contrasted starkly with Luther's theological foundations. Calvin's rejection of universal salvation took a somewhat different form, but the contrast was equally sharp. For the French Reformer, it denied that biblical process of election whereby God had chosen Israel from among the nations under the old dispensation, and had decreed in the new that only some would be chosen for everlasting bliss, with others eternally predestined to hell.[12]

In noting all this, however, we should remember that the Reformation had a radical as well as a magisterial wing. This radical wing, as represented by the Anabaptists, was characterised by an ecclesiology centred on the idea of the church as a covenanting community of the faithful.[13] On the whole, this ecclesiology went hand-in-hand with the doctrine that only some, and not all, would be saved. Yet it was on the fringes of the same radical Reformation that universalism would re-emerge as a force to be reckoned with.

The South German Anabaptist Hans Denck (c.1495–1527) not only opposed paedobaptism: even before he formally joined the Anabaptist movement he was imprisoned at Schwyz in 1525 for promoting the Origenist doctrine that at the Last Judgement even Satan will be spared. Later the same year, he was reported to have disturbed the moderate Swiss Anabaptists of St Gall with the same doctrine.[14] By 1526 Denck moved to Augsburg, where tradition has it that he was baptised by the Anabaptist leader Balthasaar Hübmaier. Hübmaier himself never embraced universalism, but does seem to have been more generally influenced by Denck's emphasis on the universality of God's salvific will, and by his commensurate stress on the freedom of all to choose salvation.[15] On some assessments, indeed, this is closer to what Denck himself actually taught.[16]

As it turned out, Denck's soteriology failed in any decisive way to penetrate those Mennonite and Hutterite movements which would subsequently develop as the main strands of Anabaptism. Traces of it did, however, resurface in the mystical writings of the German Lutheran Jakob Boehme (1575–1624). Coloured by a theosophical interest in alchemy and astrology, Boehme's work attacked the Reformed doctrines of election and reprobation as incompatible with Scripture's portrayal of a God engaged in universal revelation and renewal.[17] In and of themselves, it would be hard to construe Boehme's idiosyncratic writings as 'evangelical'. Neither is it entirely clear that in the strict, dogmatic sense of the term, he was a universalist.[18] Still, he was read extensively by others who did operate within more structured evangelical contexts, yet who nonetheless extrapolated his ideas into systematic theologies of universal salvation. Thus Peter Sterrey (1613–72), an Independent minister who served as a chaplain to Oliver Cromwell, sought to co-opt Boehme's concepts into a detailed scheme of universal redemption, as did his protégé, Jeremiah White (1630–1707).[19] Like Talbott, both men were driven by an abiding conviction that the God whose supreme attribute is love would not finally withhold that love from any of his creatures.[20] Boehme would have an even greater impact, however, on the Pietists.

Universalism and Pietism

With their irenic spirit and expansive soteriology, it is not surprising that from their emergence in Germany in the mid-seventeenth century, the Pietists included some who were inclined to explore the universalising visions of Boehme – even if they typically declined to infer universal salvation as such from them. Jakob Spener, August Hermann Francke and Nikolas von Zinzendorf certainly drew on Boehme's work.[21] Moreover, prompted by one of Boehme's greatest champions, the English spiritual writer William Law (1686–1761), the great evangelical pioneer John Wesley would also go on to study him in some depth. Admittedly, Wesley was far from convinced by Boehme's mysticism, and followed Spener, Franke and von Zinzendorf in resisting his universalist tendencies.[22] Yet Wesley did strongly promote the work of another Pietist who was at least discreetly prepared to embrace universalism – the biblical critic Johannes Albrecht Bengel (1687–1752). Bengel's groundbreaking exegetical study *Gnomon Novi Testamenti* was much consulted and admired by Wesley[23] – but what was less well known was that while publicly upholding orthodox Lutheran soteriology, Bengel privately inclined towards a doctrine of universal reconciliation. Bengel's reticence to publish his views is explained by Helmut

Thielicke as stemming from the conviction that 'not everybody was ready' for such a doctrine: 'If it came into the hands of the wrong person – the person who would construe it legalistically – it would have a devastating effect. This effect would be much the same as that of untimely preaching of predestination. Improperly understood, this too could be taken fatalistically...'[24]

The same tension between private universalism and public orthodoxy was a feature of the moderate German Pietist grouping founded in 1708 by Alexander Mack and known as the New Baptists, or Brethren (now called the Church of the Brethren). Particularly among those of this grouping who settled in colonial America from 1719 onwards, universal restoration was well known. Yet as Donald Durnbaugh notes, it was never officially allowed to be preached, lest it detract from the Brethren's traditional evangelical emphases on conversion, personal sanctification and social activism.[25] Insofar as it was disseminated at all, it seems to have been promoted on the Brethren's behalf by leaders belonging to the more overtly radical stream of Pietism. Here, figures such as Johann Wilhelm Peterson (1649–1727), Ernst Christoph Hochmann von Hochenau (1670–1721) and George de Benneville (1703–93) married a more separatist mindset with more explicitly Boehmist ideas, and were happy on this basis to promulgate final cosmic restoration – a doctrine which, as David Ensign notes, would become a 'major distinctive' of radical Pietism.[26] Another member of this radical set, the German writer George Klein-Nicolai, psuedonymously penned a pamphlet entitled *The Everlasting Gospel* in 1700, which appears to have been taken to America by the first Brethren émigrés, and which was in effect the first universalist tract published in the New World.[27]

If the Brethren formed something of a bridge between moderate and radical Pietism, this role was confirmed by the fact that although Hochmann would later plough his own ecclesial furrow, he worked closely with Mack at the inception of the movement, and drafted a statement of faith which the Brethren used extensively in both Germany and America for several decades.[28] Similarly, while De Benneville was an avowed separatist who went on to emigrate and found his own independent house church in Oley, Pennsylvania, his services nevertheless attracted a wide range of Pietists – right wing, left wing and moderate alike. No doubt, part of his appeal to the more 'evangelical' members of his congregations was his own tireless evangelistic zeal. Confounding the later stereotype that universalists lack motivation for mission, De Benneville insisted on the obligation of any who believe in final restitution to 'proclaim and publish to the people of the world a Universal Gospel that shall restore, in time, all the human species without exception'. To leave people ignorant of this grand divine plan was, for De Benneville, to deprive them of the essential ground, joy and purpose of their life. Hence, as he put it: 'My happiness will be incomplete while one creature remains miserable.'[29] Practising what he preached, De Benneville undertook evangelistic tours throughout Germany, Holland and France, and after moving to America, travelled extensively in Pennsylvania, Maryland, Delaware and Virginia, ministering with particular effect among a number of Native American communities.[30]

A similar conversionist zeal characterised two English universalists who emerged from the archetypally evangelical stable of Methodism. James Relly (1722–78) and his disciple John Murray (1741–1815) reflected John Wesley's interest in Pietism, but unlike Wesley, followed those strains of it which pointed to the final redemption and restitution of all. Wesley's embrace of Arminian soteriology led him to assert that in God's providence all *could* be saved because Christ died for all. Relly and Murray, however, interpreted Romans 5:18 and 1 Corinthians 15:22 to mean that Christ's death had *in fact* atoned for all, and saved all, on the grounds that the universality of Adam's sin in humanity must be matched by nothing less than the universality of humanity's salvation in the New Adam, Jesus Christ.[31] In this, they foreshadowed the treatment of the same Pauline texts offered by Talbott in chapter 5 of his core treatise, *The Inescapable Love of God*, and in Chapter 2 of this present book.[32]

A native of Pembrokeshire, Relly had been converted in the early 1740s under the ministry of George Whitefield. From 1746 he distinguished himself as a leading Calvinistic Methodist preacher across the West and the Midlands. Over time, however, he developed a zeal for the possibility of universal salvation which eventually led to the so-called 'Methodist Disruption' of 1751 – a dispute which compelled Relly to pursue his convictions independently. A sect known as the Rellyites resulted from this, and it was at one of their meetings in London in the early 1760s that Murray, then a Methodist preacher, became convinced of Relly's position – a move which led to his own excommunication from the Methodist connexion. In 1770, Murray emigrated to New England, and at Barnegat Light, New Jersey later that year preached a sermon which paved the way for the establishment of the first church to style itself as explicitly 'Universalist', rather than as incidentally or implicitly drawn to universal restoration – a church which he helped to found in 1793 as the Universalist Society of Boston.

Once officially formed in this way, the Universalist Church appears to have been less inclined to check itself against the doctrinal orthodoxy of mainline Protestantism in general, and of evangelical Protestantism in particular. This turn from orthodoxy was embodied by Hosea Ballou (1771–1852) – a former Calvinistic Baptist who was ordained as a Universalist minister in 1794. Freed from catholic and creedal constraints, Ballou's theological explorations led him, in time, not only to deny the punitive fires of hell, but also to disavow the Trinity, the deity of Christ and vicarious atonement. As Harry Skilton has observed, 'When Ballou arrived on the scene, most Universalists were orthodox in theology, except for their belief that all men would be saved. But his extensive preaching, writing, and training of ministerial students, influenced them towards Unitarianism.'[33] This confluence of Universalism with Unitarianism – culminating as it did much later with the formation of the Unitarian Universalist Association in 1961 – can be seen to account in no small measure for the growing resistance of evangelicals to universalism and final restitution through the nineteenth century.

Universalism and Evangelicalism in the Nineteenth Century

While various seventeenth and eighteenth century universalists came from evangelical backgrounds, and while some managed to remain discreetly within mainstream evangelical churches, universalism itself was hardly seen as compatible with evangelical belief. Indeed, as intentional universalist churches multiplied, and as universalist thought gained influence through the succeeding century, evangelicals distinguished themselves as those most vigorously opposed to incipient universalism, and to the unitarian theology with which it became increasingly yoked. There is not space here to rehearse the many polemics written by traditionalist evangelicals against universalism in the nineteenth century.[34] However, one momentous episode from the history of the Evangelical Alliance illustrates very clearly the depth of evangelicalism's retrenchment on this and related issues during this era. Keen to establish its doctrinal rectitude from the outset, the inaugural conference of the World's Evangelical Alliance in 1846 included a specific affirmation of 'the eternal punishment of the wicked' in its Basis of Faith. This clause was inserted partly in response to universalism, and partly to repudiate the spread of annihilationist views under unitarian sponsorship.[35] Yet in 1869–70 the British Organisation of the Alliance was shaken to its core after one of its Honorary Secretaries, T.R. Birks, published an esoteric study called *The Victory of Divine Goodness*.[36] An Anglican priest, Birks had distinguished himself as a leading opponent of Darwinism. In this volume, however, he argued for a semi-restitutionist view in which those consigned to hell might yet develop some sense of the new divine order, eventually possessing part, if not all, of its glory. Placed under intense pressure after a succession of fraught Alliance debates on the matter, Birks resigned his secretaryship. Even this, however, was not enough to prevent the departure of a significant number of the Alliance's Council, in protest at the fact that Birks was not also publicly censured for his views.[37]

If the 'Birks Affair' typified mainstream evangelical hostility to even quasi-universalist theology during this era, Birks was not quite alone among evangelicals in seeking to apply the benefits of the gospel to those who have died without professing Christ. More positive evangelical responses to universalism were certainly rare, but there were exceptions, and these exceptions are important – not least insofar as they offer pointers to the modern-day debate which Thomas Talbott has joined, and which this book seeks to inform.

Like Birks, F.W. Robertson of Brighton (1816–53) was an evangelical who came to favour a 'remedial' process of purgatorial sanctification over penal retribution – a process which he saw as extending beyond the grave, and which he defended on the premise that 'the law of the universe is progress'.[38] Subsequently, Robertson made a decided shift from his early evangelical context and outlook, towards a more self-consciously liberal position. Yet, as with Birks, he stopped short of actual universalist soteriology: indeed, the full-blown, absolute universalism represented by Talbott today was then still extremely rare in the mainline churches, let alone among evangelical theologians. One evangelical above all, however, bucked the trend.

Along with his friend John MacLeod Campbell, Thomas Erskine of Linlathen (1788–1870) was honoured by the respected Tübingen scholar Otto Pfleiderer for having made the 'best contribution in dogmatics' from Britain between 1825 and the early 1890s.[39] From our point of view, however, he stands out as one of the very few serious, consistent, self-declared universalists of the nineteenth century who nevertheless sought to maintain an evangelical identity.[40]

The development of Erskine's soteriology needs to be set in philosophical context. As the nineteenth century progressed, the ideas of Immanuel Kant, Friedrich Schleiermacher and their followers in Germany, coupled with the increasing impact of Romanticism, slowly began to provoke change on the British theological scene. One manifestation of such change was an increasing sense of moral disgust at the idea of endless divine retribution. Rejecting the Augustinian-Calvinist defence of eternal damnation, Schleiermacher asserted a new eschatology based on the election of all humanity to salvation in Christ. More specifically, he sought to assimilate Platonist, Romantic and pantheist concepts within a doctrine of final restoration which stressed the ability of human beings ultimately to recover from the deleterious effects of sin. In this respect, he effectively further radicalised that 'left wing' German Pietist tradition which had leant towards universalism in the later seventeenth and eighteenth centuries.[41] For his part, Erskine was one of the first British theologians to undertake theological fact-finding tours of Europe following the end of the Napoleonic wars, and it was on these trips that he came under the influence of key German theologians who were following in Schleiermacher's footsteps.[42]

Erskine's theological formation was not, however, exclusively continental. His preferred reading as a youth had included the essays of the General Baptist theologian, John Foster (1770–1843). One of the most intellectually gifted evangelicals of his time, Foster regarded eternal punishment as unjust, and developed a doctrine of progressive universal redemption based on God's unfolding 'education' of all those made in his image.[43] Certainly, Erskine read Foster's Book, *On a Man Writing Memoirs of Himself*, at the age of 17, and realised, as a kind of spiritual awakening, that life was a school, and that education was for eternity.[44]

If Foster was an early inspiration, Erskine's soteriology was also profoundly shaped by William Law.[45] We have already seen how influentially Law championed Boehmist and Pietist thought in the eighteenth century, and have noted his importance as a mentor to John Wesley.[46] Erskine read Law assiduously, quoting from his later mystical works and tracking down his sources – not least in the writings of Boehme.[47] Indeed, having been thus inspired to read Boehme in the original German, Erskine developed a noticeably Boehmist theodicy, which cast the religious life as a universal, moment-by-moment struggle between good and evil instincts, played out in a process of purification and reconciliation with God. This process was presented by Erskine as culminating in the eventual defeat of evil by good, and the victory of God's final purpose. Furthermore, it took on a 'post-mortem dimension', with the journey of salvation continuing for all beyond the point of death. This notion had been present in the early fathers, and especially in Irenaeus. However, it enjoyed a resurgence in the eighteenth and nineteenth centuries, particularly once evolutionary theory had emerged to offer new spiritual analogies for it.[48]

Following Law, Erskine invoked Romans 5:18 and 1 Corinthians 15:22 to argue that corporate humanity should be understood in terms of 'the two heads, Adam and Christ, – each being the head of all men, and therefore all men having a part in each; Adam being the corrupt fountain, and therefore rejected, Christ being the renewed fountain, and therefore elected.'[49] In this, he anticipated Talbott's claim that 'the very same "all" who died in Adam shall be made alive in Christ.'[50]

It is worth underlining that, as with Talbott the philosopher today, it was Erskine's Kantian-inspired search for a satisfactory theodicy in the 1820s and 30s which most compelled him to embrace universal salvation. Furthermore, the fact that in doing so he was prepared to depart from evangelical tradition by projecting the salvific process beyond death, is also pertinent to this book's concern with radical present-day evangelical eschatology, if not with universalism *per se*.[51] One of the more intriguing trends in current evangelical theology is the growing number of evangelical theologians since the 1960s who have either endorsed or seriously entertained the concept of 'second chance' or 'post-mortem' evangelism. This group now includes, at least, George Beasley Murray, Charles Cranfield, Donald Bloesch, Clark Pinnock, Gabriel Fackre and Nigel Wright.[52] With Millard Erickson, we suspect that the group will grow – although whether any of its living members move on to fuse the wider hope which their sympathies represent with actual universalism – as Erskine did – remains to be seen.[53]

In addition to his 'softening' of Scottish Reformed soteriology, Erskine also significantly influenced the later nineteenth century holiness movement – a movement which was steeped in German Pietist thought and peopled by figures with known universalist inclinations. His work was certainly read and discussed by those who attended the landmark Broadlands conferences, which began soon after his death, in 1874, and which continued until 1888. These Broadlands meetings cross-fertilised with the Keswick Convention – an event and a movement that would develop into the major conduit for Pietist and holiness thinking in British evangelicalism through the next century. Erskine's ideas and writings were mainly disseminated at Broadlands by Emelia Russell Gurney and Julia Wedgwood – two key organisers of the conferences who had been strongly influenced by Erskine through many years of close discipleship and visits to Linlathen. Indeed, the spiritual atmosphere of Broadlands reminded them both of Linlathen's 'spiritual power'.[54] Meetings at Broadlands were chaired by the evangelical Quakers Robert and Hannah Pearsall Smith, and hosted by Lord and Lady Mount-Temple (formerly Mrs Cowper-Temple). Although neither of the Pearsall Smiths went on record as universalists, Hannah's sympathy for universal salvation is clear from dialogues and private correspondence published after her death. Like Lady Mount-Temple, she could not believe that a God of love would consign any of his creatures to eternal torture.[55]

Another, more overt universalist in the Broadlands network was Andrew Jukes (1815–1900). Jukes had been an Anglican clergyman in Hull, but had subsequently joined the Plymouth Brethren. In 1867, he published a book entitled *The Restitution of All Things*, which caused controversy on account of its avowed universalism. Notably, Jukes cited both Erskine and Law in support of his position.[56] Like Erskine, he disavowed the notion that 'God can only save men through Christ in this present life.' Rather, citing texts such as John 12:24, Romans 6:3–5 and 2 Corinthians 11:12, Jukes construed death not as a 'point of no return' for the impenitent, but as a potential gateway into a new form of life in Christ. Jukes conceded that these impenitent would still undergo judgement: indeed, he averred that this would consign them to the 'lake of fire which is the second death', as described in Revelation 20:14. For Jukes, however, the fire in question was understood as purgatorial rather than either endlessly punitive or terminally destructive. On this basis, he repudiated both the traditional view of hell and the increasingly popular concept of annihilation for the unredeemed. Furthermore, as a variation on Erskine's post-mortem evangelism, he proposed that in God's restitution of the cosmos, those who have known Christ prior to judgement might, as the 'Firstfruits', minister salvation to those who have not hitherto believed. [57] Jukes had been well regarded by the Brethren for several 'orthodox' works on the Bible, but this somewhat esoteric defence of universalism lost him a great deal of support, and he latterly returned to the Church of England.

We mentioned at the outset that Talbott cites very few historical precedents for his universalist views from within his own evangelical tradition. An important exception, however, is a novelist and spiritual writer who also became a popular speaker at Broadlands: the Scottish Congregationalist George MacDonald (1824–1905).[58] Talbott pays particular tribute to MacDonald's *Unspoken Sermons*, recognising in them a template for his own version of universal salvation. MacDonald also promulgated universalism in popular fantasy epics like *Lilith*.[59] Raised in a strongly Calvinist home, MacDonald was ordained in 1851, and was linked with various evangelicals throughout his life. Later, he was commended by C.S. Lewis, who did not finally embrace his universalist outlook, but who took the epigraphs for his best-selling books *The Problem of Pain* and *The Great Divorce* from MacDonald, and who drew extensively from his insights on the last things.[60] Despite all this, it should be noted that MacDonald was dismissed after just two years in pastoral charge for his unorthodox views.[61]

Evangelicals and Universalism in the Past Century

Possibly the most important conduit of universalistic influence on evangelicals in the past hundred years or so is a scholar who was neither fully aligned with evangelicalism nor finally committed to dogmatic universalism. Karl Barth (1886–1968) is a towering figure in modern theology – widely revered by evangelicals, as well as by others, for his re-presentation of creedal orthodoxy and Reformed doctrinal principles over against theological Liberalism, for his insistence upon the centrality and uniqueness of Christ, and for his opposition to Nazism.[62]

Evangelical scholars continue to debate the nature and extent of Barth's universalist sympathies and whether in this sense his thinking on hell and salvation is compatible with an evangelical perspective.[63] The debate is a complex one, but centres on an apparent tension in Barth's recasting of the Reformed doctrine of election. Barth is keen to redefine the 'double decree' proposed by John Calvin, whereby God predestines certain individuals to heaven and others to hell. Recognising the potentially dualistic and 'arbitrary' strains in this view of election, Barth seeks to reconfigure it by focussing not on the eternal fate of particular human persons, but on the redemptive person and work of Jesus Christ, the Saviour of the world. From the Pauline concept of our being 'in Christ', Barth construes a soteriology in which the Son himself is elected *on our behalf*. As the universal 'elected man', his election is at once both an election to damnation (as he is accursed for us on the cross) and to eternal life (as his death makes atonement for the sin of the cosmos and as he is raised to glory). By concentrating divine damnation on the cross in this way, Barth argues that what appears to be God's reprobation is in fact an act of 'rejecting love'. Moreover, being divine, this act is so pervasive in its effect that there is no 'hiding' from it: all are implicated in the redemption it achieves:

> For in [God's] union with this one man [Jesus Christ] He has shown His love to all and His solidarity with all. In this One He has taken upon Himself the sin and guilt of all, and therefore rescued them all by higher right from the judgment which they had rightly incurred, so that He is really the true consolation of all. In Him He is our Helper and Deliverer in the midst of death. For in the death of this One it has

> taken place that all we who had incurred death by our sin and guilt have been released from death as He became a Sinner and Debtor in our place, accepting the penalty and paying the debt.[64]

While this undoubtedly looks like universalism, it must be understood in terms of an 'objective' change which still calls for a response of faith. What is either unclear, or so complexly wrought that it has appeared unclear to many evangelicals since, is the extent to which Barth understands this faith-response to be decisive in *effecting*, rather than merely *disclosing*, divine salvation for any particular person. Given the cosmic scope of election 'in Christ', Barth is mostly reluctant to envisage the possibility that anyone might either reject it or be rejected from it. At certain points, however, he does appear to countenance such rejection on the grounds that God's all-encompassing love must be a love that liberates people to isolate themselves from his reach if they are insistent on so doing.[65] As Barth sums it up: 'To the man who persistently tries to change the truth into untruth, God does not owe eternal patience and therefore deliverance.' The doctrine of final restitution, or *apokatastasis*, may have appeal in terms of 'theological consistency',[66] but to insist upon it is, for Barth, to risk 'arrogating to ourselves that which can be given and received only as a free gift'.[67]

As Roger Olson notes, Barth has particularly influenced 'self-identified progressive evangelicals who reject fundamentalism and liberal theology', and who have found in the Swiss theologian a way through the Scylla and Charybdis which they perceive these two modes of thought to represent.[68] Prominent among the first wave of these 'progressive' evangelicals were Bernard Ramm (1916–92) and Donald Bloesch (1928–). A conservative Baptist, Ramm spent a sabbatical year under Barth at Basel in 1957–58 and thereafter sought to assimilate his insights into a self-consciously evangelical framework.[69] While upholding not only the reality of hell, but also the validity of preaching it from time to time,[70] Ramm's absorption of Barth nevertheless clearly prompted him to shift from the traditional emphasis placed on damnation by evangelicals:

> Every sensitive evangelical is a universalist at heart. He agrees with Peter when he wrote that 'the Lord…is not wishing that any should

perish, but that all should reach repentance' (2 Pet. 3:9). In perhaps that passage of Scripture which represents the sovereignty of God the strongest – Romans 9 – God's attitude towards Pharaoh is that he endured him with much patience (Rom. 9:22). The idea that God is as much glorified by the damnation of the lost as by the salvation of the saints as held by some Calvinists is hard to reconcile with Ezekiel 18:23: 'Have I not any pleasure in the death of the wicked, says the Lord God, and not rather that he should turn from his way and live?' No person on the face of the earth wants everybody in heaven more than an evangelical. Only an evangelical really knows in depth the meaning of sin, the wrath of God, the reconciliation of the cross, the victory of the resurrection, the tragedy of judgment, and the glory of the New Jerusalem. Every person who fails of this final beatitude can only be of pain to him.[71]

Ramm's implication that hell awaits only those who persistently resist God's call is reflected and intensified in the work of Bloesch. Schooled in Reformed and Lutheran Pietism by a father who ministered in the German evangelical Church at Bremen, Indiana, Bloesch was later profoundly shaped by Barth's thinking while studying at Chicago Theological Seminary in the 1950s. He has since projected Barth's soteriological optimism beyond the grave, into post-mortem evangelization, and even into a qualified form of restitutionism:

We do not wish to put fences around God's grace... and we do not preclude the possibility that some in hell might finally be translated to heaven. The gates of the holy city are depicted as being open day and night (Isa. 60:11; Rev. 21:25), and this means that open access to the throne of grace is possible continuously. The gates of hell are locked, but they are locked from within... Hell is not outside the compass of God's mercy nor the spheres of his kingdom, and in this sense we call it the last refuge of the sinner. Edward Pusey voices our own sentiments: 'We know absolutely nothing of the proportion of the saved to the lost or who will be lost; but this we *do* know, that none will be lost, who do not obstinately to the end and in the end refuse God.'[72]

Another American theologian from the evangelical Reformed community who has argued for the salvation of all but those who intentionally and finally reject God, is Neal Punt. In a series of studies beginning with his 1980 volume *Unconditional Good News*, and continuing through *What's Good about the Good News?* (1988) to *So Also in Christ* (2002), Punt has set out a case for what he calls 'biblical universalism'. Punt's key contention is that all persons are elect in Christ *except* those whom the Bible explicitly confirms will be eternally lost – namely, those who consistently repudiate or ignore God's revelation of himself in gospel presentation, in creation, or in the witness of conscience.[73] As Punt puts it, 'For those who are finally lost, the Bible reveals no other cause than their own wilful, persistent unbelief and sin. For those who are saved, it is God alone who graciously, sovereignly elects and saves them.'[74] In other words, humans cannot earn their salvation – but some humans do earn their damnation. Claiming a precedent in the Reformed dogmatician Charles Hodge, Punt dismisses as unscriptural the concept that anyone is destined to hell solely because of their solidarity with Adam, and the original sin which accrues from that solidarity. Rather, he argues, they fail to 'inherit the kingdom' on the basis of their own 'actual, wilful and persistent sin' (cf. 1 Cor. 6:9–10; Rev. 22:15).[75]

Punt's thesis is perhaps weakest in the area that concerns Talbott most: that of theodicy. Specifically, he appears to leave unresolved the *inevitability* or otherwise of the persistent, wilful sinning committed by stubborn sinners. Is such sinning chosen purely by those few who in doing so deliberately forfeit the election to heaven they once shared with everyone else on the basis of Christ's 'universal' redemption? Or is this sinning foreknown, and/or foreordained by God? Punt stresses that 'no one conceived and born in sin has the capacity within himself or herself to choose the good', and maintains, in true Reformed fashion, that we have this capacity purely as a gift of divine grace.[76] Yet the logical consequence of his position is that this gift must either be ineffective in the case of those who finally reject God, or else actively withheld from them by God in the first place.

The same moral problem preoccupied a scholar whose designation as an 'evangelical' would be tendentious to say the least, but who has been widely read and appreciated by evangelicals. Following his conversion at the age of eighteen, Jacques Ellul (1912–1994) maintained an active involvement in the Reformed Church of

France while pursuing an influential career as a social philosopher and lay theologian – engaged as deeply with Karl Barth as with Karl Marx. Best known among evangelicals for his books *The Technological Society* (ET 1964), *The Meaning of the City* (ET 1970) and *The Politics of God and the Politics of Man* (ET 1972), Ellul also published a testimony called *What I Believe* in 1989.[77] In this credo, he proposes an absolute universalism which, while not presented as 'doctrinally taught truth', is nevertheless at least as robustly asserted as that expounded by Talbott.

For Ellul, the fact that God is love is taken to mean that he 'cannot send to hell the creation which he so loved that he gave his only Son for it. He cannot reject it because it is his creation. This would be to cut off himself.'[78] Quoting the standard universalist 'proof texts', 1 Corinthians 15:28 and John 12:32, Ellul echoes Barth when he argues that while the consequences of Adam's sin must clearly be dealt with in judgement, 'all our teaching about Jesus is there to remind us that the wrath of God fell entirely on him.' Jesus thus satisfied the demands of justice in his death and atonement, thereby overcoming the need for 'a second condemnation of individuals.'[79] Hence, maintaining Reformed language but maximising its reach, Ellul concludes that 'in and through Jesus Christ all people are predestined to be saved'. Furthermore, he anticipates Talbott's argument in Part III of *The Inescapable Love of God* when he goes on to declare that our free choice is 'ruled out' in this regard:

> We have often said that God wants to free people. He undoubtedly does, except in relation to this last and definitive decision. We are not free to decide and choose to be damned. To say that God presents us with the good news of the gospel and then leaves the final issue to our free choice either to accept it and be saved or to reject it and be lost is foolish. To take this point of view is to make us arbiters of the situation. In this case it is we who decide our own salvation. This view reverses a well-known thesis and would have it that God proposes and man disposes.[80]

Echoing these concerns but starting from a rather different position, Jan Bonda's universalist apologia *The One Purpose of God*, was published in 1993. A pastor in the Dutch Reformed Church, like Ellul Bonda owed a significant debt to Barth. His soteriology, however, was less dogmatic than Ellul's, while being far more detailed and careful in its construction.[81] Bonda bases his position on a close exegesis of Paul's Letter to the Romans. For example, Romans 3:29–30 is interpreted as confirming that God means to save all people – not just those who currently believe, but all Jews and all Gentiles. The final salvation of Israel, which Bonda infers particularly from Romans 11 and takes to include Jews who currently refuse the gospel, is, he says, a clear indication of God's universalistic purpose for the world as a whole. Hence the 'coming of the kingdom' in the New Testament is applied to the time when God will draw all – dead and alive – back to himself. Bonda readily concedes the same problems of human freedom and salvation with which Talbott grapples, but unlike Talbott and Ellul, is thereby led towards a hopeful, rather than an absolute universalism – one based on a general rather than a 'limited' model of atonement.

Just as Bonda develops his universalism from a particular text of Scripture, so with the growth of systematic universalist theologies across various traditions in recent years, evangelical biblical scholars have been led to re-investigate the key verses cited in defence of the view that all will be saved. The majority of such evangelical exegetes, from Tom Wright to Howard Marshall, have ended such investigations by reaffirming the traditional distinction between the salvation of some to eternal life and the condemnation of others to hell.[82] A few, however, have been persuaded that certain texts do genuinely point in a universalist direction. Writing for broadly evangelical publishers and having taught and trained at evangelical seminaries in America and England, Andrew Lincoln, although only addressing the issue in passing in his various books, has inclined towards the view that certain biblical texts and themes (e.g. God's surpassing grace) lend support to a hopeful universalism though he is clear that the New Testament does not, in his view, support a dogmatic universalism.[83] Similarly, Richard Bell, a New Testament scholar and priest formed in the evangelical Anglican tradition, has developed his earlier Pauline studies to argue in a recent paper on Romans 5:18–19 that since Paul believes all human beings participate both in Adam's sin and in Christ's 'righteous act', a universal salvation is affirmed there.[84] This is, claims Bell, 'the natural reading of the text and the context supports it.'[85] Indeed, Bell goes on to suggest that these two verses do not bear an isolated witness to universalism: as he puts it, '2 Cor. 5:19 speaks of God being in Christ, reconciling the world to himself [and] Phil. 2:11 says every tongue will confess that Jesus Christ is Lord.'[86] Bell concedes, however, that such universalist teaching is 'clearly at variance' with other parts of Romans – most notably 11:25–32, which implies the condemnation of at least some Gentiles, even while affirming a full salvation of Jews.[87] In attempting to explain and resolve this difference, Bell suggests that Romans 5 offers an a-temporal, mythical representation of the reconciling act of Christ, whereas Romans 9–11 is more immediately focussed on the historical contingencies of Paul's missionary project. Hence, while the earlier text assumes the perspective of eternity, in which God will eventually reconcile all people and all things to himself, the later text is seeking to account for the fact that some of the Gentiles to whom Paul has been sent are *currently* rejecting his message, and is not occupied by whether or not they might eventually be saved:

> ... Rom 9–11 is concerned with the bringing of the reconciling word to human beings through the mission of the Church: Rom. 10:8 speaks of the word which creates faith... and 10:14–18 is about the necessity of bringing the gospel to Jews and Gentiles... Rom. 5:18–19, on the other hand, has as its central focus the reconciling act of Christ (and the act of Adam which brought enmity between God and man). And Paul in speaking of this reconciling act of Christ which brings justification for all does not trouble himself here with the problem as to how the reconciling word is actually brought to human beings. Again, his perspective is mythical rather than historical.[88]

If all this is evidence that certain reaches of evangelical scholarship may be edging somewhere towards his own view, Talbott seems reluctant to acknowledge the idea. As we have seen, inasmuch as he cites 'evangelical universalists' at all, he does so not to commend them, but to critique points in their work at which they fall short of his own more absolute model of universalism.[89] Even Neal Punt is presented by Talbott himself not as an ally, but as a mistaken expositor of the last things.[90] Likewise, Talbott's various articles on universalism for *Faith and Philosophy, Religious Studies* and *The Reformed Journal* during the past decade or so have occasionally referenced work done by evangelicals on the subject, but the sources he quotes there are critical rather than sympathetic to universalism.[91]

If this reinforces the sense that Talbott is not very concerned about *rapprochement* with his own evangelical tradition, it also recalls the central problem which we raised at the beginning of this paper, and which must attend any account of 'evangelical universalism' – namely that for most evangelicals, and for many non-evangelicals besides, the very concept itself is an oxymoron. However conservative a person's background and theological formation has been, the historic evangelical norm is that once that person embraces universalism, he or she *de facto* forfeits any authentic claim to the description 'evangelical'. The same outlook also tends to hold that however orthodox someone may be in other areas, affirming universalism effectively cancels out their evangelical credit, and leaves them short of the doctrinal standard required to belong to the evangelical constituency. In this sense, while those we have cited as 'evangelical universalists' may be defined as evangelicals *historically* and *socio-culturally* in relation to their background, education and church allegiance, many would argue that they cannot be regarded as evangelical in a *theological* sense once they have advocated universalism.

We have already mentioned that while Strange shows modern-day evangelicals adopting a range of positions on the fate of the unevangelized – from restrictivism, through universal opportunity and inclusivism, to post-mortem evangelism – he reports that universalism has no recognised place within evangelicalism's bounds. In this, he is undoubtedly reflecting a broad consensus – a consensus underlined by Gregory Boyd and Paul Eddy's recent study *Across the Spectrum: Issues in Evangelical Theology*. Boyd and Eddy also list evangelical proponents of views stretching from restrictivism to post-mortem salvation, but implicitly bracket universalism off with that pluralism which sees all religions leading to God, and which, as far as they know, is 'universally rejected by evangelical Christians'.[92] In 2000, the UK Evangelical Alliance's report *The Nature of Hell* acknowledged the possibility of salvation for at least some who have not heard the gospel, and while finding 'no convincing warrant in Scripture' for post-mortem regeneration, did at least recognise certain advocates of it to be genuine evangelicals.[93] However, when it came to universalism, the verdict was far harsher – it was not only 'divergent from authentic evangelical faith', but would seriously undermine the integrity of any evangelical who advocated it while claiming still to be an evangelical.[94]

The Alliance report did envisage that some of those evangelical theologians who had embraced 'wider hope' and 'post-mortem' models might in time move further, towards outright universalism.[95] But such a prospect was hardly welcomed. Indeed, it was viewed with a concern similar to that expressed by Millard Erickson seven years previously, when he suggested that the more radical evangelical soteriologies of John Sanders, Gabriel Fackre, Clark Pinnock and others might become routes through which universalism could pass into evangelical terrain.[96] As things stand, however, it needs to be stressed that Sanders, Fackre and Pinnock themselves remain opposed to universalism.[97]

Despite all this, the review which we have conducted here confirms that determining whether anyone might be defined as a *bona fide* 'evangelical universalist' depends as much on what is meant by the term 'universalist' in any particular instance, as on what is meant by the term 'evangelical'. A little before attesting that he knows of no published evangelical who has embraced universalism, Strange tellingly writes: 'I do not believe that "universalism" can be a credible option for evangelicals of whatever background.' He then adds that 'any serious evangelical theologian whose ultimate authority is Scripture, cannot ignore the clear passages which refer to the reality of judgement and hell and the prophetic element which declares that some will never come to repentance.'[98] Hence, when Strange posits his apparently unoccupied category of 'evangelical universalists', he is in fact positing something which, on his very own terms, is at best an abstraction and at worst an impossibility, since to advocate universalism is from his perspective to deny evangelicalism – or at least to present evangelicalism in an 'incredible' or 'non-serious' way. Strange does concede that not all universalisms are of the 'dogmatic' sort represented by Talbott: he defines Barth, for instance, as a 'quasi-universalist'.[99] Yet since Strange also asserts that any 'quasi-universalism' which strongly hopes that all will be saved also 'goes against too much biblical evidence to the contrary', it is unclear from his viewpoint which, if any, of the various more subtle gradations of universalism we have surveyed here, might still be deemed 'evangelical'. Would T.R.

Birks' palliative semi-restitutionism qualify? Significantly, while he resigned as an Honorary Secretary of the Evangelical Alliance, he was maintained on the Alliance's membership roll. What of Andrew Jukes, who wrote many other 'sound' volumes as a member of the Brethren, and even in *The Restitution of All Things* maintained a place for divine condemnation, hellfire, protracted punishment and the 'second death', albeit as means to *apokatastasis* rather than eternal reprobation? What of Punt's 'biblical universalism', which Strange does not mention, but which is clearly far from absolute, and which on his criteria probably would not even pass as 'quasi-universalist'? And what of those – implicitly recognised by Strange when he claims that no *published* evangelicals have embraced universalism – who have yet done so in their lectures, seminars, sermons, dialogues and correspondence? What of Bengel? What of Alexander Mack and the Brethren? What of Hannah Pearsall Smith? What, come to that, of the Scots Congregationalist theologian P.T. Forsyth (1848–1921), whom increasing numbers of evangelicals are claiming as an ally, but who appears at a single place in the whole canon of his work to flirt with the possibility of a final restitution?[100] And what of those several present-day evangelical figures who were identified to us in the course of researching this article as known universalists, but who have yet to declare it formally? Such questions go to the heart of what it means to be an evangelical – and are likely to become more acute if current radical evangelical models of inclusivism, post-mortem evangelism and semi-restitution move closer to universalist soteriologies, as they may well do in the next generation or so.

And what, finally, of Talbott himself? We noted at the outset that his convinced absolutist universalism, and his personal ambivalence about whether he is termed a 'true evangelical' or not, make him a less than obvious model for current universalising trends within evangelicalism. Having said this, his clear regard for Scripture, his focus on personal salvation, and the fact that he has debated his universalist position substantially with evangelical scholars like John Piper, William Lane Craig and those contributing to this volume, suggests that the question of whether that position has antecedents *of any sort* among those who have operated as self-conscious, intentional and persistent members of the evangelical community, is a question which it is both valid and useful to address. In seeking to answer it, we have seen that while universalism is both multi-faceted and particularly hard to discern among evangelicals, some in the past and present evangelical community have clearly been informed and influenced by it. Thus, insofar as Talbott can in any sense still be counted a member of this community, he stands out not because he is the first to have assimilated universalist ideas, but because, as part of a scholarly discourse which is still perceptibly evangelical, he has done so in such an unconditional, unqualified and explicit a way.

Notes

1 Some of the material in this paper is drawn from the Evangelical Alliance report *The Nature of Hell*, Hilborn & Johnston (eds.) (2000).
2 On Talbott's own account of this evangelical heritage see Talbott (1999c), pp. 1–22. See also Chapter 1 of this present book.
3 Among numerous expressions of this traditional view, see Tidball (1994), pp. 151–52; McGrath (1996), pp. 236–40; Dunavant (2000); J.D. Hunter (1987), p. 47.
4 Bauckham (1979).
5 Strange (2002), p. 31.
6 An attitude borne out, for instance, by Talbott's avowed dislike of institutional Christian labels, and by his decidedly unevangelical equivocation in describing the Christian faith as 'one of the principal sources – if not *the* principal source – of moral and spiritual enlightenment in the world.' (1999c), p. 33. Indeed, Talbott's published work does not occupy itself much at all with the question of evangelical identity and its parameters.
7 Root (2001).
8 On this debate, see Bebbington (1989), pp. 1–2; cf. McGrath (1994), pp. 10–18; Strange (2002), pp. 3–7.
9 McGrath (1994), pp. 49–80.
10 Leith (1982), p. 50.
11 Luther, 'Preface to the New Testament', in Dillenberger (1961), pp. 15–17.
12 Calvin (1960), III:24: xii-xvii, pp. 978–87.
13 G.H. Williams (2000), pp. 1289–1311; K.G. Jones (1998).
14 G.H. Williams (2000), p. 254.
15 Ibid., pp. 256–57.
16 Ludlow (2000a), p. 2.
17 Waterfield (1989).
18 Ludlow (2000b), p. 459.
19 White (1779).
20 Ibid., pp. 9–10; Sterrey, Cit. D.P. Walker (1964), p. 111. Compare Talbott (1999c), pp. 200–220.
21 The precise effect of Boehme on these Churchly Pietists is, however, a matter of scholarly dispute: see R.S. Jones (1914), pp. 153 ff; Ensign (1955), p. 21; Stoeffler (1965), pp. 10 ff..

22 Writing in 1752, Wesley reflected: 'The mystic divinity was never the Methodists' doctrine. They could never swallow... Jacob Behmen [aka Boehme], although they often advised with one that did [William Law]'. Wesley, John, Letter to Bishop Lavington (Exeter), 8 May 1752, in Wesley (1931), vol. 3, p. 321.
23 Heitzenrater (1995), p. 188; 'Bengel, Johannes Albrecht', in Cross and Livingstone (eds) (1983), p.158.
24 Thielicke (1982), p. 455.
25 Durnbaugh (1984), p. 9.
26 Ensign (1955), pp. 285–86.
27 Alexander (1987), p. 29.
28 Pierard (1978), p. 473.
29 Cit. A.D. Bell (1953), p. 62.
30 Winchester (1890), pp. 45–49.
31 Relly (1759); J. Murray (1870).
32 Talbott (1999c), pp. 55–80, esp. 56–66.
33 Skilton (1978), p. 98.
34 But see Rowell (1974).
35 Hilborn and Johnston (2000), pp. 63–4.
36 Birks (1867).
37 For a full account of the 'Birks Affair' see Randall and Hilborn (2001), pp. 122–133.
38 Stopford (1882), pp. 155–6.
39 Pfleiderer (1893), p. 382.
40 J.H. Leckie viewed Erskine as an 'evangelical' universalist (as distinct from e.g., 'Unitarian universalists') because his 'larger hope' remained based on the cross. Leckie considered that those who followed him in his belief, apart from the obvious examples of F.D. Maurice, Dean Stanley, and the poets Tennyson and Browning, included George MacDonald, Andrew Jukes, and Samuel Cox. Leckie (1922), pp. 269–72. For more on Erskine's evangelical credentials see Horrocks (2003).
41 Schleiermacher (1989), §5, 18–26; §76. 3, 317; §81. 1, esp. 333; §81.4, 338, §89. 1, 366.
42 Horrocks (2003), pp. 230 ff.
43 Needham (1990), p. 29; Froom (1966), pp. 318–20.
44 Foster (nd.).
45 Horrocks (2003), pp. 180 ff.
46 Stephen (1962), vol. 2I, pp. 331, 344.
47 See e.g., Henderson (1899), pp. 26–30.
48 Developed notably by Henry Drummond (1851–97). See also Bauckham (1979), p. 51.
49 Erskine (1837), p. 305.
50 Talbott (1999c), p. 64.
51 Erskine (1822), p. 91. Erskine admitted that, because from everyday observation the divine process of education into righteousness was not generally evident, it was logically necessary for him to extend the process for an infinite period into post-mortem experience: Erskine (1871), pp. 69–70, 75.
52 Beasley-Murray (1962), p. 258; Cranfield (1954), p. 91; *Idem.* (September 1958), p. 372; Bloesch (1978), pp. 226–28; Pinnock (1988), pp. 165–67; Fackre (1995), pp. 71–95; N.G. Wright (1996), pp. 99–102.
53 Pinnock, for one, strongly resists identification of each doctrine with the other: Pinnock (1992), p. 170.
54 Gurney (1902), pp. 11, 37, 73, 220.

55 See Pearsall Smith (ed.) (1949), pp. 27–28; Erskine's Letter to Mrs Gurney, 14 May 1862, in Hannah (ed.) (1877), pp. 253–4. Of further interest is the fact that John Ruskin, whom Erskine heard and liked, was also a close friend of Lord and Lady Mount-Temple. Ruskin's return to Christianity (though distinctly not of the evangelical variety and involving rejection of eternal damnation) came via a spiritualist séance held at Broadlands in 1875. The apparent link between Broadlands and spiritualism represents a potentially fascinating subject for investigation – though not one, of course, which is likely to enhance its historic evangelical credentials! See Erskine's Letter to Mrs Burnett, 9 November 1853, Hannah (ed.) (1877), p. 82; also Akin (1982). On Broadlands and its influence generally, see Bebbington (1989), pp. 170–71; also Price & Randall (2000), pp. 21 ff..

56 Jukes (1976), p. 190.

57 Ibid..

58 MacDonald travelled to Linlathen especially to meet Erskine, who approved of his work. See letters from Erskine to MacDonald (undated) in Beinecke Rare Book and Manuscript Library, Yale University: General *MSS* 103, Box No.2, Folder No.68.

59 Talbott (1999c), pp. 12–15; MacDonald (1886); (1971); Hein (1999).

60 Lewis (1944a); (1946).

61 For further detail, see Hein (1999).

62 Callahan (2001), pp. 143 ff.; Olson (1999), p. 589; Marsden (1991), pp. 200–201.

63 For discussion of this debate see Colwell (1992), pp. 139–60. See also Bromiley (1979), pp. 97 ff.; Berkouwer (1956), pp. 290 ff; *idem.* (1972), pp. 390; Bloesch (1979), pp. 224 ff.; Carson (1996), pp. 143–44.

64 Barth (1956–76), vol. III, p. 613.

65 Ibid., pp. 186 ff., 602–40. For more detail on this see Colwell (1992), pp. 146–60.

66 [editors: Crisp (unpublished) argues that if Barth were consistent he would have embraced dogmatic universalism]

67 Barth (1956–76) vol IV.3, p. 477.

68 Olson (1999), p. 589.

69 For a biography and review of Ramm's work, and a discussion of the influence of Barth on his thought, see Vanhoozer (1993), pp. 290–306. Also Erickson (1997), pp. 23–28.

70 Ramm (1973), p. 72.

71 Ibid., pp. 136–37.

72 Bloesch (1979), pp. 226–28. For another 'progressive' evangelical similarly influenced by Barth, see Quebedeaux (1978), p. 152.

73 Punt (2002), p. 83.

74 Punt (1988), p. 44.

75 Punt (2002), p. 83; (1988), pp. 3–4. Cf. Hodge (1888), p. 26.

76 Punt (2002), pp. 60–61.

77 [editors: for a full exposition of Ellul's theology and how his universalism is located within it see Goddard (2002)].

78 Ellul (1989), pp. 189–90.

79 Ibid., pp. 190.

80 Ibid., pp. 191; Talbott (1999c), pp. 181–99.

81 Bonda (1998).

82 N.T. Wright (1979), pp. 55–58; I.H. Marshall (2000), pp. 17–30.

83 Lincoln (1991); (1990), pp. 32–44. See also, Lincoln & Wedderburn (1993). Regarding the hell passages Lincoln writes: 'They are there and we cannot change

them. We can try to explain how they function rhetorically but it seems to me more important theologically for us to talk about how Christ experienced hell for us and what the implications of this might be. I think that in the end taking hell seriously means taking judgment seriously. And again the cross shows how seriously God takes judgment and that the judge who is judged is for us. There mercy and judgment have met in a way that must continue to be decisive for God's purposes for humanity. Barth maintained a holy agnosticism about universalism, because he didn't want people to impose their theological logic on God or derive some right to salvation from God's mercy and grace. He insisted a merciful God need not choose a single person, let alone all humanity. But one might then also say, since God has in fact chosen at least a single individual, why not hope that God will also choose all humanity? For those who have not exercised faith in this life, I would add, it is possible to think that, rather than enduring some unspecified period in hell, they would experience God's merciful judgment of purifying light in Christ at the end of history more instantaneously' (personal email to the editors dated 22/10/2002).

84 R. Bell (2002a), p. 417.

85 Ibid., p. 427.

86 Ibid., p. 429.

87 Ibid., p. 430.

88 Ibid., p. 431.

89 Talbott (1999c), pp. 60, 77, 119, 205, 206; Punt (1980).

90 Talbott (1999c), pp. 62, 63, 80.

91 E.g. John Piper in Talbott (1983); William Lane Craig in Talbott (1992b); Lorraine Boettner in Talbott (1993), p. 157; Michael Murray in Talbott (2001a); Jerry Walls in Talbott (2001b).

92 Boyd & Eddy (2002), p. 179. Discussion of 'The Destiny of the Unevangelized Debate' as a whole is on pp. 178–92.

93 Hilborn and Johnston (2000), pp. 89–92.

94 Ibid., pp. 32, 131.

95 Ibid., p. 34.

96 Erickson (1993), pp. 150–52.

97 For relevant disavowals, see Sanders (1994), pp. 106–115; Fackre (1995), p. 95; Pinnock & Brow (1994), p. 89.

98 Strange (2002), p. 31.

99 Ibid., pp. 31–32.

100 Forsyth (1957), p. 161. Elsewhere, however, Forsyth suggests that this possibility must be left unresolved: Forsyth (1965), p. 161. For commentary on this matter, compare Duthie (1961), p. 161; Hunter (1974), pp. 117–24; I.H. Marshall (2000), p. 24–25, n. 14.

PART VI

Talbott's Reply to his Interlocutors

12

Reply to my Critics

THOMAS TALBOTT

I need more space than I now have just to thank all of my respondents adequately. Thanks to their efforts, this volume fills a void in current theological discussion, particularly within the evangelical Christian tradition. Indeed, even if the doctrine of universal reconciliation should be tragically false, as some of my critics believe, a need for a volume such as this one would still exist. For though most Christians have a fairly clear idea of how the Augustinians put theological ideas together and a fairly clear idea of how the Arminians put theological ideas together, few have any clear idea, so I have found, of how the universalists put theological ideas together.

So I extend my heartfelt thanks to critics Jerry Walls and John Sanders for expressing their concerns about free will so powerfully, to Howard Marshall for setting forth his biblical argument against universalism so vigorously, and to Daniel Strange for explaining the essentials of Calvinistic theology so earnestly. Given my severe space limitations in this concluding chapter, I cannot address all of the concerns that these critics have raised. But on a few issues anyway, I shall have the 'final' word as far as this particular volume is concerned. I would therefore urge all readers not only to consider carefully how my critics might reply to anything I say here, but also to seek out additional replies in the relevant literature. For the exchanges here merely introduce some of the issues that each of us should try to think through carefully for ourselves.

As for Eric Reitan's survey of some of the philosophical discussion and his critique of freewill theodicies of hell, I can think of nothing to say except 'Bravo!' I would urge any reader who wonders how one might square so-called libertarian free will with the *certainty* of universal reconciliation to read his chapter carefully. I must also thank Tom Johnson for his fair minded weighing of the biblical evidence and for his unwillingness to close off options prematurely, Morwenna Ludlow for her scholarly historical survey of universalism in Christian theology, and both David Hilborn and Don Horrocks for pointing to universalistic themes within the evangelical Christian tradition.[1] For obvious reasons, I shall have to concentrate most of my own efforts here replying to my critics, but I could not possibly overemphasize how much I appreciate the contributions of those who are less critical as well.

Finally, I must also thank our editors, Chris Partridge and Robin Parry, for their exceptionally fine work in putting this volume together. Robin Parry, with whom I have coordinated most of my own efforts, seems to have read almost everything relevant to our topic, at least on the biblical studies side, and he has called to my attention lots of material that I would otherwise have ignored. So thank you Chris and Robin for making this volume possible and for contributing so much to it.

Sharpening the Issue

Consider again the inconsistent set of propositions with which we began:

1 God's redemptive love extends to all human sinners equally in the sense that he sincerely wills or desires the redemption of each one of them.
2 Because no one can finally defeat God's redemptive love or resist it forever, God will triumph in the end and successfully accomplish the redemption of everyone whose redemption he sincerely wills or desires.
3 Some human sinners will never be redeemed but will instead be separated from God forever.

Because at least one of these propositions is false, anyone who accepts (3) must reject either (1) or (2); that is, anyone who accepts the traditional understanding of hell must either deny that God wills (desires) the redemption of all human beings or deny that he will successfully accomplish his will in this matter.[2]

Now on the basis of such texts as John 3:16, 1 Timothy 2:4, and 2 Peter 3:9, Marshall agrees with me that God at least wills or desires the salvation of all human sinners and hence agrees with me that proposition (1) is true.[3] Sanders and Walls also accept proposition (1) – not just tentatively, but with strong conviction. Sanders thus writes: 'with other Arminians I affirm that God intends to save everyone and reject the view that God eternally decreed specific individuals to damnation…'[4] And Walls is likewise most emphatic on this point, stressing the extent to which he and I agree on both the nature and the extent of God's love for the lost. I concur. Not even his 'hair's breadth' of difference seems to lie between us on this particular matter. For Walls explicitly states that he is 'more certain of (1) than of (3)' and in effect suggests that he would give up the doctrine of everlasting separation before he would give up our shared understanding of God's love.[5] Though he intentionally speaks only for himself here, I suspect that he in fact speaks for all of us who accept proposition (1). We all agree that love is the very essence of God and hence that it is logically impossible for God to act in an unloving way towards anyone.[6]

But on the other side, Strange is just as emphatic in his insistence that God will successfully redeem all of those whom he wills (or desires) to redeem (proposition (2)). For 'God is perfectly free', he insists, 'to have a saving mercy on all if He so desires.'[7] This, together with his stress upon God's freedom in both creation and redemption, suggests that Strange feels even more certain of God's sovereignty in redemption (proposition (2)) than he does of everlasting separation (proposition (3)); I am guessing, in other words, that he would give up (3) before he would give up (2). He also denies, of course, that God so much as wills or desires the salvation of all. So the only insurmountable obstacle to the redemption of all, given his understanding, is God's own 'decretive will'.[8] Because many Christians now find such a view morally repugnant and contrary to their own understanding of divine love, they sometimes fail to appreciate, I suspect, the extent to which the Bible itself affirms God's sovereignty in both election and salvation. When Jesus declared: 'For mortals it is impossible, but for God all things are possible' (Mt. 19:25), he was speaking of salvation in a context where a person's own choices had made it seem utterly impossible, like a camel passing through the eye of a needle. And his meaning was clear: There are no obstacles to salvation in anyone, not even in the most recalcitrant will or the hardest of hearts, that God cannot eventually overcome. That is why, according to Paul, our destiny 'depends not on human will or exertion, but on God who shows mercy' (Rom. 9:16); it is also why the New Testament generally credits even repentance (2 Tim. 2:25), faith (Eph. 2:8–9), and belief (Acts 13:48) to the work of God within. Strange and I agree on all of that.

Accordingly, this volume illustrates nicely the hermeneutical problem that I initially set forth in Chapter 1. It also illustrates why I find some of the prevailing attitudes towards universalism among evangelicals so perplexing. Walls finds 'nothing at all odd about the fact that Augustinians and Arminians each may regard the other merely mistaken, even if profoundly so, while both regard universalists as not merely mistaken but heretical'.[9] But I find this altogether perplexing. One can easily formulate, no doubt, an inconsistent set of three propositions where those who agree, with respect to one of them, that it is true nonetheless disagree concerning which of the other two is false; Walls is right about that.[10] But neither the Arminians nor the Augustinians are in a position to make such an argument. For according to most Arminians, God's love for all and his desire to save all (proposition (1)) is a *clear and obvious* teaching of Scripture, at least as clear and obvious as a doctrine of everlasting separation;[11] and according to most Augustinians, God's sovereignty in the matter of salvation (proposition (2)) is likewise a *clear and obvious* teaching of Scripture, at least as clear and obvious as a doctrine of everlasting separation. So why should either Arminians or Augustinians be any less tolerant of universalism than they are of each other?[12] And why, I ask again, should an assumption about everlasting separation be the only sacred assumption in a context where some are limiting God's love and others are limiting the scope of his ultimate victory? My own reflection upon such questions has led me to conclude that something other than biblical exegesis lies behind the fierce opposition to universalism that we find in the tradition.

Be that as it may, let us now collapse (1) and (2) into a single statement of universal reconciliation:

UR: All human sinners will eventually be reconciled to God.

And let us say that we have *biblical evidence* or a *biblical warrant* for UR if something like the following condition obtains: We have historical and exegetical evidence that certain texts in the Bible either explicitly *endorse* UR or endorse some other proposition *p* that, if true, would itself qualify as evidence for UR.[13] With this (rather rough) understanding in mind, let us now consider the positive case for UR in light of some objections that have been raised against it.

The Theme of Victory and Triumph Revisited

James Packer once tried to dismiss all of the universalistic texts in the Bible with a single, almost off-handed remark:

> All these texts are juxtaposed with texts in the documents from which they are drawn which refer specifically to the prospect of some perishing through unbelief. And unless we assume that the writers did not know their own minds, we have to conclude that they cannot in the texts quoted, really have meant to affirm universal final salvation.[14]

But isn't this an obvious non sequitur? Suppose we replace Packer's second sentence above with the following: 'So unless we assume that the writers did not know their own minds, we cannot suppose that by "perishing" they had in mind an everlasting separation from God.' Such an inference is, to be sure, quite fallacious, but no more so than Packer's own inference. From Packer's premise (about the juxtaposition of texts), nothing whatsoever follows concerning which set of texts should be reinterpreted in light of the other.

Had Packer at least considered how universalists understand the concept of *perishing*, moreover, he might have come to appreciate the position he was criticizing a little better. For, of course, no Christian universalist would deny that we perish through unbelief. But the state of *having perished* (or of 'being lost') is simply that of *not yet having been found*. In the parable of the lost sheep, for example, the shepherd goes after the one sheep *having perished* until he finds it (Lk. 15:4); in the parable of the prodigal son, the father likewise says of the prodigal that, *having perished*, he was found (Lk. 15:24); in Matthew 10:6 Jesus commands his disciples to go to certain sheep in the house of Israel, namely those *having perished*; and in Luke 19:10, we read that the Son of Man came to seek and to save (literally) 'the thing *having perished*.' Perhaps Packer would argue that Paul (or some other writer) used the verb 'to perish' ('*apollumi*') in a different sense from this. But even if he could demonstrate this, which I doubt he could, he would still need to explain how his point about the juxtaposition of texts supports *his* interpretation rather than a universalist interpretation, which is equally consistent with his own premise.

Whereas Packer tries to dismiss all of the universalistic texts without so much as examining them, Marshall appears to accept the standard Arminian interpretation of them. He thus interprets Romans 5:18 in light of 5:17, which 'refers to those who receive the gift of God', and this, he says, 'clearly limits the scope of those who are saved through Christ to those who believe.'[15] According to his interpretation, then, 5:18 implies only 'that all individuals will be saved provided that they believe, and it is left open whether they will do so'. Marshall also points to my own statement that God 'will *eventually* bring justification and life' to all human beings (his italics). That I should slip in the word 'eventually' is a 'telltale giveaway', he suggests, that I have smuggled into the text a foreign idea.[16]

But just what is the force of this supposed 'telltale giveaway'? Romans 5:18 is an ellipsis with no verbs in the original Greek, and the relevant verb in verse 19 must therefore determine the proper tense to be supplied in verse 18. That verb ('will be constituted') is indeed in the future tense. Would Marshall object if I were to interpret verse 19 as implying that 'the many' will *eventually* be sanctified or will *eventually* be constituted righteous? I doubt it. Few Christians believe that sanctification is fully accomplished during our earthly life. So why should anyone object when I interpret verse 18 as implying that all humans will *eventually* be brought to justification and life?

As for Paul's reference in 5:17 to 'those receiving' the free gift, there are two decisive reasons why this could not possibly count against a universalistic interpretation of verse 18. First, as I pointed out in Chapter 2, Paul's affirmation in 5:18 that Christ brings 'justification and life' to all sinful humans already entails that all the conditions of such justification and life will be met. So you cannot challenge the universal scope of 5:18 merely by claiming that verse 17 sets forth a supposed condition to be met.[17] But second, and this goes beyond what I said in Chapter 2, it is nearly certain that 5:17 does not set forth any such condition. For it is nearly certain that Paul was here using the word 'receiving' in a passive sense. In the words of John Murray, the 'word "receiving"...does not refer [in 5:17] to our believing acceptance of the free gift but to our being made the recipients' of it.[18] Indeed, Paul rarely used '*lambanō*;' ('to receive') in the sense of 'to take hold' or 'to accept believingly'. To receive something in his sense is simply to be the object or the recipient of it, as Murray says. We see this clearly in Romans 13:2, where those who *receive* (or incur) judgement are the objects or the recipients of it; they receive judgement in much the way that a boxer might receive severe blows to the head. Similarly, in Romans 1:5 those who 'have received grace' and in Romans 5:11 those who 'have now received reconciliation' are clearly the recipients of these effects in the same passive sense that a newborn baby receives life. My point is not that, according to Paul, salvation is possible apart from belief or faith; far from it. My point is that in 5:17 Paul was merely describing the *effect* of Christ's righteous act upon its recipients, namely all humans, and comparing it to the effect of Adam's disobedience; he was also pointing out that the former is far greater than (and therefore at least coextensive with) the latter.[19]

Accordingly, I still see no way to explain away the clear universalistic thrust of Romans 5:12–21. Neither do I see any way to explain away 1 Corinthians 15:20–28. For, as Tom Johnson points out, the suggestion that in 15:22 'the second "all" does not mean "all", while the first "all" ("as all die in Adam") does, is patently unsatisfactory.'[20] The syntax of Paul's sentence, its parallel structure, and the construction 'For as...even so' seems to me to put the matter beyond dispute, quite apart from any other consideration. Both 'alls' refer to exactly the same group of individuals.

Lest any confusion should arise, however, I should perhaps repeat a point already made in Chapter 2. I not only do not deny, but would also insist, that the second 'all' in 15:22 refers to 'those who belong to Christ'. It refers, in other words, to Christian believers. At any given moment prior to 'the end', both 'alls' no doubt include many who, at that moment, do not yet belong to Christ. But Paul's whole point here, as in Romans 5, is that the 'all' who die in Adam and the eschatological 'all' who belong to Christ both include exactly the same individuals. Why else would he have referred to Christ as the second (or the last) Adam? Even as the first Adam represents the entire human race in its initial corrupted state, so the second represents the very same human race in its redeemed and therefore transformed state. What the second Adam does for every human being is thus equal to and, according to Romans 5:17, even greater than what the first Adam has done.

If any doubt should remain concerning Paul's intention in 15:22, verses 24–26 should, I believe, lay it to rest. For here we read that Christ will turn his kingdom over to God only *after* he has annihilated every competing power and authority and has destroyed the last enemy, which is death. Not one word here implies the annihilation of those *individuals* for whom Christ suffered and died.[21] To the contrary, Christ will destroy all of the cosmic forces inimical to our human interests, including the power of death itself; he will destroy, in other words, everything that might have had the power, were it not destroyed, to render Paul's second 'all' more restrictive than the first. That is why, quite apart from any grammatical consideration, Paul's second 'all' is not more restrictive than the first. Death is destroyed (and all of its bad effects nullified) only to the extent that those subject to death are made alive. Indeed, if death should achieve a final victory in the life of a single person, then that would provide a clear answer to Paul's rhetorical question: 'Where, O death, is your victory?' (1 Cor. 15:55). But the question is not supposed to have an answer.

Finally, consider again Paul's telescoped three-stage sequence in verses 23–24: Christ the first fruits, then those who belong to Christ at his coming, and then the end. At the very least, 'the end' represents the completion of Christ's redemptive work, and the end comes only after death is finally destroyed. So if resurrection (or re-vivification), on the one hand, and the destruction of death, on the other, are logically equivalent concepts in Paul, as they surely are, then 'the end' must represent a third stage, or perhaps the completion of a third stage, in the sequence of resurrections. That is just what the expression 'each in its own order' already implies, and it accords perfectly with the idea that '*to telos*' (the end) represents the final act in the three-stage cosmic drama being described.[22]

The Argument from Silence

Given the hermeneutical problem, as I have described it here, we must all get used to the fact, I presume, that what *we* might regard as a clear and obvious teaching of Scripture, *others* might reject altogether. So let us consider now Marshall's primary argument against UR, which appears to be an argument from silence and appears to rest upon a series of claims about the absence of evidence on specific matters. In his concluding section, for example, Marshall writes: 'There is nowhere any suggestion [in the New Testament] that the final judgement still leaves the door open for repentance.'[23] He repeats essentially the same claim many times throughout his chapter, and towards the beginning he expands upon it as follows: A universalist, he insists, must either 'offer evidence that there will ultimately be nobody' who experiences post-mortem judgement 'or argue that "final judgement" is not really final. It is precisely the evidence for these possibilities which is lacking.'[24]

The form of Marshall's argument, however, has some serious weaknesses. Observe first that a proponent of UR could employ an argument of similar form against the very idea of a final judgement; indeed, I have encountered several universalists on the net who seem prepared to do just that. 'There is no suggestion anywhere in Scripture', they claim, 'that God's forgiveness has a built-in time limit or that the judgement associated with the parousia eliminates every possibility of repentance in the future. It is precisely evidence for this kind of *final judgement*[25] that is lacking.' Of course, Marshall will no doubt reject this latter claim even as I reject his claim (see below). But in a context where one side of a dispute insists that nothing in the New Testament sanctions the idea of post-mortem repentance and the other side insists that nothing there sanctions the idea of a time limit on repentance, neither claim is likely to advance the discussion very far.[26]

Observe also that in many contexts the *absence* of biblical evidence for some proposition *p* is no evidence at all against *p*. As an illustration, the absence of biblical evidence *for* the proposition that sentient races exist on other planets, or *for* the proposition that those who die in infancy nonetheless obtain fellowship with God, would be no evidence at all *against* these propositions. And similarly for Marshall's claim: The absence of biblical evidence for a doctrine of post-mortem repentance would be no evidence at all against such a doctrine. Nor would it be evidence that, according to teachings in the Bible, a time limit on the opportunity to repent exists.

But the real problem with Marshall's argument lies even deeper. For given the logical relationship between salvation and repentance, as Christians have traditionally understood it, and the New Testament teaching concerning post-mortem judgement, Marshall's oft repeated claim that no biblical evidence exists for post-mortem repentance is a simple exercise in begging the question.[27] Suppose we concede, as non-controversial in the present context, the reality of post-mortem *judgement*. Within the context of that concession, we can reason as follows: Any evidence against post-mortem repentance is evidence against universal reconciliation, and, for exactly the same reason, any evidence for universal reconciliation is evidence for post-mortem repentance. Now Marshall sees the relevant evidential relation going in the one direction, and even tries to exploit it; he recognizes that evidence against post-mortem repentance would constitute evidence against universal reconciliation. But he fails to appreciate the equally valid evidential relation going in the opposite direction; he fails to recognize that any evidence for universal reconciliation, such as we find in Romans 5:12–21, provides the very evidence that he claims to be lacking. So in claiming the absence of such evidence, he simply begs the question concerning the correct interpretation of such a text.

It seems to me, therefore, that Marshall has misconstrued some important evidential relationships. The *absence* of a clear statement in the Bible affirming post-mortem repentance would be no evidence at all against such repentance. But within the context of a shared assumption concerning the reality of post-mortem judgement, the *presence* of a clear statement that Christ's one 'act of righteousness leads to justification and life for all' humans could be conclusive evidence that such judgement will terminate in post-mortem repentance.[28] Beyond that, we have additional strands of evidence even in the words of Jesus, as we shall see shortly, and we have that magnificent vision in Revelation 21 of the New Jerusalem with its gates never closing and a continuous stream of incoming traffic. As I wrote in Chapter 3, 'even the kings of the earth, those most vile of all men who had stood with the beast and the false prophet (Rev. 19:19)', are seen entering the New Jerusalem. So from whence do they come? 'Outside are the…fornicators and murderers and idolaters, and everyone who loves and practices falsehood (22:15)'; outside is the lake of fire, the only reality left apart from the New Jerusalem itself. 'But nothing unclean will enter' (21:27), we are also told. So something must happen in the lake of fire to enable the kings of the earth and others to enter the City from the only possible position outside its gates, and that something is surely repentance and a thorough cleansing of a kind that implies a proper relationship with Jesus Christ.[29]

Now Marshall does have a reply to all of this, though it consists of additional appeals to the absence of evidence. If I have understood him correctly, Marshall thinks that, if Jesus himself had believed in post-mortem repentance and in the salvation of all, he would have declared this openly to his friends; and if Jesus *had* declared this openly to his friends, it would have been recorded clearly in the Gospels. 'But there is no hint in the Gospels that he [Jesus] continues to seek out sinners in the next world until he is completely successful.'[30] Therefore, it is unlikely that Jesus believed in post-mortem repentance or in the salvation of all. It is also unlikely that Paul would have held a position at variance with Jesus' own beliefs on this matter. Therefore, it is also unlikely that Paul believed in post-mortem repentance or in the salvation of all.

What should we make of this line of argument? Consider first Marshall's claim that we have no hint in the Gospels that Jesus will continue 'to seek out sinners in the next world until he is completely successful.' Did not Jesus compare himself to a good shepherd who pursues the one sheep 'that is lost *until he finds it*' (Lk. 15:4 – my italics)? This hardly implies that he pursues a lost sheep until it is finally lost forever. So why is this not a hint of the kind that Marshall says does not exist? In one of the very texts that Marshall cites, Jesus declared: 'Truly I tell you, you will never get out *until you have paid the last penny*' (Mt. 5:25). If the one debt that every sinner owes is repentance, as the New Testament consistently declares, then why is this not a strong suggestion of post-mortem repentance, or at least of its possibility?[31] The whole thrust of Jesus' teaching, moreover, pointed in the same direction. He categorically rejected the prevailing understanding of retaliatory justice (Mt. 5:38–42), the prevailing understanding of limited forgiveness (Mt. 18:21–22), and the prevailing understanding of a limited obligation to love (Mt. 5:43–48). Why, according to Jesus, are we to love our enemies as well as our friends? So that we might be perfect even as our Father in Heaven is perfect (Mt. 5:40). Why should there be no limit to our forgiveness? So that we might be perfect even as our Father in Heaven is perfect. Why must we forsake retaliation of a retributivist kind? So that we might be perfect even as our Father in Heaven is perfect. As I see it, then, we have here overwhelming evidence that God, as Jesus understood him, never ceases to love his own enemies, never ceases forgiving them, and sees no ultimate justice in punishment of a retributivist kind.[32] Even while hanging on the Cross, Jesus uttered the words, 'Father, forgive them; for they do not know what they are doing' (Lk. 23:34). His whole life, in other words, revealed the true meaning of his teachings.

Marshall contends further that, according to the prevailing Jewish view, punishment in Gehenna was indeed everlasting.[33] But even if this should be true, it would merely help to explain why so many of Jesus' contemporaries also rejected his teaching in the Sermon on the Mount. The very form of his words, repeated there several times, reveals just how far Jesus had departed from the prevailing pattern of thought: 'You have heard it said…', he declared, 'but I say to you…'. As radical as these words may have sounded to his contemporaries, however, their full import would not likely have been appreciated until after the crucifixion and the resurrection. For Jesus first had to *endure* the cross before its full significance could be *explained* and *understood*. How could he have explained, in a way that Paul was able to explain after the fact, the full extent and nature of his coming victory over sin and death? And how could those who still thought of the Messiah as a conquering hero, rather than as a suffering servant, or those who could not even imagine the Christ hanging on a Cross have received his explanation? When Marshall writes: 'We are left… to hypothesise that universalism was a belief held by Jesus that he did not communicate directly to his friends,'[34] he seems to intimate that, if true, such a thing would be both odd and perplexing. But I see nothing odd or perplexing here at all. Did not Jesus himself declare to his disciples and closest friends: 'I still have many things to say to you, but you cannot bear them now' (Jn. 16:12)? That single statement undermines any argument from silence – or silence in the Gospels – that Marshall (or anyone else) might try to make against UR. None of us can receive more revelation than we are able to bear at a given time, and the things that we cannot bear are usually the most important truths of all.

We may rest assured, moreover, that not even the original twelve could have understood, much less have accepted, an explicit statement of universal reconciliation until after they had contemplated the meaning of Jesus' death and resurrection for a while. Think of the opposition that Paul encountered, sometimes even from Christian brothers and sisters, in his role as an apostle to the Gentiles. To the mindset of the time, the very idea of universal grace was an outrage. When Paul defended himself before a large gathering of his people, they listened respectfully, so we are told, until he declared that he had been called to preach to the Gentiles, at which point 'they lifted up their voices and said, "Away with such a fellow from the earth! For he should not be allowed to live"' (Acts 22:22). So angry were they that they also began 'shouting, throwing off their cloaks, and tossing dust into the air' (v. 23), in effect starting a riot. They no more wanted God's grace to reach the Gentiles than Jonah wanted it to reach the Ninevites. But though Paul countered such exclusiveness by explaining the full significance of a crucifixion and a resurrection *that had already taken place*, Jesus merely hinted that such great events were on the horizon and said nothing about their wider implications. Instead, he lived the life and endured the death that carried these wider implications, and he thus laid the groundwork for Paul's later explanation of them – an explanation that Paul at least claimed to have received from the risen Lord himself.

The Nature of Divine Grace

Christians have traditionally held that, because they are saved by grace, they can take no credit for their own salvation or even for a virtuous character (where such exists). All credit of this kind goes to God. Or does it? Once you postulate a final division within the human race between the redeemed, on the one hand, and those who are hopelessly lost, on the other, an inevitable question arises: Just what finally accounts for this division? According to Daniel Strange and other Augustinians, the explanation lies in the mystery of God's freedom to extend his mercy to some and to withhold it from others. But along with Walls, Sanders, and other Arminians, I reject this explanation, which flatly contradicts, I contend, Paul's explicit teaching that God, being merciful to all (Rom. 11:32), shows no partiality to anyone. So how, then, do the Arminians explain the supposedly final division within the human race? Presumably by an appeal to *human* freedom: *We* ultimately determine our own destiny in heaven or hell.[35] But if that is true, then the redeemed are also in a position to boast, it seems, along the following lines: 'At the very least, some of my own free choices – my decision to accept Christ, for example – were a lot better than those of the lost, and these choices also explain, at least partially, why my character ended up to be a lot more virtuous than theirs.'

So the question I would put to Walls, Sanders, and Marshall is this: Do you really believe that the difference between you and those who will supposedly be lost forever, or even between you and the world's worst criminals, lies in the superior character of your own free choices? For my own part, I can find nothing either in myself or in the New Testament that would justify any such belief as that.[36] I also find it revealing that few first person accounts of conversion sound anything like libertarian free choices. To the contrary, a persistent theme in such accounts is how the Hound of Heaven[37] gradually boxes someone in and closes off every alternative. Even C.S. Lewis, despite his emphasis upon libertarian freedom in other contexts, employed the term 'checkmate' to describe his own conversion and explicitly denied that he retained a genuine power of contrary choice at the moment of conversion. He did say, as Walls correctly points out,[38] that 'before God closed in on me, I was in fact offered what now appears a moment of wholly free choice'.[39] But he immediately qualified this remark with the words 'in a sense' and went on to write: 'I say, "I chose", yet it did not really seem possible to do the opposite.'[40] That he had in mind a *voluntary* choice, but not a libertarian *free* choice, is clear from the following words: 'You might argue that I was not a free agent, but I am more inclined to think that this came nearer to being a perfectly free act than most that I have ever done. Necessity may not be the opposite of freedom...'[41] When Lewis thus described his own conversion, he ceased using the term 'freedom' in the standard libertarian sense.[42] He even described himself as 'a prodigal who is brought in kicking, struggling, resentful, and darting his eyes in every direction for a chance of escape.'[43]

That hardly sounds like someone who could justifiably credit himself for having determined his own destiny. It sounds a lot more like the words of Jesus, as recorded in John 6:44: 'No one can come to me unless drawn [or dragged] by the Father who sent me.' The crucial verb here is '*helkuō*;' and literally means 'to drag', as when a fisherman drags in or hauls in a net filled with fish (see Jn. 21:11). God drags people to Christ by closing off their options and by undermining over time every conceivable motive for resistance.[44] In that way God gradually restricts and then eliminates altogether one's power to resist his grace; and contrary to what Walls represents, I hold that the decision to submit one's will to God – to the true God, that is – is rarely, if ever, free in the standard libertarian sense. It may indeed be the freest of all decisions, given a proper analysis of 'freedom', but it is not free in the standard libertarian sense. For the process that Lewis described – quite correctly, in my opinion – was one of having resisted God at every turn, and at every turn being forced against his will to see some truth more clearly. Then, once he came to apprehend the truth about God clearly enough, all resistance melted away like wax before a flame.[45]

It is important to see, then, that God often corrects us against our will. If I should act upon the illusion that I have the skill to ski down a treacherous slope, for example, a fall and a broken leg might shatter the illusion to pieces. But such an accident would no doubt occur entirely against my will even as it provides compelling evidence, let us suppose, for my lack of skill. Similarly, when God brought all of Hitler's evil plans and ambitions to ruin, that too occurred against Hitler's will and, for that very reason, was probably a source of unbearable suffering for him. So in that sense Hitler may have endured, even during his earthly life, a forcibly imposed punishment for some of his tyrannical actions.

But how, Walls in effect asks, do I square such forcibly imposed punishment with my own 'repudiation of compulsion by physical threats such as the sword'? Why isn't a 'forcibly imposed punishment that produces unbearable misery...the wrong kind of compulsion'?[46] The answer requires two clarifications. First, the 'right' kind of compulsion rests upon the idea of *compelling evidence*, by which I mean (roughly) evidence that both *justifies* a belief and removes one's power on some occasion to reject the given belief.[47] If I experience excruciating pain every time I come into direct contact with fire, that may indeed be compelling evidence that the fire causes the pain. But if a man should torture me in an effort to convert me to his religion, my unbearable suffering would hardly qualify as a good reason, much less as compelling evidence, for believing that his religion is true.[48] Accordingly, if union with God is bliss and separation from him an objective horror, as C.S. Lewis contended, then one would expect the following: The more I separate myself from God, the more miserable I become, on the one hand, and the closer I come to compelling evidence, on the other, concerning the ultimate source of my misery. Alternatively, the more closely I am drawn to God, the closer I come to compelling evidence concerning the ultimate source of joy.[49]

Second, I freely admit that the expression 'forcibly imposed punishment' is misleading, if it is taken to imply a source of misery other than the sin that lies within. In Romans 1, Paul described God's wrath as his giving people up 'to impurity' (1:24), 'to degrading passions' (1:26), 'to a debased mind and to things that should not be done' (1:28); that is, God imprisons people in, or shuts them up to, their own wickedness. God refuses to protect us forever, in other words, from the consequences of our continuing to sin; instead, he forces us to experience (and thus to confront) the life we have chosen to live. Or, as amounts to the same thing, he forces us to endure the very consequences of our bad choices that reveal their true character, and he does so as a means of correcting us. Had Paul stopped writing at the end of Romans 1, we might never have guessed that, in his view, God's wrath is simply the most severe form that his mercy can take. But fortunately, Paul did not stop writing, and in Romans 11:32 he went on to declare that 'God has imprisoned *all* in disobedience [several instances of which are enumerated in Romans 1] so that he may be merciful to *all*' (11:32).

The Appeal to Free Will

Over against the Pauline understanding of divine grace stands the widespread libertarian assumption that, in the words of Laura Ekstrom, 'the agent's good character is ultimately of his own making'.[50] But even if a libertarian could make coherent sense of such an assumption, which seems unlikely,[51] the very idea that one's irredeemably bad character could be of one's own making is, I believe, riddled with incoherence.

Consider first John Sanders' suggestion that 'God will allow some people to be deceived and make an irrational decision for damnation.'[52] According to Sanders, sin is 'fundamentally irrational', 'makes no "good" sense', and is 'intrinsically inexplicable.'[53] But if that is true, then in what sense do we sin *freely*?[54] How could an action be both irrational and intrinsically inexplicable, on the one hand, and truly free, on the other? Suppose that a young boy should irrationally and inexplicably shove his hand into a fire and hold it there, all the while screaming his lungs out. Would we regard such an irrational and inexplicable act as free? Of course not. If we suppose further that nothing causes the boy to thrust his hand into the fire, then his totally inexplicable act is more like a random occurrence or a freak of nature than a choice for which he is morally responsible.[55]

There is a serious problem here. Sanders and other libertarians appreciate why an absolute determinism would undermine moral freedom, but they sometimes fail to appreciate the extent to which indeterminism and irrationality also threaten moral freedom. Note the word 'threaten'. Some philosophers have argued that freedom is incompatible with *both* determinism *and* indeterminism,[56] so that no coherent account of it is possible.[57] But though I think there is a way out of the quagmire,[58] neither Sanders nor anyone else has shown how an utterly irrational decision could qualify as a *free* decision. For freedom surely requires, among other things, a minimal degree of *rationality*, including an ability to learn from experience, an ability to discern reasons for acting, and a capacity for moral improvement.

With good reason, therefore, do we exclude small children, the severely brain damaged, paranoid schizophrenics, and even dogs from the class of free moral agents: They all lack the required rationality. And if, as Walls seems to imagine, those choosing damnation for themselves have no ability to learn important moral lessons and cannot even appreciate the horror of the outer darkness, then they are no less delusional and out of contact with reality than the most delusional of the schizophrenics.[59] Such individuals could not possibly qualify as free moral agents and could not possibly be morally responsible for their actions. Nor does it help to insist that the delusions of the damned are self-imposed. For as Eric Reitan points out (following Marilyn Adams),[60] even self-imposed delusions arise within a context of ambiguity, ignorance, and bondage to unhealthy desire. That some should delude themselves in such a context is hardly surprising. But such self-imposed delusions no more render someone competent to choose an eternal destiny than the self-imposed delusions of an eight year old render the child competent to choose a future career.[61]

Paul, at any rate, seems to have believed that we have no power to save ourselves and no competence to determine our eternal destiny. Isn't that the whole point behind his doctrine of grace? In order to rescue us from our delusions, God must also rescue us from our unwillingness to be rescued, which is itself the product of a delusion. According to Paul, therefore, all of those whom God foreknew – that is, all of those whom he has loved from the beginning – 'he also predestined to be conformed to the image of his Son' (Rom. 8:28). But as we saw in Chapter 3, Paul also showed how free choice and moral effort could play an essential role in the process of reconciliation. For according to Romans 11, the consequences of our bad choices are themselves a means of grace (and a source of revelation); they reveal the true meaning of separation and enable us to see through the very self-deception that makes evil choices possible in the first place. We may think that we can promote our own interest at the expense of others or that our selfish attitudes are compatible with enduring happiness; but so long as we retain enough rationality to qualify as a free moral agent, we cannot act upon such an illusion, at least not for a sufficiently long period of time, without shattering it to pieces. So in that sense, all paths have the same destination, the end of reconciliation, but some are longer and windier (not to mention more painful) than others. Because our choice of paths in the present is genuinely free, we are morally responsible for that choice; but because no illusion can endure forever, the end is foreordained.

Contrary to what Sanders suggests, therefore, God has no need to risk an ultimate disaster in creation.[62] For, however well worn the analogy, it remains as apt as ever to compare God to a grandmaster in chess who permits a novice to move freely, perhaps even allows the novice to 'get away with' some ill-advised moves, and still manages to checkmate the novice in the end. Because God has truth and reality on his side, he can permit his loved ones to choose freely, perhaps even shield them from painful truths for a while, and still undermine over time every possible motive for disobedience. He can do for every other sinner, in other words, exactly what he did for Paul on the road to Damascus and exactly what he did for Lewis when this self-described prodigal was 'brought in kicking, struggling, resentful, and darting his eyes in every direction for a chance of escape.'

The Glorious Truth That Sets Us Free

As the universalists understand it, then, the gospel is truly good news, the best possible news for those in our present condition. It is the good news that Christ has achieved a complete victory over sin and death, that there is therefore no such thing as a hopeless condition, and that the ultimate truth about the universe is glorious, not tragic. However heroic it may initially appear, the idea that God risks an ultimate disaster in creation or an ultimate defeat of his loving purposes seems to me inconsistent with everything that the New Testament teaches about Christ's victory and triumph.[63] I have no doubt that God could, if necessary, foist upon us an elaborate deception and thereby conceal from us the full dimensions of some terrible tragedy. But even if he could deceive us in this matter, he could hardly deceive himself. Nor is such deception compatible with true blessedness or the most worthwhile forms of happiness, which, unlike blissful ignorance, could never rest upon a lie. As Jesus himself declared, it is the truth, not an elaborate deception, that will eventually set us free.

Several critics have argued, however, that God will so transform the redeemed that the fate of the lost will no longer threaten their own happiness; in the words of Marshall, they 'will be sufficiently sanctified that they share the attitude of God towards the lost...'[64] But just what is God's own attitude towards the lost? If, as Strange insists, God never loved them in the first place and never so much as willed or desired their salvation, or if, as Calvin claimed, 'Esau, as yet undefiled by any crime, is [even while still in the womb] hated',[65] then God need only bring the attitudes of the redeemed into conformity with his own. He need only make them as callous as he is, in other words, and cause them to despise – and therefore to disobey Christ's command that they love – those whose sins against God are no worse than their own. But if God's love for the lost is far greater than any human love, as it surely is, then the more our love reflects his boundless love the more we will come to regret the loss of a single loved one. For it is simply not possible both to love someone *even as you love yourself* and, at the same time, to remain happy knowing that your loved one has come to a bad end. You might as well try to remain happy even as *you* come to a bad end yourself.[66]

So here, as I see it, is why Paul so often spoke in terms of corporate wholes, the most important of which is the human race as a whole. Because love is inclusive and ties peoples' interests together, because we are not isolated monads whose salvation is possible apart from the salvation of our loved ones, and because a faithful remnant (or even faithfulness in a single individual) is always a pledge on behalf of the human race as a whole, Paul understood that any worthwhile salvation must incorporate the entire human race. Paul therefore proclaimed the good news that no failure, no deceitfulness, and no lack of faith on our part can 'nullify the faithfulness of God' (Rom. 3:3). God promised unconditionally to establish *his* righteousness in us, and you can bet your life that he will always keep his promises.

Notes

1 Because Hilborn and Horrocks express surprise that I have failed to cite more 'precedents within the evangelical tradition for the universalism' I espouse, I should perhaps reassure them that I truly appreciate having allies within this or any other tradition. I also appreciate the scholarship of Hilborn and Horrocks in pointing out some of the less well-known examples. But unfortunately, some of the older material that should be readily available is hard to find. One of the texts that Hilborn and Horrocks emphasize is Andrew Jukes' little classic *Restitution of All Things*, and information about Concordant Publishing Concern is available at the following URL: http://www.concordant.org. At another web site called Tentmaker you can also download a wealth of older universalist material, including works by Hannah Whitall Smith, J. W. Hanson, Thomas Whittemore, and Thomas B. Thayer. Just go to the following URL: http://www.tentmaker.org, and follow the links to the relevant books in electronic format.

2 Indeed, if Jesus himself accepted the traditional understanding of hell and his beliefs were not blatantly inconsistent, then Jesus also rejected either (1) or (2) above; and alternatively, if Jesus accepted both (1) and (2) and his beliefs were not blatantly inconsistent, then he also rejected (3) and was a universalist himself, whether he explicitly said so during his earthly life or not.

3 Marshall, p.55.
4 Sanders, p. 170.
5 Walls, p. 108.
6 Strange insists that 'God does not have to love all of humanity... for Him to be love' (p. 157). But you might as well say: 'God does not have to believe all true propositions in order to be omniscient.' If it is so much as possible that God should not believe a true proposition, then omniscience is not one of his essential properties; and similarly, if it is so much as possible that God should not love someone, then love is not one of his essential properties either.
7 p. 158.
8 p. 161.
9 p. 108.
10 Indeed, I made essentially the same point in Chapter 1 when I commented that, 'as a matter of logic, there is a possible answer' to my question about heresy. 'For if the biblical warrant for proposition (3) were overwhelmingly greater than that for our other two propositions,' I wrote, 'then one might be in a position to argue that... anyone who wants to escape heresy would have to reject one of the other two propositions in our inconsistent triad' (see Chapter 1).
11 Recall that Walls himself is more certain of (1) than he is of (3), and, as quoted in Chapter 1, Marshall writes: 'The question is not really one of the extent of God's love; that he loves all and does not wish any to perish is *clear biblical teaching*' (my italics).
12 Walls' own example illustrates my perplexity nicely. Suppose that a religious community somewhere should have two respectably orthodox groups, one of which believes that their scriptures *clearly and obviously* teach '(4) Capital punishment is an appropriate punishment to administer for some crimes', and the other of which believes that their scriptures *clearly and obviously* teach '(5) Capital punishment is cruel and degrading'. As Walls points out, the conjunction of (4) and (5) entails '(7) Some crimes are such that it is appropriate to administer cruel and degrading punishment for them.' And a possible retributivist view is, of course, that those who commit cruel and degrading crimes deserve a cruel and degrading punishment in return. It seems to me, therefore, that those who regard (4) as a *clear and obvious* teaching of their scriptures should not regard (7) as any more heretical than (5), and those who regard (5) as a *clear and obvious* teaching of their scriptures should not regard (7) as any more heretical than (4). Why should those strongly committed to the view that capital punishment is cruel and degrading, for example, be any less opposed to the view that capital punishment is sometimes appropriate than they are to the view that a cruel and degrading punishment is sometimes appropriate? And if they are prepared to tolerate the one view as simply mistaken, but not heretical, why not the other as well?
13 It follows that an author might provide evidence for UR even if the author had never thought of UR and therefore had expressed no explicit beliefs about UR itself. As an illustration, suppose that an author should endorse some proposition *p* and *p* would, if true, qualify as evidence for the one substance theory of the Trinity. In that case, the author would have provided evidence for this theory even if the author had no clear understanding of it.
14 Packer (1998), p. 176.
15 p. 65.
16 p. 63.

17 Contrary to what Marshall suggests, Paul's universal affirmation in Romans 5:18 no more leaves open the possibility that, for some humans, a relevant condition of their acquiring 'justification and life' will never be met than the statement, 'All Christians will be sanctified,' leaves open the possibility that, for some Christians, a relevant condition of their sanctification will never be met. I believe that the process whereby we are sanctified involves a lot of hard work and a lot of free choices on our part and requires that a number of conditions be met. But whatever these conditions may be, the statement, 'All Christians will be sanctified' entails that they will all eventually be met.

18 Murray (1960), p. 198. So once again we see that the universalist interpretation of a specific text dovetails nicely with that of either some Augustinian or some Arminian scholar. This time it is an Augustinian scholar. More recently Bell, following Boring, has made essentially the same point in Bell (2002a), p. 429.

19 And even if 5:17 by itself does not entail that the recipients of the two effects are co-extensive groups, 5:18 and 19 explicitly state as much.

20 But Johnson also goes on to suggest, albeit cautiously, that the two 'alls' might be 'compatible if not exactly coordinate' (p. 89). My reasons for rejecting even this cautious suggestion should emerge in my remarks about death below.

21 I presume that Strange and other Augustinian exegetes will agree with me in this: Not one word in 1 Corinthians 15:24–26 implies the destruction of any individual for whom Christ suffered and died. But Strange will simply deny that Christ suffered and died for all human sinners.

22 Against my suggestion in Chapter 2 that 'the end' refers, among other things, to the remainder of those being resurrected, or to those who come to Christ after his return, Marshall points out, even as I did, that the majority of scholars reject such an interpretation. But Marshall nowhere addresses, I think it fair to say, my reasons for rejecting the majority opinion in this matter (see note 25 in Chapter 2). According to Thiselton, such a view as I have expressed 'does not reflect the lexicographical scope of '*to telos*' (2000, p. 1231). But once lexical considerations have established that the end of a play is its final scene, the range of possible endings is almost limitless; and similarly, once lexical considerations have established that '*to telos*' can mean something like 'the final scene in an unfolding drama', the range of possible reference is again almost limitless. So lexical considerations alone could never determine whether 'the end' to which Paul refers in 15:24, or the final act in the cosmic drama, completes the sequence of resurrections, on the one hand, or seals the fate of the wicked, on the other. The context, however, favours the former interpretation and, in my opinion, excludes the latter.

23 p. 73.

24 p. 59.

25 Indeed the term 'final judgement' is not itself a biblical term.

26 In fact, most of the standard arguments against UR suffer from a similar weakness. As a further illustration, consider how Marshall summarizes the case against UR in the following quotation: 'The major weakness in the universalist view is thus that in attempting to explain the few texts which it interprets to refer to the salvation of all people it has to offer an unconvincing reinterpretation of texts about God's judgement and wrath and to postulate an unattested salvific action of God in the future' (p. 73). But of course a universalist might also summarize the case against everlasting separation by simply altering Marshall's words slightly: 'The major weakness in the traditional view is that, in attempting to explain the few texts that it interprets as

teaching everlasting separation, it has to offer an unconvincing reinterpretation of texts about Christ's victory and triumph and to postulate an unattested limit to God's salvific actions in the future.' Once again, neither a universalist nor a proponent of everlasting separation will likely find the other's case persuasive. But it is nonetheless worth contemplating how easy it is, with respect to so many exegetical arguments against universalism, to construct arguments of similar form in the opposite direction. It is a simple matter of learning how to perform the trick. When Marshall suggests, for example, that Romans 5:18 is 'the lens through which' I view 'the rest of the NT' (p. 61), one could reply with the observation that Matthew 25:46 is the lens through which he views the rest of the New Testament. For additional examples drawn from John Murray and Charles Hodge, see Talbott (1999c), pp. 76–80.

27 An argument begs the question when it assumes as a premise the very thing it needs to establish as a conclusion.

28 Marshall claims that the burden of proof lies with those who affirm post-mortem repentance and the salvation of all (p. 73). But in the presence of Paul's clear statement affirming that justification and life comes to all, the burden of proof, it seems to me, is just the opposite of what Marshall claims it to be. If someone should affirm that, according to Paul, those who fail to repent before their 50th birthday will never be saved, then that person must bear the burden of proof; and similarly, if someone should affirm that, according to Paul, those who fail to repent during their earthly lives will never be saved, then that person must also bear the burden of proof. Where, I ask, does Paul say anything remotely like this?

29 See fn 15, Ch. 3. For more on Revelation 21 see Rissi (1972) and Eller (1974), *idem*. (1975).

30 p. 57.

31 Marshall observes, correctly, that one should not allegorize the details of a parable. But the problem is that those from different theological perspectives are rarely able to agree on what the main point of a parable is.

32 People sometimes cite Romans 13:19 in support of the view that, according to Paul at least, God is indeed a retributivist, even though he requires us to give up our own urge to retaliate. For here we read: 'Beloved, never avenge yourselves, but leave room for the wrath of God; for it is written, "Vengeance is mine, I will repay, says the Lord".' But what we have here, in fact, is just the kind of remark that loving parents make to their children all the time. If Suzie should swipe a cookie from her brother Johnnie and Johnnie should retaliate by striking her, loving parents would no doubt instruct Johnnie not to retaliate in that way. 'Leave room for us to work things out', they would say. 'We will take care of it, and we will repay when that is necessary.' Such a remark is no endorsement of retaliation for its own sake; it is instead a way of insisting that punishment should be left to the parents or to those who are wise enough and loving enough to correct Suzie in a way that serves the best interest of all concerned.

33 The remarkable thing is that, as an annihilationist, Marshall rejects, no less than I do, the Jewish view that he here claims to have been current in Jesus' day. For as an annihilationist, he must agree with me that eternal punishment is not an unending temporal process; it is instead a temporal event that terminates in an irreversible state. His remarks about '*aiōnios*' and its correct translation, moreover, have no obvious relevance to the point I made in Chapter 3 – which is that '*aiōnios*' is an adjective and must therefore function like an adjective. As such, its meaning will vary depending upon the noun that it qualifies. An everlasting struggle, for example, may be an

unending temporal process, one that is never completed, but an everlasting change or an everlasting transformation is hardly a temporal process that is never completed. The latter is a process of limited duration that terminates in an irreversible state. So whether eternal punishment is an everlasting annihilation, as Marshall holds, or an everlasting correction, as I hold, it will be an event of limited duration that terminates in an irreversible state.

34 p. 59.

35 According to Walls, it is entirely appropriate to hope for universal reconciliation or even to pray for it. But what point is there in praying to God for something that, in fact, he may have no power to bring about?

36 I have no confidence at all, for example, that in Hitler's shoes I would have fared any better than he did. I had the good fortune to be reared in one of the most loving families that you could possibly imagine. My mother constantly cultivated a sense of empathy in her children, constantly taught us to consider the other person's feelings, constantly asked questions like, 'How would you feel if...' Had I been switched as a baby and placed in a very different home, perhaps that of a white racist family, or had I been exposed to various kinds of physical and sexual abuse as a child, or had I been exposed to the same forces that shaped Hitler's personality, I have no confidence that I would have turned out any better than he did.

37 See Francis Thompson's famous poem, 'The Hound of Heaven', widely anthologized in volumes on English literature.

38 p. 124, note 12.

39 Lewis (1955), p. 224.

40 Ibid.

41 Ibid.

42 According to this conception, a person acts *freely* only when it remains within the person's power, at the time of acting, to refrain from the action; and it is within the person's power to refrain from an action only when it is causally and therefore psychologically possible for the person to do so. In a word, freedom is incompatible with determinism.

43 Lewis (1955), p. 229.

44 The logical form of John 6:44 implies only that 'being dragged' is a necessary condition of someone's coming to Christ, not a sufficient condition. But the verb is also an achievement verb. One does not drag to shore a net full of fish unless the net is successfully landed (see Jn. 21:2); and, in view of John 6:37, it seems clear that God's dragging someone to Christ is both a necessary and a sufficient condition of the person's being brought to Christ successfully.

45 As Walls points out, 'Lewis was committed to following the truth, and previous to his moment of conversion he had already begun to accept, however reluctantly, truths that profoundly altered his thinking' (see p. 124, note 12). But of course the atheist Bertrand Russell also seemed committed to following the truth and was famous for his willingness to follow arguments wherever they seemed to lead. Walls goes on to note: 'Had Lewis not made the decision to be honest with the truth on previous occasions, he would not have felt compelled as he did when the whole matter of God's existence came to a head in his experience and thinking.' But why suppose this true at all? Had Lewis refused to deal with the truth honestly at some earlier time, then for all we know he might have come to a point of crises and have found himself totally boxed in even sooner than he did. See the following section, especially note 50.

46 p. 114. The question is in response to a distinction I drew in 'Freedom, Damnation, and the Power to Sin with Impunity' between two kinds of compulsion. I wrote: 'A sword, as employed in typical cases of persecution, provides no evidence for the belief its wielder seeks to influence and therefore has no power to alter such a belief in some rational way. It typically alters behavior without altering basic convictions. But some freewill theists seem almost as leery of clear vision and compelling evidence as they are of more sinister forms of compulsion.' (2001b, pp. 427–28). See the entire section.

47 So putative evidence for some belief can fail to qualify as *compelling evidence* in one of two ways: either by failing to justify the relevant belief or by failing to remove one's power to reject it.

48 Such torment would, of course, qualify as a good reason for *something* – for trying, perhaps, to escape from or even to kill my tormenter, if I could. Barring that, it might qualify as a good reason to *pretend* to convert. But far from providing a good reason to convert to the man's religion, it might even provide a good reason to reject it.

49 Sanders writes: 'After all, exactly who is it that is standing before God in a state of full knowledge, total wisdom and moral purity? It sure is not most of us. It seems that this would involve God so altering my identity that it would be difficult to know who I am at that moment for I am made like God' (p. 180) But I could just as easily write: 'Exactly who is it that has written Sanders' critique? It sure is not that two year old who used to hide behind his mother's knee!' If I were to take Sanders' remark seriously, moreover, I would have to conclude either that those in heaven will not have 'total wisdom and moral purity' or that they will not be identical to anyone who had previously sinned.

50 Ekstrom (2000), p. 165. For similar statements, see also Kane (2002), p. 72 and Sennett (1999), p. 74.

51 I know of no satisfactory libertarian account of how our free choices supposedly determine our own character. Sanders speaks of 'the culmination of our present libertarian choices' (p.180), but he makes no effort to explain the relevant causal relationships or even to explain what he means by 'culmination', which is by no means clear. The problem is that our free choices too often have unexpected and unforeseen consequences in our lives, and more often than not these depend upon intervening factors totally outside our control. Indeed, a pattern of bad choices may sometimes be more effective than a series of good choices in producing a good character. Suppose, for example, that a person lies and cheats in pursuit of wealth and fame, only to discover that the result is emptiness and misery. If the circumstances surrounding this discovery should causally determine (even compel) a life transformation, as sometimes appears to happen, would such a life transformation be 'the culmination' of earlier libertarian choices? And if not, why not? Or suppose that someone should sincerely cultivate moral integrity and inadvertently produce some of the worst character traits: moral rigidity, self-righteousness, and a lack of compassion. Would this person's bad character be the product of some good choices? Until such questions are answered with some degree of precision, all talk about choosing a character or 'the culmination of our present libertarian choices' is apt to conceal a lot of confusion.

52 p. 180.

53 Ibid.

54 Sanders suggests that not even God can understand the relevant decisions. See p. 180.

55 For we sin freely only when we have intelligible, albeit selfish, motives for our sins.

56 Part of the problem is that indeterminism may seem to introduce an element of sheer chance into the decision making process, and chance seems incompatible with both free will and moral responsibility.

57 See, for example, Double (1991) and van Inwagen (2001). The latter article is extremely important, because van Inwagen has been a great champion of libertarian freewill. But he here concedes that, though he hopes to be proved wrong, freewill (and therefore moral responsibility) appears to be just as incompatible with indeterminism as it is with determinism.

58 Here very roughly is how I now view the matter. As free moral agents, we are not mere extensions of the physical universe, nor are our free actions the product of sufficient causes that lie either in the distant past or in eternity itself. I see no reason to suppose, moreover, that we could have developed self-awareness, or could have become aware of ourselves as distinct from God and from each other, or could have developed a will of our own, in a fully deterministic universe. So perhaps God had no choice but to start us out in a context of ambiguity, ignorance, and misperception, where indeterminism could play a huge role in the choices (or quasi-choices) we make. But indeterminism, however essential it may be in providing a break from the past and from God's direct causal activity, also introduces an element of sheer caprice into the process of deliberation, which in turn severely restricts our freedom. We must therefore distinguish between the role that indeterminism plays in our *creation* as free moral agents and the role it continues to play *after* we have come into being and have begun to interact with our environment on our own, so to speak. As we continue to make choices, to experience the consequences of our choices, and to learn moral lessons for ourselves, our freest choices, provided that our cognitive faculties are functioning properly, are fully determined in this sense: Given our own judgement concerning the best course of action, a contrary choice is no longer psychologically possible. But all of this requires, of course, a much longer story.

59 In fairness to Walls, I should point out that, in his view, the damned do get a sort of perverse satisfaction from their decisive choice of evil and indeed do display a kind of distorted rationality. But Walls does not deny that those who prefer hell to heaven suffer from a 'profound illusion' (p. 120), and neither would he deny, I presume, that schizophrenics also display a kind of distorted rationality. What I fail to see, therefore, is how a 'distorted rationality' that cannot even appreciate the horror of the outer darkness differs from the kind of irrational delusion that excludes moral responsibility. As I see it, no choice made in a context of ambiguity and ignorance, where one could rationally have chosen otherwise, will suffice to render one morally responsible for the illusions and the blindness that Walls attributes to the damned. See Talbott (2001b).

60 p. 134. See also Adams (1993), pp. 313–314.

61 According to many freewill theists, God's hiddenness and a context of ambiguity are essential in order that we might respond to God *freely*. But in fact, these metaphysically necessary conditions of our emergence as free moral agents are also obstacles to full freedom; if anything, they make us *less* rather than more responsible for our failure to love the One whose true nature and very existence supposedly remain hidden from us.

62 As I see it, God draws the line at *irreparable harm* – by which I mean (roughly) harm that not even omnipotence could repair or cancel out. God may risk temporary tragedies of various kinds, but he will not risk irreparable harm. Suppose, by way of illustration, that God should know the following: If he should grant me the freedom

to annihilate the soul of my brother and I should exercise that freedom, then thousands of people who otherwise would not freely repent of their sin would, under these conditions, freely repent of their sin. We might imagine that the horror of such irreparable harm would induce these people to re-examine their own lives. Even so, God could not permit such irreparable harm to occur; an injustice such as I have just imagined (the complete annihilation of an innocent person) would outweigh any conceivable good that God might use it to achieve.

63 According to Walls, my willingness 'to employ the rhetoric of divine defeat when talking about the love of God is cleverly misleading at best.' Why? Because the 'only meaningful sense in which God's love could be defeated would be if he ceased to love those who rejected him and his love turned into hate' (p. 122). But even if Walls has specified a coherent sense of 'defeat', which I doubt, it is hardly the *only* coherent sense. In general, you do not defeat a loving purpose by bringing it about that the loving purpose no longer exists; you defeat such a purpose by preventing it from being realized. Now according to Walls, God wills (or desires) the salvation of all human sinners, but not all human sinners will be saved. So that particular aspect of God's will surely is frustrated and defeated. Indeed, if someone's rejecting God forever does not count as a defeat, why should someone's repentance and faith count as a victory? Or suppose, as is logically possible on Walls' view, that all human sinners should freely and irrevocably reject Christ, despite his best efforts to save them. Would that not count as a defeat? It would hardly count as a victory.

64 p. 60. [Editors: the most detailed defence of Talbott's argument from the blessedness of the redeemed is now Reitan (2002)]

65 Calvin (1960), Bk. III, Ch. XXII, Sec. 11.

66 Sanders suggests that, because there is no marriage of a human kind in heaven, he will have to get used to a very different relationship with his wife. He speaks of 'a kind of divorce' and hints that God may have to erase some memories in order to prevent them from tormenting him (p. 172). We may rest assured, however, that Sanders' future relationship with his wife will be far more intimate, far more honest, and far more loving than is even feasible within an earthly marriage. It will incorporate all of his memories and will be nothing like an eternal separation. Sanders' analogy thus strikes me as delightfully curious, to say the least.

Bibliography

Texts which include a sustained, direct discussion of universalism are marked with a ★.

Some can be found online at www.universalsalvation.net

Achtemeier, P.J. (1996), *1 Peter*, Minneapolis: Fortress Press.

★ Adams, M.M. (1975), 'Hell and the God of Justice', *Religious Studies* 11, pp. 433–447.

★ —— (1993), 'The Problem of Hell: A Problem of Evil for Christians', in E. Stump (ed.), *A Reasoned Faith*, Ithaca, New York: Cornell University Press, pp. 301–327.

★ —— (1996–97), 'Divine Justice, Divine Love, and the Life to Come', *Crux* 13, pp. 12–28.

★ —— (1999), *Horrendous Evils and the Goodness of God*, Ithaca & London: Cornell University Press.

★ Alexander, J. (1987), 'Universalism Among the Early Brethren', *Brethren Life and Thought* 32, pp. 25–32.

Almond, P.C. (1994), *Heaven and Hell in Enlightenment England*, Cambridge: Cambridge University Press.

Anderson, B.W. (1999), *Contours of Old Testament Theology*, Minneapolis: Fortress Press.

Anderson, H. (1976), *The Gospel of Mark*, New Century Bible; R. Clements and M. Black (eds.), London: Marshall, Morgan, and Scott.

Anselm (1938–68), *Cur Deus Homo* in F.S. Schmidt, *Sancti Anselmi Opera Omnia*, 6 Vols., Edinburgh.

★ Atkinson, J. (1967), 'Universalism' in A. Richardson (ed.), *A Dictionary of Christian Theology* Philedelphia: Westminster.

Augustine (1931), *The City of God*, J. Healy, (tr.), London: J.M. Dent, and New York: E.P. Dutton.

——(no publication date given), *Enchiridion on Faith, Hope, and Love*. In W.C. Outler (ed. and trans.), *Confessions and Enchiridion*, Philadelphia: The Westminster Press.

Baillie, J. (1934), *And the Life Everlasting*, London: Oxford University Press.

★ Ballou, H. (1849), 'A Short Essay on Universalism' www.jjnet.com/archives/documents/ballou.htm

★ Balthasar, H.U. von (1988), *Dare We Hope 'That all Men be Saved?'* with *A Short Discourse on Hell*, San Francisco: Ignatius Press.

—— (1990), *Mysterium Paschale*, Edinburgh: T & T Clark.

Barclay, W. (1974), *New Testament Words*, Philadelphia: The Westminster Press.

★ —— (1977), *A Spiritual Autobiography*, Grand Rapids: Wm. B. Eerdmans Publishing Co..

Barker, J.W. (1966), *Justinian and the Later Roman Empire*, Madison: The University of Wisconsin Press.

Barrett, C.K. (1957), *A Commentary on the Epistle to the Romans*, New York: Harper & Brothers.

—— (1968), *A Commentary on the First Epistle to the Corinthians*, Harper's New Testament Commentaries, New York: Harper and Row.

Barth, K. (1949), *Dogmatics in Outline*, London: SCM Press.

—— (1956), 'The Humanity of God' in Barth *God, Grace and Gospel*, J.S. McNab (tr.), Scottish Journal of Theology Occasional Papers, Edinburgh: Oliver and Boyd.

—— (1956–1976), *Church Dogmatics*, G.W. Bromley & T.F. Torrance (trs.), Edinburgh: T & T Clark.

★ Bauckham, R. (1979), 'Universalism – A Historical Survey', *Themelios*, vol. 4, no. 2, pp. 48–54.

—— (1983), *Jude, 2 Peter*, Word Biblical Commentary 50, Waco, TX: Word.

Bavinck, H. (1996), *The Last Things: Hope for This World and the Next*, J. Bolt (ed), and J. Vriend (tr.), Grand Rapids: Baker Books/Carlisle: Paternoster Press.

★ Beale, G.K. (1999), *The Book of Revelation: A Commentary on the Greek Text* (The New International Greek Testament Commentary), Carlisle: Paternoster/Grand Rapids: Wm. B. Eerdmans Publishing Co..

Beasley-Murray, G.R. (1962), *Baptism in the New Testament*, London: MacMillan/ Grand Rapids: Wm. B. Eerdmans Publishing Co..

Bebbington, D. (1989), *Evangelicalism in Modern Britain: A History From the 1730s to the 1980s*, London: Unwin Hyman.

Bell, A.D. (1953), *The Life and Times of Dr George de Benneville*, 1703–1793, Boston: Department of the Universalist Church of America.

★ Bell, R. (2002a), 'Rom 5.18–19 and Universal Salvation', *New Testament Studies* 48, pp. 417–432

★ —— (2002b), 'The Myth of Adam and the Myth of Christ in Romans 5:12–21' in A. Christophersen, C. Claussen, J. Frey and B. Longenecker (eds.), *Paul, Luke and the Graeco-Roman World: Essays in Honour of Alexander J.M. Wedderburn* (JSNT Supp 217), Sheffield: Sheffield Academic Press, pp. 21–36.

★ —— (2003), *The Irrevocable Call of God: An Inquiry into Paul's Theology of Israel*, Tübingen: J.C.B. Mohr Siebeck.

★ Beougher, T.K. (2000), 'Are All Doomed to be Saved? The Rise of Modern Universalism' in P.R. House & G.E. Thornbury (eds.), *Who Will Be Saved?*, Wheaton: Crossway, pp. 83–101.

★ Berkhof, H. (1969), *Well-Founded Hope*, Richmond: John Knox Press.

—— (1977), *Christ and the Powers*, J.H. Yoder (tr.), Scottdale, Pennsylvania: Herald Press.

Berkouwer, G.C. (1956), *The Triumph of Grace in the Theology of Karl Barth*, Grand Rapids: Wm. B. Eerdmans Publishing Co..

—— (1960), *Divine Election*, Grand Rapids: Wm. B. Eerdmans Publishing Co..

—— (1972), *The Return of Christ*, Grand Rapids: Wm. B. Eerdmans Publishing Co..

★ Bettis, J.D. (1967), 'Is Karl Barth a Universalist?' *Scottish Journal of Theology* 20, pp. 423–36.

★ —— (1970), 'A Critique of the Doctrine of Universal Salvation', *Religious Studies* 6, pp. 329–344.

Birks, T.R. (1867), *The Victory of Divine Goodness*, London: Rivingtons.

Blanchard, J. (1993), *Whatever Happened to Hell?* Durham: Evangelical Press.

Blocher, H. (1991), 'The Scope of Redemption and Modern Theology', *Scottish Bulletin of Evangelical Theology* 9, pp. 80–104.

—— (1992), 'Everlasting Punishment and the Problem of Evil' in N.M. de S. Cameron (ed.), *Universalism and the Doctrine of Hell*, Carlisle: Paternoster Press/Grand Rapids: Baker Book House, pp. 281–312.

Bloesch, D. (1978), *Essentials of Evangelical Theology: Life, Ministry and Hope*, vol. 2, San Francisco: Harper & Row.

★ Blum, E.A. (1979), 'Shall You Not Surely Die?', *Themelios* vol. 4, no. 2, pp. 58–61.

★ Boer, M.C. de (1988), *The Defeat of Death: Apocalyptic Eschatology in 1 Corinthians 15 and Romans 5*, Sheffield: Sheffield Academic Press.

Boettner, L (1992), *The Reformed Doctrine of Predestination*, Philipsburg: Presbyterian and Reformed Publishing Co.

★ Bonda, J. (1998), *The One Purpose of God: An Answer to the Doctrine of Eternal Punishment*, R. Bruinsma (tr.), Grand Rapids: Wm. B. Eerdmans Publishing Co..

Borchert, G.L. (1993), `Wrath, Destruction,' in G.F. Hawthorne and R.P. Martin (eds.), *Dictionary of Paul and His Letters*, Downers Grove/Leicester: IVP, pp. 991–93.

★ Boring, M.E. (1986), 'The Language of Universal Salvation in Paul', *Journal of Biblical Literature* 105, pp. 269–292.

—— (1989), *Revelation* (Interpretation), Louisville, KY: John Knox.

Boyd, G.A. & Eddy, P.R. (2002), *Across the Spectrum: Understanding Issues in Evangelical Theology*, Grand Rapids: Baker Book House.

★ Braybrooke, M. (1983), 'Universalism' in A. Richardson & J. Bowden (eds.), *A New Dictionary of Christian Theology*, London: SCM, pp. 591–92.

Brinsmead, R. (1983), 'The Scandal of God's Justice', Parts 1–3, *The Christian Verdict* 6, 7, 8.

Bromiley, G.W. (1979), *Introduction to the Theology of Karl Barth*, Edinburgh: T & T Clark.

Bruce, F.F. (1982), *1 & 2 Thessalonians*, Waco, TX: Word.

Bultmann, R. (1960), 'Is Exegesis Without Presuppositions Possible?' in S. Ogden (ed.), *Existence and Faith*, New York: Living Age, pp. 289–96.

Burd, Van Akin (1982), *Ruskin, Lady Mount-Temple and the Spiritualists: An Episode in Broadlands History*, London: Brentham Press.

Burson, S. & Walls, J.L. (1998), *C.S. Lewis and Francis Schaeffer: Lessons for a New Century From the Most Influential Apologists of our Times*, Downers Grove: IVP.

Cain, J. (2002), 'On the Problem of Hell', *Religious Studies* vol. 38, no. 3, pp. 355–362.

Caird, G.B. (1966), *A Commentary on the Revelation of St John the Divine* (Harper's New Testament Commentaries), New York: Harper and Row.

Callahan, J.P. (2001), 'Karl Barth' in W.A. Elwell (ed.), *Evangelical Dictionary of Theology* (2nd ed.), Grand Rapids: Baker Book House, p. 143.

Calvin, J. (1948), *Commentaries on the Catholic Epistles*, Grand Rapids: Wm. B. Eerdmans Publishing Co..

—— (1960), *Institutes of the Christian Religion*, F.L. Battles (tr.), Philadelphia: The Westminster Press.

* Cameron, N. (1987), 'Universalism and the Logic of Revelation', *Evangelical Review of Theology* 11, Oct. pp. 330–32.

Carnell, E.J. (1959), *The Case for Orthodox Theology*, Philadelphia: Westminster.

Carson, D.A. (1990), *How Long, O Lord?*, Grand Rapids: Baker Book House.

—— (1996), *The Gagging of God: Christianity Confronts Pluralism*, Grand Rapids: Zondervan/Leicester: Apollos.

—— (2000), *The Difficult Doctrine of the Love of God*, Leicester: IVP.

* Cassara, E. (ed.) (1971), *Universalism in America: A Documentary History*, Boston: Beacon.

Ciocchi, D.M. (1994), 'Reconciling Divine Sovereignty and Human Freedom', *Journal of the Evangelical Theological Society*, vol. 37, no. 3, pp. 395–412.

Clark, E.A. (1992), *The Origenist Controversy*, Princeton: Princeton University Press.

Clark, G. (1987), *Predestination*, Phillipsburg: Presbyterian and Reformed.

Clark, K.J. (2001), 'God is Great, God is Good: Medieval Conceptions of Divine Goodness and the Problem of Hell', *Religious Studies* 37, pp. 15–31.

Cohn, N. (1991), *The Pursuit of the Millennium* (2nd ed.), London: Paladin.

* Colwell, J. (1992), 'The Contemporaneity of the Divine Decision: Reflections on Barth's Denial of "Universalism"' in N.M. de S. Camerson (ed.), *Universalism and the Doctrine of Hell*, Carlisle: Paternoster Press/ Grand Rapids: Baker Book House, pp. 139–160.

—— (2000), 'The Glory of God's Justice and the Glory of God's Grace: Contemporary Reflections on the Doctrine of Hell in the Teachings of Jonathan Edwards' in J. Colwell (ed.), *Called to One Hope: Perspectives on the Life to Come*, Carlisle: Paternoster Press, pp. 113–129.

Conzelmann, H. (1975), *A Commentary on the First Epistle to the Corinthians*, J.W. Leitch (tr.), Philadelphia: Fortress Press.

Costen, M. (1997), *The Cathars and the Albigensian Crusade*, Manchester/New York: Manchester University Press.

Craig, W.L. (1989), '"No Other Name": A Middle Knowledge Perspective on the Exclusivity of Salvation Through Christ', *Faith and Philosophy* 6, pp. 172–188.

* —— (1991), 'Talbott's Universalism', *Religious Studies* 27, pp. 297–308.

* —— (1993), 'Talbott's Universalism Once More', *Religious Studies* 29, pp. 497–518.

Cranfield, C.E.B. (1954), *First Epistle of Peter*, London: SCM.

—— (Sept 1958), 'The Interpretation of 1 Peter 3:19 and 4:6', *Expository Times* 69, pp. 369–372.

—— (1975), *A Critical and Exegetical Commentary on the Epistle to the Romans: Volume 1: Romans I-VIII* (International Critical Commentary), Edinburgh: T. & T. Clark.

* Crisp, O. (forthcoming), 'Divine Retribution: A Defense', *Sophia*.

* —— (2003), 'Augustinian Universalism', *International Journal for Philosophy of Religion*, 53, pp. 127–45.

* —— (unpublished), 'On Barth's Denial of Universalism'.

* Crockett, W.V. (1991a), 'Will God Save Everyone in the End?' in W.V. Crockett & J.G. Sigountos (eds.), *Through No Fault of Their Own: The Fate of Those Who Have Never Heard*, Grand Rapids: Baker Book House, pp. 159–166.

—— (1991b), 'Wrath That Endures Forever', *Journal of the Evangelical Theological Society*, pp. 195–202.

—— (1996), 'The Metaphorical View' in W. Crockett (ed.), *Four Views on Hell*, Grand Rapids: Zondervan, pp. 41–76.

Cross, F.L. & Livingstone, E.A. (eds.) (1983), *The Oxford Dictionary of the Christian Church* (2nd ed.), Oxford: Oxford University Press.

Crouzel, H. (1990), *Le fin dernière selon Origène*, Aldershot: Variorum Reprints.

Daley, B. (1991), *The Hope of the Early Church*, Cambridge: Cambridge University Press.

Dalton, W. (1977), *Salvation and Damnation*, Wisconsin: Clergy Book Service.

Daniélou, J. (1935), *Origen*, London: Sheed and Ward.

Dante A. (1935), *The Divine Comedy*, H.F. Cary (tr.), New York: The Union Library Association.

Davis, S. (1983), *Logic and the Nature of God*, Grand Rapids: Wm. B. Eerdmans Publishing Co..

—— (1993), *Risen Indeed: Making Sense of the Resurrection*, Grand Rapids: Wm. B. Eerdmans Publishing Co./ London: SPCK.

Dixon, L. (1992), *The Other Side of the Good News: Confronting the Contemporary Challenge to Jesus' Teaching on Hell*, Wheaton: BridgePoint.

Donelly, E. (2001), *Heaven and Hell*, Edinburgh: Banner of Truth.

Dorner, I. (1890), *A System of Christian Doctrine*, Edinburgh: T. & T. Clark.

Double, R. (1991), *The Non-reality of Free Will*, New York & Oxford: Oxford University Press.

Douglas, J.D. (ed.) (1962), *The New Bible Dictionary*, London: IVP.

* Dunavant, D.R. (2000), 'Universalism' in A.S. Moreau (ed.), *Evangelical Dictionary of World Missions*, Grand Rapids: Baker Book House, pp. 988–89.

Dunn, J.D.G. (1988), *Romans*, Word Biblical Commentary in 2 vols., Waco, TX: Word.

—— (1996), *The Epistles to the Colossians and to Philemon: A Commentary on the Greek Text*, Carlisle: Paternoster Press/ Grand Rapids: Wm. B. Eerdmans Publishing Co., pp. 83–104.

Durnbaugh, D.F. (ed.) (1984), *Meet the Brethren*, Elgin III: The Brethren Press for the Encyclopaedia Inc..

*Duthie, C.S. (1961), 'Ultimate Triumph', *Scottish Journal of Theology* 14, pp. 156–171.

* Du Toit, D.A. (1992), 'Descensus and Universalism: Some Historical Patterns of Interpretation' in N.M. de S. Camerson (ed.), *Universalism and the Doctrine of Hell*, Carlisle: Paternoster Press/ Grand Rapids: Baker Book House, pp. 73–92.

Edwards, J. (1865), 'The Justice of God in Damning Sinners', *The Works of Jonathan Edwards*, vol. 1, London: Henry G. Bohn.

—— (1966), 'Sinners in the Hands of an Angry God', reprinted in O.E. Winslow (ed.), *Jonathan Edwards: Basic Writings*, New York: The New American Library Inc.

Ekstrom, L.W. (2000), *Free Will: A Philosophical Study*: Boulder: Westview Press.

—— (ed.) (2001), *Agency and Responsibility*, Boulder: Westview Press.

* Eller, V. (1974), *The Most Revealing Book in the Bible: Making Sense Out of Revelation*, Grand Rapids: Wm. B. Eerdmans Publishing Co., pp. 188–205.

* —— (1975), 'How the Kings of the Earth Land in the New Jerusalem: The World in the Book of Revelation', *Katallagate/Be Reconciled* 5, pp. 21–27.

* Ellul, J. (1989), *What I Believe*, Grand Rapids: Wm. B. Eerdmans Publishing Co..

Ensign, C.D. (1955), *Radical German Pietism*, Boston: Boston University Th.D. Thesis.

Erickson, M. (1983), *Christian Theology*, Grand Rapids: Baker Book House.

—— (1993), *The Evangelical Mind and Heart: Perspectives on Theological and Practical Issues*, Grand Rapids: Baker Book House.

—— (1997), *The Evangelical Left: Encountering Postconservative Evangelical Theology*, Grand Rapids: Baker Book House/Carlisle: Paternoster Press.

Erskine, T. (1822), *Essay on Faith*, Edinburgh: Waugh and Innes

——, (1837), *The Doctrine of Election*, London: James Duncan.

——, (1871), *The Spiritual Order and Other Papers Selected From the Manuscripts of the Late Thomas Erskine of Linlathen*, Edinburgh: David Douglas.

Fackre, G. (1995), 'Divine Perseverance', in J. Sanders (ed.), *What About Those Who Have Never Heard?* Downers Grove: IVP, pp. 71–95.

Farmer, H.H. (1936), *The World and God: A Study of Prayer, Providence and Miracle in Christian Experience* (2nd ed.), London: Nisbit

—— (1948), *God and Man*, London: Nisbit.

Farrar, F.W. (1878), *Eternal Hope*, London.

Fee, G. & Stuart, D. (1993), *How to Read the Bible for All Its Worth* (2nd ed.), Grand Rapids: Zondervan.

Feinberg, J.S. (1995), 'God, Freedom and Evil in Calvinist Thinking' in T. Schreiner & B. Ware (eds.), *The Grace of God, the Bondage of the Will: Historical and Theological Perspectives of Calvinism*, vol. 2, Grand Rapids: Baker Book House, pp. 459–485.

Fernando, A. (1991), *Crucial Questions About Hell*, Eastborne: Kingsway.

★ Ferré, N. (1951), *The Christian Understanding of God*, New York: Harper.

—— (1971), *Evil and the Christian Faith*, New York: Books for Libraries.

Fischer, J.M. and Ravizza, M. (1998), *Responsibility and Control: a Theory of Moral Responsibility*, Cambridge and New York: Cambridge University Press.

Forsyth, P.T. (1957), *The Justification of God*, London: Independent Press.

—— (1965), *The Work of Christ*, London: Collins.

Foster, J. (n.d.), *Essays*, London: The Religious Tract Society.

Frame, J.M. (2001), *No Other Gods: A Response to Open Theism*, Phillipsburg: Presbyterian and Reformed.

—— (2002), *The Doctrine of God*, Phillipsburg: Presbyterian and Reformed.

Frankfurt, H. (1969), 'Alternate Possibilities and Moral Responsibility', *Journal of Philosophy* 66, pp. 829–839.

Froome, L.E. (1966), *The Conditionalist Faith of Our Forefathers*, vol. 2, Washington: Review and Herald.

Fudge, E.W. (1994), *The Fire That Consumes: The Biblical Case for Conditional Immortality* (2nd ed.), Carlisle: Paternoster Press.

—— (2000), 'The Case for Conditional Immortality' in E.W. Fudge & R.A. Peterson, *Two Views of Hell: A Biblical and Theological Dialogue*, Downers Grove: IVP.

Geach, P. (1977), *Providence and Evil*, Cambridge: Cambridge University Press.

Gelston, A. (1992), 'Universalism in Second Isaiah', *Journal of Theological Studies*, vol. 43, pt. 2, pp. 377–398.

Gilkey, L. (1981), *Reaping the Whirlwind*, New York: Seabury Press, pp. 296–299.

Goddard, A. (2002), *Living the Word, Resisting the World: the Life and Thought of Jaques Ellul*, Carlisle: Paternoster Press.

Gregory of Nyssa (1917), *The Catechetical Oration of Gregory of Nyssa*, J.H. Srawley (tr.), (Early Church Classics), London: SPCK, 1917.

—— (1978), *The Life of Moses*, A.J. Malherbe & E. Ferguson (trs.), Classics of Western Spirituality, New York: Paulist Press.

——, (1988), *On the Soul and the Resurrection*, W. Moore (tr.), (Nicene and Post-Nicene Fathers Series vol. V), Edinburgh: T & T Clark, pp. 428–468.

—— (1995), *Treatise on the Inscriptions of the Psalms*, R. Heine (tr.), Oxford: Clarendon Press.

Grudem, W. (1994), *Systematic Theology*, Grand Rapids: Zondervan/Leicester: IVP.

★ Gundry-Volf, J.M. (1993), 'Universalism' in G.F. Hawthorne, R.P. Martin & D.G. Reid, (eds.), *Dictionary of Paul and His Letters*, Downers Grove/Leicester: IVP, pp. 956–961.

Gunton, C. (2000), 'Salvation', in J. Webster (ed.), *The Cambridge Companion to Karl Barth*, Cambridge: Cambridge University Press.

Gurney, G.M. (1902), *Letters of Emelia Russell Gurney*, London: James Nesbit & Co.

Habermas, G. and Moreland, J.P. (1992), *Immortality: The Other Side of Death*, Nashville: Thomas Nelson.

* Hall, L. (2003), *Swinburne's Hell and Hick's Universalism*, Aldershot: Ashgate.

Hamilton, I. (2000), 'The Puritan Doctrine of Sin and the Wrath of God' in *Seeing the Lord: Papers Read at the 2000 Westminster Conference*, Stoke: Westminster Conference.

Hanna, W. (ed.) (1877), *Letters of Thomas Erskine of Linlathen*, 2 Vols., Edinburgh: David Douglas.

Harrington, W.J. (1993), *Revelation* (Sacra Pagina 16), Collegeville: Liturgical Press.

Harris, M. (1983), *Raised Immortal: The Relation Between Resurrection and Immortality in the New Testament*, London: Marshall, Morgan and Scott.

* Hart, T. (1992), 'Universalism: Two Distinct Types', in N.M. de S. Camerson (ed.), *Universalism and the Doctrine of Hell*, Carlisle: Paternoster Press/ Grand Rapids: Baker Book House, pp. 1–34.

Hayes, Z. (1996), 'The Purgatorial View' in W. Crockett (ed.), *Four Views of Hell*, Grand Rapids: Zondervan, pp. 91–118.

Hays, R. (1997), *First Corinthians*, Louisville: John Knox Press.

—— (2001), *The Faith of Jesus Christ: The Narrative Substructure of Galatians 3:1–4:11* (2nd ed.), Grand Rapids: Wm. B. Eerdmans Publishing Co..

Hebblethwaite, B. (1984), *The Christian Hope*, Basingstoke: Marshall, Morgan & Scott.

Hein, R. (ed.) (1974), *Life Essential: The Hope of the Gospel*, Wheaton: Harold Shaw Publishers.

—— (ed.) (1976), *George MacDonald: Creation in Christ*, Wheaton: Harold Shaw Publishers.

—— (1999), *The Harmony Within: The Spiritual Journey of George MacDonald*, Chicago: Cornerstone Press.

Heitzenrater, R.P. (1995), *Wesley and the People Called Methodists*, Nashville: Abingdon Press.

Helm, P. (1985), 'The Logic of Limited Atonement', *Scottish Bulletin of Evangelical Theology* 3, no. 2.

—— (1994), *The Providence of God*, Leicester/Downers Grove: IVP.

—— (2001), 'Can God Love the World?' in K. Vanhoozer (ed.), *Nothing Greater, Nothing Better: Theological Essays on the Love of God*, Grand Rapids: Wm. B. Eerdmans Publishing Co., pp. 168–185.

Henderson, H.F. (1899), *Erskine of Linlathen: Selections and Biography*, Edinburgh and London: Oliphant Anderson & Ferrier.

Hick, J. (1976), *Death and Eternal Life*, London: Collins/New York: Harper and Row.

—— (1978), *Evil and the God of Love* (2nd ed.), New York: Harper and Row.

* Hilborn, D. & Johnston, P. (eds.) (2000), *The Nature of Hell*, (ACUTE Report), Carlisle: Paternoster Press

* Hillert, S. (1999), *Limited and Universal Salvation: A Text Oriented and Hermeneutical Study of Two Perspectives in Paul*, Stockholm: Almqvist & Wiksell International.

Hodge, C. (1888), *Systematic Theology*, New York: Scribners.

Hoekema, A.A. (1979), *The Bible and the Future*, Grand Rapids: Wm. B. Eerdmans Publishing Co..

* Horrocks, D. (2003), *Laws of the Spiritual Order: Innovation and Reconstruction in the Soteriology of Thomas Erskine of Linlathen*, Carlisle: Paternoster Press.

* Hughes, P. (et al), *Dictionary of Unitarian and Universalist Biography*, www.uua.org/uuhs/duub

Hultgren, A.J. (1987), *Christ and His Benefits: Christology and Redemption in the New Testament*, Philadelphia: Fortress Press.

Hunter, A.M (1974), *P.T. Forsyth: Per Crucem ad Lucem*, London: SCM.

Hunter, J.D. (1987), *Evangelicalism: The Coming Generation*, Chicago/London: University of Chicago Press.

Inwagen, P. van (1983), *An Essay on Free Will*, Oxford: Clarendon Press.

—— (2001), 'Freewill Remains a Mystery' in R. Kane (ed.), *The Oxford Handbook on Freewill*, Oxford & New York: Oxford University Press, pp. 158–78.

Jensen, P.T. (1993), 'Intolerable but Moral? Thinking About Hell', *Faith & Philosophy* vol. 10, no. 2, pp. 235–241.

John Paul II (1994), *Crossing the Threshold of Hope*, V. Messori (ed.), New York: Alfred A. Knopf.

Jones, K.G. (1994), *A Believing Church: Learning From Some Contemporary Anabaptist and Baptist Perspectives*, Didcot: Baptist Union of Great Britain.

Jones, R.S. (1914), *Spiritual Reformers of the 16th and 17th Centuries*, London: Macmillan.

Jukes, A. (1976), *The Restitution of All Things*, W. Knochaven, California: Scripture Studies Concern and Concordant Publishing Concern.

Justinian (1949), 'Anathematisms Against Origen'. In J.C. Ayer, *A Source Book for Ancient Church History: From the Apostolic Age to the Close of the Conciliar Period*, New York: Charles Scribner's Sons.

Kane, R. (ed.) (2002), *Freewill*, Oxford: Blackwell.

Käsemann, E. (1980), *Commentary on Romans*, G.W. Bromiley (tr. & ed.), Grand Rapids: Wm. B. Eerdmans Publishing Co..

Kelly, J.N.D. (1960), *Early Christian Doctrines*, New York: Harper and Row.

Kiwiet, J.J. (1957), 'The Life of Hans Denck', *Mennonite Quarterly Review* 31.

Klein, W. (1990), *The New Chosen People: A Corporate View of Election*, Grand Rapids: Zondervan.

* Knight, G. (1997), 'Universalism and the Greater Good: A Response to Talbott', *Faith and Philosophy* 14, pp. 98–99.

Kronen, J.D. (1999), 'The Idea of Hell and the Classical Doctrine of God', *The Modern Schoolman* LXXVII, pp. 13–34.

Künneth, W. (1965), *The Theology of the Resurrection*, London: SCM.

* Kvanvig, J.L. (1993), *The Problem of Hell*, Oxford: Oxford University Press.

* Lacy, L. (1992), 'Talbott on Paul as a Universalist', *Christian Scholar's Review* XXI:4, pp. 395–407.

Lane, T. (2001), 'The Wrath of God as an Aspect of the Love of God' in K. Vanhoozer (ed.), *Nothing Greater, Nothing Better: Theological Essays on the Love of God*, Grand Rapids: Wm. B. Eerdmans Publishing Co., pp. 138–168.

Lead, J. (1891), *The Enochian Walks with God* (1694), Glasgow: J. Thompson.

Leckie, J.H. (1922), *The World to Come and Final Destiny*, (2nd ed.), Edinburgh: T.&T. Clark.

Leff, G. (1967), *Heresy in the Later Middle Ages*, vol. 1, Manchester: Manchester University Press/ New York: Barnes and Noble.

Leith, J. (ed.) (1982), *Creeds of the Churches* (3rd ed.), Louisville: John Knox Press.

Lewis, C.S. (1944a), *The Problem of Pain*, New York: The MacMillan Company.

—— (1944b), *The Last Battle*, New York: The MacMillan Company.

—— (1946), *The Great Divorce*, New York: The MacMillan Company.

—— (1955), *Surprised By Joy*, New York: Harcourt Brace Jovanovich.

Lightfoot, J. B. (1963), *Saint Paul's Epistle to the Philippians*, Grand Rapids: Zondervan.

Lincoln, A. (1990), *Ephesians*, (Word Biblical Commentary), Waco, TX: Word.

—— (1991), *Paradise Now and Not Yet: Studies in the Role of the Heavenly Dimension in Paul's Thought, With Special Reference to His Eschatology*, Grand Rapids: Baker Book House.

Lincoln A. & Wedderburn, A.J.M. (1993), *The Theology of the Later Pauline Letters*, Cambridge: Cambridge University Press.

Lindbeck, G. (1974), '*Fides ex auditu* and the Salvation of Non-Christians: Contemporary Catholic and Protestant Positions,' in V. Vajta (ed.), *The Gospel and the Ambiguity of the Church*, Minneapolis: Fortress Press, pp. 92–123.

—— (1984), *The Nature of Doctrine: Religion and Theology in a Postliberal Age*, Philadelphia: Westminster Press.

⋆ Ludlow, M. (2000a), *Universal Salvation: Eschatology in the Thought of Gregory of Nyssa and Karl Rahner*, Oxford: Oxford University Press.

⋆ —— (2000b), 'Universal Salvation and a Soteriology of Divine Punishment', *Scottish Journal of Theology* vol. 53, no. 4, pp. 449–471.

⋆ —— (forthcoming), 'Why was Hans Denck Thought to be a Universalist?' *Journal of Ecclesiastical History*.

Luther, M. (1961), *Martin Luther: Selections From His Writings*, J. Dillenberger (ed.), New York: Anchor Books.

MacCulloch, J.A. (1930), *The Harrowing of Hell*, Edinburgh: T. & T. Clark.

MacDonald, G. (1867), *Unspoken Sermons*, Series 1–3, London: Alexander Strahan.

—— (1886), *Unspoken Sermons*, London: Longman.

—— (1892), *The Hope of the Gospel*, London: Ward, Lock, Bowden and Co..

—— (1971), *Lilith: A Romance*, London: Ballantine.

MacLeod, D. (1995), *Behold Your God*, Fearn: Christian Focus.

Marsden, G.M. (1991), *Understanding Fundamentalism and Evangelicalism*, Grand Rapids: Wm. B. Eerdmans Publishing Co..

Marshall, C. (2001), *Beyond Retribution: A New Testament Vision for Justice, Crime, and Punishment*, Grand Rapids: Wm. B. Eerdmans Publishing Co..

Marshall, I.H. (April 1988), 'An Evangelical Approach to Theological Criticism,' *Themelios* 13, pp. 79–85.

—— (1989), 'Universal Grace and Atonement in the Pastoral Epistles' in C. Pinnock (ed.), *The Grace of God, The Will of Men*, Grand Rapids: Zondervan, pp. 51–69.

★ —— (2000), 'Does The New Testament Teach Universal Salvation?' in J. Colwell (ed.), *Called to One Hope: Perspectives on the Life to Come*, Carlisle: Paternoster Press, pp. 17–30.

★ Maurice, F.D. (1853), 'Concluding Essay: Eternal Life and Eternal Death' in *Theological Essays*, Cambridge, pp. 442–478.

McCheyne, R.M. (1979), 'The Eternal Torment of the Wicked, Matter of Eternal Song to the Redeemed' in *A Basket of Fragments*, Fearn: Christian Focus.

McGrath, A. (1994), *Evangelicalism and the Future of Christianity*, London: Hodder & Stoughton.

—— (1996), *A Passion for Truth: The Intellectual Coherence of Evangelicalism*, Leicester: Apollos.

Michaels, J.R. (1988), *1 Peter* (Word Biblical Commentary), Waco, TX: Word.

Milton, J. (1962), *Paradise Lost*. M.Y. Hughes (ed.), Indianapolis: The Odyssey Press.

★ Moltmann, J. (1996), *The Coming of God: Christian Eschatology*, London: SCM.

★ Moltmann, J. (1999), 'The Logic of Hell' in R. Bauckham (ed.), *God Will Be All in All: The Eschatology of Jürgen Moltmann*, Edinburgh: T & T Clark, pp. 43–47.

Moo, D.J. (1996), *The Epistle to the Romans*, (The New International Commentary on the New Testament), Grand Rapids: Wm. B. Eerdmans Publishing Co..

Moore, R.I. (1985), *The Origins of European Dissent*, Oxford: Blackwell

★ Morgan, J.C. (1995), *The Devotional Heart: Pietism and the Renewal of American Unitarian Universalism*, Boston: Skinner House Books.

★ Morris, K.R. (1991), 'The Puritan Roots of American Universalism', *Scottish Journal of Theology* 44, pp. 457–87.

Morris, L. (1959), *The First and Second Epistles to the Thessalonians*, Grand Rapids: Wm. B. Eerdmans Publishing Co..

Morris, T.V. (1992), *Making Sense of it all: Pascal and the Meaning of Life*, Grand Rapids: Wm. B. Eerdmans Publishing Co..

Moule, H.C.G. (1975), *The Epistle to the Romans*, Washington: Christian Literature Crusade.

★ Müller, G. (1958), 'Origenes und die Apokatastasis', *Theologisches Zeitschrift* 14.

★ —— (1964), 'Die Idee einer Apokatastasis ton panton in der europaïschen Theologie von Schleiermacher bis Barth' in *Zeitschrift für Religions und Geistesgeschichte* 16:1.

★ Murray, J. (1870), *The Life of Rev. John Murray, Preacher of Universal Salvation, Written by Himself, With a Continuation by Judith Sargent Murray*, Boston: Universalist Publishing House.

Murray, J. (1955), *Redemption: Accomplished and Applied*, Edinburgh: Banner of Truth.

—— (1960), *Epistle of Paul to the Romans* vol. 1, Grand Rapids: Wm. B. Eerdmans Publishing Co..

—— (1977), *Collected Writings of John Murray*, vol. 2, Edinburgh: Banner of Truth.

★ Murray, M. (1999), 'Three Versions of Universalism', *Faith and Philosophy* 16, pp. 55–68.

Nash, R.H. (1999), *When a Baby Dies: Answers to Comfort Grieving Parents*, Grand Rapids: Zondervan.

Needham, N.R. (1990), *Thomas Erskine of Linlathen: His Life and Theology, 1788–1837*, Edinburgh: Rutherford House Books.

★ Neuhaus, R.J. (Aug/Sept 2001), 'Will All Be Saved?' *First Things*, pp. 77–82.

Newton, J. (1808), *Works*, vol. 4, London.

Neyrey, J.H. (1993), *2 Peter, Jude* (The Anchor Bible), New York and London: Doubleday.

★ Nicholls, B.J. (1979), 'The Exclusiveness and Inclusiveness of the Gospel: Some Reflections on Contemporary Trends Toward Universalism in the Asian Context', *Themelios*, vol. 4, no. 2, pp. 62–69.

Nicole, R. (2002), *Our Sovereign Saviour*, Fearn: Christian Focus.

★ Norris, F.W. (1992), 'Universal Salvation in Origen and Maximus' in N.M. de S. Camerson (ed.), *Universalism and the Doctrine of Hell*, Carlisle: Paternoster Press/ Grand Rapids: Baker Book House, pp. 35–72.

O'Brien, P.T. (1982), *Colossians, Philemon*, (Word Biblical Commentaries), Waco, TX: Word.

★ Okholm, D.S. & Phillips, T.R. (1995), *More Than One Way? Four Views on Salvation in a Pluralistic World*, Grand Rapids: Zondervan.

Olson, R.E. (1999), *The Story of Christian Theology: Twenty Centuries of Tradition and Reform*, Downers Grove: IVP.

Origen (1936), *On First Principles*, G.W. Butterworth (tr.), London: SPCK.

—— (1976–77), *Homelies on Jeremiah*, Homélies sur Jérémie, Sources Chrétiennes Vols. 232 and 238, P. Husson and P. Nautin (trr.), Paris: Éditions du Cerf.

Osborne, G.R. (1991), *The Hermeneutical Spiral*, Downers Grove: IVP.

Ovey, M. (1995), 'The Human Identity Crisis: Can we do Without the Trinity?' Cambridge: *Cambridge Papers* 4, no. 2.

Owen, J. (1959), *The Death of Death in the Death of Christ*, Edinburgh: Banner of Truth.

Packer, J.I. (1973), *Knowing God*, Downers Grove: IVP.

★ ——, (1995), 'The Love of God: Universal and Particular' in in T. Schreiner & B. Ware (eds.), *The Grace of God, the Bondage of the Will: Historical and Theological Perspectives of Calvinism*, vol. 2, Grand Rapids: Baker Book House, pp. 413–428.

★ —— (1998), 'The Problem of Universalism Today' in J.I. Packer, *Celebrating the Saving Work of God*, Carlisle: Paternoster Press, pp. 169–178.

—— (2002), *What Did The Cross Achieve: The Logic of Penal Substitution*, Leicester: RTSF Monographs.

★ Partridge, C.H. (1998), *H.H. Farmer's Theological Interpretation of Religion: Towards a Personalist Theology of Religions*, Lewiston: Edwin Mellen.

Pascal, B (1966), *Pensees*, A.J. Krailsheimer (tr.), London: Penguin.

★ Patrides, C.A. (1967), 'The Salvation of Satan', *Journal of the History of Ideas* 28.

Peters, E. (1980), *Heresy and Authority in Medieval Europe: Documents in Translation*, London: Scholars Press.

Peterson, D. (ed.) (2000), *Where Wrath and Mercy Meet: Proclaiming the Atonement Today*, Carlisle: Paternoster Press.

Peterson, R.A. (2000a), 'The Case for Traditionalism' in E.W. Fudge and R.A. Peterson, *Two Views of Hell: A Biblical and Theological Dialogue*, Downers Grove: IVP, pp. 115–81.

—— (Oct 23rd 2000b), 'Undying Worm, Unquenchable Fire', *Christianity Today* 44, no. 12, pp. 30–40.

Pfleiderer, O. (1893), *The Development of Theology in Germany Since Kant and its Progress in Great Britain Since 1825* (2nd ed.), London: Swan Sonnenschein & Co..

Phillips, T.R. (1991), 'Hell: A Christological Reflection' in W.V. Crockett & J.G. Sigountos (eds.), *Through No Fault of Their Own? The Fate of Those Who Have Never Heard*, Grand Rapids: Baker Book House.

Pierard, R.V. (1978), 'Hochmann Von Hochenau, Ernst Christoph' in J.D. Douglas (ed.), *The New International Dictionary of the Christian Church*, Grand Rapids: Zondervan, p. 473.

Pinnock, C.H. (1988), 'The Finality of Jesus Christ in a World of Religions' in M. Noll & D.F. Wells (eds.), *Christian Faith and Practice in the Modern World*, Grand Rapids: Wm. B Eerdmans Publishing Co., pp. 152–168.

—— (1992), *A Wideness in God's Mercy: The Finality of Jesus Christ in a World of Religions*, Grand Rapids: Zondervan.

Pinnock, C.H. & Brow, R.C. (1994), *Unbounded Love: A Good News Theology For the 21st Century*, Downers Grove: IVP/ Carlisle: Paternoster Press

Piper, J. (April 1983), 'How Does a Sovereign God Love?' *Reformed Journal*.

—— (1995), 'Are There Two Wills in God? Divine Election and God's Desire For All to be Saved' in T. Schreiner & B. Ware (eds.), *The Grace of God, the Bondage of the Will: Historical and Theological Perspectives of Calvinism*, vol. 2, Grand Rapids: Baker Book House, pp. 107–132.

Plantinga, A. (1974), *God, Freedom, and Evil*, Grand Rapids: Wm. B. Eerdmans Publishing Co..

—— (1980), *Does God Have a Nature?* Milwaukee: Marquette University Press.

* Powys, D.J. (1992), 'The Nineteenth and Twentieth Century Debates About Hell and Universalism' in N.M. de S. Camerson (ed.), *Universalism and the Doctrine of Hell*, Carlisle: Paternoster Press/ Grand Rapids: Baker Book House, pp. 93–138.

—— (1998), *Hell – A Hard Look at a Hard Question: The Fate of the Unrighteous in New Testament Thought*, Carlisle: Paternoster Press.

Price, C. & Randall, I. (2000), *Transforming Keswick: The Keswick Convention, Past, Present and Future*, Carlisle: Paternoster Press.

* Punt, N. (1980), *Unconditional Good News*, Grand Rapids: Wm. B. Eerdmans Publishing Co..

* —— (1988), *What's Good About the Good News? The Plan of Salvation in a New Light*, Chicago: Northland Press.

★ —— (2002), *So Also in Christ: Reviewing the Plan of Salvation*, Chicago: Northland Press.

Quebedeaux, R. (1978), *The Worldly Evangelicals*, San Francisco: Harper & Row.

Rahner, K. (1966), 'The Hermeneutics of Eschatological Assertions' in K. Rahner, *Theological Investigations* vol. 4, London: Darton, Longman & Todd, pp. 323–46.

—— (1978), *Foundations of Christian Faith*, London: Darton, Longman & Todd

Ramm, B. (1973), *The Evangelical Heritage: A Study in Historical Theology*, Grand Rapids: Baker Book House.

Randall, I. & Hilborn, D. (2001), *One Body in Christ: The History and Significance of the Evangelical Alliance*, Carlisle: Paternoster Press.

★ Reitan, E. (2001), 'Universalism and Autonomy: Towards a Comparative Defense of Universalism', *Faith and Philosophy* 18, pp. 222–240.

★ —— (2002), 'Eternal Damnation and Blessed Ignorance: Is the Damnation of Some Incompatible with the Salvation of Any?' *Religious Studies* vol. 38, no. 4, pp. 429–450.

Relly, J. (1759), *Union: Or a Treatise of the Consanguinity and Affinity Between Christ and His Church*, London.

Reymond, R. (1998), *A New Systematic Theology of the Christian Faith*, Nashville: Thomas Nelson.

★ Richards, J.W. (2002), 'A Pascalian Argument Against Universalism' in W.A. Dembski & J.W. Richards (eds.), *Unapologetic Apologetics*, Downers Grove: IVP, 2001/ Carlisle: Paternoster Press.

★ Rissi, M. (1972), *The Future of the World*, London: SCM.

Ritschl, A. (1966), *The Christian Doctrine of Reconciliation and Justification*, H.R. Macintosh & A.B. Macaulay (eds.), Clinton, N.J.: Reference Book Publishers, pp. 125–139.

★ Robinson, D. (1985), *The Unitarians and the Universalists*, Westport, Connecticut: Greenwood Press.

★ Robinson, J.A.T. (1949a), 'Universalism – Is It Heretical?', *Scottish Journal of Theology*, vol. 2, no. 2, pp. 139–155.

★ —— (1949b), 'Universalism – a Reply', *Scottish Journal of Theology* vol. 2, no. 4, pp. 378–380.

★ —— (1969), *In the End God*, London & Glasgow: Collins Fontana (1968; New York: Harper & Row).

★ Root, J.R. (2001), 'Universalism' in W.A. Elwell (ed.), *Evangelical Dictionary of Theology* (2nd ed.), Grand Rapids: Baker Book House, p. 1232–33.

★ Rowell, G. (1971), 'The Origins and History of Universalist Societies in Britain 1750–1850', *Journal of Ecclesiastical History* 22.

★ —— (1974), *Hell and the Victorians: A Study of the Nineteenth Century Theological Controversies Concerning Eternal Punishment and the Future Life*, Oxford: Clarendon Press.

Rust, G. (attrib.) (1933), *A Letter of Resolution Concerning Origin and the Chief of his Opinions* (1661), New York: Colombia University Press.

★ Sanders, J. (1992), *No Other Name: Can Only Christians Be Saved?* Grand Rapids: Wm. B. Eerdmans Publishing Co.

★ —— (1994), *No Other Name: Can Only Christians Be Saved?* London: SPCK.

—— (1998), *The God Who Risks: A Theology of Providence*, Downers Grove: IVP.

Schaff, P. (1886), *History of the Christian Church*, vol. III., New York: Charles Scribner's Sons.

Schleiermacher, F.D.E. (1948), *The Christian Faith*, H.R. Mackintosh and J.S. Stewart (eds.), Edinburgh: T & T Clark.

—— (1989), *The Christian Faith*, translation of the 2nd German edition [1830], Edinburgh: T & T Clark.

Schreiner, T.R. & Ware, B. (eds.) (1995), *The Grace of God, the Bondage of the Will: Historical and Theological Perspectives of Calvinism*, vol. 2, Grand Rapids: Baker Book House.

Schreiner, T.R. (2001), *Paul: Apostle of God's Glory in Christ*, Downers Grove: IVP/Leicester: Apollos.

Schwartz, H. (2000), *Eschatology*, Grand Rapids: Wm. B. Eerdmans Publishing Co..

★ Seaburg, A. (1972), 'Recent Scholarship in American Universalism: A Bibliographical Essay', *Church History* 41, pp. 513–523.

Sennett, J.F. (1999), 'Is There Freedom in Heaven?' *Faith and Philosophy* vol. 16, no. 1, January, pp. 69–82.

Seymour, C. (1989), 'Hell, Justice, and Freedom', *International Journal for Philosophy of Religion* 43, pp. 69–86.

—— (1997), 'On Choosing Hell', *Religious Studies* 33, 1997, pp. 249–266.

—— (2000a), 'A Craigian Theodicy of Hell', *Faith and Philosophy* 17, pp. 103–115.

★ —— (2000b), *A Theodicy of Hell*, Dordrecht: Kluwer Academic Publishers.

Shogren, G. (1997), 'Hell, Abyss, Eternal Punishment' in R.P. Martin and P.H. Davids (eds.), *Dictionary of the Later New Testament and Its Developments*, Downers Grove/Leicester: IVP, pp. 459–62.

★ Shutt, R.J.H. (1955–56), 'The New Testament Doctrine of the Hereafter: Universalism or Conditional Immortality?', *Expository Times* 67, pp. 131–135.

Skilton, H. (1978), 'Ballou, Hosea' in J.D. Douglas (ed.), *The New International Dictionary of the Christian Church*, Grand Rapids: Zondervan, p. 98.

Smith, L.P. (ed.) (1949), *A Religious Rebel: The Letters of Hannah Pearsall Smith*, London: Nisbitt & Co..

★ Stauffer, E (1955), *New Testament Theology*, London: SCM, pp. 222–225.

Stendahl, K. (1976), *Paul Among Jews and Gentiles*, Philadelphia: Fortress.

Stephen, L. (1962), *History of English Thought in the Eighteenth Century* (3rd ed.), London: Harbinger Books.

Stoeffler, E. (1965), *The Rise of Evangelical Pietism*, Leiden: E.J. Brill.

Stopford, A.B. (ed.) (1882), *Life and Letters of Fred W. Robertson*, vol. II, London: Kegan, Paul Trench, & Co..

Stott, J. (1986), *The Cross of Christ*, Leicester: IVP.

Strange, D. (2001), 'The Reality of Wrath: Towards a True Understanding of God and the Gospel', *From Athens to Jerusalem* 3, no. 1, pp. 1–6.

—— (2002), *The Possibility of Salvation Among the Unevangelised: An Analysis of Inclisivism in Recent Evangelical Theology*, Carlisle: Paternoster Press.

Stump, E. (1986), 'Dante's Hell, Aquinas' Moral Theory, and the Love of God', *Canadian Journal of Philosophy* 16, pp. 181–196.

Swinburne, R. (1977), *The Coherence of Theism*, Oxford: Oxford University Press.

—— (1983), 'A Theodicy of Heaven and Hell' in *The Existence and Nature of God*, A.J. Freddoso (ed.), Notre Dame: University of Notre Dame Press.

* Talbott, T. (June 1983), 'God's Unconditional Mercy: A Reply to John Piper', *Reformed Journal*, pp. 9–13.

* —— (1987) 'C.S. Lewis and the Problem of Evil' *Christian Scholar's Review* XVII:1, pp. 36–51.

—— (1988a), 'On the Divine Nature and the Nature of Divine Freedom', *Faith and Philosophy* vol. 5, no.1, pp. 3–24.

—— (1988b), 'On Free Agency and the Concept of Power', *Pacific Philosophical Quarterly* 69, pp. 241–254.

—— (1990a), 'What Jesus Did For Us', *Reformed Journal* vol. 40, pp. 8–12.

* —— (1990b), 'The Doctrine of Everlasting Punishment', *Faith and Philosophy* 7, pp. 19–42.

* —— (1990c), 'Providence, Freedom, and Human Destiny'', *Religious Studies* 26, pp. 227–245.

* —— (1992a), 'The New Testament and Universal Reconciliation', *Christian Scholar's Review* XXI, pp. 376–394.

* —— (1992b), 'Craig on the Possibility of Eternal Damnation', *Religious Studies* 28, pp. 495–510.

* —— (1993), 'Punishment, Forgiveness, and Divine Justice', *Religious Studies* 29, pp. 151–168.

* —— (1995), 'Three Pictures of God in Western Theology', *Faith and Philosophy* 12, 1995, pp. 43–52.

* —— (1999a), 'Universalism and the Greater Good: Reply to Gordon Knight'. *Faith and Philosophy* 16, pp. 102–105.

* —— (1999b), 'The Love of God and the Heresy of Exclusivism', *Christian Scholar's Review* XXVII:1, pp. 99–112.

* —— (1999c), *The Inescapable Love of God*, Parkland: Universal Publishers/uPublish.com.

* —— (2001a), 'Universalism and the Supposed Oddity of Our Earthly Life: Reply to Michael Murray', *Faith and Philosophy* 18, pp. 102–109.

* —— (2001b), 'Freedom, Damnation, and the Power to Sin with Impunity', *Religious Studies* 37, pp. 417–434.

Temple, W. (1951), *Nature, Man and God*, London: Macmillan.

Thielicke, H. (1982), *The Evangelical Faith*, vol. III – The Holy Spirit, the Church, Eschatology, Grand Rapids: Wm. B. Eerdmans Publishing Co./ Edinburgh: T & T Clark.

Thiselton, A.C. (2000), *The First Epistle to the Corinthians*, (The New International Greek Testament Commentary), Carlisle: Paternoster Press/ Grand Rapids: Wm. B. Eerdmans Publishing Co..

Thompson, F. (1962), 'The Hound of Heaven' in *The Norton Anthology of English Literature*, New York: W.W. Norton & Company.

Tidball, D.J. (1994), *Who Are The Evangelicals? Tracing The Roots of Today's Movements*, London: Marshall Pickering.

Tillich, P. (1963), *Systematic Theology*, vol. 3, Chicago: University of Chicago Press.

Toplady, A. (1837), *The Works of Augustus Toplady*, London.

* Torrance, T.F. (1949), 'Universalism or Election', *Scottish Journal of Theology* vol. 2, no. 3, pp. 310–318.

Townsend, C. (March 1997), *An Eye For an Eye: The Morality of Punishment*, Cambridge: Cambridge Papers 6, no. 1.

—— (1999), *Hell: A Difficult Doctrine We Dare Not Ignore*, Cambridge: Cambridge Papers.

Travis, S. (1980), *Christian Hope and the Future of Man*, Leicester: IVP.

Trumbower, J.A. (2001), *Rescue for the Dead: The Posthumous Salvation of Non-Christians in Early Christianity*, Oxford: Oxford University Press.

VanArragon, R.J. (2001), 'Transworld Damnation and Craig's Contentious Suggestion', *Faith and Philosophy* 18, pp. 241–260.

Vanhoozer, K. (1993), 'Bernard Ramm' in W.A. Elwell (ed.), *Handbook of Evangelical Theologians*, Grand Rapids: Baker Book House, pp. 290–306.

Verduin, L. (1964), *The Reformers and Their Stepchildren*, Grand Rapids: Wm. B. Eerdmans Publishing Co..

* Walker, D.P. (1964), *The Decline of Hell: Seventeenth Century Discussions of Eternal Torment*, Chicago: University of Chicago Press.

Walker, W. (1959), *A History of the Christian Church*, New York: Charles Scribner's Sons.

* Walls, J. (1992), *Hell: The Logic of Damnation*, Notre Dame: University of Notre Dame Press.

—— (2002), *Heaven: The Logic of Eternal Joy*, Oxford: Oxford University Press.

Walvoord, J.F. (1996), 'The Literal View' in W. Crockett (ed.), *Four Views on Hell*, Grand Rapids: Zondervan, pp. 9–28.

Ward, W.R. (1993), 'German Pietism 1670–1750', *Journal of Ecclesiastical History* 44, pp. 476–504.

* Ware, K. (2000), *The Inner Kingdom: Volume 1 of the Collected Works*, New York: St. Vladimir's Seminary Press, pp. 193–215.

Warfield, B. (1897), 'The Development of the Doctrine of Infant Salvation', in *Two Studies in the History of Doctrine*, New York: Christian Literature Co., pp. 143–239.

—— (1952), *Biblical and Theological Studies*, Philadelphia: Presbyterian and Reformed Publishing Co.

Waterfield, R. (ed.) (1989), *Jacob Boehme: Essential Readings*, Wellinborough: Crucible Books for the Aquarian Press.

Watson, D.L. (1990), *God Does Not Foreclose*, Nashville: Abingdon.

Wesley, J. (1931), *Letters of John Wesley*, (8 Vols.), J. Telford (ed.), London: Epworth Press

* White, J. (1779), *The Restoration of all Things or, A Vindication of the Goodness and Grace of God to be Manifest at Last in the Recovery of his Whole Creation Out of Their Fall.* (1712), London.

* —— (1851), *The Restoration of all Things or, A Vindication of the Goodness and Grace of God to be Manifest at Last in the Recovery of his Whole Creation Out of Their Fall.* (1712), introduction by D. Thom, London: The Universalists' Library.

* White, V. (1991), *Atonement and Incarnation: An Essay in Universalism and Particularity*, Cambridge: Cambridge University Press.

Whitely, D.E.H. (1964), *The Theology of St. Paul*, Philadelphia: Fortress Press.

Williams, G. (2001), 'The Cross and the Punishment of Sin' in D. Peterson (ed.), *Where Wrath and Mercy Meet: Procaliming the Atonement Today*, Carlisle: Paternoster Press, pp. 68–99.

Williams, G.H. (1962), *The Radical Reformation*, London: Weidenfeld and Nicholson.

—— (2000), *The Radical Reformation* (3rd ed.), Kirksville: Truman State University Press.

Willis, D. & Welker, M. (eds.) (1999), *Toward the Future of a Reformed Theology*, Grand Rapids: Wm. B. Eerdmans Publishing Co..

Wilson, H.B. (1860), chapter in *Essays and Reviews*, London.

* Winchester, E. (1809), *The Universal Restoration Exhibited in a Series of Dialogues Between a Minister and his Friend* (1788) (Fifth edition: with notes by W. Vidler), Glasgow: A. Napier.

—— (1890), *Some Remarkable Passages in the Life of Dr. George de Benneville*, Germantown: Converse Cleaves.

Wolf, S. (1990), *Freedom Within Reason*, Oxford: Oxford University Press.

Wright, C (1955), *The Beginnings of Unitarianism in America*, Boston: Starr King/Beacon.

* Wright, N.G. (1996), *The Radical Evangelical: Seeking a Place to Stand*, London: SPCK.

* Wright, N.T. (1975), 'Universalism and the World-Wide Community', *The Churchman*, vol. 89, no. 3, pp. 197–212.

* —— (1979), 'Towards a Biblical View of Universalism', *Themelios* Vol. 4, No. 2, pp. 54–58.

* —— (1988), 'Universalism', in S.B. Ferguson & D.F. Wright (eds.), *New Dictionary of Theology*, Leicester: IVP, pp. 701–03.

—— (1992), *The Climax of the Covenant: Christ and the Law in Pauline Theology*, Edinburgh: T & T Clark/ Philadelphia: Fortress.

Wright, R.K.M. (1996), *No Place for Sovereignty: What's Wrong With Freewill Theism*, Downers Grove: IVP.

Zeis, J. (April 1986), 'To Hell With Freedom', *Sophia* 25, pp. 41–48.